THE SOCIAL IMPLICATIONS OF ROBOTICS
AND ADVANCED INDUSTRIAL AUTOMATION

IFIP TC 9 International Working Conference on
The Social Implications of Robotics and Advanced Industrial Automation
Tel-Aviv, Israel, 14–16 December, 1987

organized by
IFIP TC 9 - Relationship Between Computers and Society
Israel Information Processing Association

with the support of
The General Federation of Labour in Israel
The British Council
Israel Institute of Productivity
Digital (Dec.) Ltd., Israel
IBM Research Center, Haifa
Intel Electronics Ltd.

NORTH-HOLLAND
AMSTERDAM · NEW YORK · OXFORD · TOKYO

THE SOCIAL IMPLICATIONS OF ROBOTICS AND ADVANCED INDUSTRIAL AUTOMATION

Proceedings of the IFIP TC 9 International Working Conference on
The Social Implications of Robotics and Advanced Industrial Automation
Tel-Aviv, Israel, 14–16 December, 1987

edited by

D. MILLIN
Computer Science Studies
Beit Berl College
Israel

B. H. RAAB
Israel Center for Information Systems
The Israel Institute of Productivity
Israel

1989

NORTH-HOLLAND
AMSTERDAM · NEW YORK · OXFORD · TOKYO

ISBN: 0 444 87320 1

Published by:

ELSEVIER SCIENCE PUBLISHERS B.V.
P.O. Box 103
1000 AC Amsterdam
The Netherlands

Sole distributors for the U.S.A. and Canada:

ELSEVIER SCIENCE PUBLISHING COMPANY, INC.
655 Avenue of the Americas
New York, N.Y. 10010
U.S.A.

Library of Congress Cataloging-in-Publication Data

IFIP TC 9 International Working Conference on the Social
    Implications of Robotics and Advanced Industrial Auto-
    mation (1st : 1987 : Tel Aviv, Israel)
    The social implications of robotics and advanced in-
dustrial automation.

    1. Automation--Social aspects--Congresses. 2. Robo-
tics--Social aspects--Congresses. 3. Industry--Social
aspects--Congresses. 4. Technology and civilization--
Congresses. I. Millin, D. (Daniel) II. Raab, B. H.
III. IFIP Technical Committee 9. IV. Title.
HC79.A9I45 1987   303.4'83   88-36261
ISBN 0-444-87320-1

PRINTED IN THE NETHERLANDS

PREFACE

The first International Conference on Social Implications of
Robotics and Advanced Industrial Automation held in Tel-Aviv
14-16 December 1987, was an attempt to draw public attention to
one of the most crucial issues of modern society, namely to what
extent rapid introduction of advanced technologies and robots
can improve the quality of life and decrease the magnitude of
dichotomy between the information poor and information rich.
The Conference was sponsored by IFIP Technical Committee on
Relationships between Computers and Society (TC-9) and the
Israeli Information Processing Association (IIPA).
This event brought together scholars from the social sciences
and computer experts from many countries, all of them expressed
deep concern over the human outcomes of the "second industrial
revolution".
Three major areas were discussed at the conference: impact of
artificial intelligence and robots, vulnerability of the
information society and impacts of advanced technology on
kibbutz life.

These proceedings are organized under seven key headings.
Part I includes the keynote speakers who presented three
different points of view concerning the impact of advanced
technologies on society.
Ysrael Keisar, Member of the Parliament and Secretary-General of
the Histadrut (the General Federation of Labor in Israel) was
the guest of honor and welcomed the delegates.
In his address he explained the unique role of the Histadrut as
a labor organization which supplies not only protection for
workers and agreements with employers but medical-care,
financial services and a variety of cultural services as well.
From his point of view advanced technologies and robots do not
necessarily bring only benefit to the society but also cause
unemployment, particularly within the age group of 20 to 25.
Only a comprehensive approach which will provide education and
overall care for workers will suite the future needs of
society.
Barrie Sherman (UK), delivered the keynote address in which he
stressed the influence, of the process our society is going
through, as the result of the "second industrial revolution".
He stated that technology changes but the institutions governing
our lives remain static. This leads to conflict, stress and
strains within society.
Sherman said: "Within manufacturing industries robots and
carrying systems will diminish the need for human labor. Until
and unless companies start to expand their services the
skilled/semi-skilled manual worker has a bleak future".
Yisrael Meidan (IL), was the second keynote speaker and he
presented a slightly different approach concerning the impact of

advanced technology on the industry. and stated that there is no
significant change in the relative share of capital and labor in
the production function. This type of change does not affect the
quantity of labor required. it only affects the character of
labor.

Part II deals with artificial intelligence and robotics.
examining the issue from various aspects.
Harold Sackmans' (USA). general conclusion was that AI and
robotics currently generally tend to accelerate existing trends
in positive and negative social impacts of computers that have
long been documented prior to the current efflorescence of AI.
In particular, AI and robotics developments tend to exacerbate
the ever-growing gap between the information rich and the
information poor at international, national, regional,
institutional and individual levels.
Yosef Regev (IL), raised the question, what will be the outcome
if we do succeed in giving computers and robots the gift of
intelligence. His response concerning the ability of AI and
expert systems to see a more comprehensive picture than that of
humans was rather skeptical. Inanimate environment where
computer programs. robots. communication lines and computerized
data all work together to determine the environment in which
human being operate. Such an environment can eventually become
more and more capable of inputting incorrect data, drawing wrong
conclusions and immediately transferring a flawed decision to
every point in a country or in many countries.

Part III deals with the impact of Advanced Technology and
Robotics on Kibbutz life.
Menachem Rosner (IL). presented some findings which came out
from studies carried out on the introduction of high-tech into
kibbutz society. At present there are 260 kibbutz communities,
with a population of 120.000.
 The members collectively own the means of production and share
the income. Introduction of robots led in many plants to an
increase in the autonomy of different sub-units and due to the
relatively high level of participation and limited hierarchy.
only rather small organizational changes will be needed to adopt
to the new circumstances.

Part IV deals with advanced technology and its impact on Labor
relations.
In his article. Paul Kolm (A)refers to the dynamic part played
by industrial robots in the automation of the industrial
production process. This article/report turns to those countries
which have treated the problem of industrial robots directly.
however the background in any case show technical development
generally is estimated by the various and which ideas have been
developed by them in this respect.
Ozer Carmi(IL) states that developed industrial societies in the
west. including Israel, have been characterized since WWII by a
continuous rapid change, affecting all aspects of existence;
with the most dramatic changes accruing in the realm of
technology resulting from the need to improve productivity and
efficiency.

Part V focuses on the influence of technology on organizations
society and the individual.
Ilan Meshulam(IL) speaks of the need to deal with maintaining
innovation. suggesting an approach to innovation rooted in

system perspective. "Successful implementation" he says, "requires the organization to invest its efforts in reaching a fit between the various components of the organization and its organization culture."

Oded Shenkar(IL) believes that one of the major problems in large scale robotization is the reduction in the level and intensity of social interaction and its adverse behavioral correlation.

Lior Horev (IL) attorney of law, took a legalistic point of view and pointed out three areas of conjunction between computer and law such as: 1) Abuse of computer - aspects of "human individual rights", aspect of "computer crime" temptation to commit such crimes.

2) The "Need of Survival" - active self defense by software creators which causes damage.

3) Responsibility - special responsibility which is typical of the computerized services and devices.

Alexander Matejko (Ca) debates the problem areas of the sociotechnics of technical innovations.

Gert Schmidt (FDR) presents and discusses findings of research on the implementation of new information and communication technologies in industry in the Federal Republic of Germany.

Part VI turns to the subject of training in the age of constant technological change.

Yacov Hecht (IL) suggests that the economical-technological effectiveness of the labor market is measured today by its flexibility, as manifested by the extent of labor and occupation mobility.

The ORT automation and robotics Literacy Project has been the subject of Dan Sharons'(UK) contribution to the conference.

Part VII: At the final panel the speakers expressed their hopes and anxieties concerning the innovation in state of the art technology, hoping that they will improve our lives and make the world better and more human. The real challenge is to use the technologies in an appropriate way but not to impose them. Many of the speakers expressed their deep concern regarding unemployment due to the introduction of high-tech. Moreover they felt that the state and society as a whole must take steps to adjust and provide measures which will alleviate the employment problem - thus facilitate the acceptance of the benefits of advanced technology in our society.

Therefore the challenge has to assist poor families and children far more than to provide those that already have with yet more.

Each presentation was followed by a question and answer period and was also discussed by working groups.

The editors wish to thank the authors of papers, the participants and all those organizations and persons who contributed to the success of the conference.

The Editors

CONTENTS

CONTRIBUTORS AND PARTICIPANTS

PROGRAMME COMMITTEE

Chairman: Dr. D. Millin
Head Computer Science Studies
Beit Berl College
Israel

Co-Chairman: Prof. K. Brunnstein
Fachbereich Informatik
West Germany

Members: Prof. J. Berleur
Belgium

Prof. G. Halevi
Israel

Prof. K. Fuchs-Kitowski
East Germany

I. Meidan
Israel

Dr. M. Palgi
Kibbutz Studies Institute
Israel

Y. Shalom
Israel

Z. Yanai
IBM (Israel) Ltd.
Israel

ISRAEL ORGANIZING COMMITTEE

Chairman: Dr. D. Millin
Head Computer Science Studies
Beit Berl College
Israel

Co-Chairman: B. Raab
Israel Center for Information Systems
The Israel Institute of Productivity
Israel

Members: S. Bukshpan
Municipality of Petach Tikva
Israel

Dr. O. Carmi
Institute of Labor Relations
Israel

S. Dolev
Israel

R. Halevi-Segal
EGGED
Israel

M. Gottlieb
Israel Information Processing Association
Israel

Austria: P. Kolm
                Gewerkschaft der Privatanges
                Deutschmizterplatz 2
                1010 Wien

Canada: A. Matejko
                7623-119 Street
                Edmonton T6G 1W4

France: N. Alter
                Ministere Des Postes et Telecomm.
                DGT-ISPES
                20, Avenue de Segur
                75700 Paris

Israel: U. Agami
                Reshet Amal
                Vaad HaPoal
                Rehov Arlozoroff 83
                Tel Aviv

                Dr. Y. Ben-Schlomo
                ORT Pedagogical Center
                Hatayasim Road
                Yad Eliahu, Tel Aviv

                S. Bukshpan
                Municipality of Petach Tikva
                Box 1
                Petach Tikva

                Dr. O. Carmi
                Institute of Labor Relations
                Israel Institute of Productivity
                30 Shderot Yehudit
                Tel-Aviv

                Dr. M. Dror
                World Future Society
                Israel Chapter
                P.O.Box 60
                Yeroham 80500

S. Dolev
Rehov Keren Hayesod 1
Givat Schmuel 51905

J. Gattegno
Israel Manufacturers Assiciation
Beit Hatasiya
Kaufman Street
Tel Aviv

E. Golan
Kibbutz Industries Association
Sociatechnical Department
107 Hashmonaim Street
Tel Aviv

A. Golfisher
ORT Technical High School
15 Golomb Street
Givataim 53466

M. Gottleib
Managing Director
Israel Information Processing Association
Kfar Hamacabiah
Ramat Gan

Prof. G. Halevi
Cunsultant
Rehov Hanardaya 19
Tel Aviv

Prof. M. Hannani
Rehov Eshel 28
Omer, Beer Sheva

S. Hashbi
Israel Institute of Productivity
30 Shderot Yehudit
Tel Aviv

Y. Hecht
Ministry of Labor and Social Welfare
P.O.Box 915
91008 Jerusalem

R. Halevi-Segal
EGGED
Derech Petach Tikva 142
Tel Aviv

L. Horev
Attorney at Law
Rehov Bloch 5
64161 Tel Aviv

J. Koavchik
ORT School "Melton"
Bat Yam

Dr. I. Kolomer
ORT ISRAEL
29 King David Blvd.
61160 Tel Aviv

M. Krindler
P.O.Box 78
20292 Karmiel

R. Kuperman
IPA
Kfar Hamacabbiah
Ramat Gan

M.A. S. Laor
Researcher
Vaad Hapoal
Rehov Arlozoroff 93
Tel Aviv

A. Lior
Institute of Labor Relations
30 Shderot Yehudit
Tel-Aviv

I. Meidan
Rehov Yoav 6
Tzahala, Tel-Aviv

M. Merdler
ORT Technical High School
2 Prof. Shor Street
Holon

Dr. I. Meshulam
Intel Electronics Ltd.
P.O.Box 3173
Jerusalem

Dr. D. Millin
Vice-Chairman IFIP TC-9
Head Computer Science Studies
Beit Berl College

U. Osri
Kibbutz Industries Association
Sociotechnical Department
107 Hashmonaim Street
Tel Aviv

Dr. M. Palgi
Kibbutz Studies Institute
University of Haifa
Haifa

I. Polak
ORT Technical High School
Industrial Zone
Netanya

Prof. M.A. Pollatschek
Faculty of Management
Technion
32000 Haifa

B. Raab
Director, Israel Center for Information Systems
Israel Institute of Productivity
30 Shderot Yehudit
Tel Aviv

J. Regev
Department of Mechanical Engineering
Ben Gurion University of the Negev
84105 Beer Sheva

J. Richter
School of Business Administration
Tel Aviv University
Rehov HaUniversita
Ramat Aviv, Tel-Aviv

Prof. M. Rosner
Kibbutz Studies Institute
University of Haifa
Haifa

Z. Scherz
Weizmann Institute of Science
Rehovot

Y. Shalom
Rehov Yesurun 30
452000 Hod Hasharon

O. Shenkar
School of Business Administration
Tel Aviv University
Rehov HaUniversita
Ramat Aviv

R. Soffer
ORT ISRAEL
29 King David Blvd.
61160 Tel Aviv

A. Winger
ORT Technical High School
ORT St.
Industrial Zone
Natanya

Z. Yanai
IBM (Israel) Ltd.
Shaul Hamelech Blvd.
Tel Aviv

Ireland: J. Drumm
                  214 Grace Park Heights
                  Drumconda
                  Dublin 9

Italy: A. Dina
                        Observation & Research on Advanced Technology
                        Italian Metalworking Trade Union
                        c/o FIOM-CGIL Corso Triest 36
                        Rome 00198

                        Prof. P. Maggiolini
                        Politecnico di Milano
                        Dipartmento di Electronica
                        Piazza Leonardo Di Vinci 32
                        20020 Arconate (Milano)

                        Prof. G. Valle
                        Universita di Milano
                        Science Della Informazione
                        Via Moretto 9
                        20133 Milano

The Netherlands: G. Noltes
                        Ministerie van Welzijn
                        Volksgezondheid en Cultuur
                        Den Haag

                        F. van Rijn
                        University of Amsterdam
                        Ruysdaelkade t.o. 225
                        1072 BA Amsterdam

United Kingdom: Y. Kahn
                        14 Greenarce Walk
                        Cannon Hill
                        London N14 7DB

                        B. Sherman
                        16, Camden News
                        London NW1 9DA

U.S.A.:   Dr. T. Perl
                        T. Perl Ass.
                        525 Lincoln Ave
                        Palo Alto, Ca 94301

Part 1
OPENING AND KEYNOTE ADDRESSES

The Social Implications of Robotics and Advanced
Industrial Automation / D. Millin and B.H. Raab (Editors)
Elsevier Science Publishers B.V. (North-Holland)
© IFIP, 1989

Opening Address

HISTADRUT'S LEADING ROLE

IN ISRAEL ECONOMY AND SOCIETY

Israel Kesar
Secretary-General of the Histadrut
General Federation of Labor in Israel

Before I speak on the subject of the Conference, I would like to introduce
the Histadrut to our guests from abroad in order to show its contribution to
Israel social and economic development.

Histadrut - the General Federation of Labour in Israel was founded in 1920
by 87 delegates, representing 4,433 members. Today, 68 years later, their
number reached 1.6 million.

Since the British Mandate (1917-1948) regarded Israel (then Palestine) as
just another colonial possession, the Histadrut was obliged, during those
per-state years, to attend to all the essential needs of its members -
including employment, housing and medical assistance. Histadrut acted,
hence, not only as a trade union, but founded agricultural settelments, a
Sick-Fund, a building company, industrial enterprises, a bank, an
agricultural produce marketing company, consumer cooperatives, etc. It also
took responsibility for the education of workers' children and set-up a
daily newspaper and publishing house.

Thus its unique structure developed - a combination of trade unions, a
social security system, and a workers' economy - all within a single
comprehensive framework.

The founders of the Histadrut determined in its constitution its being open
to every worker - irrespective of nationality, race, religion or political
views. The elections to its General Conventions, once in four years, are
carried out on a political representation basis.

Whereas the trade unions and shop committees represent the Histadrut at the
place of work, the Labour Councils are the representatives of the Histadrut
in the community. Today the histadrut network comprises of is comprised 72
local labour councils and thousands of shop committees.

Following the establishment of the State of Israel, in 1948, the Histadtut
transferred most of its educational network, the labour exchanges and other
functions to the State. On the other hand, it took upon itself a central
role in the absorption of mass immigration arriving in the country. It also
took part in the founding of hundreds of new agricultural settlements as
well as industial enterprises. Kupat-Holim (the Workers' Sick-Fund) absorbed
most of the newcommers. At present the insured population in Kupat Holim
numbers over 3.3 million - about 75% of Israel's total population.
Histadrut's pension funds insure hundreds of thousands of its members in
comprehensive pension schemes.

A great number of labour and social laws, whose provisions were already in practice due to the Histadrut's efforts - were passed by Parliament and become obligatory. An extensive system of basic social security was established by the State. Labour courts were set up to deal with matters of National Insurance and implementation of the said labour laws.

Freedom of Association and freedom of industrial action were strictly observed. The Histadrut, however, does not spare efforts in order to settle labour disputes through negotiations and mutual understanding, and only where no alternative is left, does it resort to industrial action. Thus, the Histadrut also agreed to set up a panel of agreed arbitration, but strongly objects to compulsory arbitration, which, in its opinion, has no place in a democratic society, and only tends to worsen labour relations.

The labour Economy established by Histadrut is comprised of about 22% of Israels GNP and labour force. It consists of the cooperative sector which includes the agricultural coopratives - Kibutzim and Moshavim and urban cooperatives; and the administrative sector - owned directly by the Histadrut, constituting the Worker' Bank, the industrial concern "KOOR", the construction company "SOLEL BONEH", an insurance company, department stores, etc.

The fact that a trade union federation is also an employer creates a serious dilema. However - the workers employed in the labour economy prefer this framework to any other system of ownership, since they share advantages in salaries, social benefits and work conditions. Great efforts are being made to strengthen their feeling of solidarity with the enterprise - especially through workers' participation on managerial boards, profit sharing, as well as through social welfare and cultural activities.

A cornerstone of the Histadruth's wages policy is the automatic cost-of-living adjustment, which is customary in our country since the outbreak of World War II. Agreements for the payment of C.o.L. adjustments are signed periodically between the Histadrut and the Manufacturer's Association and then extended, by Government decree, as general practice in the country. These agreements are imperative to the protection of the standard of living of the workers, thus helping to stabilize labour relations and prevent social unrest. It should also be remembered, that the Histadrut's policy had a decisive effect on the curbing of the inflation in Israel, which reached its peak in 1985, but now tends to stabilize itself close to the inflation rate prevailing in Western Europe.

Wage agreements in Israel are signed once in two years between the Histadrut and the Manufacturers Association in the private sector and with public employers in the public sector. These are basic agreements, which determine wage increases, improvements in social benefits and work conditions on the national level. In addition - there remains a large scope for intiative at the trade union and plant level.

The Histadrut also maintains a youth organization, the leading sports association in the country - "HAPOEL"; the "AMAL" vocational education network; a cultural and education centre, and a women's organization - "NA'AMAT" - operating child-care centers and various educational institutions.

The Histadrut has developed a wide-ranging network of international activity. It has established close ties with free trade union federations and cooperative movements all over the world. Its Afro-Asian Institute and Latin American Centre in Tel-Aviv have trained thousands of trade-unionists and cooperators from developing countries.

In the 68 years of its existence the histadrut's unique structure proved its vitality and stood up to the test of time. It faces the future trusting that it will maintain its leading role in the social and economic development of the country.

And now, briefly, to some of the questions relating directly to automation and robotics.

We live in an era of a rapidly changing economy. We have new, but also still some relatively old industires, with a great variety of occupations and wages. Constant development in technologies, rapid changes in international as well as domestic markets - have a decisive impact on the occupational structure and workers' income, secutiry of employment, and on the economic and social situation in the country as a whole.

Old and prestigious trades disappear and new ones develop; skilled professional workers lose their positions if they cannot adapt themselves to the demands of new technologies. Thus young computer operators often replace skilled veteran manual workers whose machines become obsolete.

We have to support - on the one hand - development and progress, without which there is no rise in the standard of living and no chance to compete on international markets. On the other hand, however, we have to cope with all the difficulties created by the rapid technological and scientific progress.

It is far from being obvious that the introduction of new sophisticated technological processes necessarily leads to the workers' direct benefit. If its immediate result is a loss of jobs and employment opportunities - it creates severe problems for the workers as well as for the Trade Unions as their representatives and spokesmen.

The fast penetration of the most advanced technolgies into our economy is, as aforesaid, largely changing our occupational structure, thus committing our educational system to cope with new demanding and even critical challenges.

This inevitable process of technological progress may also raise exaggerated and unjustified expectations for additional jobs and better income. However, the number of new openings created by it is rather limited and, in many instances, insecure and unstable. Simultaneously we face an extensive problem of youth unemployment, in particular among the 20-25 age group. That means that a substantial part of our future work force in far from having its employment safe and guaranteed.

It seems, therefore, that there exists an inherent conflict between the new era of technological progress and development and the young generation's need for new and satisfactory jobs. In Israel, in fact, we need some 60,000 new employment openings per year to safeguard jobs for all those joining the work-force.

Thus, the principal stress in our investments should be directed towards developing human resources, through planned education and training of young workers in trades and skills with the best chances of offering employment and helping the ecomomy at the same time. Education and vocational training must be improved and expanded in a way which will offer everbody a fair chance of getting it; and so that everyone should be able to express, develop and realize his creative capacity.

We have to insist on creating new jobs, preserve the existing ones as far as possible, and share the results of increased productivity among all of us. It is vital for us to support new technologies for the benefit of the community as well as of the individual and advance the quality of work life. At the same time we have to be on guard constantly so as to always keep control ever new technology and not to let it rule our lives.

The Social Implications of Robotics and Advanced
Industrial Automation / D. Millin and B.H. Raab (Editors)
Elsevier Science Publishers B.V. (North-Holland)
© IFIP, 1989

WORKING AT LEISURE

Barrie Sherman

This is a conference about robotics and advanced industrial
automation, which really means it is concerned with general and micro-
electronics of all descriptions. It is tempting to believe that these
technologies exist as an entity in themselves, divorced from the
ambitions and prejudices of human beings; a subject that can be
discussed and dissected in the comfortable vacuum of a conference or
academic seminar. They cannot be, indeed they must not be. Neither
must the newer automation production technologies be divorced from
the service information and analytical technologies. They interact with
one another, they compete for the same scarce resources (especially
that of skilled workers), and often the underpinning technology is
identical.

These newer technologies exist in a world of competition and
regulation; a world where employment is becoming scarcer and where
the rich are becoming richer and the poor, poorer: and this applies to
countries as well as people. Furthermore, these technologies are being
introduced into societies which have evolved but little from the first
industrial revolution; the one driven by the steam engine; and the
combination of new technology and the old existing culture is not
always a happy one.

There can be no doubt that robotics and advanced automation have the
potential for inestimable good; there can equally be no doubt that they
can be used for apallingly evil purposes. Technologies do not decide
which route is taken for themselves, the Artificial Intelligence (AI)
systems have not reached that point as yet, if indeed they ever do.
People decide what technology is used for; it does not matter what type
of technology, high or low, new or old. By people I mean you and me,
this conference, designers, engineers, workers, businessmen, generals
and politicians.

I will argue that the new technologies amount to another industrial
revolution, the second or third, depending how you regard the
combination of electricity, chemical production and the internal

combustion engine. Revolutions imply great changes, and I shall argue that the changes in production methods and service delivery, let alone who is employed, where and how (indeed on which continent they are employed), and the types of products and services available, will have to be matched by corresponding changes in social and political life.

But to start, bear with me while I take you back a couple of hundred years, to when the steam engine was driving the new factories and mills, changing agriculture and revolutionising transport and distribution, amongst other things. It was not only a time of great industrial change but also of enormous social and demographic upheavals. New towns and cities appeared where none had been before, older power centres like the market towns dwindled and new power centres arose. New housing, new education systems, new health measures and a new capitalist ethos were being developed. Although people did not go around muttering, "Gosh, isn't this a marvellous thing, aren't we lucky; we're living in the industrial revolution," it was exciting to live through.....unless you happened to be a worker. Then you suffered.

In fact it was a time of suffering. Infant mortality rates were staggeringly high, as were the numbers of industrial accidents, not surprising with no protective laws and children as young as eight years old working in facories and mines. It was a time when political upheaval was endemic across Europe and later in North America. Britain needed seven political reform acts to keep its Parliamentary system together, the year of revolutions in Europe saw power change hands fundamentally while the American Civil War was between the old agrarian society and the newer industrial one.

It was a time of massive slumps when Eastern Europe decanted its populations into Western Europe and America. One hundred years ago there was a slump so severe (1876 to 1894), and unemployment so massive, that the policy of most European governments', insofar as they had a policy at all, was to encourage their workers to emigrate, and they did to the USA and Canada, Autralasia and the empires of the industrialised states. Overproduction had created the slump. It was a triumph for ingenuity and technology leading to increases in productivity, but it was a disaster based on these increases outstripping possible demand for the products. The entire century was kept trading by colonial expansion and war. It was a time par excellence of revolutions and of wars.

I'm telling you this for two reasons. The first is to demonstrate that despite the often proclaimed view that technology has been introduced without any problems the first industrial revolution shows that the problems were immense. The stresses and strains were enormous in all of the industrialising, and ultimately industrialised, countries. If you think about it carefully, you would not expect any less from a revolution.

The second reason is the more important of the two, however. I will argue that micro-electronics is the only technology since the steam engine to have the same two basic characteristics. There has been nothing like it this century. The steam engine's first characteristic was that it was a ubiquitous technology; as I have said it was everywhere: it was the motive power. All production, most transport and distribution, agriculture and mineral extraction depended on steam, water or wind power, and the latter two, being far less flexible, lost out. There was no service industry in those days, except for 'service', maids and skivvies.

Steam engines were also a supply side technology. In themselves they added but little to demand, and that was as capital goods. In the nineteenth century no-one turned to their family after tea and said, "Wont be long, just going down to the shops to buy a steam-engine." Steam engines were used to increase efficiency and raise productivity, and they did so throughout the century. This century we have had technologies which were ubiquitous (electricity), and technologies which were supply side (NCM's), but never the two together; untll now.

Now think about micro-electronics. It is a ubiquitous technology. It is everwhere in the formal sector, in fact, try to think of an area where it is not now in use, or will soon be used. You cannot, can you? There are some personal services immune from micro-electronics, but even here, many of them are illegal. Like the steam engine it is everwhere, including the armed forces and the service industries. How many people do you know, other than computer buffs who will go to buy integrated circuitry?   If people as at home with computers as yourselves don't know many, then there cannot be many of them, can there?   Like the steam engine, micro-electronics is a supply side technology. We all know that it is used to increase efficiency, increase effectiveness, and raise productivity.

Productivity is defined as output per head of worker.   It can be increased either by increasing output, or by decreasing the number of workers. Now, if a technology comes along which increases the rate of productivity in certain industries an enormous amount, then, by definition, output has to rise at least as much if employment levels are to be maintained.   It is a simple arithmetical fact. Clearly by the end of the nineteenth century, output could rise no further.   Micro-electronic based technologies raise productivity levels substantially, but a cursory look around the industrialised world today will show that output is not increasing by anything like as much in the established industrialised countries.   Unemployment stays high, even with economic growth....both the classical and Keynesian economists say that cannot happen....but it is happening.

It is true that there are some consumer products with micro-electronics incorporated in them.   But to add to employment numbers, they have to be new products for new markets. Sure there are some like this, personal computers, video cameras, VCR's, and credit cards are examples, none of which could exist without micro-electronics. But they are far outnumbered in volume, and as a percentage of world product, by new products for old markets and plain amended products.

The digital watch was a new product for an old market.   The traditional analogue European watch industry was decimated as the Far East (Japan and Taiwan) swept the board.   Watches became cheaper, and far more of them were sold, yet worldwide fewer workers overall were needed to make them. Indeed, those that were employed were unskilled assemblers, rather than Swiss, French or German skilled operatives.....and they were half a world away.   You only have look at cars, washing machines, cookers, bathroom scales, or any other white goods, to realise that the major use of intregrated circuitry is to amend a product. Far from increasing employment, this tends to reduce it drastically, over time.

Let us look at industrial processes. Robots reduce the number of workers; they are intended to. Computer controlled machine tools, and integrated systems, reduce the need for skilled labour; they are intended to. While there are other benefits, enhanced quality control for example, the new industrial technologies directly reduce the need for labour. This is how they increase productivity. But the use of micro-electronic components reduces it still further, Not only are fewer people needed to assemble the components, there are fewer of them to assemble. This means fewer people are needed to assemble the sub-components. It also means that fewer invoices, bills and wage statements have to be made out, and as the production process is truncated, so the need for supervisors and managers diminishes.

In the last fifteen years we have seen the loss of jobs worldwide in manufacturing industry, it is starting even to affect Japan. Over this period the workers who would have had jobs in the manufacturing sector have been working in the expanding service industries. But what happens when the same employment effects start to hit the service sector....and they will before the mid 1990's. All we are awaiting is the network revolution; we are waiting for the PTT's to produce telecomm systems which will match the sophistication of the existing office-based computer systems.

If you look at the great commercial centres like London or New York and analyse what the majority of the workers actually do, it is clear that they shuffle, amend, and then transmit, information. They excercise no real discretion and their decision making is confined to a smallish number of variables, all which are known beforehand. Externalities, therefore judgements, play no part in the process. Not a pleasant thought if a new technology which is designed to do exactly the same tasks, only faster, more accurately and more cheaply, is just around the corner. We already use a host of electronic equipment, including PC's, computers, processors, and clever exchanges to improve productivity within offices. But, all that is needed is the full implementation of an all electronic, cheap, reliable network and switching system, at which point a considerable increase in clerical and administrative work can be done by far fewer employees from anywhere, cheaply and efficiently. From home, from shops, from overseas: the era of world trade in letter writing is about to unfold, imports and exports of clerical work are already a reality.

Few goods or services are immune from this process. It is affecting libraries, publishing, shops, transport, health care and education, law and order, entertainment and newspapers, war and defence, you name it and the jobs are changing, both in quantity, and quality. But there are also a series of wider changes starting. They are covering the widest of spectra--from attitudes in industry and commerce through to community groups, politics and international relations and trade. Yet, as in the nineteenth century, the fact we are living through an industrial revolution is passing people by. The current changes are seen as a series of unconnected (and probably reversible) events, rather than as part and parcel of a larger and more fundamental change.

But, in the shorter run, the psychological effects that are now appearing, are the more important. The certainties that we knew we could hold onto are evaporating into doubts, and the precepts on which we have based our lives no longer seem to be as relevant today as they were a mere five years ago. These effects are being felt in all of the industrialised and industrialising countries. Individuals find it increasingly difficult to keep up with the changing circumstances, trade unionists become more defensive whilst many businessmen find both the changing environment and technologies hard to comprehend and exploit. As the technology changes what we do, and how and where we do it, the institutions and precepts governing our lives remain static. This mismatch of yesterday and today, leads to conflicts, stresses and strains within society.

However, the other side of any problem is a challenge. Only by taking this positive view will the technologies (except perhaps the in their military uses, where ordinary people have little or no control) have a chance of being used optimally. This must not mean that the social and community costs which may well arise should be glossed over or ignored, indeed to do so may well be to court disaster in the longer run. These costs must be identified, and then tackled. One of the major costs will be the diminution of employment opportunities, especially for young people.

Recent attitude surveys have shewn that 7 out of every 10 persons in Britain believe that the new technologies will destroy more jobs than they will create. This belief is held despite all the major political groupings, and both the central union and employers organisations, denying the proposition. The feeling is held because so many people have first hand knowledge of job losses (and the reasons for them). Given the arguments outlined above, it is not difficult to see why this should be so.

What has been happening is that new systems have been put in place, output has expanded, but no new workers have been needed. There have been few redundancies. The job losses should be designated more accurately as potential job losses. They come about from natural wastage (attrition), early retirement and the resulting inability of schoolleavers to get jobs. If, and when, they are needed, the tendancy is for them to be part-timers, temporary employees, or a combination of the two. Throughout the industrialised world new robotic systems, new information and new office systems are going hand in hand with the diminution of the full time/permanent labour force--and the unions have been powerless to stop it.

There are three misconceptions about employment and technology that it would be as well to clear up at this point. The first is that unions oppose the introduction of new technologies. This is in fact the reverse of the truth. Most unions appear to have gone overboard in a love affair with computer and electronic technologies. For example, outside of the print industries there has been very little strike action and none over the introduction of robots. In my judgement unions have actually aquiesced too much, too often, they have failed to represent their members best interests. Most research is now pointing to managers as the source of mistrust and inaction.

The second misconception is that small companies can introduce technologies with no adverse employment effects. Not so. The company introducing the technology may do well, but its competitors will either shed labour or go to the wall. Company A, with 25% of the local bed-leg market introduces a new computer system. Companies B C and D do not; they all employ 10 people. Company A increases its productivity 50% and also provides a better service to its customers. It increases its market share to 40%. Unless the total market for the bed legs has increased by more than the extra $12\frac{1}{2}$% (and the odds are that it is growing at best at a GDP rate of about 3%), there have to be job losses, and/or bankruptcies. In small companies the firms which do not use the technologies lose the jobs <u>but</u> if they all introduced the technologies there would be overproduction. In theory the price of bedlegs will then fall. But bedlegs are components and the impact of a fall in their price on the total cost of a bed will be minimal, therefore there will no extra demand for beds...and therefore one or two of the companies will go bankrupt, losing half of the jobs. Jobs will have to be lost whichever route is taken, and this applies to the generality of small companies, most of which are component manufacturers or the providers of intermediate services.

The third misconception is that by not using the technlogies jobs will be saved. This used to be a trades union standpoint, but at best it is a very short term argument. It is true, but only in monopolies or monopsonies, or in areas where the price reductions or service improvements are not significant for the customers. The Civil Service and other public services are examples of the first type, newspaper publishing or supermarket lazar check-outs are examples of the second. By and large, the companies not using new technologies will be at a comparative disadvantage...they will lose market share, and they will lose jobs. <u>But</u> it is Catch 22. If a company invests in new technologies jobs will be lost in that company or a competitor company; if it does not invest then jobs will be lost because it is no longer competitive!

This second industrial revolution is in its infancy. Not only are the present generation of computers, information systems and robots primitive (when compared with their currently known potential) but there are two extra waves just around the corner. It is rather like the period around 1915 when we had the motor car but were still awaiting Henry Ford and his mass production methods for it to start to reach its potential. The first new wave will be the network explosion led by a combination of electronic national telecomm networks and more sophisticated satellite technology. The second wave, a combination of 5th generation and bio-computers, should become commercially viable early in the 21st century; the combination of these waves will lead to another tranche of changes.

The amount of work that people will be able to do from a variety of different places will expand, <u>but,</u> the amount of time spent at work will diminish overall, and for some a very great deal. In other words leisure time will increase. The role of managers and professionals will change (especially when artificial intelligence systems and the 5th generation equipment merge). International trade patterns will change, along with alliances and emnities. Finally, information will become synonomous with power.

All of these factors open new opportunities for politicians, managers, entrepreneurs and for employees and their unions. Telecommuting, especially transnationally, is likely to become a standard procedure, leading to a subcontracting of clerical and administrative work. Given the lower cost of labour, indeed the plethora of non-unionised 'captive' labour, in the Newly Industrialising Countries (NIC's), the possibility of these countries becoming net exporters of clerical work and information havens must be quite high. The other side of the coin is that employment for women in the industrialised country's commercial centres will collapse. Within the manufacturing industries robots and carrying systems will diminish the need for human labour. Until, and unless, companies start to expand their customer/client services the skilled/semi-skilled manual worker has a bleak future.

As leisure time increases so the need to find ways in which this time can be filled grows with it. The current situation is that those with leisure time do not have the wherwithal to use it properly, while those with the resources do not have the leisure time. This may be simplifying the problem, as it is far from clear that the unemployed have leisure time in the way it is normally recognised. It appears that leisure has to be earned, either by current employment, or in the case of the retired, their past employment. Whether it is to cope with the increased leisure time or with the rapidly changing systems at the workplace the education and training systems of many countries will have to adapt.

However the work ethic is still strong, although it is not really about work anymore---it is all about paid employment. When people work hard at DIY, digging gardens or even helping others, it does not satisfy the ethic, unless it attracts a wage. This paid employment ethic is not the natural state of mankind, it was imposed during the first industrial revolution; before that the original 'work ethic' was really a usefulness ethic: we needed to be useful to others and to ourselves. Our work ethic (employment ethic) stemmmed from the fact that the first industrial revolution processes were not only very labour intensive, they were also extremely unpleasant, especially for someone used to the more seasonal open air life in the country. Employers needed labour in vast quantities and all the organs of the establishment coalesced around propaganda to get people to need employment spiritually rather than just economically. This differed from the original work ethic, which was about personal and group survival, rather than the employment ethic, which is about profits and 'looking busy'.

Our present industrial revolution is demanding that we return to the original ethic. Voluntary work needs to become as satisfying as paid work (and interchangeable with it), but while this sounds easy to achieve, in reality it hides a series of very difficult and fundamental political and social decisions. For example, people have to be financially secure, so that we will have to look at new measures such as 'Negative Income Tax'. We shall have to have fresh looks at how taxation can be levied and what the appropriate levels of public expenditure should be, nationally and internationally. From paying people to not-work to new welfare payments and from education to trade policy, hard (and radical) political decisions will have to be taken---precisely as they were during the first industrial revolution. Indeed we are in a position to learn from the mistakes made in the nineteenth century.

However, therein lies a problem. Because the people who run politics and government refuse to accept publicly that we are living through another industrial revolution, (they believe it would be alarmist) we look to the wrong period for help. We look to last year, rather than the last century. We look at production factors a decade ago rather than a hundred years ago. We cannot learn this way. Indeed, we are repeating history's classic mistake. <u>By and large we are getting the right answers, but we have been asking the wrong questions all the time.</u>

We must realise that workers will no longer be able to work for 47 years of their life, 47 weeks in each year and for 47 hours per week (with overtime), even if they wanted to. Employment will be in short supply, because we will be sharing it around. Three day weeks, a month on, month off, year long sabbaticals every five years; the range of possibilities is huge. It is probable that legislation attached to supranational bodies, such as OECD, GATT and the EEC will detail many of the rules by early in the next century, and they will govern international trade. The alternative to this scenario is to run an increasing percentage of long-term unemployment in the midst of affluent societies, and this would be unlikely to remain a stable situation in the longer term.

One of the consequences of this is that we shall have more free time. But our education systems prepare us for employment, not leisure. Indeed as education systems move more towards training, they equip our young people less well for employment too. Training, even if it is for a skill in current use, focusses down onto a small part of life....it narrows horizons. On the other hand, education is a widening process which is aimed at enabling people to leran how to learn. Only people who can do this will be capable of coping with a rapidly changing technology and fundamentally changing society. If I have one plea, it is for educationalists around the world to stand up and defend their profession against the predations of industrialists, politicians and trainers. Training has its place, but after education.

A good education system would allow people far more choice in their selection of leisure activities.   At present, as a result of our employment oriented training/education system, leisure is regarded as a residual after employment has finished, and residuals are scantly regarded.   We need to take leisure more seriously, if only because it will be one of the major job-providers in the future. We need to see leisure as a constructive rather than hedonistic activity; we need to view leisure as a pleasant and rewarding activity, and we need to widen the horizons of people to the ever widening options which leisure can provide.   Leisure is also becoming internationalised.   The insights provided by Satellite TV and increasing international tourism will probably change the world as radically as any technology; indeed it comes down to the technology anyway; they are both products of the same electronic technology.

We must realise that the 1960's and 1970's are not returning, however much we may wish that they would.   Given that we must stop hearking back to these 'golden days' (those living through them found them more copper than golden), and look to the future, with one eye on the more distant past. Few politicians, let alone industrialists or trade-unionists appear prepared to accept the fundamental nature of these changes. This responsibility has been shifted onto the shoulders of the technocrats and computer/cyberneticists (albeit by default). It is up to the people at this conference, it is up to the membership of IFIP in general, not only to show what can be done, but also to chart any pitfalls that can be spotted and alert the public to them.

For the full argument see "Working at Leisure", Barrie Sherman published by Methuen Ltd. London

The Social Implications of Robotics and Advanced
Industrial Automation / D. Millin and B.H. Raab (Editors)
Elsevier Science Publishers B.V. (North-Holland)
© IFIP, 1989

IMPACT OF AUTOMATION AND ROBOTICS ON
EMPLOYMENT IN ISRAEL

Israel H. MEIDAN

Chairman, Institute of Incomes and Output.
Tel-Aviv, Israel.

1. INTRODUCTION.

1.1. I am doubtful as to whether the Israeli experience of the
impact of automation and robotics on employment may have any
relevance to other countries in the industrial community. The
circumstances of our social and industrial development, the
characteristics of the population, and the political environment
governing the existence of Israeli society, created some specific
patterns of behaviour, which may not be relevant to others.
However, as our experience contradicts some of the publicised
evaluations and assesments concerning the topic, I shall try to
relate our experience after a brief description of the
chracteristics of the Israeli socio/economic environment and its
industrial development.

1.2. Economic development in Israel was effected mainly by the
following factors:

- Lack of natural resources, small area of arable land and
  limited sources of water supply.

- A small population base and political isolation from
  neighboring export markets, which hampered the establishment of
  mass producing industries.

- An economic boycott declared by the Arab states against
  Israel, intimidating international corporations and
  discouraging them from dealing with Israeli firms. This
  prevented many multinational corporations from establishing
  industrial enterprises in Israel.

- Large scale immigration, gathering people from different and
  diverse cultural, social and economic backgrounds, creating a
  society of people with little education and no industrial
  tradition, molded with groups of highly educated and advanced
  scientists and industrial leaders.

- A strong desire to pursue progress and to achieve a high
  standard of living shared by a majority of the population,
  alleviating to a great extent the reluctance to change.

- A basic inclination for learning and pursuing higher education,
  shared by a high proportion of the people.

1.3. Although the process of economic development in Israel
followed in many respects the patterns observed in most of the
developing economies, the factors listed above affected some very
significant changes.

1.3.1. The initial thrust of progress was directed towards the agricultural sector. Shortage of water and limited availability of land, directed efforts towards intensive agricultural crops. Efforts were directed to achieve high productivity by the optimal utilization of human resources, water and other production factors. These efforts were backed by significant research activities and a mechanism for the dessimination of know-how and training. The agricultural sector reached a high level of sophistication in its product policy and relatively effective and efficient marketing and production systems.

1.3.2. Industrial development was prompted by government efforts to establish labour intensive industries that will substitute for imports and provide employment for the incoming immigrants. The pattern was similar to that pursued by many developing countries. Financial and other assistance was given by the government to enterpreneurs who were ready to launch new enterprises providing employment in developing regions. Protective tariffs to secure the existence of these "Infant Industries" against potential imports were decreed, and massive government bureaucracy to control and maintain these arrangements was established.

Thus, in the 50's and early 60's many new industries were established. these included textile, clothing, food processing, cement, wood and metal fabricating industries which were needed for the building and construction programs. Employment in Industry has grown tenfold between the years 1955 and 1966, and productivity has risen by an average annual rate of 6%-7%.

The experiments to move into what is known as the second phase of industrialization, i.e. the establishment of electro- mechanical and mass producing industries, were not overly successful. The small size of the local market, the lack of managerial and technical know-how, and the reluctance of multinational firms to establish industrial plants in Israel, prevented the growth of industries such as car assembly plants, manufacturing of home appliances, television, radio and video equipment, and the like.

These developments, coupled with the particular needs of the country's defense requirements and the availability of a high proportion of highly educated human resources, accelerated the establishment and growth of the 'Third generation Industries' i.e. science based industries manufacturing products which use microelectronics, fiber-optics and other advanced technologies.

Figure 1 shows the shifts that occured in the composition of exports of the Israeli industry. these changes ilustrate the different phases of industrial development in the last three decades. We can see clearly the shift in the 1980's, from citrus and textiles to metal, electronics and fine chemical products.

Figure 1: **CHANGES OF EXPORT PRODUCTS IN MILLION US $**
(1980 PRICES)

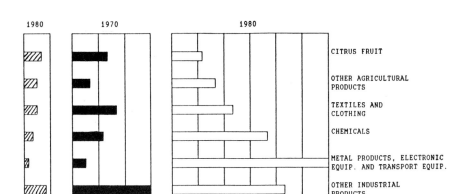

MILLION US $

2. PHASES OF PENETRATION OF AUTOMATION AND ROBOTICS.

2.1. Before discussing the effects of Automation and Robotics on
employment, let me try to describe the phases and the extent of
penetration of these technologies into the Israeli main economic
sectors.

2.2. AGRICULTURE.

2.2.1. The Agricultural sector, as mentioned in paragraph 1.2.1.,
is characterised by a strong quest for labor saving, efficiency
and high productivity. The settling authorities together with the
Kibbutz movement, developed agricultural research and established
elaborate systems of Information dessimination. These included
centers for agricultural experimentation and very effective
farmer training and extension services. Thus, this sector was
prone to an extensive penetration of innovative technologies,
including Automation and Robotics.

2.2.2. In the agricultural production systems we wittnessed among
other phenomena, the widespread automation of cowsheds, including
the process of milking, feeding, cleaning and distribution; The
Institute of Agricultural engineering together with equipment
manufacturers, developed or adapted a whole range of agricultural
devices to harvest, select, and automatically pack most of the
agricultural produce. These were put very quickly into use by
farmers and co-operatives. Automation of packing-houses included
the entire handling, sorting, dispatching, documenting, and the
quality controll processes.

2.2.3. Limited production resources, and mainly the shortage of water, initiated a whole gammut of activities to improve irrigation systems and to assure the optimal use of water, both, to secure highest yields and to save as much as possible of this precious resource. Thus, drip irrigation was developed, augmented by automated control systems which measure humidity of the ground in which crops are grown and activate the flow of water according to specific needs of each crop. all these systems are centrally controlled and save the manpower which used to tend valves positioned in the fields. Nowadays, many of these systems are used in private home gardens.

2.2.4. The information systems and administrative controls in the agricultural sector do not lag behind. To give but a few examples: The planning of crops of most of the 'Kibutzim' is determined by the use of an optimization matrix developed by a team headed by Dr. Goldshmidt. It considers available production resources in each community (land, water, human resources etc.) on one hand, as against alternative crops and their market prices on the other. It than determines the optimal planning of growth. Exporting flowers to European markets is controlled by a central system which marries demands and prices in different markets, with available fresh crops, and directs the harvesting, packing and dispatching by air to the apropriate buyers. Another example of these techniques is the feeding of cattle: In this case, the various mixes which assure the best types of cattle feed according to the characteristics of the animals, are pitted against the cost of the ingriedients. Thus, the optimal feeding mix is calculated and the results are passed to mixing silos, which prepare the mix accordingly and distribute it to the cattle sheds.

2.2.5. These developments led to a significant growth of exports of agricultural products, also freeing a large part of the labor force in this sector. The Kibbutz movement trying to provide alternative sources of employment, started to establish industries within the kibbutz structure, developing the concept of "AGRO-INDUS". In other forms of agricultural settlement some unemployment occured.

2.3. BUILDING AND CONSTRUCTION.

2.3.1. In the last two decades we witnessed a contraction of activity in this sector. These developments followed the expansion of this industry as a result of the great efforts to settle the masses of newly arrived immigrants in the early 1950's. The policies to slow economic activities as a means to fight inflation, pursued in the aftermath of the 1973 war and the oil crisis, reduced significantly the volume of building and construction. More recently, the crisis even deepened. Overall output of the construction industry was reduced by some 35% in the last five years. Employment was not reduced proportionally, thus, productivity was down during this period by some 20%.

2.3.2. Another factor which influenced the penetration of new technologies, automation and robotics into this sector, was the influx of nonskilled labour from the occupied territories in the aftermath of the 1967 war.

2.3.3. The conservative attitudes of the leaders of the Israeli construction industry, coupled with the contraction of its activity and the availability of a big supply of inexpensive labour resources, hindered investemnt in modern equipment. With the exception of mechanical cranes and some prefabricated plants which were introduced in the late fifties and early sixties, little automation (and practically no robotics) was introduced into this industry.

2.4. MANUFACTURING INDUSTRIES.

2.4.1. We have already mentioned the fact that the there are very few assembly plants in Israel. The industry is composed mainly of Textiles and clothing plants, Food processing industries, Steel, Cement and other construction related plants, Diamond processing industries, a large military goods industry (arms, munitions and aircraft) and a relatively significant proportion of science based industries including micro-electronics, electro and fiber optics, medical diagnostic equipment and pharmaceutical products. Most of the enterprises are small or medium sized. There are only few large sized plants. This industrial structure prevented the massive introduction of robots as labor substitution equipment.

2.4.2. While the use of computers and micro-electronics in industrial products and processes is widespread, a recent survey conducted by the Industrial Automation Center came out with the findings that the total number of robots in the Israeli industry does not exceed 80 - 100.

Most of these robots are in the Kibbutz industries. The attitude of introducing advanced technologies and labour saving devices in the agricultural sector was in all probability transferred to the agro-industrial sector. We also find some robots in the military industries, and many computer controlled automatic manufacturing and testing equipment in the science based industries. On the other hand, there are very few Robots in privately owned plants.

2.4.3. Chemical and process industries are computer controlled and automated. Perhaps the most interesting and significant example is that of the Dead Sea Potash Works. We can observe here three generations of technologies. The old wet process mechanical plant, which employed some 400 workers to process annually 200 tons of potash; near it, a partially computer controlled 'wet' plant, employing some 200 workers manufacturing some 400 tons. Right next to it we have the most recently built "Maklef" plant, utilizing newly invented dry process technology and completely automated. this plant processes some 900 tons of potash with 64 employees.

2.4.4. Some of the bigger industrial plants automated intensively their production processes. The Aircraft Industries trying to cope with the requirements of the Lavi plane, developed a highly sophisticated C.A.D.- C.A.M. production system. Among the other examples we find in the Bagir clothing industries, where the design and manufacture of menswear is fully automated.

2.4.5. In most of these cases, Automation and robotics were introduced to meet expanding production demands. In many cases, the sophistication of the new products and materials, necessitated the introduction of advanced processes of automated design and production. We have very few examples where automation was introduced solely for the purpose of manpower saving.

3.EFFECTS OF ECONOMIC FLUCTUATIONS.

3.1. The introduction of new equipment, automation and robotics was influenced, to a very great extent, by prevailing economic conditions.

3.2. Following the 1973 "Yom Kipur" war, the Israeli economy operated under severe strains. The oil crisis, coupled with the increased defence spending, brought about strong inflationary pressures. In 1984, inflation reached an annual rate higher than 500%. Naturally, this phenomena did not encourage investment.

3.3. Government economic policy tried to fight inflation through measures taken to slow down economic activity. Enterprises faced a contracting local market. Efforts to increase export had to overcome the limiting conditions of world trade that contracted in the aftermath of the oil crisis. All these contributed to the fact that for the last decade, GNP growth was very slow and productivity stagnated. There was little capital investment and hardly any modernization of equipment.

3.4. Figure 2 shows the comparative rates of productivity growth in the past three decades. we can see from this figure the effects of the economic slow down on productivity, following the oil crisis. The table highlights the stagnation in productivity growth in Israel during the last decade.

3.5. The new economic policy introduced by the coalition government in 1985 enacted price controlls, curtailed government spending and reduced buying power by cutting wages. These conditions contributed to a relatively high rate of unemployment.

3.6. The Israel Institute of Productivity was asked by the Ministry of Labor to conduct some 27 surveys in "Developing Towns" to analyse the causes of unemployment in these communities, and recommend steps to be taken to ease the situation. It is significant that these surveys revealed that unemployment was not caused by the introduction of automation and innovative production technologies. In most cases unemployment was caused by the inability of the firms to compete in local and international markets. This, due to the lack of capability to adapt dynamically to market change and to introduce advanced production technologies.

3.7. The conclusion of these surveys attributed the growth of unemployment in Israel to the slow-down of economic activity, to inadequate managerial skills and to the lack of capability to adapt dynamicaly to changing markets and production processes which reduced the competitive capacity of these firms. On the other hand, it was found that in many cases the adaptation of automated production technologies strenghtened the competitive capabilities of firms and enabled them to increase their sales and exports, and provide additional employment opportunities.

Figure 2: **CHANGES IN PRODUCTIVITY PER EMPLOYEE 1955-1984
AN INTERNATIONAL COMPARISON**

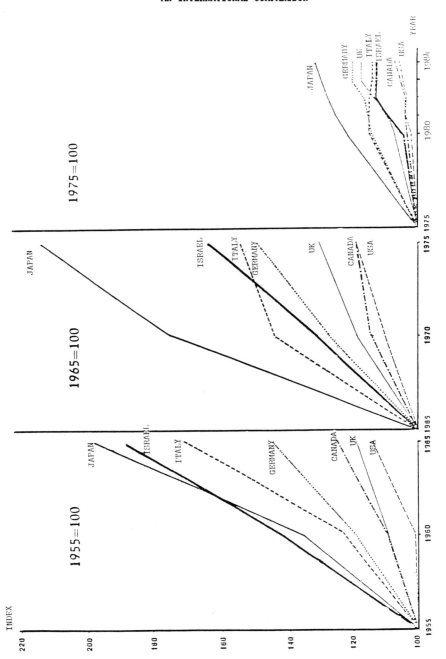

3.8 It is obvious that these conclusions may not be relevant to many of the industrialised communities. However, it should be clear that economic fluctuations and lack of productivity gains, may reduce the ability to compete in world markets and contribute to unemployment to no lesser degree than the introduction of automation and robotics.

4. SOME CHARACTERISTICS OF THE HUMAN RESOURCE IN ISRAEL.

The Israeli labor scene is characterised by certain particular conditions that affect the introduction of robotics and automation in industry. Let me mention but a few of these:

4.1.SIZE AND PARTICIPATION RATE IN THE LABOR FORCE:

4.1.1. In addition to the small size of the country, the participation rate of the Israeli population in the labor force, when compared to other industrialised communities, is relatively low. This is due to several factors:

- The relatively high birth rate and the large proportion of older people which immigrated to Isreal, leaving a smaller part of the population in the working age group.

- The low rate of participation of women, which is due to cultural values and mores.

- The high defense burden, conscripting three age groups into regular military service.

- A growing trend to continue academic studies amongst the graduates of the high school system.

4.1.2. The result of these factors can be seen in the following Figure 3:

Figure 3: **THE PARTICIPATION RATE IN CIVILIAN LABOUR FORCE FROM THE TOTAL POPULATION IN 1986 – INTERNATIONAL COMPARISON (Percents)**

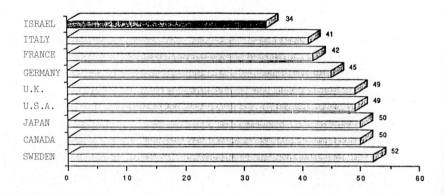

4.2. GROWTH OF THE SERVICE SECTOR.

The aftermath of the 1973 war, which cut drastically industrial development, stimulated the growth of the public service sector at a pace faster than that of developing countries and of many industrial economies. As may be seen from the following table, the proportion of the labor force employed in public and other services is as high as that of the highly industrialized communities.

Figure 4: **DISTRIBUTION OF EMPLOYED PERSONS IN ISRAEL BY ECONOMIC BRANCH - 1955-1983**

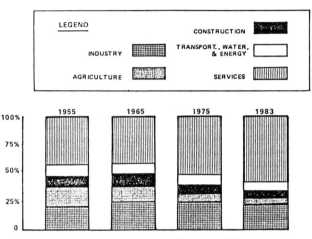

DISTRIBUTION OF EMPLOYED PERSONS IN ISRAEL
BY ECONOMIC BRANCH. — 1955 — 1983

4.3. EDUCATION, VOCATION AND SOME QUALITATIVE ASPECTS.

4.3.1. Efforts to absorb the immigrants, which arrived from varied cultural and social backgrounds, coupled with strong achievement motivation and a will to learn, shared by a great majority of the population, accelerated the growth of an educational and vocational system which changed the quality of the labor force.

4.3.2. In the early fifties, the rate of illiteracy among the working age population was relatively high. 77% of this group had 0 to 8 years of schooling. 19.1% had 9 to 12 years and only 3.7% had 13 years and more.

4.3.3. As we may see from figure 5, working age population with 4-8 years of schooling shrunk in 1985 to 17.9%. The part of those possessing secondary school certificates grew to about half of the labor force, and the share of employees with academic degrees grew to some 22.9% of the labor force.

Figure 5: **POPULATION AGED 14 AND OVER BY YEARS OF SCHOOLING**
(PERCENTAGE)

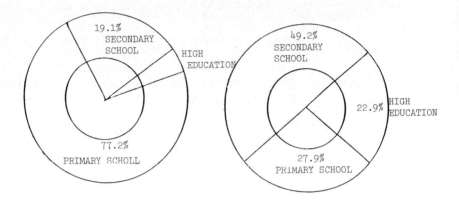

4.3.4. The growth of the vocational and professional training
system was no less impressive. It was characterised by the
establishment of a vocational training network which exceeded by
far the demands in the labor markets. A special system for
training practical engineers (two years of schooling after
graduation from high school) was established. the output of this
system provided the labor market with technicians in Electronics,
Industrial Engineering, Computer Programming, Systems Analysis,
and the like. Out of a population of aproximately four million
people, the system, which is run by various shools and training
organizations, provides some eighty thousand graduates each
year.

4.4. These activities helped to create human resources capable to
cope with change required by the process of the introduction of
new products, innovative technologies, automation and robotics.

5. IMPACT OF AUTOMATION & ROBOTICS ON SKILL REQUIREMENTS.

5.1. As already mentioned, due to the structure of the Israeli
industry, the effects of automation and robotics on the volume of
employment were relatively limited. On the other hand, the impact
of automation and robotics on the changes required in managerial,
technical and vocational skills is considerable.

5.2. In 1985, a survey was conducted by the Israel Institute of
productivity in an industrial enterprise that went through a
transition from mechanical manufacture of telephone equipment, to
automated pruduction of digital exchanges and telephones. The
findings of this survey have shown a significant growth of
Engineers and Technicians as against an even greater reduction in
the the skilled and semi skilled production labor force. While
the total value of output more than trebled, labor force was
reduced by some 20%. The following Figure 6, sums up the changes
that occured in the proffessional composition of this plant.

Figure 6: **CHANGES IN COMPOSITION OF LABOR FORCE
IN AN AUTOMATED ENTERPRISE**

Classification of Employees	Number Employed	
	1979	1984
Engineers	100	300
Eng.Technicians	100	300
Production Workers	1000	400
Management & Admin	100	80
TOTAL LABOR FORCE	1300	1080
Total Production (value in U.S. $)	30.000.000	100.000.000

5.3. The changes in the "Telrad" plant summed up in figure 6 above, as well as the surveys conducted in the developing towns, and the report of the Government Committee for the determination of policy in the field of Informatics published in 1986, point to the need of a greater effort in the formation of Industrial and Electronics Engineers, as well as the expansion of academic education in the areas of computer sciences. It also highlights the acute requirements of significant retraining systems to facilitate the transition of production workers with the required capabilities, to become technicians, and the others to recieve the required training to become operators of digital controlled equipment.

5.4. Another area requiring attention, is that of the extreme changes taking place in the content of the various skills with the introduction of automation. Let me give but a few examples: Engineers and draftsmen must be able to control C.A.D.-C.A.M. systems and posess the capability of quantifying their ideas and transmitting data, so that the computer will translate it into drawings and production orders. A machine lathe operator which required in the past manual skills to operate his machine, requires today the capability to program the operation of the automated C.N.C.system that he controls. When one goes through our "Bagir" clothing manufacturing plant, one can see designers that had to learn how to operate computers and design on their monitors, cutters that program computer controlled cutting tables, sewing machine operators that controll electronic-eye directed sewing machines, not to mention storemen and warehouse operators tackling automated transportation and storage systems.

These changes transcend the area of the production floor. The Production Engineer has to be trained in computer skills to be able to design and control automated work stations and plan and synchronise the entire logistical system around them. The accountant must have the capacity of adapting or designing an automated accounting system, which in most cases draws data directly from operating machines and on-line reporting.

5.5. These changes provide the possibility to enrich some of the more tedious and boring jobs. They require however that the educational and vocational training systems emphasise some of the following characristics and qualities in the formation process of its students. these are:

- The development of flexibility and a capability to adapt to change, togather with curiousity and the will to learn new things.

- The imbuement of the belief that quality and precision are most important values.

- An analytycal capability, and the capacity to accept the responsibility in controlling complex and expensive equipment.

- The willingness and capability to cooperate and work in and with teams.

Although these characteristics should be a part of a normal formation process, their importance with the development of microelectronics, computers and industrial automation can not be overemphasised.

6. EFFECTS OF AUTOMATION AND ROBOTICS ON MANAGERIAL CULTURE.

Most of the management training programs try to include in their syllabuses some chapters that will aquaint managers with computer operations, and give them some information pertaining to the utilization of automation and computer technology in business operations.

Very few try to prepare for the problems resulting from the introduction of automation in the organization as a whole, and the changes that it might require in its labor force. Few, if any, tackle the topic of the changes required in managerial style and culture, and the labor relation problems that organizations might face.

Let me list but a few of these changes, based on observations in industrial plants that went through this transition.

6.1. The first is the need for exact planning and formalization of requirements, so that they may be translated to computer language. Leadership in many instances, relies on hunch and acumen. The exacting needs of prescribing specifications, describing parameters of acceptance and rejection, and the need to forecast future phenomena in exact quantitive terms, require preparation and change in managerial style, which many managers find very difficult to adapt to.

In one instance in the Israel Telephone Services, the transition from informal leadership styles, to formal Computer controlled, time measured operations, created a crisis amongst the foremen, half of which found it almost beyond their capability to adapt to the new requirements. Many of them had to change jobs even after an intensive retraining period.

6.2. Another, is the need to develop team spirit and cooperation among highly diverse professionals. Automation requires a high degree of specialization in many professions. On the other hand, the success of the operation depends to a great degree on the cooperation and comprehension of the overall system by leaders and members of its different components.

6.3. The problem of managing a highly educated workforce is another problem often overlooked. Setting up an organizational structure and objectives that will provide challenge, motivating tasks and a culture of cooperation, is no easy task. A wider adaptation of participative managerial styles may perhaps alleviate some of the difficulties.

6.4. We have witnessed many transitions failing due to management not being aware of these problems, and not gaining cooperation of its labor force due to clogged communication channels and inadequate preparation of the transition. planning was mostly directed to the technical and financial requirements, while little or no attention was given to the human aspects of the transition. Although we nowadays find more awareness to these problems, management training programs should emphasize these topics in their syllabuses.

7. SOME SOCIAL IMPLICATIONS DUE TO AUTOMATION.

The emergence of computer and automation technologies, and the limited number of specialists as against the growing requirements, bear the danger of creating a social elite group, talking its own 'code' language, and earning an income much higher than that of other professionals. Before the present economic slowdown in Israel, the agreed minimum wage was 340.- shekels a month. Computer programmers earned at the time wages that run from 2000.- to 5000.- shekels a month. Nowadays, with the introduction of a minimum wage law and with the crisis faced by the electronic and computer industries, the gap narrowed considerably. However, the situation carries a potential of social explosion, especially in the development towns in Israel, and steps have to be taken to accelerate both: Industrial development programs which will provide employment opportunities in more sophisticated economic ventures, and more educational and training programs in areas related to microelectronic technology.

8. CONCLUSION.

8.1. The economic policy introduced in Israel in 1985, with the objective of fighting the inflation and creating a climate of economic stability, saw measures of success that are well known. the inflation was stemmed from an annual level higher than 500% to that of 20% a year – this, without the terrible price of significant unemployment.

Yet, we are now in a period of a slowdown of economic activity, and in addition to the danger of returning to the unbearable higher inflation rates, we may face severe social problems unless we find the way for renewed economic growth.

Extrapolating present development trends, reveals that the
employment forecasts in the Israeli economy may not provide
enough employment opportunities in the forseeable future. In
figure 7 we can that total employment growth in industry will be
less than 10% in the coming five years. The new entrants into the
labor force may not find adequte employment opportunities and we
may face higher unemployment rates or a bigger trend of
emigration from Israel. This, not due to automation and robotics,
but as a result of overall economic conditions and policies, and
the shortage of challenging positions for the newcomers to the
labor market.

8.2. The answers to economic viability in the Israeli economy,
and the alleviation of some of the employment problems, require
the establishment, expansion and growth of sophisticated
industries manufacturing competitive 'high-tech' products, with
the most advanced production methods. The small size of the
country and the characteristics of the local human resource
require that we aim to provide the most sophisticated technology
to every working hand.

8.3. To facilitate this development, we shall be required to
adapt appropriate development policies. These should provide the
conditions to attract and foster enterpreneurs, to strenghten the
educational and vocational system so that they can cope with the
requirements for change, to broaden entrepreneurial capacities
and alleviate the bureaucratic conditions that hamper growth and
investment, as well as to develop consciousness and programs to
face the social problems that may arise.

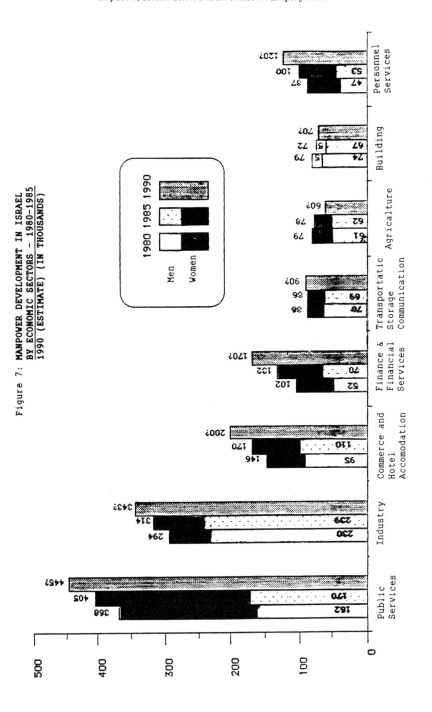

Figure 7: MANPOWER DEVELOPMENT IN ISRAEL BY ECONOMIC SECTORS – 1980-1985 1990 (ESTIMATE) (IN THOUSANDS)

REFERENCES

1. Statistical Year-Book, 1986.
   Central Bureau of Statistics, Jerusalem, 1987.

2. The Annual Report on Output and Incomes Distribution.
   The Institute for Research of Incomes and Output, Tel-Aviv.
   Report No. 24, 1987.

3. I. Meidan and D. Millin,
   National Policy and Computer Development in Israel.
   North Holland Press, Amsterdam, 1986.

4. Meidan, Israel,
   Effects of Technological Changes on Employment.
   The Israel Institute of Productivity, Tel-Aviv, May 1983.

5. A. Sagiv, B.Z. Barta and Z. Behar,
   Integrating Computer Design and Manufacture concepts into
   Curricula for Vocational and Continuing Education.
   Proceedings of the IFIP WG 3.4 Working conference, Jerusalem.
   North Holland Press, Amsterdam, 1985.

6. Final Report, The National Steering Committee for Information
   Technology, The Government of Israel. (N.C.R.D. 11a-85).
   Printiv Press Jerusalem, February 1986.

7. Reports on Employment In Developing Towns, 1982-1984.
   The Israel Institute of Productivity, Tel-Aviv. 1984.

8. Planning for Industial Development in Israel 1985 - 1990.
   Planning Department, Ministry of Commerce and Industry.
   Government Press, Jerusalem, 1985.

9. 30 Years of Computing in Israel, 1948 - 1978.
   ILTAM Publication, pp. 51-77. Jerusalem, 1979.

10. Robert Miller (ed.),
    Robotics: Future Factories, Future Workers.
    American Academy of Social and Political Sciences.
    Sage Publications, New-York, 1983.

11. Computerised Manufacturing, Automation, Employment, Education
    and Work Place. Office of Technological Assessment.
    The United States Congress, Washington D.C., 1984.

12. Evans, John,
    The Worker and The Work Place.
    Microelectronics and Society for Better or for Worse.
    Pergammon Press, Oxford, 1982.

13. Productivity and Employment, an International Prespective.
    Annual Report for 1985.
    The Israel Institute of Productivity, Tel-Aviv, 1986.

Part 2
ARTIFICIAL INTELLIGENCE
AND ROBOTICS

The Social Implications of Robotics and Advanced
Industrial Automation / D. Millin and B.H. Raab (Editors)
Elsevier Science Publishers B.V. (North-Holland)
© IFIP, 1989

SALIENT INTERNATIONAL SOCIO-ECONOMIC
IMPACTS OF ARTIFICIAL INTELLIGENCE AND ROBOTICS

Harold Sackman
Dept. of Information Systems
School of Business and Economics
Calif. State Univ. at Los Angeles, USA

This paper is aimed at elucidating some of the salient
social impacts of artificial intelligence and robotics as
distinguished from the social consequences of earlier and more
traditional forms of computerization. An attempt is made at the
outset to develop workable operational definitions of artificial
intelligence and robotics based on empirically verified system
test and evaluation. The central inquiry of the paper is then
defined -- in what ways are the social consequences of AI and
robotics different from "non-AI" computerization? Leading social
impacts for AI vs. non-AI automation are examined for: national
economies, management, labor, education, health care, and
family/individual trends and forecasts.

The general conclusion is that AI and robotics currently
generally tend to accelerate existing trends in positive and
negative social impacts of computers that have long been
documented prior to the current efflorescence of AI. In
particular, AI and robotics developments tend to exacerbate the
ever-growing gap between the information rich and the information
poor at international, national, regional, institutional and
individual levels. This survey also finds alarming trends in the
lack of quality control in establishing empirical reliability and
validity of AI services, as distinguished from robotics services
for institutional and individual users. AI products and services
are found to be characterized more by their variability than by
their central tendency, highlighting the need for more effective
regulation by vendors, computer professionals and users as well
as new areas for legal and governmental requirements to protect
the public interest. AI contains some of the seeds of potential
technical solutions to some of these problems in such areas as
voice I/O, expert systems, and natural language processing to
help make computer systems more "user friendly" and more
universally accessable.

A series of recommendations are put forth to help meet the
rapidly growing challenges of AI and robotics by improving
computer literacy, sharpening national and international planning
and policy-making, developing effective professional standards of
AI excellence, improving shared empirical test and evaluation of
AI capabilities and limitations, and greatly enhancing AI and
robotics ergonomics. The integrative moral recommendation is to
take more positive steps to use the benefits of AI to
progressively ameliorate rather than unwittingly exacerbate the
global gap between the information rich and the information poor
over the long run at all social levels.

1. Toward Operational Definitions of Artificial Intelligence
   and Robotics

   To distinguish AI and robotics from traditional forms of
automation, in working toward salient social impacts of AI, the
domain of AI and robotics needs to be defined. Findler (1986)
cryptically defines AI as the "computational theory of
intelligence". This definition begs the question of
intelligence. Philosophers and psychologists have debated the
nature of intelligence over the centuries, and now engineers and
computer scientists, among others, have joined the fray. In
grappling with this issue for the purpose of this paper, it seems
to me that the two crucial elements are: 1) intelligent behavior
in machines is analogous to similar types of behaviors observed
in human individuals or groups, and 2) such intelligent behaviors
in machines need to be operationally defined so that they can be
independently verified by empirical experimentation.

   Accordingly, the author's two-part definition of AI (and by
extension, robotics) is:

   a. AI is the interdisciplinary analysis, design and
      development of computer and machine procedures that
      behave in an operationally defined manner analogous to
      specified aspects of human sensation, perception,
      cognition, problem-solving, and motor functions.
   b. Such operationally defined measures of machine
      intelligence are verifiable by empirical test and
      evaluation in replicable experimental settings.

   The second part of the definition separates mere speculation
from serious applied scientific endeavor. It also sets the
bedrock experimental standard for AI as an applied
interdiscipline in its own right. The first part of the
definition places the burden of demonstrating intelligent machine
behavior on the investigator in an operationally replicable
manner. The implicit definition of intelligence, in man or
machine, is that it is behaviorially pluralistic, assuming many
changing, evolving forms.

   The above formulation of AI is consonant with Findler's
assertion that AI is a discipline in its own right. He states
that:

   "AI is becoming organized, is getting a theoretical
formulation, does need empirical verification, does relate to
other bodies of knowledge, does evolve according to principles
that have guided other disciplines. It has solved important
problems during its 30-odd years of history." (Findler, 1986, p.
20-6).

   What are the basic functional areas and techniques of AI?
Gevartner's chart, (1985) shown in Figure 1, reveals key
functional areas and techniques in AI. My approach, although
generally consonant with Gevartner's portrayal in Figure 1, is
somewhat different. The five key functional areas of AI, in my
view, are 1) game playing (e.g. chess and checkers), 2) problem-
solving (e.g. expert systems), 3) semantics and linguistics (e.g.
natural language processing), 4) pattern recognition (e.g.
medical imaging), and 5) robotics, which cuts across the entire
spectrum of sensation, perception, cognition and motor response.

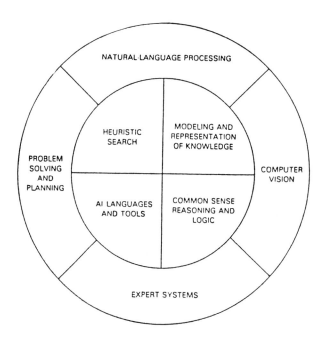

(Source: William B. Gevarter, <u>INTELLIGENT MACHINES</u>,
           New Jersey: Prentice <u>Hall, 1985, p. 5)</u>

<u>FIGURE 1</u>

Methodological and Functional Areas of Artificial Intelligence

Figure 2

USA Investment Trends in Factory Automation

and Robotics

	<u>1980</u>	<u>1985</u>	<u>1990</u>
	Millions of dollars		
Factory computers and software	$ 935	$2,861	$6,500
Materials handling systems	2,000	4,500	9,000
Machine tools and controls	3,000	4,800	7,000
Programmable controllers	50	550	3,000
Robots and sensors	68	664	2,800
Automated test equipment	800	2,000	4,000
TOTAL SPENDING ON CAM*	$6,853	$15,375	$32,300

*Computer-aided manufacturing

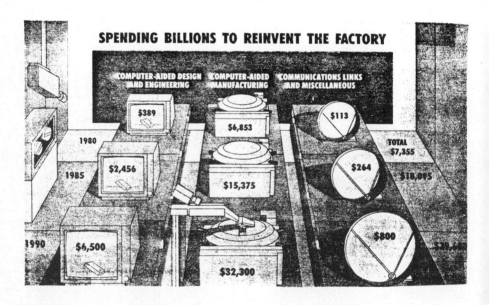

(Adapted from Otis Port, Business Week, 1986, P. 101)

(Estimates are in millions of dollars)

FIGURE 3

FOUR SECTOR AGGREGATION
OF THE U.S. WORK FORCE BY PERCENT
1860 - 1980

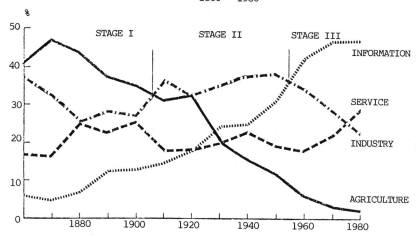

from: The Information Economy, Vol. 1
      Definition & Measurement
      OT Special Publication 77-12(1) US Dept. of Commerce

The four key AI techniques, in my view, include 1) heuristics (e.g. prioritizing), 2) search (trial and error), 3) inference/reasoning (inductive, deductive and correlational procedures), and 4) signal processing (e.g. waveform analysis).

What is the upshot of the above definition of AI, its functional areas and techniques? We have a motley conglomeration of rather strange bedfellows under the vague rubric of behavior analogous to human behavior, with amorphous boundaries between more "intelligent" and less "intelligent" behaviors. The track record of AI is cluttered with problems and pitfalls, a long string of false claims and promises, and ever-growing potential abuse. Clouding the entire scene is the charged emotional impact of "machine intelligence". Hopefully, the disciplinary requirement for applied empirical verification, if seriously observed by professionals and especially leaders in AI, may move this turbulent area into the mainstream of applied scientific endeavor. In any case, with the above caveats in mind, the stage is set for the statement of the central problem of this paper.

2. Statement of the Problem: Distinctive Social Impacts of AI vs. "Non-AI" Automation

The focal inquiry of this paper is: "To what extent are the quantitative and qualitative social consequences of AI (including robotics) different from non-AI computerization? What are the distinctive features of the social impacts of AI?"

To provide an initial answer to these questions the author employs the following approach. Leading social consequences of computers have been developed by the IFIP/TC9 Committee in its Third Conference on Human Choice and Computers (HCC3) (Stockholm, 1985). The author was editor of the Proceedings for HCC3 which was focused on comparative national problems and policies in the social use of computers (Sackman, 1986). In the main body of this paper, which follows, he explores the key national and international problem areas in social impacts of computers in national economies, management, labor relations, education, health care, and family/individual trends, using HCC3 "social impacts" as the baseline in comparing AI vs. "non-AI" consequences. These comparisons are then consolidated and generalized in the final conclusions and recommendations of this paper.

3. Worldwide Economic Impacts and Policies

A key conclusion of HCC3 was that the socio-economic impacts of computers are primarily technology-driven rather than socially planned. Technology is in the saddle and the vagaries of the marketplace guide the turbulent course of technological development and social applications. National governments have only recently and rather belatedly begun to piece together coherent policies for national computerization.

AI has been viewed as the basis for the nascent "fifth generation" of computers, especially in Japan. As such, AI is likely to quantitatively accelerate technology-driven social consequences for both AI and non-AI applications. On the qualitative side, AI, in such applications as voice I/O, natural language processing and expert systems, may make computers more approachable, accessible, and easier to use for non-specialists.

Another HCC3 conclusion was that computer technology is fueled by two types of competitive social forces--market rivalry and national defense requirements. AI enhances both types of competition by accelerating existing technological trends in fifth generation computer systems. It should be appreciated that military technology has long drawn on AI developments for its most advanced weapon systems. AI is no stranger to the defense establishment. For example, intercontinental ballistic missiles and cruise missiles require AI pattern recognition software to interpret internally stored radar maps for navigational guidance and weapon delivery subsystems. Both types of missiles, in fact, may be classified as specialized robots, capable of "sensation" (radar), "perception" (pattern recognition), "cognitive discrimination" (target selection) and "motor behavior" (navigation and weapons delivery).

Economic plans and policies for national computerization are primary objectives in virtually all nations as they shape their economies for the 21st Century. Other "social impacts", such as the effects of computers on individuals are secondary. Economic viability is seen as being contingent on achieving and maintaining competitive levels of national computerization. Nations can only neglect AI developments at their own peril for national computerization. As such, AI developments reinforce such national policies.

In HCC3 we found that smaller countries, and developing countries were virtually technological captives of the larger, industrialized nations. As such, these nations (e.g. Belgium, Holland, Scandinavia, India) have to follow the technological lead of the major industrialized nations. This has generated feelings of dependency and a drive toward greater self sufficiency in smaller and in developing nations. AI and robotics have tended to exacerbate such national feelings of dependency.

On the other hand, as AI becomes more affordable as off-the-shelf technology, greater independence may become possible in custom-tailored specialized applications. For example, this is already taking place with small-lot production in flexible manufacturing systems as illustrated in specialized kibbutz applications of robotics described in this conference.

The size of the aggregate computer and communications industry is at about 500 billion dollars worldwide today. Eonomists and computer experts have noted a doubling rate of roughly five years for this aggregate industrial complex, over the last two decades, which has been projected through the year 2000 (e.g. HCC3 estimates).

With the technological quickening provided by AI R&D, it seems reasonable to assume that this doubling rate is likely to continue, resulting in a 2 trillion dollar worldwide market in the year 2000 for computers and communications. Thus, AI is seen as reinforcing and sustaining the total thrust of all types of automation and its communications infrastructure as a major and dominant industry in its own right, in moving toward the Information Age (e.g. Venken, 1987, on AI in the European

Market).   This scenario, of course, is contingent on the absence
of major cataclysmic social events taking place,   such as   large-
scale wars   or major worldwide economic depressions.

4. Management Response

    The   HCC3   conference   noted   the   rising   influence   of
multinational   corporations,   spurred   in   part   by   worldwide
computer-communications   and   real-time   management   information
systems.   The diffusion of AI is likely to accelerate such trends
quantitatively   and   qualitatively.   For example,   the advent   of
intelligent decision support systems is being vigorously explored
(Hill,   1986).   A significant breakthrough in natural   language
processing,   linked   to more versatile voice I/O systems,   could
facilitate   international human communications by   breaking   down
age-old language barriers.

    Another   notable   industrial trend is   toward   industry-wide
networking and cross-industry networks.   For example,   worldwide
online   networks already exist in banking,   petroleum and airline
reservations.   Cross-industry   links   have   been   effected   with
electronic   fund transfer systems (EFTS) moving   industrialized
nations ever closer toward real time economies.   AI technology is
facilitating the design,   development, implementation, and use of
computer   communications   networks   (e.g.   "intelligent   network
managers", Rappaport, 1987).

    The   literature   on   social   impacts   of   automation   has
consistently   shown a trend toward increasing specialization   and
division   of   labor with increasing automation.   This   trend   is
being   accelerated by rapid introduction of robots in   smokestack
industries coupled with FMS,   CAD,   CAM and CIMS.   (See Figure 2
for   trends in US investment in CAD,   CAM,   robotics and related
automation).   The   worldwide doubling rate of robotics over   the
last decade has been approximately 3 years (e.g. three years from
now the global robot population will double).

    The   specialization and division of labor in the human   work
force   is   being   shaped   and paced   by   the   specialization   and
division   of   labor   of   associated   computer   operations.   AI
application areas, such as expert systems, seem to be trending in
the   same   direction.   For example,   expert systems for   medical
diagnosis   are   moving   away   from   generalized   to   specialized
diagnostic knowledge bases,   and similar trends are being observed
in other expert system application areas (Sackman,   1988).   This
is   not   surprising   since knowledge bases   of   well-defined   and
limited   specialized   areas are easier to design   and   implement,
compared   to generalized applications,   and are more likely to be
comprehensive and internally consistent.

    Finally, management has historically been consistently ahead
of   labor in understanding and exploiting automation in virtually
all   industrialized nations..   AI is likely to accelerate   this
trend   and   exacerbate   the   growing   automation   gap   between
management and labor.   AI   is   a   more   complex   species   of
computerization   and   requires a higher degree of   user   computer
literacy   to   master   its   direction   and   emerging   potential.
Management,   especially under   the growing pressure   of   intense
international competion in   virtually all   industrial areas,   is
compelled to keep up wrth latest advances in automation,

including AI. This leads to the response of labor.

5. Trade Union Challenges and the Quality of Working Life

It should be appreciated at the outset that there are vast worldwide differences in the role and status of trade unions. In the USA, aggressive managerial strategies and tactics have decreased unionization of the work force from about 40% after World War II to less than 20% today. Western European democracies roughly approximate 50% unionization; Scandinavian countries run closer to 70%, and, as we learned in this conference, Israel has a unionization level of 90% with Histadrut. As this percentage increases, so does the power and influence of the national union infrastructure, including the ability to anticipate and shape the introduction of AI and robotics in the work force.

A well established historical trend, reinforced by computerization, is the consistent proportionate rise of information-related jobs in industrialized economies. This is illustrated in Figure 3, from Porat's classical analysis of the information economy (1977). He subdivides the total US work force into four sectors: 1)agriculture, 2)industry/manufacturing, 3)information services (broadly considered, including government, communications and education) and 4) non-information services. Note that the trend for information services has evolved from roughly 5% of the work force over a century ago to about 50% of the work force today.

The major cause for "fear and trembling"in the face of relentless automation for labor unions has been and will continue to be the loss of jobs and the ubiquitous associated threat to job security. Automation is only one among other powerful factors influencing unemployment (e.g. inflation, interest levels, the national debt, the balance of trade, international competition, economic nationalism, and the general state of the economy). The unemployment equation is incredibly complex, with such factors as robots replacing people on the factory floor in smokestack industries, and with office automation creating new clerical jobs at computer terminals in bureaucracies. As pointed out by several speakers at this conference, the labor impact of a specific type of automation requires careful inquiry into who gets the benefits and who pays the costs, and into tracking positive and negative ripple effects throughout the economy.

This leads to impacts on the quality of working life, previewed earlier under the rubric of increasing specialization and division of labor. A key question is whether the introduction of automation leads to job deskilling or upskilling. As the HCC3 conference clearly demonstrated, deskilling seems to be the preferred choice for most managers. Deskilling usually means fewer workers, lower-skilled workers, including increased feminization of the work force, resulting in lower labor costs for employers. AI and robotics seem to be hastening this process. The semi-automated "maquiladora" manufacturing plants in Mexico, near the border of the USA, financed by American firms, with cheap (feminine) labor from Mexico, are a case in point.
From the point of view of labor unions, upskilling is generally the preferred alternative since it leads to greater job

challenges, higher skills and higher pay. Isolated cases of organizational success in job upskilling in office automation and in the factory (especially with FMS) have yet to be demonstrated on a wide scale to significantly influence employers. AI applications can be designed for upskilling or deskilling the work place; the AI knife cuts both ways depending on human choice.

A major trend that is likely to lead to a more favorable attitude toward upskilling, and more broadly, the quality of working life, is the gradual erosion of the traditional adversarial posture between management and labor in industrialized nations. In the USA, embattled firms, reeling under massive international competition, particularly in smokestack industries, are learning to bury the hatchet and foster a cooperative team spirit with labor unions. The battle cry is "Productivity!". The new spirit include such features as: the team approach, job rotation, fewer job classifications, participative management, quality circles, productivity bonuses, special incentives, increased job security, reduced absenteeism, and employee stock ownership plans (ESOP's) to mention some of the buzzwords. The quality and the challenge of working life is enhanced by such steps, and if this cooperative movement in labor relations becomes the rule rather than the exception, then it seems more likely that the team approach would gravitate more powerfully toward job upskilling. The greater complexity and challenge of AI applications would lend itself well toward upskilling with a more computer literate user population.

The feminization of the increasingly semi-automated work place is likely to be enhanced by telecommuting, or remote work. Women are especially attracted to the possibilities of work at home to keep up with their careers, and maintain their income while caring for their children. Unions are concerned that telework can be used as a "union-busting" technique by employers in isolating workers, giving them only part-time jobs, depriving them of costly union and fringe benefits, and exploiting workers with minimal job security and legal protection. AI, particularly when applied to telecommunications, can be used to strengthen the range and scope of what might be called "teleproduction", "telemanagement", or remote management. The piece-work of the notorious "sweat shops" in the textile industry going back to the beginning of this century, are cases in point which unions decry. The impact of AI on telecommuting will depend on economic conditions, social legislation, labor/management cooperation and social choice. All factors considered, increasing applications of AI are likely to reinforce existing trends for increasing deskilling and continued feminization of the semi-automated work force.

6. Educational Directions

In the educational area, a major finding of the HCC3 conference was virtually universal computer illiteracy of the general population in essentially all countries throughout the world. It was also generally agreed that educating and training the general population in computer literacy, broadly considered, was probably the most cost-effective single step that could be taken by each nation-state to facilitate successful computerization of the economy.

AI, which accelerates automation to ever-greater complexity, is likely to increase individual differences in the growing gap between computer literate and computer illiterate groups. This in turn, is likely to exacerbate the gap between the information rich and the information poor. Accordingly, the urgency for educational efforts to reduce computer literacy is likely to grow with the diffusion of AI in society.

It was also noted in the HCC3 conference that automation accelerates the tempo of contemporary technological and social change, contributing to heightened "future shock". Recommendations were made to move toward more effective real-time social response to accelerating social change, including trends toward lifelong education, the learning society and the experimental society. AI, increasingly at the forefront of the computerization of society, tends to increase the tempo of technological and social change, and as such, enhances the need to phase into lifelong education and the learning society.

In HCC3 it was found that long-range educational plans have been instituted in Israel, France, Japan and the Scandinavian countries to develop computer awareness and computer-related skills in teachers as well as in the general population. AI is likely to increase the need for such long-range educational planning for all nations for national economic viability in the face of intense international competition.

7. Family and Individual Alternatives

The possibilities for harnessing computers to increase effective individual human intelligence, creativity and problem solving have long been established in the human factors literature. As pointed out in the HCC3 conference, it would be a crime against humanity not to use computers to elevate human creativity and the quality of life. AI opens up new vistas in education, creativity and problem solving, especially in natural language processing and expert systems, that should be oriented toward the long-range public interest.

In the HCC3 conference, special stress was placed on the protection of individual human rights through systematic legislative and judicial procedures. Some of the social steps included Sweden's data protection laws for individual privacy, Austria's strong concern for protecting individual "human dignity" against the encroachments of automation in the work place, and protection against "derogatory dossiers" in personnel files in many Western European nations. AI developments are likely to make increasingly sophisticated analyses of computer-accessible information on individuals more feasible, raising new threats against the family and the individual as well as new opportunities for social benefits. The TC9 Committee has long espoused the vigorous establishment of legal informatics as a counterbalance against such threats and against computer crime broadly considered. AI poses new legal challenges to individual rights in computerized societies that need to be systematically explored and understood to protect the individual and the family.

AI is already well established in health care information systems which have great potential for alleviating the almost insurmountable and extremely expensive health care problems

pressing all nations.   The problem of mental and physical health
relates intimately with sustaining the quality of life for the
family and the individual.

Medical expert systems for diagnosing a great variety of
human diseases are undergoing rapid development (Goh, 1987).   AI
is widely used in medical imaging techniques, including CAT-scans
(Computer-Axial Tomography),   magnetic-resonance scans, PET-scans
(Positron Emission Tomography), ultrasound imaging, and DSA
(Digital Subtraction Angiography).   These imaging techniques use
pattern recognition software to analyze signal waveforms passing
through the human body.   AI is used in ICU's (Intensive Care
Units) for real-time physiological tracking of vital signs via
bedside monitors.   In medical and biological research, AI pattern
recognition with laser and spectrographic techniques is used in
"gene machines" to help decipher the genetic code for a growing
list of infectious agents and inherited disabilities.   All of
these AI applications and others in medical informatics raise
prospects for enhancing computer-aided health care and reducing
patient morbidity and mortality.   The substantive expense of many
of these techniques precludes mass applications and raises major
issues of cost containment and social equity.   The US Senate and
House of Representatives is currently grappling with these issues
in connection with Medicare and Medicaid programs for the US
population.

AI enhances the effectiveness of health care and
unfortunately, tends to increase the costs.   For example, AI
instrumented ICU's can cost $3000/day/patient.   Most nations,
often against their values and their will, are moving toward a
multi-tiered structure of health care in an uneasy compromise
between social equity and increasing health care costs.

This short odyssey through AI impacts on the family and the
individual essentially reveals that AI tends to accelerate the
same types of social impacts generated by non-AI computerization.
It also tends to complicate social impacts in new ways that raise
new challenges for the growing global gap between the information
rich and the information poor.

8. Conclusions and Recommendations

8.1 Conclusions

Five key conclusions emerge from this paper.

1. Acceleration of Technological and Social Change: AI generally
tends to accelerate existing socio-economic impacts of computers
by contributing to the acceleration of technological change,
which tends to reinforce existing socio-political conditions, and
also generates new social consequences.

2. Global Gap Between the Information Rich and the Information
Poor: AI and robotics, in generally reinforcing existing socio-
political relationships, tend to intensify the growing gap
between the information rich and the information poor at all
social levels--international, national, regional, institutional,
group, and individual levels.

3. Lack of AI Accountability: This exploratory survey finds

alarming trends in the lack of professional quality control in establishing empirical reliability and validity of emerging AI services. This is not the case for robotic services where industrial quality control is increasingly evident.

4. AI Heterogeneity and Variability: AI products and services are found to be characterized more by their variability than by their central tendency. Heterogeneity of products and applications is also rampant, especially in embryonic AI areas. This chaotic state of affairs highlights the need for more effective internal and external regulatory standards for professionals, vendors, and users as well as new legal and governmental developments to define and protect the public interest.

5. Serendipitous AI Fallout: AI contains potential technical solutions to help alleviate some of these problems in "user friendly" areas such as voice I/O, natural language processing, expert systems, and pattern recognition graphics to make reliable and validated AI systems more universally accessable to all levels of the population.

8.2 Recommendations

Four recommendations are offered to help meet the rapidly growing international social challenge of AI and robotics.

1. Improve Computer Literacy: AI and robotics are only as effective as the constructive attitudes and the ability of people who use these tools (e.g. Foulkes and Hirsch, 1984). Educational amelioration of worldwide computer and AI illiteracy is probably the most cost-effective single approach to optimize the long-term social benefits of computers, AI and robotics.

2. Facilitate International and National Long-Range Planning: This paper stressed the growing realization that viable national economies in the next century require successful national computerization. AI and robotics underscore and accelerate the urgency of this requirement which can only be met by cooperative long-range social planning at national and international levels.

3. Social Excellence of AI Services: Social acceptability of AI requires development of professional standards of AI quality control, particularly shared empirical test and evaluation of AI capabilities and limitations, and enhanced AI ergonomics for more universal social use.

4. Integrative Moral Recommendation: The above and related positive steps need to be taken at all social levels to systematically guide the development and use of AI to progressively ameliorate rather than unwittingly exacerbate the global gap between the information rich and the information poor.

9. References

1. Findler, Nicholas V.
    The Past, Present and Future of Artificial Intelligence
    SEARCC '86 Proceedings, Bangkok, Thailand
    Elsevier Science Publishers, New York, 1987, pp. 20-1/20-9.

2. Foulkes, Fred K. and Jeffrey L. Hirsch
    People Make Robots Work
    Harvard Business Review, Jan.-Feb. 1984, pp. 94-102.

3. Gevartner, William B.
    Intelligent Machines
    Prentice-Hall, New Jersey, 1985.

4. Goh, Angela E.S.
    Medical Expert Systems
    SEARCC '86 Proceedings, Bangkok, Thailand
    Elsevier Science Publishers, New York, 1987, pp. 17.1/17.9.

5. Hill, Timothy R.
    Toward Intelligent Decision Support Systems
    Proceedings of the Seventh International Conference on
    Information Systems, 1986. Editors: Leslie Maggi, Robert
    Zmund, James Wetherbe.
    ACM, New York City, 1986, pp. 195-205.

6. Port, Otis
    High Tech to the Rescue
    Business Week, New York City, June 16, 1986, pp. 100-103.

7. Porat, Mark U.
    The Information Economy
    US Dept. of Commerce, Office of Telecommunications
    OT Special Publications 77-12, Washington, D.C., 1977.

8. Rappaport, David M.
    The Intelligent Network Manager
    SEARCC '86 Proceedings, Bangkok, Thailand
    Elsevier Science Publishers, New York, 1987, pp. 19.1/19.17.

9. Sackman, Harold
    The Computerization of the USA: Winners and Losers
    in Computers and International Socio-Economic Problems
    (H. Sackman, ed.)
    North Holland Press, Amsterdam 1987, pp. 519-554.

10. Sackman, Harold
    Comparative National Plans and Policies in the Social Use
    of Computers
    in Computers and International Socio-Economic Problems
    (H. Sackman, ed.)
    North Holland Press, Amsterdam, 1987, pp. 573-586.

11. Sackman, Harold
    An Overview of Health Care Information Systems in the
    USA: Tutorial Briefing
    Proceedings of the International Symposium on Information
    Systems, Johannesburg, South Africa, 1987
    Elsevier Science Publishers, New York, forthcoming in 1988.

12. Venken, Raf
    Industrial Applications of Artificial Intelligence in
    Europe
    SEARCC '86 Proceedings, Bangkok, Thailand
    Elsevier Science Publishers, New York, 1987, pp. 18.1/18.10.

The Social Implications of Robotics and Advanced
Industrial Automation / D. Millin and B.H. Raab (Editors)
Elsevier Science Publishers B.V. (North-Holland)
© IFIP, 1989

The Inanimate and the Intelligent

Joseph Regev

Ben Gurion University of the Negev
Beer Sheva, Israel

Abstract

This paper discusses the basic differences in the decision-making operations between the human mind and computer systems, with an emphasis on their ability to cope with the unexpected. This is linked to the problem of bureaucracy: division between decisions and operations. The combination of bureaucracy, computers and Murphy's rule may lead to unpleasant situations when an exceptional case occurs and a person gets caught in a "talk to the wall" situation. A possible conclusion can be that every system must have some channel of problem handling and correction. In other words: *computer systems are always imperfect and should never be given absolute power. There must always be some human power whose function is to detect problems in the functioning of every system and correct them.* The question whether AI and robots are going to improve the situation is also discussed.

Introduction

Suppose AI (Artificial Intelligence) is successful. Suppose we do succeed in giving computers and robots the gifts of intelligence. What will be the outcome of such a situation? Many Science Fiction books envisage all sorts of horrible results. In this paper we will discuss the outcomes which are real in the sense that they do not depend on some system going wild as in "2001: Space Odyssey". In an appendix, several case histories are described and the reader may prefer to start with these stories before learning their moral: *nobody can ever come out with a rule which will always be correct and compatible with every possible combination of events.*

Human and Mechanical Decision Making

Even today we can computerize and robotize any process whose rules are known. Sometimes doing it may be prohibitive from the point of view of the effort required to formulate the rules or to build the system that will carry out the required processes in the physical world - in other words too expensive to implement. Of course there is the basic difference between processes which operate according to a fixed algorithm in a rigid procedure and processes which require more heuristic-type logical operations or inference of conclusions from a given body of knowledge with different data relevant to different situations. But all cases, conventional programming as well as expert systems, all require an inanimate entity to carry out operations, i.e. decisions, that up to some time ago were the privilege of men only.

Now it's true that we should not kid ourselves about the marvelous decision-making capabilities of the human mind. The mistakes of human judgement can be found in the reports of the growing number of car accidents and in the books of history. Yet there are certain aspects which are unique to human decision making that are worth our scrutiny. For the purpose of this discussion let's compare the human mind with that of inanimate entities (IE in short) be they computer systems, CNC-type machines or sensored "intelligent" robots:

a. The human mind is not always predictable, it works intuitively and in jumps and it can come to altogether new ideas. The IE is operating according to a given set of rules and information base and hence, in principle can only get to conclusions which were allowed by the person or persons who programmed it.

b. The human mind operates upon the whole realm of knowledge and experience gathered from the day a person is born. A human problem solver also uses all the information he can find in books and journals, sometimes seemingly irrelevant to the problem (used for analogy and models). He can and he does ask the advice of his colleagues. IEs use a limited (though powerful) body of knowledge which is the essence of what the creators of that IE think it ought to know.

c. The human mind is capable of making changes in the procedures of activities. IEs cannot change their procedures unless programmed to do so by a human mind, which is rarely the case.

d. The pattern recognition capabilities of any IE known today are amazingly poor compared to those of a 3 year old child.

e. The human mind is built to create new entities in our minds, make hypotheses about these entities, refute them and confirm them all the time, with every face we see in the street. IEs work with fixed number of procedures and conceivable entities. Changing the basic procedures and the underlying concepts is quite difficult. Expert Systems are much more flexible and changeable but even their changeability is rather limited. Other AI systems may also be quite difficult to change when it comes to the basic elements of the systems.

f. The human mind is capable of dealing with the unexpected and making changes on the run. IEs will usually either fail or go on doing the old procedure when an unexpected event occurs.

g. The human mind can discern the occurrence of an unexpected event and will work out a new decision compatible with the new situation. IEs in many cases will not detect this occurrence and may do the wrong thing, sometimes even with destructive results.

All these may lead us to the conclusion that *IEs should always be restricted in their decision powers and that in any set-up there must always be a channel where unexpected or incompatible behavior of the IEs can be detected and corrected before too much damage is done.*

Mistakes and Lack of Responsiveness

Most of the computer-resident systems in operation today (counting heads and not operations) are Data Processing systems and Personal Computer systems (whatever that term may mean). Both groups of computer-resident systems exhibit the same annoying characteristic: they make mistakes and they are not responsive enough to the needs of the non-professional naive user. When such a naive user comes to the system (either from free will or because of some external motivation) he comes with a specific requirement in his mind. What the system does may be different - making it into a rendezvous of misunderstanding. The worst part of it is that the naive user has no way of making the system do what he thinks it ought to do. Every one must have been witness to situations when something wrong was written in a DP (Data Processing) file or a word processor would not come out with the right results in the required format. Let's look at the various causes to that "talk to the wall" situation:

a. Lack of instructions how to operate the IE or rather work with it. Some IEs do not have manuals. Many do not have on-line help. Most of the instructions are written in a language which is best described as Computerese. Most naive users are not fluent in this language and in the craft of reading computer instructions.

b. Error in data supplied by one of the input sources to the system (the most prevalent cause). In DP it is well known that the longer the distance between the originator of the data and the person typing it in - the higher the rate of wrong data produced. But even when the originator is the typist - he may type in some input which is in principle totally wrong.

c. Typing errors (of the user) and situations of no return when a return is needed. Thus the naive user who wants to type one thing, mistypes and then presses the ENTER (or CARRIAGE RETURN) key, finds himself in places in the menu jungle which he did not want to access with no way of going back to the former step and correcting the input.

d. Programming errors (bugs) in one of the computer programs which are part of the IE. It's human to err. Only when a person starts programming the computer does he learn the meaning and the scope of this saying. Some legendary programmers are believed to be able to program a sizable program without a single bug. Most real-life programmers can't do that. With interactive programs the number of different situations possible in a single computer system - becomes unbelievably large and hence the difficulty to test all the cases and debug the system completely. We can and we do divide each program into modules but the coupling between these modules is too strong to allow perfect debugging of any module by itself.

e. Incompatibility in the assumptions and the requirements between programs which comprise the IE or in formats of files and messages. Although many methods have been devised to ensure good communication between the programmers who work on a single IE - none has proved to be a perfect solution to this problem. Sometimes even a single programmer may forget what he had decided upon two weeks ago.

f. Malfunction (inherent or occurring) of one of the technical components of the IE. Most systems assume all the electronic and mechanical parts to function perfectly. When this is no longer true - most systems have severe difficulties in diagnosing the situation, let alone coping with it. The naive user is even in a more bewildered state.

g. The version (release) symptom. Every system has several versions and releases which have different operating system, programs, data files, input formats and manuals. It's not unusual to have incompatibility problems between all these, thus making the situation time-dependent, i.e. you cannot be sure that something that works today will work tomorrow or in three years from today. The only thing you can be sure of is that the computer you are using today will not be the computer you will be using in 10 years from today. Here we also find the phenomenon that every problem and bug which is notified to the vendor, is said to be corrected in the next release. In reality some releases follow the 2nd law of Thermodynamics (in Computerese it would be: the number of bugs always becomes larger) and some follow the law of the odd release (every odd-number release is full of bugs which are corrected in the even-number release).

h. The recovery symptom. Every now and then failures cause the system or some disks (or diskettes) to crash (i.e. to fail). When the system is rebooted (i.e. restarted). some files may be missing and have to be recovered. The recovery process sometimes may not recreate the pre-failure situation exactly. Typical of that symptom are cases where some details in the data have disappeared or some erased details reappear mysteriously.

i. Bugware or imperfect software. This is that kind of software which is released and sold by people who know they have not put in the effort required to debug it enough to make it usable. That phenomenon is well known in CBE (Computer-Based Education) but is actually quite common in other branches of the computer and information industry because very rarely do companies bother to do a really thorough debugging phase with many naive users and learn of their cognitive problems. Only large companies keep problem handling services called PSR, PTF, SPR and other acronyms. Usually these services are notorious for their slowness.

j. Some official trying to make the system do something which it was not designed to do. That official may be a decision-maker under pressure, an irresponsible programmer, an unknowledgeable dispatcher down in the hierarchy or a devious fiend.

k. Lack of understanding by the naive user as to what the system is supposed to know and to do and as to what it cannot perform.

l. Murphy's law: if anything can go wrong - it will go wrong at the worst possible moment. This will need a special consideration.

These problems appear in computer-enclosed programs. Adding the capabilities of computer vision, computer voice input , robot motion and robot manipulation of articles - the capabilities of many robots - will make the problems more acute because of the relatively poor pattern recognition of computers. One should have in mind devices that allow entrance to high-security offices and that record each entrance to a working place and each going out of them and think what situations can happen when these malfunctions of systems described in this paragraph are combined with such devices. Thus robotics may well aggravate the situation and turn problems in the information world into problems in the physical world.

Is AI any Better

These phenomena are clearly typical to non-AI systems. The question that rises is whether AI can eliminate most of these sources of problems. It certainly can decrease significantly their number and prevalence but there is no reason to believe and no proof that I know of, that it can bring their numbers down to insignificance. As much as I know, AI programs are not verifiable today and there are reasons to doubt whether they will ever be verifiable in the sense that it can be proven that they will not produce results which are incompatible with the intents of the people who designed it. The basic phenomenon is still there and Parnas [1] even says about heuristic programming: "I trust such programs even less than I trust unstructured conventional programs. One never knows when the program will fail. On occasion I have had to examine closely the claims of a worker in AI I have always been disappointed. On close examination the heuristics turned out to handle a small number of obvious cases but failed to work in general". In AI systems you can never predict exactly how the system will respond to any input in the future. The behavior of the system is dependent on the knowledge base which may be (and should be) constantly changing and on it's learning capabilities.

One may even claim that AI makes the wrong system more convincing because it looks quite intelligent and the naive user tends to treat it more reverently than a wrong simple-minded program whose faults come out clearly when the program and the user are out of phase. Every communication that any two human beings are having, is in terms of constructs which are in their minds. Communication with an IE is less meaningful because the constructs in the memory of the computer are only a representation of the constructs in the mind of the creator of the IE. And even worse, the person communicating with the IE must assume that the IE has these constructs which are actually missing i.e. the intelligence which is not there. In other words: *an intelligent-looking IE is more dangerous than a simple-minded IE.* Weizenbaum's book [2] dwells more on this subject.

Inherent Causes

There are some points which make this situation even more problematic:

a. IEs do not work alone. Networks and diskettes pass information as data files and programs. Mistakes in data or programs move from one installation to another in a manner similar to a new Flu virus (see case histories).

b. Data in computer files are never the real thing. They are always some representation and more so a condensed summary of the essence of the complicated real facts. Making decisions on the basis of such data is similar to judgement of trial cases without seeing the person on trial and without knowing the circumstances and the whole picture.

c. In many cases computer data come from different sources which are not compatible in their criteria of data reduction. Decisions are made after comparing two such pieces of data and the conclusions may be totally erroneous.

d. Every optimization process must have an evaluation function which allows it to decide which actions are better than others. The evaluation function is always an imperfect way of putting in programming something we have in mind. The differences between the evaluation function and the real value in human terms may be not large but it may bring about big differences in the results. i. e. in the optimal points arrived at.

e. Most real-life evaluation functions are actually a combination of several evaluation functions each one having a different goal, combined together by giving weights to every component function and summing them up. These weight functions are not really part of the problem but an artifact to allow reconciliation of different or even contradictory desirables. In some cases they may corrupt the optimization process significantly.

f. Computer crimes cannot be overlooked. Not every willful change in the data files and computer programs is the work of a villain. Some may be done by people who are usually law-abiding citizens but who regard tempering with these files as a prank and not a criminal offense. To some people it is also quite tempting because no signs are left after a change is made in the magnetic storage media. This problem has to do with our need to be able to recreate information which was lost by a power failure, a computer crash, a crime or one mistyping during a computer interactive session.

g. Abuse of power: There is an implicit assumption in most of our hierarchies, that every person will do his best to serve the system. Some people may use their power to serve their own needs or whims.

Because of these points, decisions made by IEs may sometimes be very bad decisions. Now I don't claim that human decisions are any better, I claim that in situations involving human beings, one can talk, one can argue, one can bribe, one can intimidate, one can complain to a higher authority. In situations involving IEs only - nothing can stop the on-going car. It's this "talk to the wall" situation which makes things much more distressing even than the most Kafkaesque human situation.

Division between Decisions and Operations

The problem is actually more basic than just the utilization of IEs to make decisions that ought to be made by people only. The real problem lies in a phenomenon which has been with us ever since bureaucracy appeared on earth, presumably in the time of the Pharaohs. The problem is that of the division between the decision maker and the operator that carries out these decisions. The person who makes the rules usually tries to make the best rules from his point of view. The clerk who works according to these rules, in most cases, tries to carry out these rules as best as he can, with Maupertius Principle as a contradictory agent (a principle in theoretical Physics that says that every body behaves so as to make the least action). Why then are there so many cases where things go wrong? Because to every rule there must be exceptional cases which the rule-maker didn't take into account. And there are those border cases where the criteria fit and the rule can be applied, yet most human beings with any consideration in their hearts would decide not to apply the rule, because the results to the person affected would be more severe than expected generally. As clever as the rule-maker may be, he cannot take into account all the possible cases with all the combinations of data. He can never think of those cases where a certain accumulation of circumstances causes the rule to be clearly (or even somewhat) incompatible with common sense or with the spirit of the law. That to me is the real Murphy's law. The person who writes a program or a system, makes decisions which work well in those cases which he tests. It's only in other cases, exceptional yet which are bound to occur sooner or later, that the system fails or what is worse, produces wrong results. A minor point which deserves mentioning here is that Murphy's is so popular because of a psychological amplification effect. Cases confirming this law are bound to be noted and remembered while all the other cases go without anybody ever giving any notice to them. Now the clerk which serves as the performer of certain rules, can see that the case is such that the rule causes wrong actions to be carried out or defaulted, but he usually claims that he doesn't have the authority to change the rule or circumvent it. With a computer it's worse - the machine really cannot change the program which it carries out nor can it discern the need to do so.

One point here is that the computer has made the clerks less responsive than they were before the advent of computers. They can hide behind the computer as an excuse for their lack of action. Lack of action is something most clerks are prone to because of too much work, forgetfulness, a repressive boss or just inherent laziness. But that's just part of the story. They are among those naive users who feel so helpless when faced with the whims of the computer system which is supposed to serve them. They may truly feel anxiety and frustration. But that is not the main issue. Computers today allow those clerks to assemble and later access, huge amounts of information, retrieve from it easily anything that may seem relevant and finally make decisions and send them to be effective all over the country and sometimes even all over the world.

Modern computer systems have given all the clerks immensely penetrating eyes and unbelievably long hands to see and to hold. A clerk using the computer doesn't see the person with the whole picture of his case, only a file of data. The computer did not augment the minds of the clerks but made them quick at the trigger. One small decision and immediately 10,000 low income citizens in Israel got an additional Income Tax note that they have to pay more than $13,000 additional tax ,which was a deliberate decision (see more about that in the appendix). If the clerks were all saints that shouldn't have bothered us. But being what they are, there is some room for apprehension. Actually we should be very apprehensive because computers allow clerks and decision makers to take actions not only on single occasions but decide upon stupid actions which will keep popping up again and again, possibly even forever. In most of the set-ups there is nothing that will stop the wrong decisions or wrong data from reappearing, once they were implanted into the system.

One can argue that AI would allow us to improve things in the sense that the intelligent IEs would be more capable of seeing the whole picture and taking more things into account. In the appendix there is a whole compendium of cases which I took from newspapers and out of my own personal experience. Most of these cases show us the stupidity of the seemingly intelligent human beings. The purpose of this compendium is not to demonstrate how stupid is the computer but rather that no one can think about the strange exceptional cases that will eventually occur and make the rule invalid or inhuman. In the short run, the addition of AI and computer networks would be beneficial. It would eliminate those cases that come out of lack of information. Then we would be left with those cases that are truly exceptions, not taken into account by the decision makers. Can we hope that AI can eliminate these cases and bring their occurrence down to insignificance? Looking at my former arguments, I don't see any basis for that hope. Does an AI program working with natural language really understand the language in the sense that people understand it? Of course not. It can only translate many constructs in the natural language (or in other sources of input) to computer-manageable quantities which are contained in its knowledge base and that knowledge base is always limited. As Fried [3] has put it: "The present day knowledge-based system are not creative - i.e. they do not create knowledge more than is already contained in them. The significance of it is that the process of their understanding fails on the limits of their knowledge. A small child knows that if a glass of milk has broken, the milk will flow out, stain the table and will wet his mother. Such simple logical knowledge can be available to a knowledge-based system only if all the steps of this action and the inferences of each step, are contained or can be derived from the knowledge base."

AI will most probably allow clerks find more cases which they think need to be taken care of. Today what is holding many clerks from taking care of many problems - is only the amount of data or the amount of work that they have to deal with in order to do it. With AI that is no obstacle. IE here really stands for Inanimate Environment where computer programs, robots, communication lines and computerized data, all work together to determine the environment where we operate as human beings. Actually this environment is not inanimate at all. It contains also the clerks who carry out whatever they are instructed to do, the officials who make the decisions, the programmers who stuff these decisions into the computers and sometimes the typists that feed the computer. Such an environment allows wrong data to enter the system, wrong rules to be decided upon, wrong conclusions to be drawn and transferred immediately to every point in the country or in the world.

Present Day Expert Systems

Most of expert systems (and even other AI systems) built to date are not really full scale operative systems. Some are experimental systems. Some were built for demonstration purposes. Some are still in their initial stages. Some work on a very limited domain or body of knowledge. If you come to the sites of operations, you will find very few systems that are being used on a daily basis by many people who access a substantial body of knowledge. As Stephen C-Y. Lu says in [4]: "Very few robust techniques have been developed to apply these theories to the real problems faced by practicing engineers. AI technology has not matured enough to handle elaborate engineering problems". Actually we know today very little about how such systems behave in real-life conditions and how do naive users behave in an environment involving such systems.

Preiss in [5] discusses the shortcomings of the present day expert systems. He demonstrates them to be no more than Technical Assistants. He explains that the body of knowledge given to a computer is always partial and fragmented and that the system works according to rules given before and never produces any new rules because an expert system always works deductively and never inductively. He says: "We need a program which can learn from the accumulated experience of working" but he continues to add "and from interaction with the human user (not the programmer)". We know enough about systems that work on rules given to them by some real human expert to make us feel uneasy, let alone systems that would create their own rules. We all know all the jokes about wrong conclusions made based upon a reasonable body of facts. Induction is best carried out with deep understanding and with intuition - both of which are not typical of IEs. Preiss says there: "New situations are dealt with by reasoning by analogy, by using knowledge to create new rules and data and by trying new rules and correcting them (reasoning by debugging)". It seems we have still to learn a lot until we are able to build systems that can implement these ideas. My concern is mainly about the building blocks out of which those systems are created and these building blocks are what the imagination of the originator could come out with. Yet the buildings themselves, buildings that cannot be predicted exactly beforehand, these buildings can also be a source of unexpected phenomena.

A reader who is not familiar enough with computer systems might get the impression from this paper that computers and computer systems are something quite unreliable. That of course is not so. In terms of arithmetic operations, it is inconceivable that computers will perform any error. In terms of IF statements and PROLOG inferences, it is quite seldom that computers produce wrong results. Statistically computers are very reliable. But that does not help Aviva Nesher, the father of Erez Shitrit, the Rabinowich sisters or Pinchas Avkhazar in their plight (see case histories). There are a few cases there of people who tried to commit suicide!

Necessary Channels of Corrections

Should all IEs be put in chains before they strangle us? Not at all. The point I'm trying to make is that we should never take the human part out of any system. Some people think that the computer is the most important invention of this century. I tend to think that in the long run, the ombudsman will prove to be more important. The ombudsman, as everybody knows, is that person or official body whose task is to accept complaints from those who feel they have been wronged, to check the matter and if the complaint is found to be warranted, to force the clerks to change their actions. The same mechanism should be applied to IEs as well. Every inanimate entity must have a channel whereby complaints can be accepted and remedial action taken in due time if the need arises. The idea is to have with every IE some kind of electronic mailbox where users can enter their complaints and misunderstandings and have some person of authority check the messages, supply answers (preferably in the form of a file open for reading by everybody) and means where corrections in data or programs can be enforced by the ombudsman. Other more conventional methods of complaint handling can be used instead. A person to whom you can apply can also be quite effective, provided he has really the authority to change things and not just PR the angry customer.

Even without any formal administration to handle complaints and corrections, things can be a lot better if we realize that every system is never a final version and that every system should always be subject to constant revision and improvement. Every expert system should always be open for additions and omissions by the experts who put their knowledge inside the system or other experts who inherit them in this office. The question whether expert systems should be giving advice to naive users or only to a "small" expert, is not yet resolved. The example of information retrieval in large data banks (including Easynet) can tell us that some naive users can do it, most of them can't do it without wasting a lot of time (and money) and getting partial results and some are not successful in doing it but they don't know it. Suppose someone gets the advice of a commercial expert system and the advice is harmful. Who should he sue: the hardware vendor, the basic software producer, the expert system designer, the various experts that put their minds in the file, the PTT that operates the communication line, or maybe the optometrist that gave him bad eye-glasses. Of course there is also the basic right of every citizen to know what is written about him in every data base. This right ought to be made part of the constitution (or legislation) of every free country and there should be a minimal number of limitations to that right. Some people claim that no unique identification number should be given to any citizen and that transfer of data between files should be prohibited by law. I don't think that such techniques of putting sticks in the wheels of the carriage can be useful for long. We won't be able to prohibit data transfer but we can, if we understand the importance of it, insist that *methods for correction must become a necessary part of any system whatsoever.*

Even if that idea becomes standard, that will not be enough. Some authority must be made responsible for the enforcement of this principle. Also ombudsman personnel may be overloaded, not clever enough or lazy thus rendering their action ineffective. So we must have other hierarchies of ombudsman institutions, as in courts of justice, where a person can appeal again and again until justice is done. Also hasty corrections made under pressure of time may well become the source of the next cases of Murphy's law, i.e. an IE doing something which is clearly wrong. So procedures for corrections, some immediate and not permanent and some permanent but well tested - such procedures must be part of the ombudsman institution. It seems that programming style becomes something which we cannot leave to the whims of every person who got hold of a computer. Now, this sentence looks to me as something which may be a source of bureaucracy and troubles, which leads me to the conclusion that common sense will always be required, human common sense and not the inflexible sense common to all IEs I know of.

Conclusion

Every system which works according to a set of rules, must have a mechanism whereby faults in the rules and in the data can be found out and corrected. That is especially important in systems which employ AI techniques or robotic manipulators. If we don't realize that soon enough, we can make life miserable for our offspring or even for ourselves.

References

1. Parnas D.1. Software Aspects of Strategic Defense Systems, Communications of the ACM, Vol. 28, No. 12 (Dec 1985) pp. 1326-1335
2. Weizenbaum J., Computer Power and Human Reason (W.H. Freeman and company, San Francisco, 1976)
3. Fried I., The Dangers of Superficial Treatment of Expert Systems, Computerworld (29 Jun 1987). Translated into Hebrew in: Maase Choshev, Vol. 14, No. 5 (Oct 1987) pp. 9-12
4. Decision-Level Automation for Engineering Design and Manufacturing, Engineering Outlook, Vol. 29, No. 2 (Sep 1987) pp. 3-4
5. Preiss K., Artificial Intelligence in Manufacturing Systems, Annals of the CIRP, Vol. 35, No. 2 (1986) pp. 443-444

APPENDIX: CASE HISTORIES

All these cases have been taken out of newspaper items, out of my own experience and from stories told to me by people I know, as their own experience. Some of them may be exaggerated, colored or misinterpreted but not all of them. I didn't include all the clips I had, only the interesting ones, yet the number of cases here may be considered exceedingly large. I put in so many cases in order to show that *it's not on rare occasions that an exception makes a rule either invalid or inhuman or both.* The point here is not the stupidity of men, bureaucracy or computer systems but the inadequacy of rules and procedures to cover all possible cases. I hope I wasn't carried away in describing the misery of the people who got into trouble, usually through no fault of their own. I divided the items into chapters according to the principal source of problem but almost every item could be fitted into many places. The names may be misspelled as I transcribed them back from Hebrew transcription to Latin alphabet.

Information Transfer

A person who is now an owner of a world-wide known computer firm, one day, many years ago found out that all the banks in USA wouldn't give him any money. He couldn't understand it but he had to struggle his way to success without ever getting any credit from any bank. When he became very famous and very powerful he took his name out of the black list and found out how he got there in the first place. He once ordered some small item to be sent collect. When the delivery boy arrived with the parcel, he happened to be out of the office and the girl who was there was a new employee and said she neither knew anything about it nor did she have the money to pay for it. The parcel was sent back and his name was entered into the black list.

The police computer in New Zealand is used by some policemen to get the addresses of good looking young women drivers when their cars pass near a police post. It has been claimed that the computer of the army in Israel is being used by private investigators to get private medical information about new would-be employees of companies who employ the services of these private investigators. probably this is done by private investigators who are ex-policemen or ex-soldiers and still have access to the files.

The army in Israel got permission to access the database of the psychiatry department in the ministry of health with the names of all the people who applied to psychiatric treatment. Psychiatrists claimed that there are cases where perfectly healthy people have been dismissed from the army or sent to highly undesirable positions in the army because of that. Prof. Hanan Munitz also claimed that this is a disaster because now people would avoid psychiatric treatment for fear it will affect them later. This will defeat the purpose of the army as these people could get a psychotic attack in the army and start shooting everybody on sight. He also expressed his fears that once the information is divulged to the army, it won't stop there.

A member of a municipal council of one of the towns in Israel made use of the government population data base and sold it to a publicity company. This is against the law in Israel and he was caught because a programmer working in the government in this domain noticed his daughter getting an envelope addressed to her with some details which are unknown except in that data base.

Three cases have been reported of planes which developed problems because one of the passengers was using an electronic game which influenced the electronic systems in the cockpit.

An elderly lady was living alone in her department and nobody was ever seen visiting her. One day, the postman who brought her mail, noticed that a few weeks had passed since she removed her mail. He rang at her door and no answer came. The neighbors didn't know anything and there was not that awful smell which comes from a corpse. The postman concluded she was dead and notified the national social security that kept on sending her checks which were never cashed (their computer never noticed that). From there the information passed to other computers which recorded the fact that she was dead. A few months later she showed up again.

She was ill and went straight to her daughter who lived far away. She was so ill she didn't bother to think about mail, neighbors or burglars so she just took the bus and went away without telling anybody. Later she had a tough time going to all the places and making them believe she's still alive and is entitled to get water, electricity, telephone, etc.

A man who wanted a job with a public firm was declined without explanation. A high official who intervened for him found out the reason was he was recorded in the computer files as a person having a police record. The contents of that record were that at the age of 15 he played soccer with his friends and broke the window-glass of a neighbor who called the police and filed a complaint against him.

Wrong Conclusions out of Partial Information

A law-abiding citizen came out of his own workshop in Beer Sheva and went home in his car which had some of his tools in the back. On his way he saw a neighbor who raised his hand asking for a lift. he took the guy who happened to be a person known to the police, not for his good deeds. On their way they were seen by a sharp-eyed policeman who was passing by with his fellows and they asked them to stop. When the policemen saw the tools, they naturally thought them to be burglars on their way to some mischief. The policemen told them to come with them to the police station. The driver was upset and in an angry voice said: "What's the problem? Why do you detain me?" Hearing this, the policemen became quite angry, twisted his hand and took him by force to the station, giving him a few kicks to make him go. They kept him there for a few hours until they realized that he is a regular citizen, making a nice livelihood from of his own workshop, with no police record. So they let him go saying it's ok. The citizen didn't think it's ok. The day after that, he came back to the police station, bruised as he was and said he wanted to file a complaint against the policemen who treated him so brutally. The policeman on duty refused to accept the complaint, telling him for his own good to go home. He went to his lawyer and sent the complaint through him. The police reaction: they put him in jail for a few days to interrogate him thoroughly. The story appeared in the local newspaper and the police claimed that it was all lies. If the guy will be strong enough and will not admit in some crime, he will go out of there with a police record of detention in jail for several days. This story is from the local newspaper of Beer Sheva of the very week this paper was written. Connected to the former story one can see the implications of it.

Some time ago I went from Israel to USA and there I was to take a few inter-city flights. I booked all these flights from Beer Sheva. At the last moment I changed the time of my first flight from Israel to a flight two hours earlier. Whenever I came to an airport in the States I always found that my flight reservation had been cancelled by the computer. As I had not been on my original flight it promptly proceeded to cancel all my ensuing reservations without looking to see if I was on another flight. This caused me a great deal of trouble. When I tried to complain, somebody explained to me that it was not a bug in the program but probably a way the airlines put people on the wait list so that they would not be caught overbooked.

The police got information that on a certain date in a certain place a meeting of some drug-pushers was to take place. The source also mentioned that some of them are known to keep the heroin inside their bodies. The policemen in that town got the information through the police computer or some other channel of information but could not get any more details about the participants of that meeting. On the prescribed time the policemen came to the meeting place and found there four youngsters with long unkempt hair. The policemen grabbed these youngsters, told them to take off their pants and in the middle of the street, with a crowd of people looking at the scene, put their hands in nylon gloves and searched inside their bowels. The youngsters were innocent high-school kids travelling around in the summer vacation. Never mind the country.

Iris Kempner from Israel went for a trip in UK. Her passport was in a somewhat shabby state and the immigration officer in the airport decided that it was forged. She was arrested for two days and then expelled from England. An Israeli police officer who came to identify her, didn't manage to persuade the British she really was Iris Kempner, nor did her husband and the Israeli consul.

Erez Shitrit was a 18 years old youngster from Tiberia, Israel drafted to the army and after the recruitment course sent to an army camp in the northern part of Israel, not very far from his home. Two days after that he was told to be on night watch, an order which he resented for reasons unmentioned in the newspaper (probably felt he was treated unjustly by his superiors). So he ran away from the camp. His commander and the sergeant major became very angry and went after him with a jeep. They caught him on the road and took him by force on the jeep, back to the camp. He didn't sit still on the jeep and they told him to sit down and then started the jeep moving. That action made the soldier fall off the jeep, fall on his head and lose consciousness. A civilian who had a kiosk nearby, told them not to touch him and to call an ambulance urgently but they thought they knew better, So they took the unconscious soldier on the jeep and brought him to the army doctor telling him that he was feigning injury. They did not mention the head concussion. The doctor helped him somewhat and the soldier regained consciousness but was rather bewildered. They tried to talk to him but when he was still acting strangely so they called his home and told his father to come and take him home for the night. The father came and was told that his son was a little bit in shock but that it was nothing. The son told his father that he was awaiting trial but couldn't say more than that. They took him home and there his mother touched his head, felt how swollen it was and called an ambulance. The ambulance came immediately and took him to hospital and on the way, the ambulance crew notified the hospital in Tiberia to make ready an army helicopter to take him to a larger hospital in Haifa for brain surgery. When they got to the hospital in Tiberia the helicopter was ready but couldn't be used because a proof was needed that the wounded person was indeed a soldier. His brother had to drive home and back and bring his army papers. The helicopter brought Erez Shitrit to the operation room 8 hours and 4 minutes after he got the blow and that was too late. He died some time later. Had he gotten the treatment in time, he could been back on his feet a few weeks after the operation. The army refused to acknowledge ErezShitrit as killed during his service. Their records say he was sent home in good health and brought back with a broken head. Conclusion: his father murdered him. The police was sent against the father with this absurd accusation! The story got to the newspapers a few days ago and became a scandal for a few days.

Mass Decisions

In Israel there is a big workers union called the Histadrut which also gives medical services (like Blue Shield) to 80% of our population. There is another workers union, mainly Jewish Orthodox which has an agreement with the Histadrut to use their medical services. A few weeks ago, all 150,000 members of the smaller union got a computer-printed message telling them they cannot go on using these medical services as they are not members of the Histadrut. It turned out that someone had decided to set the computer loose to find out who gets the medical services without being a member of the Histadrut. This affiliated union was forgotten and thus 150,000 letters were printed out and sent without anybody noticing anything suspicious about it.

A high official in the income tax department in Israel decided once that within the group of citizens who declared themselves as employees earning less then a certain yearly sum (and thus exempt of detailed income declaration), there must be people who cheat. Although all these people had all their taxes deducted directly from their salaries, he gave the computer orders to issue notice of additional tax they would have to pay on about $13,000 which was much more than these people did earn. Within a week 10,000 low-income citizens got these mortifying tax assessments. The income tax clerks had difficulty in answering all these people who swarmed to the offices. People had to ask for the annulment of these notices and that took about three rounds of trials from the income tax clerks until the notices were really annulled. The story appeared in small letters in the newspapers but no scandal was created. The strange thing is that every tax-payer got a different sum of money to pay. As there were no data to base these sums upon, my only assumption is that they used a random number generator to decide upon these numbers!

Computer Out to Get the Criminals

An Israeli called Joseph Naor was working in Nigeria where he had a local bank account. At the end of 1984 he came back to Israel for a short vacation which became long because he became seriously ill. When he recovered and was ready to go out of Israel he was detained because the computer found out he had a bank account in foreign currency for a time too long to have it if you are an Israeli living in Israel. He was supposed to ask for a permission but he couldn't do it or forgot to do it because he was ill. His passport was taken away from him and the police wanted him available for interrogation and kept him in Israel for 7 months (out of his job). He went to a lawyer who made a judge sign a writ that the passport be given back but the police went to another judge who was busy and without looking, signed another writ revoking the former one. This unusual change of decisions was cycled one more time until Naor was allowed to go back to his job - after paying for 7 months of court and lawyer expenses (without having a salary for more than a year).

Aviva Nesher from Tel Aviv is divorced from her husband. She gets a welfare allowance from the national social security. Her ex-husband who is a used-car dealer managed to put a car on her name and a few days later sold it. The computer of the national social security found this out and stopped her allowance because a car owner is not entitled to a welfare allowance. She tried to commit suicide.

Computer Crime

The present prime minister of Israel, Mr. Itzhak Shamir, once found out somebody had played around with the speech he had prepared with a word-processor on the computer of his department. It was changed so that he would seem a fool when reading it in the Knesset. The woman who did it, belonged to another faction in his own party, Kherut, and there was a bitter dispute between the two factions.

An electrician in Kiriat Tiv'on in Israel was amazed to read in "Yediot Aharonot" (the newspaper with the largest distribution in Israel) in June 1986 a news item from USA saying he was caught there in some huge drug smuggling felony. All his friends called him to ask how come and he had to tell them again and again that he had not been to the USA for some time and knew nothing about this crime. After a detailed investigation the editors of the newspaper together with the police found out that a high-school kid from this town who was using the computer of the Technion in Haifa, Israel - went in the network from Haifa to the States, then accessed the communication channel of the newspaper from there to Israel and had planted this false item as if it came from there. The kid did it as a hoax against the electrician who was also a part-time teacher in his school.

A group of children had a computer club where they used to collect computer telephone numbers and passwords so that they could trespass and enter computers from their home computers and do what they like with these computers (very much like the movie "War Games"). A journalist learned about it and wrote the whole story in his newspaper. They were very angry with this journalist so they decided to "kill him electronically". They didn't cause him any physical damage but they went to all the computers they gained access to, and they changed his status in all the records to "deceased". They also put a note in the file of an undertaker to go there and collect his body. I heard this story from the father of one of these children.

A number of elderly and lonely people had been cheated using a computer list. A clerk who was working in the municipal company which does rehousing of the poor in Tel-Aviv, Israel made a plot with a contractor and a lawyer. The clerk supplied the list of the poor and the contractor came to them and promised to help them get a new apartment. The lawyer made them sign the necessary papers and then the contractor got the money and gave these people some new apartments, in bad condition, worth only part of the money. They were successful with 24 cases of illiterate or ill people who were living alone with nobody to help them deal with the authorities.

This story is the only one here which I did not get from first instance. Yet it is so relevant, I cannot leave it out of this collection especially since I heard many mutilated versions of it: A programmer who was working in one of the banks in Chicago got the task of writing a program to compute the interest for money kept in the bank accounts by the clients. He decided to perform the perfect crime and steal something nobody would ever look for - the fractions of cents in the interest of every bank account. But he had a problem: how could he transfer the money to his own account without having this account number appear explicitly in the computer program discernible for everyone who wanted to look at the program. He devised a mechanism which would look innocent enough to anyone looking at the program: His program would start with the operation which sorted all the bank accounts according to the alphabetic order of names of clients. Then it would add all the sums in all the accounts and compute the interest for all the accounts put together. Then it would compute the interest for each account separately, truncate it to an integer number of cents and subtract it from the general interest. That operation was performed for all the accounts save the last one. This last account got what was left - which had all the fractions of cents that all the other accounts did not get. The programmer opened an account there under the false name of Zylberman and was always the last account in alphabetic order and thus got every time a considerable enhancement to his salary. That went on for a few years until a refugee from Poland came to this bank. His name was Zhigmund which is written in Polish with a Z with an accent below. The clerk in the bank didn't know how to write this strange Z so he wrote it as ZZ . Now this refugee became the last one in the alphabetic order and he got this leftover of fractions of cents. After some time he came to the bank to ask who was the benevolent person giving him money all the time and that is how the perfect crime was discovered. As I said above, I would not vouch for the authenticity of this story but it is still a nice story and a relevant one to our discussion.

Dangers of Networking and Information Transfer

One day I got a public message from Greece saying that electronic mail from Israel to the States will be suffering delays and losses because students have been seizing the University of Crete for three weeks and the network management cannot route the messages through Montpelier, France and they have to go on routing the messages through Pisa, Italy where the lines are in bad shape.

An electronic mail public message about a program that proliferates like rabbits. The first message was: Someone somewhere has written an exec that prints a Christmas tree on the screen. Then it goes and reads your netlog and names file and sends the exec to all those it finds. It doesn't succeed at getting all the entries but enough to make it proliferate faster than a rabbit.

We have purged over 300 of these files from RSCS when we were investigating the Ohio State backlog (which it helped cause) and deleted over 100 of them from our system already today. Please be on the lookout for this file, it is called CHRISTMA EXEC.
Later came other messages about this epidemic:
From: Hank Nussbacher <HANK@TAUNIVM>
Subject: CHRISTMA EXEC continues to spread
I just pulled a copy out of RSCS that was being DISTRIBUTEd via Listserv's
MEDINF-L list. The clever originator was CHIRUR2 at IPRUNIV. What will
users think up next!!!
Hank

From: Hank Nussbacher <HANK@TAUNIVM>
Subject: CHRISTMA EXEC
I think I have created a solution to the rapidly spreading CHRISTMA EXEC.
I have created a virus to eat a virus. This new CHRISTMA EXEC does
the following:
- it scans your NETLOG file
- if it sees a CHRISTMA EXEC sent to another node, it sends itself to
  the same user. This is known as a chaser.
- if it sees that CHRISTMA EXEC was sent to a local user, it does a
  CP TRANSFER of all that users files to your rdr. This retrieves
  possible 'bad' virusi.
- it then scans those new files, returning those that are not CHRISTMA EXEC
- if it finds a CHRISTMA EXEC of 42 lines, it purges it forever
- if it doesn't find a CHRISTMA EXEC it assumes the user has already
  been infected and proceeds to send a copy of itself to the infected user
- around January 15th, this CHRISTMA EXEC will just ERASE itself and not
  send itself after infected targets.
Hank

From: Hank Nussbacher <HANK@TAUNIVM>
Subject: Hankophyte
To those users who fear that my hankophyte will clog up the links even more:
as long as one virus is out there, lurking in some corner of the network,
sitting in some guy's reader until he comes back after winter recess, we
are in trouble. The only way to combat a virus is to build a stronger
virus and to infect the network with the stronger virus. My virus is
stronger since it looks to destroy the original and not itself. The
original virus is not out to destroy my virus.
The added safety factor is that my virus expires on January 15th.
Hopefully it can kill off all the CHRISTMAs EXECs by then. With Eric's
CLEANXMA and Bill Rubin's RSCS mods, I think we just might be able to
beat it. Should be interesting, while it lasts.
Hank
Virus Invades Lehigh University (from an electronic mail public message): Last week, some of our student
consultants discovered a virus program that's been spreading rapidly throughout Lehigh University. I thought
I'd take a few minutes and warn as many of you as possible about this program since it has the chance of
spreading much farther than just our University. We have no idea where the virus started, but some users have
told me that other universities have recently had similar problems. The virus: the virus itself is contained in the
stack space of COMMAND.COM. When a PC is booted from an infected disk, all a user need do to spread the
virus is to access another disk via TYPE, COPY, DIR, etc. If the other disk contains COMMAND.COM, the
virus code is copied to the other disk. Then, a counter is incremented on the parent. When this counter reaches
a value of 4, any and every disk in the PC is erased thoroughly. The boot tracks are nulled, as are the FAT
tables, etc. All Norton's horses couldn't put it back together again... :-) This affects both floppy and hard
disks. Meanwhile, the four children that were created go on to tell four friends, and then they tell four friends,
and so on, and so on.
I urge anyone who comes in contact with publicly accessible disks to periodically check their own disks. Also,
exercise safe computing - always wear a write protect tab. :-)
This is not a joke. A large percentage of our public site disks has been gonged by this virus in the last couple
days.
Kenneth R. van Wyk, User Services Senior Consultant,
Lehigh University Computing Center

Abuse of Power

Some clerks in China who work in the electricity company, use their power in order to extort money and
expensive presents from the customers. They stop the electricity in the middle of an opera show or irrigation
pumps if they don't get what they want. Because power failures in China are quite common, It's difficult to
prove there was malpractice in any of these cases.
Jean Eve Moutenage from Douey, France was a lazy policemen. Instead of looking for real breaches of the
law, he used to write down license numbers of cars he saw around and later he would write down tickets of all
sorts of offenses the drivers of these cars had allegedly committed. Most of the drivers paid the fines without

remembering whether they have done it or not. Some tried to talk to the judge but I suppose that in France traffic courts are like traffic courts in Israel: A single judge may sit and pass judgement on many many cases on one day. So who listens to the defendant? It took some time before the police was ready to look into the matter.

In one of the democratic countries in the world there lived 30 years ago a leader who was very popular in this country. One day this leader went abroad and did something which some people thought was a disgrace. Very few politicians and journalists dared say anything against it because he was really very popular. One tiny party decided that this act cannot be left unnoticed so they organized a protest in the airport when he came back. This made him very angry so he gave orders and all the known members of this tiny party were recorded in the files of the secret service as security menace to their country. This party was neither left nor extreme right and all her members were as patriotic as that leader. Yet they all had been labelled secretly as traitors, a fact which probably influenced their lives and which they had no way of knowing about it.

Bugs in Programs

A person in Israel had problems with his electricity meter and it was replaced. Next month he found out that a huge sum of money (about $10,000 I believe) was taken out of his bank account. The reason is this: The new meter showed a number lower than the former record kept by the computer. The computer computed the amount used as the difference between the numbers and got a negative "amount used". But the program was not designed to cope with such rare cases. It was written in Cobol which keeps negative numbers such as -15 in the form of 99985 (called the complement). This program made him pay for the huge number of kilowatts which was the complement of the negative number which was computed. The money was taken out of his bank account as many bills are paid directly from the bank accounts. It took about two months for the clerks of the electricity company to find out how it happened and return the money back without interest. The overdraft which they caused was none of their business.

I once put some money in a bank to be kept in a foreign currency account. The clerk mistyped one numeral in the number of the bank account by writing a 3 which looked very much like an 8 (it was before they had online terminals). The money was thus put in a non-existent bank account and there dissolved with inflation that was here in those days. That computer program didn't have any measures to detect such a common mistake or detect money being kept in nowhere. When I found out what happened and complained about it, all the bank was ready to do was to give me back my worthless nominal sum of money.

Some computer programmer found out that the interest-computing programs in most of the banks in Israel are incorrect. Nobody would bother to take the bank report and compute the interest by hand to find that out and ask for extra money. He wrote his own version of it, to be run on a PC and sold it to many institutes who used it to recompute the interest and claim more money. The banks had to pay all these claims and the damage to them was in tens of millions of dollars.

In Kolbotek, which is a very popular TV program in Israel, accountants explained to the public that the IRS computer program is incorrect and how to check it and avoid paying baseless details in the assessment.

There is a well known story about the guy who was away from home for several months and received a bill to pay $0 for electricity and when he didn't pay it he got a reminder and then a letter saying they would disconnect him because he didn't pay his bill. The story goes on that he sent them a check for $0 and got a receipt saying all debts have been cleared. That is only a story but I did see a municipal tax note in Eilat, Israel sent to "Empty Apartment". I wonder what they would do to it if it didn't pay its taxes.

Here is an excerpt from some correspondence in the public messages service of the Bitnet electronic mail. It tells the details of an instance when two computers rejected an electronic message and kept sending it back and forth, each time with an additional rejection note, making it into a bigger and bigger file looping back and forth:

Date: Wed, 29 Jul 87 11:32 PDT
Sender: Tom Mlay <TS0070@OHSTVMB>
Subject: Re: Mailer loops

Today I discovered another quite trick. A loop between my Croswell's mailer and the VMMAILER at DJUKFA11. I have often suspected this with other mailers. It seems someone sent a file to a user at OHSTVMB. But it failed the validity check. The mail was returned to VMMAILER at DJUKFA11, who immediately returned it because you cannot send mail to a mailer. Upon returning it to MAILER at OHSTVMB, he complained about mail addressed to MAILER and returned it. The file is now over 8,000 records - 12 records of note and 7,888 records of headers and errors.

Could we (i.e. someone) look into this to see if there is a way to eliminate such loops.
Tom Mlay
Answer:
I suggest all of the following:
(1) Run a more reasonable mailer, although I don't know that one
    exists for VM.

(2) Fix the mailer. Mail to MAILER should 'never' be
answered. It should be forwarded to your local postmaster for
manual action. This is the approach that UCLA/Mail
takes. I have had bounced mail that would have been
looping if not for this feature.
Leonard D. Woren
MVS Postmaster <LDW@USCMVSA.BITNET>
University of Southern California

The computer of the Israeli Bezek company (the telephone company) is doing some mischief sometimes. Once it sent inflated bills to many subscribers. When they paid these bills, their accounts were credited but the balance was not zero, so it sent all of them letters "before disconnection" because nobody ever pays more than is due. On another occasion it noticed that nobody pays the bills for the telephones of the company itself. It issued a disconnection order which was promptly carried out by the technicians. All the telephones of the headquarters were disconnected and the director general had to go in person to the nearby exchange and tell them to reconnect because he couldn't do it by telephone.

Wrong data

The clerks of income tax in Israel have stop checks in the streets, where they stop cars, check the records of their owners and confiscate the cars of people who are written down as owing money to income tax. Once they did it to Rabbi Nissim Zeev, a deputy mayor of Jerusalem who owed them nothing. The rabbi was so angry he shouted and probably tried to hit them. Due to his being an eminent personality in Jerusalem, they didn't arrest him but they did take away his car.

Claudia Argalles from Ashkelon, Israel was called to be drafted to the army at the age of 9. A simple error in the records of the army computer. It's not the only case but in this case the clerks couldn't fix it and the computer kept sending her letters with appropriate threats.

When I wrote this very paper which you are reading, I was using a speller to correct my spelling mistakes and my typing errors. When this paper was nearly finished, I noticed that in one place the word "conclusions" was mistyped as "conlusions". As this paper was passed through the speller several times, I wondered why wasn't it found out by the speller. It turned out that the dictionary incorporated in this speller had this word (and maybe other words as well) misspelled. The guys who wrote this speller didn't think about this possibility and allowed no method of correcting the dictionary.

A man called Shalom Blaustein from Israel who happens to be a rather rich man, went on a trip abroad taking with him no money except a Visa credit card. Wherever he got, he always found the computer claiming his credit card is invalid. Whenever he managed to talk to the people of Visa in Israel they promised him it's a mistake which has been fixed and will not occur again and yet it did occur again and again. He sued them 10 million shekels for sorrow, disgrace and ill fame.

The clerk of a lawyer wrote down a complaint in Beer Sheva against one person. She wrote down the name and the identification number of the guy. She mistyped one digit in that number and the policemen managed to find the guy with that identification number who happened to live in Beer Sheva, in another street not far away from the first guy and the name had a very Russian sound like the first guy. The second guy showed them that the name on the arrest warrant and the address were different but the policemen just looked at the identification number and arrested him. After five hours he was allowed to go home. The policeman explained to the journalist: "Who the hell can differentiate between all these Russian names".

A Yugoslavian called Milorad Yoanowich working in Vienna broke his leg and entered a hospital. Because of an error in a computer record he had a heart pace-maker planted in his bosom. The problem stemmed partly out of his lack of knowledge of German.

Wrong identification

Joseph Haviv had a debt which he had difficulties in paying. A few days after the due date he was arrested and wasn't allowed to contact anybody outside the prison and ask that his beloved dog be taken care of. After 3 days, his employer looked for him and when he found out the reason for his disappearance, he immediately paid the debt. The police by mistake, freed another prisoner with the same name and poor Haviv was kept in prison 11 more days until he was allowed to go home. By that time the dog had starved to death. He sued the state and got 2500 shekels as damages.

Randolph Miller of USA started getting all sorts of strange letters and couldn't get any job because of some unknown felonies. After some time the police informed him that they caught a guy by the name of Derin Giro who assumed the name of Miller for 5 years and had used it in order to get a driving license and a social security card, opened bank accounts, used them to buy many items without paying for them and did several other nasty deeds. Giro, a psychotic case, said "he didn't want to be the person he was" and took the identity of

Miller whom he met once. The banks did not care who the real Miller was and kept pressing Miller to pay the huge debts. The police advised him to assume a new identity as the only solution to the problem.

Binyamin Brosh of Arad, Israel did not agree to sign a guarantee for a loan one of his colleagues at work had asked him to sign. The colleague forged his signature, got the money and eventually didn't pay it back. To the police the forger admitted to the crime but that doesn't help Brosh. His salary is confiscated every month by the bank, he has nothing to eat, yet being a person with a salary he is not entitled to any welfare.

Difference in Criteria

Rachel Dotan from Israel got a special permission to get married below the age of 17 (maybe she was pregnant) but when she and her husband went to buy an apartment they couldn't do it because she was legally under age to get a mortgage.

My own son is to go now on a trip with the Society for Nature Preservation to Sinai, Egypt. The clerks on the border won't let him go out of the country without a certificate from the army saying he's not supposed to be called for army service in the near future. The clerks in the army won't issue such a certificate because he's only 15 years old and they are not allowed to issue such certificates for people below 17. The clerks on the border claim that he looks big enough to be a soldier and therefore they must have the certificate. We know that he's bound for trouble because a former group was detained for almost a day because of that difference in criteria.

Sara and Varda Rabinowich from Rehovot paid their property-tax in 1979 in full. After some time they got a new tax note for less than a Shekel and when they came to the clerk to pay it, he laughed at them and told them to disregard it. Three years later they got a new tax note based on the original one. With interest, inflation and accumulated fines the sum expanded to become 18,206 shekels! When they came to the property-tax office, the same clerk wasn't working there any more and the new clerk said they would have to pay it because they had no right to defer payment of even that tiny sum of money.

David Levy is an important minister in Israel today who wishes to become prime minister in the coming years. One day the newspapers were full with news items about one of his sons being accused of getting two salaries at the same time and being summoned to the police for interrogation. The father announced pathetically that it's a plot against him. Later the minister for police apologized and said there was nothing in the charges. He explained that the computer got reports of the salary paid to Levy junior on several months and a salary of one period was paid later and taken by the computer to be the salary of the second period when he had another source of income. Looking at the whole picture there was one salary for every month, no more no less. The followers of Levy senior still believe it was a plot.

In 1971 I came to Beer Sheva and bought an apartment for the price of 35,000 Israeli pounds which is not a high price. The apartment was registered as mine only in 1975 because of some procedure which I had to undergo and which took all this time. In 1977 I got an enormously lengthy form from income tax to fill, where I was to declare all my income for the past years, all my capital and all my worldly possessions. I tried to tell them that I'm only a university employee and no big-shot capitalist but to no avail. I filled that lengthy form in detail and brought all the necessary documents which I had a hard time collecting and gave the whole pack to them in person. I was called for an interrogation in which the clerk cross-examined me on every detail, asking me if I wanted to correct it before I'd be accused in giving false information and hiding my income. When I didn't admit in having any other source of income, the clerk looked at me with stern eyes and asked where did I get the money for what I bought in 1975 for the price of 175,000 Israeli pounds. I told her that I couldn't buy anything for that sum of money because it's more than I've earned in my whole life. She insisted I did buy it and she had my name and the name of my wife attached to that purchase. She admitted that the computer doesn't know what is this property but the price looks like a second apartment. I told her that if she finds a second apartment connected to my name, I'm ready to split it with income tax but that even didn't make her smile. She told me the IRS information force would look into the matter and she let me go. I came home dejected and told my wife who started laughing. She explained to me that it is our one and only apartment and the sum came from the current value of it. This arose because of the inflation and rise in prices of apartments which happened in Israel in these very years. I went back to IRS and left them a note and never heard any more about my alleged second apartment.

Talk to the Wall

Perry Samy from Netanya, Israel had a problem with the income tax office. Again and again he applied to them but to no avail. He was told by the clerk that only the court can help him. He went there and found out that the courts can not do anything to help him. He was so frustrated that he went back to the the income tax office and raised a scandal by shouting and breaking things. He was brought to trial but the judge said she wholly sympathized with him and asked the case to be sent to the manager of income tax to draw conclusions of.

Pinkhas Avkhazar of Tel-Aviv was going to fly to a furniture fair in Milano in May 1986 when the computer in Lod airfield said there is a arrest warrant against him and wouldn't allow him to go out of the country. The computer didn't have any other information except that the arrest warrant was issued in 1975. He had to check with every court and every police station in Israel but nothing was found as the relevant record, if one existed, was destroyed some years before. His lawyer managed to get a letter from the police saying that no one wants his arrest and then he was able to
go to the fair.

No Applicable Law

One family in Israel does not think highly of hospitals and when their son was born, they preferred to do it at home. When they wanted to register the newborn, the ministry of the interior wouldn't do it. Only a hospital can register births. The clerks said that they cannot just accept "anybody who comes and claims he has a newborn baby".

In Siudad Bollivar a child was born with two heads and two hearts but one body. There was a big dispute whether he should be registered as one person or two.

The rule is Invalid

In november 1984 in Petakh-Tikva, Israel a person called Menachem Gazit parked his car in the evening in a permitted parking place in a street near his home. He slept rather late and when he came out he found that his car had disappeared. Instead he found there a taxi station and the taxi drivers told him that early in the morning, the workers of the municipality moved their station from across the street. They painted the sidewalk with the yellow color of the station. A few minutes after that painting, a police towing car passed by and towed away the car of Gazit. The taxi drivers told the policeman that the car was parked there before the change in status, but the policeman didn't think it had any relevance to the situation and proceeded with the towing. Mr. Gazit went to the police and he was told to pay a fine and for the towing. He showed them the yellow paint on the tires but to no avail. He got to the commandant of the police unit. The guy realized Gazit was right, so he shrugged and was ready to let him go with his car without the fines. He was not ready to ask forgiveness from Gazit or pay any damages.

In Campolinio, Italy the citizens rushed out of their houses to see one person being marched out all over the village, totally naked, by another person who was walking behind him with a pointed rifle. The man with the rifle was a husband who came home and found his wife in bed with one of his neighbors. He took his gun and thus punished the person in this peculiar manner. Why do I include this story here? Because the person who was disgraced, was summoned some time later to the court to be tried for immodest exposure in public.

In Israel a husband who prefers to stay at home and take care of his children while his wife goes to work and becomes the breadwinner of the family - is bound for many problems because he is a non-working head of a family and a woman cannot be a head of a family. The situation is now so impossible that under the present regulations he is bound to lose his rights for medical services from the Histadrut.

Giorgio Altoballi from Ortona, Italy got in 1983 a postcard sent to him from Napoli in 1962. He had to pay a fine of 600 lirettas because the stamp was no longer valid.

Ovadia Salman of Holon, Israel made a living by going around with a small cart and a horse and selling vegetables. He was registered in the national social security office as self-employed as if he was an independent businessman. Then the horse died and he didn't have the money to buy a new one. Now he is unemployed but the national social security still claim income reports for all the past years with a signature of a certified accountant. Neighbors wrote to them and explained the situation but the clerks of the national social security didn't come to see two old hungry people living in a poor state. Instead, they sent the bailiff department to confiscate their last belongings.

Yeheskiel Abbers from Jerusalem, Israel saw a motorcycle driver cause some damage to a car. He wrote down the license number of the motorcycle and left a note on the car with his name and telephone number. He was summoned to the court to testify against the offender. On the night before the day of the trial, his pregnant wife was taken suddenly to a hospital to be operated upon but the operation was unsuccessful and they lost their child. He forgot all about the trial. The court issued a new summons to be enforced by the police. He was was called to the police to pay 2000 shekels as a security measurement to ensure his appearance in the second trial. He didn't know that the police don't accept checks and when he came immediately to the police without hard cash money, he was arrested until the date of the second trial, with his wife left alone in hospital and his other children left alone at home. Luckily for him, he was seen by a police officer who was a friend of his brother and he brought the money to bail him out.

Greg Hammond is an invalid swimmer in Australia. He participated in a swimming race with normal healthy swimmers and managed to get to the first place but he was not recognized by the sports authorities. The rules say a swimmer has to touch the end line with both hands but Hammond is an invalid with only one hand.

In Holon, a husband left his wife and four children and disappeared. It turned out he left significant debts and the creditors went to the bailiff department to get their money back. The officers of that unit went to the apartment, broke the door when this wife didn't open it and took away every belonging they had. The woman and a welfare worker named Tova Tevet tried to plead and to explain that the husband doesn't live there any more but to no avail. For two years the bailiff department would take away whatever the welfare gave them. After two years of misery the oldest daughter, aged 12, tried to commit suicide and that made the mother and one of the other children try to do the same.

After reading all these cases, I suggest you read again my paper, having these real cases in mind all the time.

The Social Implications of Robotics and Advanced
Industrial Automation / D. Millin and B.H. Raab (Editors)
Elsevier Science Publishers B.V. (North-Holland)
© IFIP, 1989

On the Impact of Industrial Automation,
Robotics and Artificial Intelligence
on the Vulnerability of Information Economy

Klaus Brunnstein

Faculty for Informatics, University of Hamburg
Hamburg, Federal Republic of Germany

Abstract: In many institutions and enterprises, rather
complex Edp systems develop as the formerly singular
application programs are enhanced and combined to
"integrated solutions". Moreover, a growing variety of
hardware&software system architectures is connected,
with often incompatible structures.

In "von Neumann"-systems, growing complexity implies
growing dependency and, in case of improper working or
misuse, growing vulnerability of the enterprise. Though
many "accidents" (misbehaviour of systems and programs,
illegal use by insiders, criminal action such as
invasion from outside) enlarge the related risks,
further steps are undertaken to connect and (at least
partially) integrate such systems of different enterprises thus cumulating the risks.

As Artificial Intelligence techniques are applied, the
correctness of the Knowledge Bases as well as the
correctness of the Logic Algorithms presents another
class of unsolved problems which may further enlarge
the vulnerability of an institution. To master these
problems, careful analysis and controlled progress
should be preferred over precipited "innovation" steps.
Moreover, designers, managers and users must be educated to cope with unavoidable faults and unforseseen
situations.

1. Introduction: Vulnerability of Computerised Economies:

Since John von Neumann's "First report of an EDVAC", which
described the principles of the algorithmic system architectures, on which todays (large to small) computers as well as
application programs were developped, Edp systems become
ever more essential for institutions and enterprises,
economic sectors as well as national and international
activities. This rapid process of Computing applications,
unparalled in its velocity in the history of technical
civilisation, implies opportunities and risks at the same
time (as two sides of the same coin, unavoidably connected
to one another).

With the rapid development of Computing applications, the
dependency of the affected institutions and enterprises from
the proper functioning of their Edp systems grows. Since
ever spreading parts of the economy depend on the correctnes
of Edp-generated results, which rather often can no longer
be controlled by humans, the respective part of the economy
becomes vulnerable when Edp services are not availbale. As
the propagation of erroneous actions or data and the
related consequences for the World economy demonstrate to a
surprised public (such as in the October 1987 Crash), parts
of international economy like banks, insurances, trade and
industry have yet reached a high level of Edp involvement
and dependency, with a corresponding adoption of rich
opportunities and often unforeseen risks.

Generally, a society (an economy) us <u>vulnerable</u>, if any of
its essential structures or processes can be influenced in
its ordinary behavior by unforeseen or unavoidable, comparatively simple means. Through use of Information and Communication Technologies, the (previously existing) vulnerability
of civilized societies grows significantly, especially with
the integration of new parts and methods, if no curative
action has been planned.

Examples of (non-Edp) dependencies are well-known in the
history of civilized societies and economies: energy production ("Oil crisis"), availability of Electrical Energy
("Blackoputs"), transportation of goods (esp. regarding
those needed for the daily life) etc. Nevertheless, the
propagation of faults could be limited, in former phases of
technical civilisition, to specific branches and localities.
With the application of Computing and Communication,
limitation of risks becomes more difficult: the connection
and, as a consequence the system dependency, which develops
in Computing and Communication applications worldwide
(though with different velocities in developed and developing countries) will not allow "localisation" of the risks
(as the October 1987 Crash or the problems of computerized
airtraffic show).

2. Riks Factors in Edp Systems:

In todays Edp systems following the classical "von Neumann
architecture", proper functioning of computerized environments depend on several <u>assumptions</u>:

- Algorithms, modules, programs and systems are
  correctly designed, specified, implemented and used.

- Failures in hardware/software can be detected (if not
  excluded by design), and remedies are available to
  minimise the consequences of failed processes.

- "Malignous use" (inadvertantly by legal user,
  willingly by criminal actors, inside/outside the
  institution) and use of illegal software techniques
  (like: unauthorized software changes, implantation
  of "software bombs", like a Virus or Worm) can
  either be excluded or be detected, trapped and
  remedial action can minimise the negative effects.

- Networks and locally "intelligent" workstations
  can be controlled separately to avoid that formerly
  isolated risks spread into different parts of
  the connected systems.

Though many system egnineers and managers try to minimise
the Edp risks, several of the given assumptions are not
justified in practice, either due to basic problems, or
following human unability to design and implement - as
system/program engineers - error-free large software packages (of several thousand to million instructions), to
control - as users - the plausibility of the results of
large programs (without deeper insight into their structure
and behaviour), or even - as Edp organisers and managers -
to control and guarantee the "proper" use (that it a use
only in cases where the built-in assumptions are applicable)
of the systems. The rich literature gives surprising and
often shocking cases of error propagation and system and
user mis-behaviour, with practical impacts also on innocent
"usees" (those people being affected by Edp methods, but
unable to control what goes on: e.g. states' citizen as
objects of public data storage/processing).

As long as proper theory is missing which proves whether a
given piece of software solves the specified problem
("verification"), extensive and permanent control of the
status of every systems' component as well as of every
users' action and data is the only way to minimise the risk
of misbehaviour and illegal action. Unfortunately, Risk
Control becomes yet more difficult through distributed Edp
systems and "Personal Computers", with (decentralised and
rather often improperly advised) users almost totally unaware and uneducated to cope with the problems mentioned.
The case of "Computer Virusses" shows the dilemma: while
users want personal control over their equipment, they are
often unable (or unwilling) to maintain "clean" software
(which they rather often "get" from unidentified, obscure
sources) and to control the plausibility of their results.
While Virusses, for some time, were mainly problems of
students and hackers, the risk is now escalating as virusses
have recently been detected in hospitals (e.g. in Intensive
Care PCs).

Because of the lack of theoretical models, it is virtually
impossible today to calculate the risk of a given software
package like: a book-keeping system, a CAD or CAM package.
Nevertheless, practical "Risk Analysis" and case studies
about experienced failures may help to detect and classify
many of the built-in risks. As this is applicable to a
precisely described system environment, a "Risk Vector" R
may be constructed which contains information about the
several risk components. Without going into detail, let us
generally assume that R is known (in a normalised, mathematical form) which describes the risk components of every
singular system. How does the risk propagate when several of
the (formerly indepently designed and used) systems are
connected to other such systems (as is the case of the
development of Industrial Automation systems)?

3. Vulnerability of Industrial Automation

In Industrial Automation, the integration of formerly independently designed systems produces risks of advanced
dimensions and complexity. In first phases of Industrial
Automation, isolated solutions have been planned and
implemented, rather often with incompatible hardware and
software techniques. Tools used to design products (CAD) and
to prepare the engineering aspects (CAE), to plan and
control the production processes (CAP/CAM) use very
different programming techniques (e.g. programming
languages), and moreover they are implemented on different
kinds of (operating) system architectures (e.g. realtime-
and transaction-oriented systems), which moreover differ
widely from traditional (often COBOL-based, batch- or
transaction-processed) programs used for inventory, financial calculations and quality assurance.

The cumulated risk of a system consisting of singular non-
interfering components can essentially be calculated from
the risk of the most vulnerable system, and a first
estimation can be expressed by the maximum risk valid in the
system:

$$Rl_{total} = \sum_{I=1}^{N} Rl_I \leq N * \max_{I=1}^{N} Rl_I$$

This measn, that the risk of a system connected from N
formerly independent subsystems is not greater than N times
the maximum risk of the singular subssystems; but it is
always greater than the highest singular risk. The risk
grows with the number of independent components (e.g.
different user populations, storage size, processing
complexity), but is (in this stage) "only" additive (that
is: it grows in a controlled manner).

In a second phase of Industrial Automation, formerly
isolated "island solutions" are stepwise connected to each
other to finally achieve an "Overall Enterprise System"
where all information and communication processes shall
give, at any time and location, maximum information related
to every part of the enterprises' processes. The benefit of
a progress from several isolated system components to
(finally) one combined solution seems to allow control of
every step of the development as well as the conservation of
the investments in and experiences with (earlier) subsystems. The progress from isolated to subsequently combined
systems seems natural and adequate, because it follows the
same paradigm which underlies the construction of every
singular subsystem: modularity.

At a first glance, the "only" problem seems to be the
construction of "proper" interfaces between the respective
modules, which now have to exchange the information produced
or consumed by each other. As figure 1 indicates, the demand
for new or differently designed goods, as experienced in the
Distribution Department and stored in a related databank,
provides input information for the Design Department and the
related CAD system; after the design process and the
construction of a production plan, the respective data have
to be transferred to the Manufacturing Department where the

Picture 1: Integration of Industrial Planning&Production

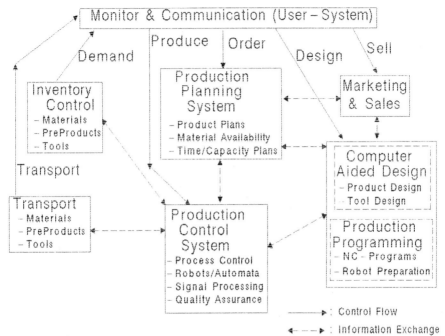

respective good will be produced depending on a plan or demand data retrieved from the Distribution Department.

Moreover, the communication paths seem to be restricted to a given set of commands (e.g. Order, Produce, Construct); unfortunately, the respective singular processes have significant demand for data and information stored and processed also by the concurrently active other systems. Shared storage and processing is a major source for additional system complexity, dependency and thus risks.

The complexity of the combined system is not simply a superposition of the singular subsystems. Since the respective singular systems' architectures are widely incomprehensive and imcompatible, the interaction is much more difficult in unforeseen system situations. As many experiences in Computer Integrated Manufacturing show, the propagation of faults in such a complex system is often less predictable and comtrollable than in large single-purpose architectures. Essentially, the risk of a "phase 2" system grows proportionally with the risk of its component systems:

$$R2_{total} = \bigcap_{J=1}^{M} R2_J = R2_1 * R2_2 * R2_3 * .. * R2_M$$

where

$$R2_I = (\sum_{J=1}^{N} R1_I), \text{ i-th component (of N)}$$

As compared to the (merely additive) behaviour of "Phase 1" systems, risk propagation in such integrated ("Phase 2") environments is so much faster that significantly more intelligence must be invested into risk avoidance and detection as well as fault control. As many examples (also in enterprises with rich Edp experience) show, adequate, advanced methods of Risk Analysis and Control are either missing or not applied.

In a <u>final (third) phase</u>, integrated industrial systems of different enterprises are connected to each other and exchange information and data. Due to each partners own Edp history, the architecture of the "single" (phase 2) systems will be very different from one another; moreover, the "phase 2" integration produces very different enterprise-specific system structures. Under the super-imposed "phase 3" integration, the complexity of the "total" system grows into yet another dimension. Consequently, architectural misbehaviour of a small part of one subsystem may propagate, by exchange of data and control information, in unforeseen and even hardly controllable manner into other systems, with sometimes unforeseen effects. The risk of an economy based upon coupled "phase 3" systems will grow exponentially with the number of components:

$$R3_{total} = (\prod_{K=1}^{L} R2_k)^Z \text{ ,with Z coupled system}$$

While integration of singular ("phase 1") systems components to ("phase 2") "Computer-integrated manufacturing" (CIM) system is underway, at least in medium and large scale enterprises, and not yet finished, several (mainly large and internationally operating) enterprises have also begun to connect their systems, at least with "Electronic Data Interchange" (EDI) techniques. Several enterprises (e.g. in printing industry, in banks and insurances) have yet experienced the sharply risen vulnerability of such connected systems.

An illustrative example of severely grown vulnerability happened to the international banking community (and to the Western economies) on October 17, 1987, which since the 1970's has built large Edp controlled Information Interchange in the 1970's (e.g. the S.W.I.F.T network). International banks argue that actual information about any stock exchange at any place in the world would be of great value to any other stock dealing institute; (nearly) every international bank has therefore connected its own stock supervising system to an international stock exchange network.

Most of the stock control programs follow a loss minimizing strategy ("program trade") according to which stock values have to be "sold" when the value drops below certain (oftenly built-in, that is compiled-in) limits. On October 19, 1987, the drop of certain values startled a built-in devaluation process: when the first program, after having detected the descending value of its stock, "offered" a packet from its portfolio, this furthermore decreased the value of the respective packet so that the lower limit of other trading programs fell under their (specific) limits.

Though no specific economic reasons (e.g. bad management or production news of the affected enterprises) were visible, and despite a comparingly excellent international economic perspective (apart from some Western politicians speculations about the respective economies), the Dow Jones index fell by 25% on the first day, as compared to "only" 7% in October 1927, then in an extremely bad situation of the internatuional economies: "Black Monday 1987" clearly demonstrated the vulnerability induced by unforeseen "side-effects" of "phase 3"-system coupling.

4. Vulnerability of Artificial Intelligence Systems

In sytems based on Artificial Intelligence techniques, the assumption of properly stored and used Knowledge as well as organisational adequacy is accompanied by another kind of vulnerability. While traditional "von Neumann"-kind programs and systems assume correctness of algorithms as well as input data, AI techniques based on "stored knowledge" assume correctness of the logical operations ("A implies B", "From A Follows B, Otherwise C", etc.) as well as the correctness of the stored information and structures. Unfortunately, the correctness of stored knowledge (or a piece of it) is yet more difficult to prove than the correctness of a von Neumann-algorithm. Human history demonstrates moreover that "knowledge" depends on time, location, as well as social, economic and intellectual backgrounds which is often difficult to determine, describe and store. Moreover, different (maybe controversila) "sets of knowledge" may co-exist in a society at a time: in every case, it must therefore very carefully be analysed whether and how "knowledge technologies" (like AI) are applicable.

A "Knowledge Base" has to be constructed from knowledge "melted" out of the heads of experts: the adequacy and correctness then becomes a problem growing with the amount of information and structural interdependencies stored as well as with the numbers of experts "melted". Moreover, a useful knowledge base will significantly change (mainly grow) over time: permanent consistency checks must guarantee, that no contradictions between new and old knowledge element come into the Base. A rigid access and usage control must moreover guarantee that illegal changes of the Knowledge Base (which will lead to wrong conclusions) are excluded.

Unfortunately, many contemporary AI systems are equipped with only rudimentary access control, auditing and monitoring facilities (much below the - also often inadequate - level of "von Neumann"-systems!). Moreover, only very rough methods are known which exclude inconsistencies; at this time, no automatical test of the correctness and completeness of a singular Knowledge Base (or a combination of different KBs) for practical purposes (in industry, economy or health care) is visible. In this situation, it is therefore impossible to classify the risk of an AI system; Moreover, only very special analyses of the "vulnerability" of an organisation which relies itself on such AI-based systems, seem possible.

Regardless of this - inadequate - situation, some scientists and enterprises suggest (and begin) even to couple such AI systems (used in larger industrial enterprises, at least experimentally, for Diagnosis and Decision Support, Analysis of technical Faults, Ressource and Configuration Management), with traditional "Von Neumann"-Systems, like Databanks, CAD- and CAM-packages, or Portfolio Management Systems. At this time, an estimation of risks attributed to system architectures combined from "von Neumann" and "Artificial Intelligence" based components, is impossible due to lack of any methodological basis.

5. Consequences and Remedial Action:

As everyday practical experience in Industry and Economy, Science and Health Care demonstrates, growing integration of Edp services and tools at the same time produces more problems and a higher vulnerability. The growing risk can only be minimized and unforeseen events mastered (if not excluded)

- by careful analysis of the institutions need, combined with the analysis of the vulnerability before and after installation of an Edp system,

- by very careful analysis of the risks and hazards of each system component, as well as the risks and hazards introduced through integration and combination of other systems, those in the own environment as well as those from different architectures (in other parts of the same enterprise, or in totally different systems),

- generally by a conservative, careful approach to new Edp methods, avoiding uncalculatable risks introduced by precipitate innovative steps,

- by careful control of the systems development and of its working environment (e.g. monitoring, auditing), and by proper analysis of the development of the systems use,

- by education of the responsible managers to calculate the balance between opportunities and risks of every new architecture, method and tool (with enough mis-trust in the Edp-professional promissions), and finally

- by proper user education: badly educated users are a severe source of many system failures, and such users are mostly unable to detect system errors at all; on the other side, well-educated users allow for brain-based plausibility control and thus for less undetected systems errors and side-effects and for graceful behaviour in cases of system failures.

Though users, to a certain degree, introduce risks (not only willingly as criminal actors, but also unwillingly as victims of systems' misconceptions) into Edp systems, they also help, when educated to a certain degree of "mastery", to detect and minimize system failures and thus to minimize (or at least "smooth") the institutions' dependency from the Edp system.

Part 3
THE IMPACT OF
ADVANCED TECHNOLOGY AND ROBOTICS
ON KIBBUTZ LIFE

The Social Implications of Robotics and Advanced
Industrial Automation / D. Millin and B.H. Raab (Editors)
Elsevier Science Publishers B.V. (North-Holland)
© IFIP, 1989

HIGH-TECH IN KIBBUTZ INDUSTRY:
STRUCTURAL FACTORS AND SOCIAL IMPLICATIONS*

Menachem Rosner
The Institute for Research of the Kibbutz
and the Cooperative Idea University of Haifa, Israel

Contrary to the fast pace of technological innovation there are big
differences in the rate of diffusion and appplication of those technologies in
advanced industrial nations. An illustration of such differences is the case of
industrial robots. The number of robots in Japan in 1982 was roughly four times
the number in the U.S. (14,000 versus 3,500 in 1982). The ratio of robots per
capita is the highest in Sweden.

The number of C.N.C. machines in U.S. industry is also considerably lagging
behind the number in Japan and in several European countries. In addition to
widely-discussed economic factors, are there also social factors which can help
explain such differences?

There is considerable controversy over the organizational implications of the
use of new industrial technologies and over their impact on the skill level of
the industrial worker.

New approaches in organizational and management theory stress the need for a
transition from hierarchical control to worker commitment (Welton 1985;
Welton-Sussman 1987). In Germany, Kern and Schuman (1986) even foresee the
possibility of an end to the division of labour and they stress the need "new
concepts of production" overcoming the old Tayloristic approach. "Higher
producitivity cannot be attained under present conditions without a more
considerate, enlightened treatment of human labour - that is something that
capital too must learn" (Kern and Schuman 1986, p. 1621).

On the other hand, a series of researchers stress the "de-skilling"
implication of the new technologies. Following Bravermann (1974) they believe
that management will use the new technologies to further its control over
production at the expense of worker's skill and autonomy (Shaiken 1984; Nobel
1984).

In her cross-national comparative study, Kelley (1986) found no conclusive
evidence to support neither the de-skilling nor the skill-upgrading theories.
The differences in work organization and degree of division of labour can be
explained by a series of nation and plant specific factors. She distinguishes
between three basic strategies in the use of new technologies: (1) the
scientific management approach leading to de-skilling; (2) the techno-centric
participative approach leading to skill-upgrading; and (3) a worker centered
participative approach. This last approach "implies a radical decentralization
of control and responsibilities in production, providing for an unambiguously
skill-upgrading effect on production roles and allowing for the greatest
flexibility in adapting the technology to new uses and in speedily solving
implementation problems" (p. 240).

While Kelley did not find cases in which the worker-centered participatory
approach was fully implemented it seems that the process of introduction of new
technologies in kibbutz industries fits this approach.

---

* The factual background for this article is based on an on-going research on
the implications of the introduction of new technologies in kibbutz industry
conducted by the author and M. Palgi with the participation of J. Weiss.

In the 260 kibbutz communities, with a population of 120,000, the members collectively own the means of production and share the income. The management of the communities and of the economic organizations, such as factories which are part of them, is based on direct and participatory democracy. Decisions are taken by assemblies and committees, and officers and managers are elected for limited periods. Following a fast process of industrialization, most of members active in production, work in factories.

Cross-national comparative studies have shown the relatively high degree of worker participation in decision making, the relatively high level of worker commitment and motivation and the contrasting low level of alienation (Tannenbaum et al. 1974; Bartolke, et al. 1985; Leviatan and Rosner 1980).

The rate of introduction of advanced computerized automation in the small and medium-sized kibbutz factories has been outstanding in comparison with the overall rate in Israeli industry. While the 300 kibbutz plants employ only 6% of the total industrial workforce in Israel, they use 60% of the industrial robots. The diffusion of computerized numerical control devices is also much larger than in the overall industry level. (The rate of investment out of the gross income is generally superior to that in the overall Israeli industry).

An analysis of the structural factors that can explain this fast introduction of new industrial technologies reveals interesting similarities with countries, like Japan and Sweden, that have the highest rates of diffusion.

Some of the social factors pushing toward the introduction of new technologies in the kibbutz are similar to Sweden:

1. Out of value-based considerations, the kibbutz system limits severely the use of foreign labour, e.g. the employment of hired workers from outside the kibbutz. While the values guiding the Swedish policy to minimize the employment of foreign workers are different, the outcome is similar: a voluntary shortage of labour in industry.

2. A rather high level of education and social welfare creates a high level of aspiration toward self-realization in work and reluctance to perform routine and alienating tasks. In both settings these factors led in the past to the development of a socio-technical approach aiming at organizational and technological changes: e.g. avoidance of assembly-line technologies, introduction of autonomous and semi-autonomous work groups, etc. The introduction of new technologies was therefore seen as another way to attract educated young adults to industrial work.

There are societal similarities between the kibbutz and Japan which help to overcome some of the major obstacles to the introduction of new technologies, such as: organizational rigidity, adversary relations between management and worker, job insecurity, etc.

The features of the Japanese system of industrial organization which can be compared with the kibbutz can be found mainly in the large corporations. Among them are: (a) lifelong working-place security; (b) a sophisticated system of professional education to assure adaptation to rapid technological changes; (c) open opportunities for mobility within the enterprise - both horizontal, through job enlargement, and vertical, through ascent in the hierarchy; (d) relatively small hierarchical differences, there being little distance between the various levels of hierarchy; (e) the "quality circle" approach representing only one example of unofficial possibilities of workers' participation at a place of work. (Shira, 1983).

All these characteristics can be found - although on a much more intensive level - in the kibbutz enterprises:

(a) The kibbutz is responsible for lifelong statisfaction of the demands of
    all its members, the change of place of work having no influence on the
    degree of this satisfaction - in particular not on material living
    conditions.
(b) The kibbutzim have a sophisticated system of adult education. A change of
    the place of work is not exceptional but rather common. There is an
    official system of rotation for public office and management.
(c) The formal hierarchy is flat. Since the office of manager brings with it
    more difficulties than advantages, there are more opportunities for
    mobility than there is the readiness to use them.
(d) The differences between the levels of hierarchy manifest themselves only
    in work. Since the manager is elected and since he is ony able to
    implement jointly taken decisions, he generally enjoys a high degree of
    legitimation. Social relations are informal and not restricted to working
    hours.
(e) Participation of the members in decisions is both direct and indirect -
    through voting for manager and management - and both informal in the
    working group and formal through participation in the assembly of factory
    and kibbutz. The "self-management" in a kibbutz is thus integrative since
    it unites the different levels of participation, not only of workers on
    the board of directors, but also the decision-making process at all levels
    (Tannenbaum et. al. 1974).

In conclusion, the relatively high rate of diffusion of new technologies in
kibbutz industry can be explained both by factors motivating management
towards the introduction of new technologies - as is the case in Sweden - and
by factors helping to overcome social obstacles in this process - as in the
case in Japan.

Relatively high rate of diffusion in kibbutz industry

This rate has been high in spite of a number of limitations resulting from
the kibbutz structure, such as the difficulties of finding in a single, small
community the professional manpower needed, limitations in risk-taking and in
availability of investment-capital.

Due to the support of nationwide and regional organizational kibbutz
movement networks in financing and professional training, it has been possible
to at least partially overcome these difficulties.

But from a theoretical point of view, we can conclude that there seems to
be a high degree of structural compatibility between the kibbutz structure and
values and the social conditions that can facilitate the introduction of new
technologies.

The implementation of the worker-centered participation approach

An important feature of the worker-centered approach is worker's
participation in the decisions about the introduction of new technologies.
Generally new and important investments will be discussed first with the
workers concerned and then the decision will be taken by the plant assembly.
The first approval will be given by the kibbutz economic committee and
afterwords by the general assembly in the framework of the overall investment
plan.

In the process of introducing new technologies, and in particular
industrial robots, additional forms of participation have been devised.
Following the initiative of the federation of kibbutz industries, an institute
for industrial robots was established to promote the introduction of this new
technology. Before a decision is taken to introduce such industrial robots,
the kibbutz members are informed of the advantagee and problems of using this

technology, assisted by explanations by the institute, to avoid arousing fears and prejudices. The institute aims to provide information to kibbutz plants about the opportunities offered by industrial robots and other advanced technologies and to advise them in the decision-making process related to their introduction. They seek to assist the kibbutz plants in the choice of technologies that are the most appropriate to the solution of their problems, and devise programs for training the necessary technical personnel.

The expectation that the introduction of new technologies will help to overcome the labour shortage problem has generally worked out. In an exploratory survey in 14 plants that introduced high tech, there is overall agreement about the rise in productivity effect. Informants in five plants reported that after the technological change they have no more labour shortages; in seven other plants, the situation improved. While all the plants report a rise in output, only in one plant the number of workers increased and in six it decreased. Seven plants report an increase in the number of younger workers, and in nine plants the readiness of kibbutz members to work in industry has increased (Weiss 1987).

We have no details about the factors that contributed to this change in attitude, but we can at least partly relate it to an improvement in work conditions and work content (Eleven out of 14 plants reported an improvement in working conditions, while six reported an improvement in work content and shift work. There was almost no change in the number of shifts, but in nine plants the number of worker in each shift decreased.

Although we have no conclusive evidence on the impact of new technology on the division of tasks and utilization of skills, it seems that an integrative, non-Tayloristic approach was strengthened, especially for C.N.C. technology. As reported in M. Palgi's article in this volume, in the plant studied, the programming is performed in the production department and not in a special and separate department. Technicians and engineers take an active part in production work. A similar situation was found also in other kibbutz plants (Rosner 1986).

It seems that the introduction of new technologies led in many plants to an increase in the autonomy of different sub-units. This trend toward decentralization and increased worker-participation in the framework of work groups and departments fit also the recommendations of the socio-technical department of the kibbutz industrial association. E.g. one of the kibbutz plastic plants has recently installed a new fully automated and computerized extension producing p.v.c. compounds used as raw materials for various plastic products.

Following these technological changes a team of the kibbutz industry association's socio-technical department was asked to study the organizational structure of the plant and to suggest changes, if necessary. The main suggestion has been the decentralization of the decision-making process, by dividing the plant in two autonomous units: (a) division producing reinforced flexible hoses with 30 workers in four different departments; (b) the compound-producing automated division with only ten workers. The reasons for the creation of this division seems to be not only the difference in products and market conditions that also existed before the technological changes. The higher degree of autonomy is probably needed to deal with the specific requirements and problems of the new technology.

Previously, the main formal participatory decision-making body was the worker-assembly convening once a month. The new recommendations are to convene once a month worker-assemblies in the framework of the divisions and only once in three months the general plant-wide assembly. More authority is also given to the division-managers, and the major functions of the central plant-wide office-holders, e.g. the production-manager, is now of coordination between relatively autonomous units.

This single example might illustrate a certain potential of decentralization and even de-hierarchization of the new technologies, but no conclusive evidence is available at this stage.

But even in this single case in a small kibbutz factory, we can remark similarities with findings reported after visits in 16 large American plants that have introduced advanced manufacturing technology (Walton and Susman 1987): "Most of the plants we visited have reduced the number of (hierarchical) layers ... They have upgraded supervisors and assigned them functions previously performed by second-level managers."

Although the trends are similar, we can assume that in kibbutz plants, due to the relative high level of participation and limited hierarchy, only rather small organizational changes will be needed to adapt to the new conditions.

There is also almost no evidence of conflicts related to the introduction of advanced manufacturing technologies and to their implementation. On the other hand, these processes create other and new problems for the kibbutz and its industry, such as higher dependence on professional and scientific knowledge held by a certain part of the workforce, dependence on the ability to mobilize financial resources, and greater dependence on the changes in the international market.

But it seems that even in this early stage the encounter between the kibbutz and high-tech can be seen as a valuable experiment to overcome the conflict between human and business values.

Bibliography

Bartolke, K. W. Eshweiler, D. Flechsenberger, M. Palgi and M. Rosner, 1985. Participation and Control. Spardorf: Wilfer Publ.
Kelley, M.R. 1986. Programmable automaions and the skill question: A reinterpretation of the cross-national evidence. Human Systems Management, vol. 6, No. 3.
Kern, H. and Schumann, M. 1986. Limits of the division of labor: New production and employment concepts in West German industry. Economic and Industrial Democracy. Sage, Vol. 8.
Leviatan, U. and M. Rosner, 1980. Work and Organization in Kibbutz Industry. Darby, Pa: Norwood Editions.
Nobel, D.F. 1984. Forces of Production. New York: Alfred A. Knopf.
Rosner, M. 1986. New technologies in the kibbutzim. The Jerusalem Quarterly, No. 39.
Shaiken, H. 1984. Work Transformed. New York: Holt, Rinehart and Winston.
Shira, T. 1983. Contemporary Industrial Relations in Japan. Madison: University of Wisconsin.
Tannenbaum, A., B. Kavcic, M. Rosner, M. Vianello and G. Wieser, 1974. Hierarchy in Organizations. San Francisco: Jossey and Bass.
Walton, R. 1985. From control to commitment in the workplace. Harvard Business Review, March-April.
Walton, R. and Sussman, S. 1987. People policies for the new machines. Harvard Business Review, March-April.
Weiss, J. 1987. Social and organizational aspects of robomation and advanced technologies in kibbutz factories. MA dissertation, Tel Aviv University (Hebrew).

The Social Implications of Robotics and Advanced
Industrial Automation / D. Millin and B.H. Raab (Editors)
Elsevier Science Publishers B.V. (North-Holland)
© IFIP, 1989

HIGH-TECH AND THE KIBBUTZ INDUSTRY: A CASE STUDY

Michal Palgi

Institute for Social Research on the Kibbutz
Sociology Department
University of Haifa
Mt. Carmel 31 999, Haifa
Israel

The emergence of new technologies has brought with it pessimistic and
optimistic predictions as to its effects on the workers and the organization. Both workers and employers might expect positive and negative results from its introduction.

Looking at this process from the workers point of view, the positive
and negative outcomes are mainly, but not only, to do with their
quality of working life. The jobs that they will be doing will be
more varied as a result of smaller series of production and the manufacturing more flexible. They might be "reskilled" - i.e. learn new
types of work, to control and manage new types of machines and also
use different manual and mental skills at work - in their workplace.
For some this might be a challenge for others it could be a threat to
the orderly, secure, stable lifestyle they lead.

In the "new technologies era" the workers could control the machine
and their line of production by the computer. Thus they could get
more information about their own work and the work of others. This
on the one hand may give them more leeway for autonomous decision-
making but on the other hand their employers would be able to super-
vise them more closely through their control on the general computer
system.

Writing all this in the conditional tense is because the way the
organization functions with the introduction of high-tech depends on
the ideology and policy of the employers. If the employers believe
that the workers are to be trusted both in the programming of the
machine and keeping the secrets of the company then they would let
them have full control of the machines. If the employers come from a
standpoint that does not trust the workers then they would "deskill"
them. The workers would be allowed only to press the buttons and
keep an eye on the machine. When trouble occurs or a change in production is necessary, the experts will have to be called in.

Maybe the greatest negative effect, from the workers point of view, of
the introduction of high-tech to the workplace is their fear of unemployment. The machines are much faster, produce more accurately
with less waste and can do almost all the work people do. The insecurity in employment and the need to change the type of work or
occupation several times in a life time (as a result of changing
technologies) bring about a resentment towards the "new machine age".

Looking at these effects from the employers point of view, we can see that their hopes and fears are focused mainly on issues of efficiency: a. Efficiency in production - from the point of view of production they hope for better quality, higher quantity, less waste, less workers and more flexibility in the products they can manufacture. They fear the heavy investments that high-tech incurs and the difficulties in adjusting the organization to the new machinery. b. Efficiency in management - from this point of view they hope to be better informed, to know what is going on in their organization, to be able to control the workers and the relatively complex production from their own office. On the other hand they fear the experts who might try to control the whole organization, who might demand to be more involved in decision-making and the general running of the firm and upon whom they are so dependent. In addition, also the workers at the shopfloor level would have access to many secrets of the firm and thus deprive the employers of the power of knowledge. The difficulties in recruiting expert workforce and the expense of the new machines are additional burdens.

We can sum all that has been written above about the anticipated effects of the introduction of high-tech to the production process in the following chart.

ANTICIPATED EFFECTS OF HIGH-TECHNOLOGY

	POSITIVE	NEGATIVE

WORKERS:	- varied job opportunities
	- reskilling
	- more control and autonomy
	- more information
	- better work conditions:
	  clean, not heavy, flexible
		- unemployment
		- deskilling
		- totally controlled
		- frequent change of
		  occupation

EMPLOYERS:	- better information and
	  communication
	- more control
	- development of new production lines
	- more accurate products
	- less waste
	- flexible manufacturing:
	  small series
	- less workers
		- no secrecy
		- not enough skilled labor
		- heavy investments
		- difficulties in acclimatizing to tech changes
		- decentralized organization
		- less control
		- dependency on experts

All in all, it can be seen that the policy of introducing the high-tech and the type of organization of work that will evolve from it depends on the fears and hopes, trust and mistrust between the different bodies in the plant.

In view of the above written, it would be of utmost interest to check how these effects emerge in communities that have no direct salary for their workers and no fear of unemployment - the kibbutzim.

The kibbutzim have started out as agrarian communities governed by some basic values that have in many ways moulded its structure and living norms. These values, relevant to the present discussion, are, socialism (which includes the idea of self labor and self management), and equality.

The communities that were built in order to fulfill these and other values are self-managed, with no salaried work. Work and consumption are organized on a cooperative basis and there is no direct dependency between work and the satisfaction of needs. The consumption expenses for all members represent the price of labor. Labor costs are considered fixed costs, since the labor market is relatively closed, with 90 percent of the workers coming from among the kibbutz members. In face of these conditions, the use of labor saving technologies will not reduce the cost of salaried work. Also, new labor-saving technologies will not cause unemployment, but rather a different social distribution of work such as, increase in services or shortening the working hours. Therefore, the question whether to introduce high-tech has a slightly different meaning in the kibbutz. Looking at the introduction of robots for industrial use in Israel, we find the share of the kibbutzim is 60% while their percentage in the Israeli population is 3.5%.

The questions we wanted an answer to were:
a. What are the considerations for introducing high-tech in plants of the kibbutz? Are they the same as in other places?
b. How does the new technology affect the people in the plant, their adjustment, feeling of belonging, their participation in decision-making and their influence on what happens in their work place?

THE STUDY*

This study has been divided into two parts. The first was a small survey that has been carried out in 14 kibbutz plants. It tried to find out why they have introduced high-tech, what were their expectations from it, and to what extent they were fulfilled. The questionnaires were sent to key-personnel and were to give us some ideas for questions asked in the second part of the research.

The second part was a case study of one plant. We have decided to start with an in-depth study of one plant in order to get an insight of the issues relevant to the introduction of high-tech to kibbutz industry. The plant chosen is one that has been studied by us twice before. Once in 1969 and once in 1977. All the data from the previous studies is available to us. In this paper we shall concentrate on the comparison of the plant of 1987 with the plant of 10 years earlier. We realize that not all changes in the plant are due to the technological ones. We shall describe the social and organizational changes that have occured and try to give them our interpretation. In this part of the study we used questionnaires for the workers, which were similar to those distributed in the earlier study, we have interviewed the manager, the production manager on the organizational and social changes in the plant. We still need to interview some of the workers who have been working in the plant during both studies.

THE FINDINGS

The findings from the 14 kibbutzim survey will serve us in order to answer our first question. Why is high technology introduced to kibbutz plants? Table 1 will show the answers given by kibbutz plants.

* I want to thank Menachem Rosner and Israel Weis who have been my partners in this study

M. Palgi

Table 1: Considerations for Introducing High Tech in Kibbutz Plants according
to its importance (1 the most important, 3 the least)

THE CONSIDERATIONS	T H E R A T I N G S		
	1.first	2.second	3.third
increased production	7	2	0
improved quality	5	3	3
cheaper costs per product	0	3	4
better work conditions	2	4	3
change in shift work	0	1	2
better quality of work	0	1	2
total number of plants	14	14	14

Each plant could give three ratings. The first was the most important consideration. It can be seen from the table that the total number of times
that issues of work efficiency have been mentioned (27) is higher than the
total number of times that QWL issues have been mentioned (15). Also, only
two plants have mentioned work conditions as their first consideration, while
all the rest mentioned theirs as increased production and improved quality of
product.

All in all, we can see that the considerations for introducing high-tech to
kibbutz plants are similar to those out of the kibbutz, but the weight of
those not connected directly to production is relatively high (more than a
third).

The second question that the plants were asked to answer was: To what extent
do you find the introduction of high-tech has brought about the anticipated
changes?

Table 2: The Extent to Which the Introduction of High Tech in Plants has
Brought About the Anticipated Changes in Kibbutz

THE CHANGES	T H E I R F R E Q U E N C Y				
	not at all	a little	a certain extent	very much	total
increased production	0	1	3	10	14
improved quality	0	2	6	6	14
cheaper costs per product	2	0	6	6	14
better work conditions	3	0	9	2	14
changes in shift work	3	3	6	2	14
better quality of work	1	7	3	3	14

It can be seen from table 2 that the expectations concerning production have
almost always been realized while those concerning the work of people have in
some cases not been.

Let us combine the two lower categories (not at all and a little) and the two
upper categories and then look at all the efficiency consideration in comparison to all the QWL considerations. We find that in the efficiency categories
only 5 out of 42 cases the anticipated changes have not occured or occured to
a small extent while in 37 they did occur. In the QWL categories we find that
in 17 out of the 42 cases the anticipated changes have not occured or occured
to a small extent.

These findings might be the outcome of the relatively low place that QWL considerations take in the overall considerations. In the previous table (table 1) we saw that QWL considerations were usually not among the first for introducing high-tech. This can be as a result of the relatively high QWL that already existed in the kibbutzim or that efficiency considerations were also higher in the kibbutz. We have no other research results from other societies to compare it with but believe that they might show the same trend. We assume that they might even score lower on the weight they put on QWL issues.

After examining selected results from the small survey we have carried out, we shall now consider the case-study in Kibbutz Nof.

Nof Industries are among the oldest in the Kibbutz Haartzi federation. They began in 1944 as a small workshop with three to five workers producing parts for water taps. The workshop was originally situated in a neighboring community, but in 1949 it was moved into the kibbutz yard with its 15 workers, slowly developing both the variety and type of its products.

Today, it is a well-established metal factory with 120 workers from two different kibbutzim. During the last ten years, five manipulators with two degrees of freedom were introduced to aid production. In addition, during the last five years a robot with six degrees of freedom and a few C.N.C. lathes were acquired. The store-room was also completely computerized. The factory, during the last ten years has:
a. physically grown - the buildings are spread on a third more area than previously;
b. grown in the number of workers - from 80 workers in 1977 to 120 workers in 1987;
c. ownership is now split among two kibbutzim whose members are the workforce of the plant;
d. new, computerized machinery has been introduced to the factory.

The following chart outlines the organizational layout of the factory. It shows its structure in 1977 and in 1987.

NOF INDUSTRIES - ORGANIZATIONAL CHART
1977 - 1987

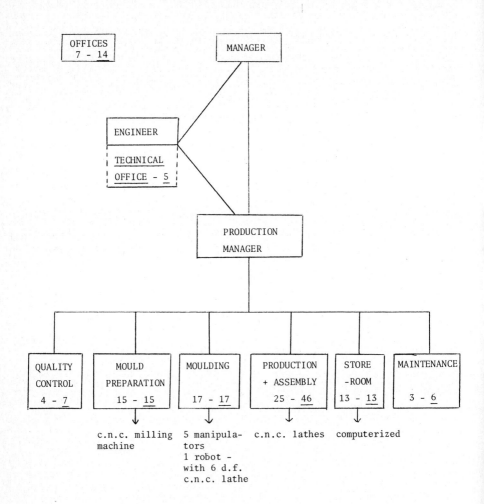

All underlined typing represents numbers and departments of the 1987 plant.
All the departments apart from the technical office have already existed in
1977.

From the chart it is possible to see the production process. The plans for the new products are prepared in the technical office. From there they are brought to the mould preparation department where the engineer and technicians program the milling machine for the preparation of the new mould. From there the mould passes on to the moulding department where almost all the work is computerized. In the past the workers had to install the material and moulds into the furnace but now all this is done by the manipulators and the robot. From there the products go to the production and assembly department where they get their finishing touches, and are assembled and packed. From there they are put into the storeroom. Also some of the products from the other departments are kept in the storeroom until they are needed. Quality control is done several times during the production processes. First when the products pass from the mould preparation department to the moulding department, then when they pass from the moulding to the production department and lastly when the finished product comes out.

The organizational changes during the last ten years are quite clear from the chart. The number of workers in the offices and production services have increased by 90% (17 in 1977 and 32 in 1987). In the actual preparation of the moulds and the moulding department there was no increase in workers. There the machines have replaced people. This is relevant to our discussion as the work in these departments was mostly physical and uncomfortable. There was always a problem to find workers to man them and the outcome was that all young men had to give half a year turn there.

Each of the departments that has computerized machines is able to do its own programming. If in 1977 there was one engineer, in 1987 there were eight engineers and highly qualified technicians.

In Nof Industries, the main considerations for introducing the new machinery were two:
1. The machines used in the factory became old and had to be replaced.
2. With the old machinery there was much physical work and ecological hazards.

The plant invited the kibbutz federation socio-technical team to assess the possibilities of change. The team, together with the workers, looked at the technological options that were feasible from both the economic and social points of view. After deciding which machines they wanted, they started to introduce them by stages. It can be seen that in this particular industry the economic and human considerations were interlinked. The plant found it hard both to produce with old machines and to recruit workers for them.

After describing the organizational changes in the plant we shall examine what happens to the workers in this plant. It is important to remember that in the kibbutz society there are no material rewards for work. The only rewards are either connected to the content of work or to the social environment (intrinsic and extrinsic). It can, therefore, be understood why these rewards are so valued. We shall examine here work monotony and autonomy in the plant, opportunities at work and democratic practices in the plant.

In order to examine the monotony of the work and the autonomy of the worker we have asked a few questions:
1. Do you do the same type of work all day long?
   (The scale goes from 1. always to 5. never).
2. Can you leave your machine unattended? 1. never, 5. always.
3. To what extent is the pace of your work determined by the machine? 1. to a small extent, 5. to a great extent.
4. To what extent is the quality of your work determined by the machine? Categories as in 3.
5. How is your work load? 1. very light, 5. very heavy.

Table 3: Monotony and autonomy at work - a comparison between 1977 and 1987

	1977				1987		
	MEAN	SD	N		MEAN	SD	N
1. Do the same work	3.26	1.08	50	*	2.74	1.32	35
2. Leave the machine unattended	3.56	1.05	51		3.14	0.93	35
3. Pace machine determined	2.33	1.26	51	*	3.48	1.14	35
4. Quality machine determined	2.51	1.00	51	*	3.53	1.06	35
5. Work load	2.54	0.71	51		2.90	0.68	35

* In a t-test the difference between the two sample means is significant
(0.05)

From the table it is very clear that the workers perceive their work now as
more monotonous more binding and more machine determined than they did in
1977. People are more dependent on the machine for their freedom to leave,
for the pace and quality of their work. Also they report a heavier work load
in 1987.

When we looked at the social relations among the workers and between the
workers and their supervisors we found no difference between the two times of
measurement. Also there were almost no conflicts reported between the different groups and individuals in the plant.

Another issue we have tried to measure was the opportunities given to the
workers in their work. Again we found no difference between the measures of
1977 and 1987 in the opportunities for doing interesting work, for using ones
skills and for learning new things. At least from this respect it does not
seem that the technological changes have deskilled the workers in this plant.

One of the most important aspects of kibbutz life is self-management. It has
tried to maintain it both in the social and the production spheres. One of
the dangers of the introduction of new technologies is that many issues would
be decided by the "experts" and not be brought to public discussions. We have
tried to examine this point by asking several questions about the authority of
the workers assembly on different issues. The workers assembly is the central
decision-making body in the plant, and we wanted to see if its power has diminished, stayed the same or increased during these ten years.

The question was: In what way does the workers assembly deal with the following
issues? On each issue there was the possibility to answer one of the following:
1. Does not deal at all.
2. Hears information.
3. Approves decisions.
4. Discusses and recommends.
5. Discusses and decides.

Table 4: Authority of Workers Assembly - A Comparison Between 1977 and 1987

	1976				1986		
	MEAN	SD	N		MEAN	SD	N
Yearly production plan	2.66	1.02	42	*	2.19	0.63	35
Investment plan	3.35	1.09	43	*	2.87	0.99	35
Training plan	3.02	1.13	43	*	2.06	0.96	35
Election of management	4.29	0.93	42	*	3.27	1.37	35
Election of committees	4.10	1.08	43	*	3.21	1.14	35
Internal work organization	2.50	1.41	41	*	1.97	1.34	35

* In a t-test the difference between the two sample means is significant
(0.05)

It can be seen from table 4 that the authority of the assembly on all issues has been reduced. Even on issues such as the election of the committees active on the plant and on the election of the manager its authority is diminished. It does not seem possible that this is only a result of the introduction of advanced technology. It seems more feasible that the size of t^e factory (which has increased by 50%) and the partnership with another kibbutz are at least partially to account for it.

CONCLUSIONS

After looking at the optimistic and pessimistic expectations from the introduction of high-tech to the factory, we have tried to look into the process and its effects in the kibbutz industries. First we looked at the general considerations for this technical change and in view of them their outcomes. Then, we examined some of the findings of a case study of an industrial plant in the kibbutz. In this plant, which had been studied in 1977 and in 1987, we saw that the introduction of high-tech has not brought with it unemployment, on the contrary, employment increased and so did production. The opportunities for workers to do interesting work, use their skill and learn new things have not diminished during the years, but also have not increased. On the other hand we found that workers did more repetitive work and their quality and quantity of work was mainly determined by the machine. The seemingly contradictory findings of more repetitive work but not less interesting can be explained if one does not forget that we are dealing with averages. Some of the work is very repetitive and some is but a little. This we can see from the relatively high S.D. of this variable.

The workers have a heavier work load now and are more constrained by the machine. The participation of the workers in decision-making is lower than it used to be in 1977.

All in all, it can be seen that there are many issues that Nof Industries have to take into consideration. It seems that it has not by-passed many of the ill effects that could occur with the introduction of new technologies. We are well aware that other factors (like size and joint ownership) have also contributed to the present situation.

REFERENCES

(1) Bell, D. The Coming of Post-Industrial Society Basic Books, NY, 1973).
(2) Cohen, S.S. and Zysman, J., Manufacturing Matters - The Myth of Post-Industrial Economy (Basic Books, NY, 1987).
(3) Levin, H.M. and Runberger, R.W., The Educational Implications of High Technology (School of Education, Stanford University, 1983).
(4) Mark, J.A. Technological Change and Employment: Some Results from BLS Research. Monthly Labor Review April 1987.
(5) Piel, G., Re-entering Paradise - The Mechanization of Work, Challenge, Sept-Oct., 1983.
(6) Piore, M.J. and Sabel, C.F., The Second Industrial Divide (Basic Books, NY, 1984).
(7) Shaiken, H., Works Transformed (Holt, Reinhart and Winston, NY, 1984).
(8) Yuchtman-Yaar, E. and Gottlieb, A., Technological Development and the Meaning of Work: A Cross Cultural Perspective, Human Relations, Vol. 38, No. 7, pp. 603-621, 1985.
(9) Zuboff, S., Automate/Informate: The Two Faces of Intelligent Technology, Organizational Dynamics, Autumn 1985.

The Social Implications of Robotics and Advanced
Industrial Automation / D. Millin and B.H. Raab (Editors)
Elsevier Science Publishers B.V. (North-Holland)
© IFIP, 1989

KIBBUTZ-INDUSTRY - FUTURE FOR A SOCIALISTIC EXPERIMENT?

Michael Landwehr

Diplom-Volkswirt
University of Cologne
Cologne, West-Germany

1. The aim of the kibbutz

As mentioned above, the kibbutz is considered as a socialistic experiment, sometimes more so by "outsiders" than by kibbutzniks
themselves. But even if the pragmatic, even accidental character
of this communal settlement cannot completely be denied, the ideo-
logical aspect , the intention to practice a new communal, collective way of life became stronger. The kibbutzniks did not feel
like individualistic settlers, but like part of both the Zionist
movement and the labour movement. They wanted to combine national
liberation and self-administration in their social and economic
sphere.

Significant for the kibbutz are its aims

- self-labour
- job-rotation
- democracy
- national renaissance.

Refering to the topic of my thesis, I will concentrate on the
kibbutz' attitude towards labour and on the influence of
industrialization on that "socialistic experiment".

2. The industrialization of the kibbutz

The history of the kibbutz starts with purely agricultural settlements at the beginning of our century. In the following years
there was no industrial production but only craftswork for
producing and repairing agricultural machines for their own use.
During World War II, when the country was cut off its commercial
connections to the Western World, the need for industrial
production became obvious. The rural settlements and most of all
the kibbutzim played a good part in the protection of the country.
Therefore the kibbutzim were integrated into the economic support
of the allied forces. Because of the war necessities industrial
investments were made, which built the foundation of the further
growth of industrial work.

o The intention to industrialize the kibbutz, however, resulted
  not only in military demand or the need of repair-shops. The
  motives to introduce industry were more widely spread. Besides
  the above mentioned, some other aims of the industrialization
  of the kibbutzim were to achieve:

- full employment of the labour resources,

- supporting the economic existence of settlements located in areas, where agriculture was hard to practice,

- offering jobs for younger and higher qualified members and for old members, who could not stand the physically hard work in agriculture, but wanted to keep on working and needed some easier occupation.

Nowadays the industrial sector produces about 50 % of the kibbutz production. The main branches are:

- metall-working,
- electrics,
- plastics,
- food,
- textiles.

They all are branches, which are affected by the new industrial revolution.

3. The consequences of industrialization

From the economic point of view, industry today has become domi-nating, and that even more under the aspect of industrialized run-ning of agriculture.

That means on the one hand, that the kibbutz is offered the chance of a wider-spread economic acitvity, that it can avoid possible trouble because of agricultural monostructure, if being involved in the consequences of overproduction in the Western World, expecially in the Common Market. In the long run, industry can therefore be a stabilizing factor for both prosperity and employment.

On the other hand, there are dangers resulting from the growing economical interdependence because of an export-oriented industry. When the kibbutz can soften the consequences of agricultural crises, in the same time it has to suffer from the industrial crises, actually from the trouble on the exchange markets.

Moreover, mechanization of agriculture and industry is very capital-intensive. So the kibbutzim have to face difficulties in maintainig their until today functioning system of self-financing, so that they could get dependent on the banking sector.

But these dangers are to be faced by all kinds of enterprises. Which are the special ones for the "socialistic experiment" kibbutz?

3.1 Automation and self-labour

The industrial revolution of the kibbutz economy went along with a rising number of hired labour from outside the community, a grave offence against the kibbutz-principles. In the last years however, there have been made great efforts to reduce hired labour; a means to this end is rationalization, automation of work. So the development of the technology in the working sphere is —

superficially regarded - a factor in favour of the conservation of the kibbutz identity. But that is really only a superficial view.

What must be regarded is that reducing hired labour means reducing jobs, jobs for often unskilled workers of the surroundings of the settlements. If they cannot get new jobs, the support of the kibbutz' puritanism is payed by unemployment in the "outside" economy. According to its own principles, the kibbutz feels not to be an isolated "socialistic paradise", but to be a part of the whole, and that means a part of the nations economy _and_ social system.

3.2. The kibbutz' philosophy of work

Another aspect of enforced rationalization with its highest expression in using robotics is its revolution of work itself. The kibbutzniks wanted to restore work as an expression of human individuality, they wanted work not be only a means of earning ones life but of supporting creativity and self-determination.

Working in a system highly dependent on computerized processing, the possibilities for the single worker, except those higher qualified, are restricted more and more. This danger has its expression in the threatenings of such vital kibbutz principles as job-rotation and inner democracy or self-administration.

3.3. Democracy and participation

As it is often declared in discussions about working democracy by the protectors of the "conventional wisdom", as Galbraith called them, democratic structures and job rotation are not to combine with working efficiency.

On the other side exponents of the cooperative theory warn of the danger of _transformation_, so as Oppenheim in his work about productive cooperatives. They do not deny the possibility of success in running productive copperatives, but they proclaim the unavoidable transformation into a capitalistic enterprise with the former members as "stock-owners" and hired workers without any rights in participation.

As it seems to be demonstrated in the eigthy years of kibbutz-history, the process of transformation could be avoided. The kibbutz did not get a "closed shop", which wanted to shut the group against new members, and it seemed to be partly successful in restricting hired labour, and that not for the price of economic handicaps.

Automation in industry, however, forces a new analysis of consequences for the kibbutz values. First of all, the introduction of automation requires qualified members, who have been trained to the demands of the new techniques like data processing, organization and controlling of the working process. That offers a chance to those young members, who could not find adequate jobs in the kibbutz after their education in schools and universities. That means a higher degree of satisfaction with work and therefore the chance to keep them as members.

On the other hand, new and more complicated techniques can obstruct the possibilities for the other group of members, who is not well acquainted with this completely new kind of work. Job

rotation, especially rotation in leading positions, is restricted
to those who are able to operate the new technologies, and that is
a first step to creating a new class and to form hierachical
structures. Moreover, there appears the danger of being subdued to
"the forces of facts", which is exerciced by the demand of
industry to employ its capacities.

As it is often declared by managers of modern enterprises, the
authority is partly transferred from the subjective decisions of
the human staff to objective criterions, which are beyond
individual control.

4. Conclusion for the future of the kibbutz

The kibbutz, which now exists for about eighty years, has until
today overcome different troubles and could stabilize its popular
and economic foundation. By introducing industrial production (and
that includes industrialized agriculture) the kibbutzim could
prove their vitality and the will to get fit for the tasks of the
future. The risks, which they will run, are obvious. They have to
slip through between Scylla and Charybdis, between losing contact
to the modern world and losing their identity as socialistic
communities by complete adaptation to the society of mass-
production and mass-consumption.

As far as to show perspectives to the communities, the first
positive step is made by discussing the problems instead of
helpless subjugation to the so-called "forces of facts".

Another positive aspect seems to be the early dispute about introducing industry. This project was not at all welcomed by the
kibbutz-movement but was intensively discussed in all its pros and
contras. Furthermore industry was not started, as an industrial
project in the world of free enterprise, with the aim of profit
maximizing, but with the aims mentioned above. Rentability was one
aspect among others, it was not neglected, so as in many short-
lived productive communities, but it was also not made the
absolute maxim.

Moreover the kibbutz could demonstrate the possibilities to
accomodate the new industrial revolution to a humanized world of
working. Opposite to many of the alternative projects in the
Western World, who want to get out of the surrounding economy, the
kibbutzim are a part of it. They do not feel like missionaries and
therefore may even work better like them giving the good example,
if not for the industrialized countries, then for the developing
ones and – last, but not least – for the socialistic countries
during their process of reforming.

Therefore the kibbutz should be prepared for its future.

References

1) Engelhardt, W.W., Die Produktivgenossenschaft - Genossenschaft jenseits von Individualismus und Kollektivismus für die Landwirtschaft von Entwicklungs- und Industrieländern, in: Archiv für öffentliche und gemeinnützige Unternehmen (1972)

2) Heinsohn, G., Das Kibbutz-Modell (Frankfurt/M., 1982)

3) Kibbutz Industries Association, Kibbutz Industries (Tel Aviv, 1982)

4) Landwehr, M., Industrie im Kibbutz, Zukunft oder Ende eines sozialistischen Modells (Köln, 1984, to be revised and published in 1988)

5) Melman, S., Managerial versus Cooperative Decision Making in Israel, in: Studies in Comparative International Development AR 1970/71 (New Brunswick, 1971)

6) Palgi, M., Rosner, M., Industrial Democracy in Israel, Center for the Study of Industrial Democracy and Self-Management (Haifa, 1983)

7) Rosner, M., Leviatan, U., Work and Organization in Kibbutz-Industry (Darby, 1980)

Part 4

ADVANCED TECHNOLOGY
AND ITS IMPACT ON LABOR RELATIONS

The Social Implications of Robotics and Advanced
Industrial Automation / D. Millin and B.H. Raab (Editors)
Elsevier Science Publishers B.V. (North-Holland)
© IFIP, 1989

INDUSTRIAL ROBOTS - SOCIAL CONSEQUENCES AND UNION POLICY

Paul KOLM
Gewerkschaft der Privatangestellten, Austria

1. NEW TECHNOLOGIES AND UNIONS

Industrial robots are only one however in some fields in
fact a very dynamic part of the automation of the industrial
production process. So in the highly developed capitalistic
countries there have been statements of some unions treating
the problem of industrial robots directly - and only to them
this report is referring to - the background however in any
case is how technical development generally is estimated
by the unions and which ideas have been developed by them
in this respect.

Even if the unions have different political traditions,
organisation structures, activity patterns and strategies in
the different countries there is nevertheless a common
denominator in the unions' estimation of new technologies,
their social consequences as well as the requirements and
conceptions how to implement new technologies.

The report of the European Trade Union Institute published in
1979 "The Effects of Microelectronics on Employment in
Western Europe during the 8oies" contains a rather good
résumé of this smallest common denominator. The unions in
Europe recognize the improvement of the living standard in
the long run being dependant on the use of technological
development for the production. The apprehension of the
unions is referring to the speed of introducing new
technologies as well as to the question who will be profiting
by their advantages. (1)

2. INDUSTRIAL ROBOTS AND WORK ORGANISATION

Technique which is used in the rationalization procedure is
determined by the production's conditions in its process of
development already. Technique is not a neutral instrument
the use of which can be created in any desired manner, but
it is a system containing and transporting structural
conditions.

This is valid for the conception as well as for the large
field of application where there are higher options the more

flexible the systems are. Robots are most effective as
parts of very flexible production systems.

Considering this question one must not neglect the historical
process, a process which has been condemning a growing part
of the working people to fragmentary, repetitive, monotonous
work, often under bad working conditions. The "almost
logical" answer is the elimination of work by for instance
the robot.

Until a robot is able to fulfill a working procedure
completely many development steps are necessary. If you
ask a welder which kind of his work satisfies him most,
he presumably would answer "welding". However, it is just
this qualified task, which is taken over by the robot and
to the worker the charging of the machine is left until this
task will be automatisied too. "In order to apply the cure,
to abolish the trivialised job, one first has to create the
disease, the supply of trivialised job which can be done by
robots" (2) says Rosenbrock.

Although the unions are aware of the importance of the work
organisation a study of the European Economic Commission is
resuming in the introduction already that the representatives
of workers only have very little influence on this phenomenon.
But the social consequences of robot implementation depend
essentially on the technical and organisational context to
which robots are used and which are the effects of the
economic and social frame conditions (3).

3. INDUSTRIAL ROBOTS AND EMPLOYMENT

Robots are a technology of rationalization. The increase of
productivity is always in relation to the reduction of the
workers needed. There are considerable differences concerning
the indicated number of workers who can be replaced by a
robot. In the study of the European Economic Commission about
industrial robots for the Federal Republic of Germany 4 workers
at maximum per robot, for Great Britain 6 workers at maximum
are indicated, in Scandinavia 2 robots replace one worker.
From an inquiry of the International Metal Workers Union
resulted that in France there were replaced three workers
per robot, in Finland 5 workers at maximum (4). These differences
in part are due to the fact that robots executing different
working operations (for instance handling, welding) or
different technical conceptions of course differ also in
respect of the possible replacement of workers. In part, the
calculations included also new working places originating
from the production of robots. Last, but not least it is also
a question of unions policy to which extent enterprises can
realise their advantage.

4. INDUSTRIAL ROBOTS AND QUALIFICATION

The context between organisation and qualification is evident.
In general, there is a new distribution of necessary abilities
and professional experiences between the former and the new

work functions, and there is a tendency towards more abstract, standardized and formalized functions.

In a Danish case study four examples of the organisation of work by means of robots are described (3).

<u>Division of Labour by Robots</u>

Enter-prise	Programming, test pro-gramming	Work planning, tool prepa-ration	production, supervision of robots, charging and discharging	quality control	maintenance, repair, defect finding
A	XXXXXXXXXXXXXXXXXXXXXXXX		XXXXXXXXXXXXXXXXXXXX		XXXXXXXXXXXXX
B	XXXXXXXXXXXXXXXXXXXXXXXX		XXXXXXXXXXX	XXXXX	XXXXXXXXXXXXX
C	XXXXXXXXXX	XXXXXXXXX	XXXXXXXXXXXXXXXXXXXX		XXXXXXXXXXXXX
D	XXXXXXXXXX	XXXXXXXXX	XXXXXXXXXXX	XXXXX	XXXXXXXXXXXXX

Quelle: Clematide B. and alii, 1982, p.31.

The description shows that there is a fundamental division of work functions programming/production planning - production/ supervision/charging - maintenance/repair/defect finding. By that the supervision of the operations of production to a larger extent is transferred from the workshop (worker, foreman) to higher levels in the hierarchy of the enterprise.

Of course, many qualification possibilities depend on the configuration of the system. This configuration in many cases does not exclude the programming function of the worker, for instance in the "teach in" procedure of welding or paint-spraying robots. However, the most analysis' and own   inquiries show that the time shares for these qualified work   decreased rapidly after the introduction period and the charging and discharging remained the determining part of activity.

The polarisation of qualifications therefore is not only a problem of distributing qualification among different activities and persons, but also just in view of the robots a problem of requirements' distribution within the activity of one person. So the creation of completely unqualified rest activities caused by organizational decisions which has been observed in context with robots again and again in many cases is more inhuman than the previous heavy work without robots was (5).

5. INDUSTRIAL ROBOTS AND WORKING CONDITIONS

Enquiring the motives for the use of industrial robots in almost any case the humanization of work is pointed out besides the economic reasons, especially the removal of heavy

work and of noxious environment influence. In the enquiry
already mentioned which has been published by the International
Metal Workers Union the unions appreciate the improvement of
working conditions as well as the positive effects on health
and protection against accidents caused by the use of robots (4).

However, considering the results of research and the positions
of unions treating the problem of working conditions more
profoundly, a more differentiate impression is obtained.

Studies in Germany and Sweden analysing use of robots documente
new working conditions by the use of robots which are in
contradiction to the demand of humanization expressed before.
The robot removing previous defiles in the production flow,
and increasing the output accordingly, requires an increase
of performance from the remaining workers. Those who have to
take over the rest activities at the work stations before or
after the robot operation are concerned by an intensification
of performance as well. The deskilling problems specially
where the work at single working places was roboterized was
mentioned in section 3 already. In this and many other cases
the possibilities of the worker to plan and to arrange the
work procedures himself - referring to space as well as to
time - were reduced. At the same time the social isolation
of the workers increased (6).

In general it has to be pointed out that the trend of the
change in working conditions cannot be defined clearly, apart
form the fact that certain working places will completely be
abolished by roboterization. Complementary it has to be
mentioned that there are no legal prescriptions referring
to the operation of robots, concerning the health and work
safety, although robots frequently are used at potentially
dangerous working places, and under certain circumstances
robots may become a danger themselves.

So it is not by chance only, if the Activity Programme of
the International Metal Workers Union is demanding severe
rules for the protection of maintenance and repair workers
and effective protection appliances for new machines and
whole working areas for the workers in the machine tool
industry, an industry which at the same time is initiating,
producing and as one of the first using new technologies (4).

The working conditions essentially are also influenced by
specific working time regulations. The use of robots here is
leading to two opposite tendencies, dependant on the type of
the production system and the organisation of the production
process.

On the one hand, the extension of shift work is remarked, by
which a better exploitation of the expensive equipment is
obtained. The social consequences and strain to health caused
by shift work are well known, the unions are not only demanding
the reduction of shift work, but also measures to compensate
the strain.

On the other hand, by the use of the robot being able to work
during 24 hours per day (provided the supply of the necessary
material is assured) there is a reduction of night shift work

just in those fields where night shift work was usual hitherto.
However, this effect belongs to the problem of employment
already, for the central problem is the reduction of workers,
apart from the intensification of performance for those
workers who are busy with the preparation of the night shift.

6. CASE STUDIES IN AUSTRIA (7)

The case studies, performed in five companies, involved in
two cases robots for spot-welding, in three cases handling
robots. In all five companies workstations for single workers
were the object of the studies. Considering the Austrian
structure of the economy this is not quite arbitrary. The
big conveyor belts characteristic for the automobil-industry,
may not be found in our country.

In all cases economic considerations were the central criteria
for the purchase. Besides the immediate reduction of cost,
improvements of the quality have been considered.
Improvements in the working environment for service-personal
were described as an additional motivation by the planing
authorities.

As far as the actual impacts are concerned, the different forms
of the implementation (welding-robots, handling-robots) have
to be considered seperately.

The introduction of a welding-robot needs a longer phase of
transition until the rationalization effect is achieved. The
problems are not centered only around the optimal control of
the robot itself, but as well around the necessary adaptations
of the organisation, the control of the work procedures and
the adaption of technological constructive aspects of the
product. All the interviews took place just in this learning
phase of the manufacturing plants, the effects can therefore
not be judged in a final way. The direction of the development
was however clearly visible. Handlingrobots which are immediately
coupled with a conventional machine do not involve such an
extensive transition phase.

Welding-robots replace in the average three to five conventional
work stations. First because in the case of two - armed robots
studied, the robot can work for two by definition, second
because the robot resulted in a reduction of the welding times
between 4o and 6o%.

The programming of the robot needs a qualified welder, because
he doesn't only define the different steps, but as well the
parameters of the welding process. The more programmes will
have been stored, and the more special instruments for the
handling of the product are already present, the lower will
be the fraction of the total work time needing this combination
of welding qualification with the ability to handle the robot.
The actual feeding and serving of the robot needs concentration
in watching out for failures and for right timing, but not
a very high training of the worker. The developments of the
workingconditions are not always directed the same way. Some
dangers for instance by heat or by chemical substances, will
become lower. As well physical efforts by handling heavy parts

or welding in uncomfortable positions of the body are reduced.
On the other hand the permanent feeding procedures form a new
kind of strain for the welder. The worker has in the overall
effect less influence on his work. The increased speed of work
and the strong dependence on the robot are seen as a disadvantage
compared to the conventional work stations of welder, as well
the increased psychic strain during the control process and
during the necessary search for the reasons for failures.

The reduction of labour during the feeding of raw materials
and for the removal of the final products result out of the
possible serving of more than one machine by one operator and,
given that certain conditions are fulfiled, as well by the
introduction of so called "ghost-shifts" (no human control
of the work-process during that shift). Where the robot is
combined with a production machine this will result in a
reduction of physical stress. The qualification is primarily
determined by the needs of the machine. The kowledge
concerning the control of the robots is added. In two of the
case studies the robots, installed to produce plastic-goods,
have been programmed by the company producing the robot, the
control and the servicing of the machine is done by the people
setting up the machine. The actual female operator of the
machine performs a simplified, but seen from the cycle, further
reduced residual activity without qualifications specific
to the robot.

Let us add up: rationalization by the introduction of robots
reduces the number of jobs. There is no clear strategy of
the companies in relation to qualification and working conditions.
Improvements sometimes appear as welcome by byproducts,
deteriorations, partly as an effect of the tayloristic approach,
show very often shifts of the strain characteristic for
automation in general, and are equally often considered as
"natural". The representatives of the workers trie to reduce
the number of jobs lost and trie to stabilize the income. The
development of the work situation in general and the necessity
to control these changes lie outside the view of the people
immediately concerned. This is not very astonishing, con-
sindering the impact of the crises and the, in many domains
missing alternatives.

7.   CONSEQUENCES FOR UNION POLICY

Union policy should unfold itself on three levels:

7.1 Expansion of co-determination

The abilities of the companies to determine one sidedly the
conditions of the implementation of robot technology should be
restricted.

It is not enough to ensure the implementation of regulations
concerning results, for instance avoidance or compensation of
known results, but as well to make visible the full range
of possible implementations of the new technology, that is to
influence the procedures which are able to influence the
organisation of work (8).

The unions may point out the fact, that the implementation of
traditional concepts of work simplification and the drastic
reduction of responsibility and initiative in the computer
controlled production plant will result in a reduction of
output.

Even under these assumptions codetermination could contribute
to guarantee and to develop qualification, improve the workingconditions and to stabilize incomes. But the problem of
unemployment will only be mitigated, not solved fundamentally.

7.2 Reduction of working time with wage compensation

The use of modern machinery, especially of robots, reduces the
necessary time for the production of a given amount of goods.
In the time of the crises, during stagnating growth, the
reduction of labour time is a main alternative to the unemployment,
created by the increase of productivity. The reduction of
labour time to 35 hours/week is today an aim of the trade
unions in many countries.

7.3 Economic policy

Investment subsidies only when combined with specific demands
concerning the social consequences of the investment, which
can controlled immediately by the workers involved. Limitation
of the possibilities of tax reductions of investments, and
simultneously:

- use of the gains achieved by rationalization for the
  creation of new jobs in new domains, especially in the
  social infrastructure.

REFERENCES

1) Europäisches Gewerkschaftsinstitut (Eds.): Die Auswirkungen der Mikroelektronik auf die Beschäftigung in
   Westeuropa während der Achtziger Jahre, Brüssel 1979

2) H. Rosenbrock: Robots and People, Vortragsmanuskript 1981

3) Kommission der Europäischen Gemeinschaft (Eds.): Sozialer
   Wandel und Technologie in Europa, Informationsbulletin 1o:
   Die Robotertechnik, Brüssel 1982

4) International Metalworker's Federation (Eds.):
   Metalworkers and new Technology, Results of IMF Questionnaire
   of Industrial Robots, Genf 1981

5) K.H. Jansen: Gewerkschaften und neue Produktionstechnologie,
   in: Industriegewerkschaft Metall (Eds.): Industrieroboter
   und Humanisierung, Frankfurt 1981

6) O. Mickler: Neue Handhabungssysteme als technische Hilfen
   für den Arbeitsprozeß, in: Industriegewerkschaft Metall
   (Eds.): Industrieroboter und Humanisierung, Frankfurt 1981

   Soziologisches Forschungsinstitut Göttingen: Handhabungs-
   mechanisierung und Belegschaftsinteressen, 198o (Eds.):
   Sozialer Wandel und Technologie in Europa, Informationsbulletin 1o: Die Robotertechnik, Brüssel 1982

7) R. Dell'mour, P.Fleissner, W.Hofkirchner, P.Kolm, P.P.Sint:
   Industrieroboter in Österreich, Wien 1984

8) H. Kubicek und   P. Berger: Regelungen und Rahmenbe-
   dingungen im Bereich Arbeitgeber-Arbeitnehmer-Beziehungen
   in: P. Mambrey, R. Oppermann (Eds.): Beteiligung von
   Betroffenen bei der Entwicklung von Informationssystemen,
   Frankfurt/New York 1983

The Social Implications of Robotics and Advanced
Industrial Automation / D. Millin and B.H. Raab (Editors)
Elsevier Science Publishers B.V. (North-Holland)
© IFIP, 1989

TECHNOLOGICAL CHANGES: THEIR IMPACT ON LABOUR RELATIONS
AND ON HUMAN RESOURCES MANAGEMENT

Dr. Ozer Carmi, Institute of Labour Relations, Israel

Joseph Gattegno, Manufacturers' Association of Israel

Developed, industrial societies in the West, including Israel, have been
characterized since World War II by a continuous rapid rate of change, affecting all aspects of existence.   There are those who maintain that the rate
changes have taken place in a single decade since 1945 far exceeds the changes
recorded over thousands of years of human history.

The most dramatic changes have occurred in the realm of technology, resulting
from the need to improve productivity and efficiency, which in turn boosts
the competitive capability of organizations in terms of price, quality and
service.

What is a technological change ?

Technological change means the substitution of capital for labour.   The
subject can be best explained by the key term *production function,* meaning a
certain level of production arising from different combinations of labour
and capital input.   The implications of technological change correspond with
the degree of change along the production function, i.e. more capital and less
labour are employed for producing the same quantity of goods.

*Technological changes beget opposing emotions -- management expects increased
efficiency, whereas the workers feel that their job security is threatened.*

The Typology of Changes

Three types of technological change may be distinguished :

- Type I -- There is no significant change in the relative share of capital
              and labour in the production function. This type of change does
              not affect the quantity of labour required, it only affects
              the characteristics of labour.

- Type II -- There is a certain degree of change in the capital-labour
               combination and as a consequence some workers become redundant.

- Type III -- Here, the change in the capital-labour combination is
               significant: capital replaces a substantial quantity of labour
               and many workers become redundant.

Naturally, the type of change has an influence on the severity of the problem
it creates, and on the instruments that can be utilized for solving the problem.

The problem becomes more severe as one moves from Type I to Type II change.
The problems arising from Type I change can be solved by fostering internal
worker mobility and by suitable training programs. In Type II the remedy can
be early retirement, shorter work hours and sharing of tasks. In Type III
change, drastic measures are often required to prevent severely harming the
work force, possibly including government intervention, training programs and
large scale re-training of employees.

A. Technological Changes and Attitudes Regarding Labour Relations

Trade Unions

Trade unions seek maximum involvement in the process of introducing the change, in order to minimize as much as possible the adverse effect on the labour force.

The attitude of the trade union toward technological changes is influenced by a number of factors, the three principle ones being the following :

The characteristics of the trade union, its structure and the nature of the change. If it is a craft union (as opposed to industrial union), a stronger opposition may be anticipated. As regards structure, studies have shown that the more complex and larger the union, the greater its political resoluteness; the fewer the unions participating in the negotiations and the less dispersed the power within the union -- the more it is inclined to accept the changes. As to the nature of the change, the trade union's attitude is influenced by the number of positions affected and by the skills and responsibilities demanded of the workers.

One may sum up the response of trade unions in the West to changes as being pragmatic. Generally, there is a positive attitude towards changes. However, if the change is substantial and affects employment, the responses may range from acceptance to adaptation and sometime to opposition.

The Employers

Changes are mostly initiated by the managements as part of the managerial privileges, which include among others the right to decide on the extent of mechanization and on work methods.

Employers' organizations profess that technological changes are essential for assuring the ability to compete. Thus, for example, the CBI, the British employers' organization, adopted a series of resolutions on the subject of changes, including the statement: "Employment will not be assured by the artificial protection of jobs, but rather by economic development through the adoption of technological changes as required".

Contrary to the trade unions that demand negotiations covering all the topics involved in the introduction of changes, employers are generally in favour of the joint consultation process. In Europe, Israel and recently in the USA the doctrine is being advocated, both among employers and workers' organizations, favouring the adoption of the Scandinavian method of productivity agreements, which combine elements of high productivity (including the introduction of technological changes), quality of work life, job security and improved labour relations.

The Government

Generally, governments view favourably the introduction of technological changes being of the opinion that the rejection of changes will harm the economy and employment more than their adoption. Government intervention mostly involves various measures aimed at mitigating the negative effects of the change (statutory arrangements regulating negotiations about the changes, backing the change by financial aid or tax relief, finding ways for mitigating the damage, initiating and supporting studies for assessing the effects of the changes, aiding retraining programs, etc.).

B. Implications Regarding the Disposition of the Work Force

Negative results are not an inherent feature of new technologies. They can be reduced and it may even be possible to derive substantial benefits from changes. The problem is that in the western world the concept of technological determinism prevails -- a reluctance to face the issue squarely.

How does this deterministic approach affect the work force ?

Four main risks may be mentioned :

1. Diminished labour requirement and the need for dismissals.

2. Negative influence on the content of the task -- mainly dehumanization and impairment of the standard of skills (in practice, polarization occurs: on one side are workers highly skilled in planning and systems programming, and on the other side the majority of unskilled workers fulfilling routine tasks).

3. Stricter supervision over the work, resulting in the impairment of the bargaining capacity of the trade union.

4. Health and hygiene hazards. Whilst there is a greater awareness of physical hazards, there is an increasing risk of psychological harm, related to dehumanization, de-skilling, stricter supervision of worker by management, greater work load and less balanced judgment. All these factors increase the risk of stress and sickness.

C. The Correct Way of Introducing Technological Changes

Japan is one of the few countries that has adopted a positive attitude towards technological changes and she is considered to be one of the most innovative countries in this respect.

Nine out of ten Japanese workers believe that the success of the company contributes to their personal welfare (the ratio is reverse in the USA),hence the commitment of the management, the workers and the trade union to adopt the changes as a condition of the company's success.

Admittedly, a large part of Japan's success can be attributed to cultural and social characteristics, nevertheless, there are certain aspects that can be emulated and applied in western countries, including Israel.

The key word is "involvement" and it was interpreted as follows by a wellknown organizational consultant in Japan: "From our viewpoint the cornerstone of management is the art of attracting and recruiting the intellectual resources of all persons employed in the company... Only through the integration of the mental powers of the entire work force can the company face up to the constraints and confusion posed by present day environment. "

The Japanese model does not mean to diminish the management's prerogatives; it seeks to reinforce the involvement and responsibilities of the entire labour force.

How is this done? As opposed to the model of bargaining as practised in the western world, the Japanese posit the integrative mode of cooperation.

How do these two models compare ?

- Bargaining is a responsive, post-factum model, whereas in integrative forums (Quality Circles),influence can be exerted already in the planning phase of the change.

- Negotiation is a situation of trade-offs, whilst a cooperating group that operates mainly on the shop floor level can come up with solutions that benefit both sides, according to their needs.

- Cooperating forums involve work committees and trade unions in the process of adoption of the change.

In Conclusion: The assumption is that joint forums stand a better chance of exploiting the potential of technology, provided that they are backed by suitable skills, information, methodology and the philosophy of commitment and mutual trust.

THE ISRAELI CASE

A. *Survey of Means at the Disposal of the Parties to Industrial Relations*

The collective agreement in Israel plays an important role in defining the rights and prerogatives of the parties to industrial relations. Stipulations relating to the rights and limitations to perform such acts as dismissal or transfer of workers are included in national (general) as well as in plant (special_) collective agreements.

1. The problem of redundancy dismissals, including dismissals resulting from technological changes, had already been solved in the General (basic) Collective Agreement for the Settling of Industrial Relations, 1967. It is stipulated there that technological changes or changes in the lay-out con-stitute a just cause for redundancy dismissals. It is the management's prerogative to define the need and the extent of the reduction of staff. A list of workers to be dismissed is then handed over to the workers' representatives (local union and the plant committee), and there is a detailed procedure and criteria for the negotiations and arbitration as to the dismissed workers to be substituted for the ones proposed by management.

2. Another agreement relating to technological changes and productivity has been signed in 1979 (Collective Agreement - Agreed Rules concerning joint productivity councils in industry). The agreement defined agreed ways for time and motion measurement, the setting of incentives and way of rechecking and adjusting time measurements. There is a provision for an impartial arbitration in these matters in cases where negotiations fail.

3. There is an agreement stipulating procedures for the encouragement and the evaluation of suggestions for improvements in work organisation, in means of production, in saving of material or manpower, improvements of quality, etc., and setting the scale of prices to be given for acceptable suggestions.

4. A general collective agreement has been signed in 1976 to increase the inplant mobility of workers with a view to increasing the range of skills and flexibility of the manpower. It has been agreed that the acquisition of skills by way of completing vocational training shall entitle the worker to wage increase.

5. In 1979 two agreements were concluded. One -- for workers and members of works committees on the importance of increased productivity and on conduct-ing negotiations on labour relations -- and another on improved quality of life at work, safety and hygiene.

6. Most national collective agreements include the stipulation granting a priority to be re-engaged within a certain period of time to a worker dismissed for redundancy reasons.

7. The collective agreement on comprehensive old age pension in industry of 1979 includes criteria enabling a worker with considerable seniority to retire before the set retirement age (65 men, 60 women) with a right, however, to proportionately reduced pension.

8. The biennial negotiations -- these forthcoming negotiations on behalf of the whole business sector will include, i.a. the problem of improving productivity and the possible influence of this on the increase of wages, technological changes, changes in hours of work, etc.

B. *Government Intervention*

The Government is partly involved in the subject; it tries to stimulate technological progress and modernisation in industry by diverse tax reductions and relies on investments in means of production, especially in development areas, by allowing accelerated depreciation of machinery and by granting loans under favourable conditions. In cases of original and innovative research activities, particular monetary aid is granted by the Chief Scientist.

The vocational training division of the Labour Ministry has been active in the field of professional retraining and upgrading courses. The role of the employers' organisation in this field is in many instances quite remarkable and the cooperation with the vocational training division is positive.

There is cognisance of the fact that in-plant vocational training for the particular skills required is much preferable to outside training which is backward, both on the training and technological levels.

New standards have recently been set in the field of safety at work, and on the employer's obligation to inform his workers of the hazards connected with the new means of production and the hitherto unknown technologies. Labour inspectorate has been reinforced and the plants are bound to proffer a comprehensive safety system in respect of the complete production cycle.

The involvement of the Employment service is three-fold :

1. There is a duty on the employer's part to give the Service previous notice on dismissals involving ten or more workers, so that it can take steps to provide alternative employment for the dismissed.

2. The Service extends aid in find temporary means of workers' mobility, for instance by assisting in transportation expenses or training workers for jobs available in the receiving plant, or paying their subsistence during the training by the plant itself.

3. It is responsible (together with the National Insurance Institute) for the administration of unemployment insurance.

C. *The Histadrut (General Federation of Labour) and Technological Change.*

As might be expected, in the Israeli industrial relations system, unions and managers have been the most active actors in instituting technological change and dealing with its consequences. Government action, while important, has tended to be less powerful.

In the Israeli scene, the attitude of the Histadrut is particularly interesting because of its power and the central role of the collective negotiation process.

In Israel, as in other countries, the primary concern of trade unions in their dealings with technological changes relates to *the bearing of the changes on the employment situation, on the status of the workers and on the status of the trade unions.* Hence, one should examine the response of the union, particularly with respect to Type III changes, which have the most significant influence. What then are the pssible responses? They are related to several groups of factors, each of them worthy of separate consideration.

The classic work in this area is by Slichter et al (1960). In this study, the authors found five principal types of union response:

1. Willing acceptance.

2. Opposition.

3. Competition - attempting to keep the old method in use in competition with the new, perhaps by accepting wage cuts on the old jobs.

4. Encouragement.

5. Adjustment - doing what can be done to help the workers immediately affected, use it to the best possible advantage and suffer the least possible harm for it.

What are the determinants of the union response ?

1. The nature of the union - craft or industrial union (more opposition by craft unions).

2. Whether the industry, enterprise or occupation is facing stiff competition and whether it is expanding or contracting. (Competition makes the union more willing to accept technical change. Expanding employment oppor- tunities, usually but not always, make the union more willing to accept technical change).

3. The nature of the change: the numbers of jobs affected, the effect of the degree of skill and responsibility required of workers, the effect on the kind of skill or other qualifications required.

4. The stage of development of the change and of union policy toward it. (When a proposed change is new and when a union is first presented with it, a policy of opposition is more likely than after the union has had an opportunity to get used to the idea and adjust to it).

A study conducted in the seventies found additional factors that influence the response of trade unions to changes. Economic environment was found to be the chief variable which determined union responses to technical change. Where jobs are plentiful, resistance to change is low; where they are scarce, resistance is high. Another finding of this study was that some aspects of union structure and administration affect the union response.

A union is more likely to accept a change :

1. The broader the union's membership base;

2. The larger the union;

3. The greater the political security of the union and its leadership;

4. The smaller the number of unions negotiating in the industry;

5. The more limited the distribution of power within the union.

Another study of the late seventies by McLauglin concludes that union acceptance of change was facilitated by a healthy economy and by union leaders' perception that :

1. Only a small proportion of the jobs in the affected unit would be lost;

2. The change was inevitable;

3. A quid pro quo for lost jobs could be obtained.

Other determinants of a favourable response shown by McLauglin's data were:

1. Leader perceptions that resistance to the change would lead to loss of jobs;

2. Leader perceptions that effects of the change on remaining members would be small;

3. Member perceptions that union leaders or the employers had high credibility;

4. Non-essentiality of union members' work;

5. Diversity in union members' skill;

6. Consideration shown to the workers by the employer by cushioning the shock.

In addition, a number of aspects of the particular industry and centralization of decision-making power in the union facilitate a favourable union response to change.

Let us now examine the applications of the various criteria for the Histadrut's response to technological changes. First, the factors that influence the response:

The Histadrut includes both craft and industrial unions. When the subject was dealt with at the national or plant level, the attitude to changes was generally favourable. At the national level, important agreements were reached concerning changes; at the plant level, changes are usually accepted fairly rapidly, as a means of strengthening the competitive capability of the organization. On the other hand, in the printing industry - in Israel as in other countries - where there is considerable affinity between branch and craft, changes have been accompanied by forceful struggles, and employers had to pay a high price in terms of quid pro quo.

It is almost unthinkable to institute changes at the branch level without the active involvement of the trade union. The situation is different at the plant level, although here too the union often participates in the introduction of changes.

As to the dominant factor, namely economic conditions - in the course of the past twenty years, the state of the economy in Israel has facilitated the institution of technological changes. In fact, serious problems were encountered precisely in those industries that did not institute in time the changes required for improving their competitive capability.

*How does the structure and administration of trade unions in Israel influence
their response to changes?*

The Histadrut has an extremely broad base; the proportion of organized workers
in Israel is one of the highest in the world, a situation that favours the
acceptance of changes.

The Histadrut is definitely a political organization wielding substantial
influence on all official authorities, which affords considerable political
security both to the organization and to its members.

Only in recent years has a measure of decentralization been discernible in the
negotiation process. For many years negotiations proceeded at the national
and branch levels, facilitating the introduction of changes.

The Histadrut is a monopolistic organization with a highly centralized
structure. The decisions laid down by its central management are binding at
all organizational levels, throughout the country. One should also remember
that 20 percent of the Israeli economy is Histadrut owned. Being a large-
scale employer and having a highly centralized structure grealy facilitate the
institution of changes.

With regard to McLauglin's later findings, the Histadrut has acted flexibly,
mainly at the plant level; when the changes caused small-scale dismissals, it
often managed to secure favourable retirement conditions for the workers,
especially for Histadrut and other public employees. The Histadrut has been
less successful in obtaining quid pro quo for workers in the private sector.

The other factors listed by McLauglin also favour the acceptance of the changes
by the Histadrut. The Histadrut regards the situation in its broader aspects
and is concerned primarily with employment and not only with attaining higher
wages and better working conditions.

Generally, workers, particularly in the private sector, have faith in their
employers and in the union, which makes it easier to institute changes. The
heterogeneity of union members also serves this purpose. Finally, since
collective negotiation is a pivotal process at all labour relation levels in
Israel, in most cases every effort is being made to cushion the shock involved
in the introduction of changes.

CONCLUSIONS

Technological changes are introduced and occur in varying intensities and from
one country to another, from one industrial branch to another and even from
one enterprise to another. They may be introduced gradually and partly, or
rapidly and totally. The more rapid and drastic the introduction of such
changes, the bigger the impact on employment and consequently social and
economic crises may occur.

The proper approach for Israel, which is a small and highly socially sensitive
society, is to try and apply an integrated approach preserving at the same time
the interests and prerogatives of each sector. It is for the employers' organisations to inform the relevant workers' organisations in good time of impend-
ing technological changes and the resulting employment consequences -- and so
to moderate the " change trauma "on the part of the workers and to allow for
sufficient time for adjustment. The public, including the workers, is becoming gradually more and more aware of the fact that preventing the introduction
of new technologies is more destructive to the society and economy than
accepting the changes and trying to adjust to them.

It is in particular the responsibility of the employers' organisations to concentrate their attention and efforts on formulating a clear policy. The State of Israel, whose economy is still in the process of growing and expanding, has reasonable chances of overcoming the employment slackness arising out of technological changes, provided that a concerted activity by all will be devoted to modernisation of school syllabi, vocational training and retraining, as well as resolving and abolishing all protective anti-mobility agreements, practices and attitudes.

REFERENCES

Atkinson, J, 1985, Flexibility Planning for an Uncertain Future, *Manpower Policy and Practice,* Journal of the Institute of Manpower Studies, Vo.1, Summer, pp. 25 - 30.

Bamber, G.J, 1986, Technological Change and Trade Unions, *Proceedings of the Seventh World Congress of IIRA, Hamburg.*

Davies, A, 1984, The Management/Union Relationship in the Introduction of New Technology, in Piercy, N (ed.), *The Management Implications of New Information Technology,* London, Croom Helm.

Dror, D, 1986, Industrial Relations Implications of Government Policies towards Technological Change, *Proceedings of the Seventh World Congress of IIRA, Hamburg.*

Francis, A, William, P, 1980, Microprocessors: Impact and Response, *Personnel Review,*Vol. 9, No. 2 (Spring)

Freeman, C, 1985, Technical Change and Unemployment, *Proceedings of an International Symposium on Micro-electronics and Labour,* Tokyo, pp. 347-59.

Gill,C, 1985, Editorial of a Special Issue on the Impact of New Technology on Work and Employment, *Industrial Relations Journal,* (16) 2, pp. 5-8 .

International Labour Office, 1985, *Technological Change: The Tripartite Response,* 1982-85, ILO, Geneva.

International Symposium, 1983, Special Issue of the *Bulletin of Comparative Labour Relations,* Vol. 12 .

Kassalow, E, 1986, Technological Change:"Unions and Employers in a New Era", *Proceedings of the Seventh World Congress of the IIRA,* Hamburg.

Kochan, T.A, Tamir, B, 1986, Collective Bargaining and Technological Change: Some Preliminary Propositions, *Proceedings of the Seventh World Congress of the IIRA,* Hamburg.

Lansbury, R.D, Davis, E.M, (eds.), 1984, *Technology, Work and Industrial Relations,* Longman Cheshire, Melbourne.

McLaughlin, D.B, 1979, *The Impact of Labor Unions on the Rate and Direction of Technological Innovation,* National Technical Information Service.

Rajan, A, 1987, New Technology and Training, Missed Opportunities, *New Technology Work and Employment,* Vol. 2, No. 1, Spring, pp. 61-65.

Rojot, J, 1986, Employers' Responses to Technological Change, *Proceedings of the Seventh World Congress of the IIRA*, Hamburg.

Sarfati, H, Cove, M, 1986, The Social Implications of New Technology: An Unpredictable Future, *New Technology Work and Employment*, Vol.1, No.2, Autumn, pp. 140-151.

Slichter, S, H, Healy, J.J, and Livernash, R, 1960, *The Impact of Collective Bargaining on Management*, The Brookings Institution.

Verma, A, & Zerbe, W, 1986, Employee Involvement Programs and Worker Perceptions of New Technology, *Proceedings of the Seventh World Congress of the IIRA*, Hamburg.

Williams, R and Steward, F, 1985, New Technology Agreements: An Assessment, *Industrial Relations Journal*, 16(3), pp. 58-73.

The Social Implications of Robotics and Advanced
Industrial Automation / D. Millin and B.H. Raab (Editors)
Elsevier Science Publishers B.V. (North-Holland)
© IFIP, 1989

TRADE UNION EXPERIENCE WITH ADVANCED INDUSTRIAL AUTOMATION IN THE FRG
NEW CHALLENGES AND NEW ECONOMIC CONSTRAINTS

Dr. Ulrich Briefs MP

RSI
Posterholt (NL)
University of Bremen (FRG)

Complex industrial automation and information technology systems have
been exhibiting a considerable growth throughout the last years. The
confrontation with the effects of rationalization brought about by
these systems has let trade unions in the FRG push the policy of
shortening weekly working hours. In addition especially electronic
monitoring of working processes had led to new trade union approaches.
In the future, economic constraints of complex industrial automation
will play an even more dominant role in determining the social implications of complex industrial automation.

1. INFORMATION TECHNOLOGY AS PART OF INVESTMENT IN THE FRG

West Germany has by now had a very marked experience in advanced industrial
automation and this has very markedly been reflected on trade union policy and
practice.

To give a few key figures with regard to technological development in general
and with regard to industrial automation: More than five hundred billion US-
dollars have been invested throughout the last 15 years in advanced technological systems in the industrial sectors of the FRG. More than one hundred billion
US-dollars have been invested in information technology in investment systems
in this period in the FRG (incl. private and public services).

In the beginning of the seventies, the share of information technology investment in equipment was at about 5 per cent, it is now beyond 20 per cent - with
increasing tendency. This has been achieved in spite of the fact that information technology devices are more or less the only pieces of equipment which
have been becoming cheaper throughout this period.

The information technology industry in the FRG is nowadays the only major sector exhibiting substantial growth rates year after year.

This fact, however, has to be seen in its ensobering aspects: The rapid growth
of the information production sectors in the FRG has brought nearly no relief
to the labour market. The volume of production of the EDP-industry for example
has during the last 15 years grown by 400 per cent, employment, however, has
only increased by less than one hundred per cent. After all, it has brought less
than 40 000 new jobs - this has to be seen against an actual overall unemployment in the FRG of 2.4 million people (in reality more than three million people).

The heavy investment in information processing technology has on the other hand
reduced the number of jobs available in the FRG by at least five hundred thousand.

The advancement of industrial (and services) automation is likewise reflected
by the increasing number of jobs affected by information technologies: In the

beginning seventies, it was only about 6 per cent of the jobs which were affected by information technology systems, it is now already 25 per cent. It will
be more than half of the jobs in the beginning nineties and towards the turn of
the century, possibly more or less every job will be at least to some degree affected by information technology system and this more and more in the context
of complex automation systems.

The same process is reflected by the increase of the numbers of vdus: In the
beginning of the seventies, vdus were nearly unknown in the FRG, now more than
a million jobs (roughly 5 per cent of all jobs) are vdu-jobs. By the mid-nine-
ties every third job of about 10 million white-collar jobs in the FRG will be
a vdu-job.

On the other hand, the "degree of penetration" of information technology systems into the jobs is in many firms and organizations still very low: Many vdu-
jobs are still jobs where the workers are performing only a smaller part of
their daily worktime at the vdu.

Actual and future development will be shaped by the interaction of two major
application developments:

1. The increasing "deepening" of the use of information technology systems in
    the workplace - the (wo)man-machine-dialog will become a general feature of
    jobs and will increasingly restructure and reshape work contents, work skills
    working conditions, work organization;

2. In correspondence and adaptation to this basic process, which will in view
    of the considerable inertia of organization last by far into the next cen-
    tury, networking will take place - networking on the local level, as well
    as on a metropolitan and regional and especially on the national and inter-
    national level (via satellite communication); communications and the estab-
    lishment of very complex systems like ISDN will foster the process of "com-
    puterization" of jobs.

It is essential to understand that networking is not an isolated development,
but that it is consequently and logically developed and pushed to enlarge and
enhance the effects of computerization of jobs.

2. TRADE UNION EXPERIENCE IN THE FRG IN THE CONTEXT OF COMPLEX INDUSTRIAL
    AUTOMATION

Advanced industrial automation systems are increasingly designed and used in the
FRG in this context:

1. They bring information technology systems as components of complex automa-
    tion systems into a large number of jobs hitherto not at all or not so deep-
    ly affected by these systems: The directly productive activities in indus-
    try have only been growing in the last years into a prominent position in
    the process of overall computerization.

2. Complex industrial automation is increasingly put forward in the context of
    concatenated flexible systems which are likewise supported by networking
    structures - information technology systems especially also linking flexi-
    ble complex concatenated manufacturing systems to the general information
    processing systems of the relevant organization.

There are few data about specific systems of complex industrial automation in
the FRG. The variety of these systems is so large and of course so specific to
the conditions of the respective industry that a numerial classification - even
in investment terms - is now difficult and will be so in the future.

The element of complex industrial automation systems which can most commonly be "counted" is the number of robots installed: Between 1980 and 1986 the number of industrial robots in use in West Germany has increased from 1,255 to 12,400. 8,626 of them were tool-handling robots and 3,437 material-handling robots.

Nevertheless: The apparent successes of the West-German export-oriented industries - the FRG is still the most successful exporter of the large industrial countries - show that West Germany's industry at least has kept pace with the other major exporting countries with regard to the development and application of complex industrial automation systems. This is, of course, also telling something about the development of complex industrial automation in use in the FRG.

The general experience of trade unions in the FRG with complex industrial automation and with information technology systems in this context is:

- Computerization and complex industrial automation increase productivity; in the long run, they increase productivity even dramatically.
  Two cautioning remarks, however, are necessary:
  1. Productivity, however, is not so much increased by adding new use values (new products and new services) to the production of society; complex industrial automation and information technology systems increase productivity mainly by changing how products are produced, not so much by giving scope for the production of new products and services;

  2. In most cases, productivity is not increased immediately on the very introduction of complex automated systems or information technology systems, but only after a more or less larger and in many cases difficult period which is needed by the organization to adapt itself to the new technology.

- The first major implication is that complex industrial automation and information technology systems will reduce the amount of socially necessary labour: In the long run, this effect may dramatically increase mass unemployment. On the other hand, the reduction of the amount of socially necessary labour (on the job, in the department, in the firm, in the industry and on the national and international levels) is not new: In the FRG, from 1962 to 1982, annual g.n.p. in real terms has doubled, with the reduction of the number of working hours necessary for this increased production by 25 per cent throughout this period; the reduction of the number of working hours thus is a secular trend which, however, will get new impulses by complex industrial automation and information technology systems;

- Several major implications are linked to the structural change in work (to work contents, to work organization, to working conditions) induced especially in the context of man-machine-communication at the remaining jobs: Increasing adaptation at adoption of complex challenging work functions to and by computerized systems (enhanced by remote control and other telecommunication applications), increase in transaction speed, omnipresent electronic monitoring of work progress, night- and shift-work - artificial intelligence will in this context, but slower than it is expected generally now, contribute to complex industrial automation systems promoting the assumption of additional complex functions of control and intelligence in the working process by these machine systems.

3. TRADE UNION RESPONSE TO COMPLEX INDUSTRIAL AUTOMATION AND INFORMATION TECHNOLOGY SYSTEMS IN THE FRG

Complex industrial automation and information technology systems have throughout the last ten years contributed to considerably changing trade union policy in the FRG. The major features of this change are

- The emphasis laid by the trade unions on the demand of shortening the weekly
  working hours in correspondence to the reduction of socially necessary labour
  induced by new technologies and especially by information technologies in general and increasingly fostered also by complex automation systems. Trade unions in the FRG have become the leaders with regard to demanding the 35-hour
  week. In 1984, the largest strike movement in the after-war period in the FRG
  led to the 38.5-hour week in the metal-working and printing industries. In
  1987, a step further was done towards the 37-hour week to be reached in 1990.
  By now more than half of the jobs in the FRG are affected by collective agreements providing for a working week below 40 hours.

The discussion in the trade unions has now started about the 30 and 32-hour
week - the 6-hour working day - to be achieved in the nineties.

One cautioning remark has, however, to be made with regard to the extent of
the reduction of working hours achieved so far: The advance of working time
reduction has not been substantive enough to reduce unemployment sufficiently.
The pace of reducing working hours in the future has to be enhanced considerably if a major amelioration on the market is to be achieved.

One ecouraging remark has to be added likewise: The reduction of the weekly
working hours enforced by the trade unions movement in the FRG has not, contrary to quite a few previous apprehensions, endangered the success of the
West German export industries on the international markets. On the contrary:
The years 1985 and 1986 have been the most successful years with regard to
West German exports in all the after-war period. It is apparently not necessary to wait for other competing capitalist countries to follow the same path!

- In addition to enhancing the policy of reduction of weekly working hours the
  trade unions movement in the FRG has developed quite a few new lines with
  regard to its traditional policy of protection of workers against adverse
  effects of rationalization (controlling ergonomic effects - providing for
  more pauses at the vdu, medical examinations, training and retraining, replacement jobs, information and consultation of workers in the process of
  EDP-systems design and implementation etc. etc.)

- One new major line of conflicts between trade unions and employers has aris-
  en from the introduction of information technology systems and of first attempts in complex automation systems: The conflicts around increasing control and supervision in the working process which is fostered especially by
  the electronic monitoring features of EDP-systems. Quite a range of practical and political debates and approaches has been developed by trade union
  bodies - especially on the shop floor level - in this context: The most advanced form of worker's interest defence is the interference of work councils to whom the Work Constitution Law of 1972 gives certain codetermination rights (veto rights), if supervision and control is enhanced by technological systems, in the process of information technology design and implementation. In many cases, firms have concluded agreements with their work
  councils selecting and limiting the registration, storage, processing and
  communication of personal data in personnel information systems or in computerized production monitoring systems - these latter especially being developed as first steps to complex industrial automation systems. This has
  led to a certain practice of trade union bodies on the shop floor to contribute to the "shaping" ("Gestaltung") of information systems. It is only
  relatively late that the trade union bureaucracies have understood the importance of these steps of the trade union bases and provided for assistance
  to work councils and shop stewards committees in form of consultancy on the
  local and regional level. Right-wing forces especially in the large metalworkers union actually try to switch the debate in the trade unions from
  this threat of complex industrial automation to the more "positive aspects"
  of complex industrial automation and information technology systems.

- A perspective discussion in the trade unions in the FRG has been orienting itself towards qualitative aspects of computerization and of the future reduction of working time: A major role in the future will be played by the use of working time reduced by the productivity increases engendered by complex automation systems and information technology systems for a policy of reducing work pressure ("deintensification of work"), for reskilling on the job and especially for using more time for information, consultancy and joint determination of workers on the job, on the shop floor, with regard to all major decisions and especially with regard to the decisions about new technologies.

This latter point - steps towards a rigid democratization of work - may be especially considered as the major axis for a perspective of human work under the conditions of computerized working processes increasingly integrated into systems of complex industrial automation.

4. NEW TECHNOLOGIES - NEW ECONOMIC CONSTRAINTS

The conflicts around human work and complex industrial automation respectively information technology systems will in the future be aggravated by the increasing capital intensity and the effects of a specific sort of an economic crisis - a crisis which, however, is a crisis amidst a state of prosperity of the economy unwitnessed in history up to now.

The increase in capital intensity is the most dramatic actual development going on in capitalist economies with regard to the economic situation of human work in the context of complex industrial automation. Capital intensity (confer the data on page 1 of this text) has nearly quintupled on the average in the last 20 years in the FRG. In the automobile industry or in the industry which is producing packaging materials nowadays between 250,000 and 500,000 DM have to be invested to create one single job. In the design of electronic circuitry overhead cost (especially capital costs, i.e. depreciation, risks, interests etc.) is ten times (and more) as much as labour costs. At machining centres the ratio of fixed costs to labour costs is between 10:1 and 15:1. In one of the most advanced plants planned in the FRG - the nuclear retreatment plant at Wackersdorf the ratio of fixed costs to labour costs would be, if it was really built, at least 30:11!

With increasing high technology application and with increasing complex industrial automation and in this context also with the use of information technology systems the capital intensity and hence the ratio of fixed costs to labour costs will further increase!

And increasing will also be the pressure on the workers: At a machining centre four minutes of work are sufficient to produce the value corresponding to the wage and social benefits of the worker.

With increasing complex industrial automation and increasing use of information technology system as part of these systems thus the economic pressure not to loose a single minute of work will be made more and more pending on the worker: Firms and organizations will do everything to prevent workers from stopping to work, e.g. by going out on strike, from being idle for whatever other reason etc. This leads to approaches adopted by firms combining contradictory strategies of behaviour vis-à-vis human work in the future: on one hand they increase pressure on the worker, on the other hand they endeavour to "motivate" him (or very seldom her!)
In view of the enormous excess capacities existing in all major capitalist countries and industries and pushed by the existence of giant idle "strolling" capital masses - the economic pressure exerted by increasing fixed costs will likewise increase pressure on firms and consequently on the worker: These conditions

will induce more and more impulses to rationalize, to reduce the number of socially necessary working hours further, to tie workers to their jobs, to control and monitor operations of the workers etc. etc.

This process which is inevitable under the conditions of the capitalist "mode
of production" can particularly well be executed within complex industrial automation systems and on the bases of information technology systems as part of
them. The complex interaction of productivity increasing properties of complex
automation systems and of general economic conditions and its potential to find
economic solutions in the interests of firms and organizations will therefore
be crucial for the analysis of social implications of future complex industrial
automation and of information technology systems.

REFERENCES

(1) Briefs, U., Kjaer, J., Riagl, J-L (Eds), Computerization and work,
     Springer-Publ; Heidelberg, Berlin, New York, 1984
(2) Wobbe-Ohlenburg, W. Der Einfluß neuer Produktionstechnologien auf die
     Struktur der Automobilarbeit, eine Fallstudie zum Einsatz von Industrie-
     robotern im VW-Werk, Campus-Verlag, Frankfurt, 1982
(3) Coy, W., Industrieroboter, Rotbuchverlag, Berlin, 1985
(4) Briefs, U., Informationstechnologien und Zukunft der Arbeit, Pahl-Rugen-
     stein-Verlag, Köln, 1984, 3. Auflage 1987

The Social Implications of Robotics and Advanced
Industrial Automation / D. Millin and B.H. Raab (Editors)
Elsevier Science Publishers B.V. (North-Holland)
© IFIP, 1989

MAN, WORK and MODERN MACHINE TECHNIQUE :
DISCOURSE ON VALUATIONS

John Drumm, Irish Representative to IFIP TC-9
214 Grace Park Heights, Dublin 9, Ireland.

Much discussion of robotics and autonomous systems lacks an adequate framework for values
study. This paper presents a philosophical approach for modelling their increasing social implications on health and well-being on jobs, and the labour market. The paper suggests that we place
an overemphasis on machine techniques, to the detriment of the 'human element' notably in the
cultivation of skills, character and will power. The implicit trust put in complex systems is not
supported by sufficient research on the conflict between human and business values. Using a
model (VAL) the paper sketches one method to understand problematic effects, with society
selected as a 'novel' clinical patient for psychological assessment. The following diagnosis,
examples, symptomatology, and inter-related elements, are elaborated upon in a working paper.

1. INTRODUCTION

There are many approaches to a values discussion, and in attempting to bring out some challenging issues,
the paper threads together thoughts of prominent thinkers on high-technological transition, interspersed with
subjective opinions. The chief inspiration for the ideas is Abraham Low the pragmatic Polish psychiatrist. In
borrowing his views especially in so much as they are applicable to assessing technology impacts on
individuals and society, I hope not to have done injustice to his philosophy of taking a total viewpoint. The
strict but humane rules and procedures applied in medical diagnostic assessment are worth pursuing in social
assessment.The paper refers to Low's work because a discriminating interpretation of social impacts requires
a good understanding of human values. Low's self-help programme has stood the test of over half a century.
Its simplicity and richness in problem-solving has helped to throw light on a world shaken by momentous
liberal revolutions. His philosophy of duality and integral objectivity is useful for those attempting to draw
conclusions about social change. This humanitarian psychology, while focusing on the trivialities of everyday
living, is nonetheless of merit in building any foundation for long-term socio-economic goals and security.
A values critique is essentially a philosophical presentation. It must give due account to at least two fundamental constructions in dealing with predicaments, in society arising from modern industrial automation.

a) Philosophical assumptions are either to be understood in the domain of "Philosophies of the World", for
discerning the extent of social effects, or, in terms of a "Philosophy of Life" which help us to better interpret
effects on individual human behaviour. (24) : Chapter 14.

b) We need a model for understanding the phenomenal world that can do justice to our subject and the
character of what we mean by reality. Such a need arises in our efforts to comprehend the historical focus of
labour, and specialization of functions, that have produced the proliferation of disciplines and professions as
explained by Pruyser (23) chapter 6.

2. CRISES PERSPECTIVE

Present society is characterised by great business and social enterprise. We live in a time of exploration,
bringing multiple choices, experiences and change. It is a creative period in the history of mankind. The spirit
of commercialism abounds. Depending on ones point of view and circumstances, present events and
pioneering feats can be seen as either encouraging, threatening, or a potent mixture. For the more fortunate
they might be well summed by the attitudes of the astronaut Neil Armstrong, who viewed the next few
decades as being a tremendously lucky and exciting time to be alive, particularly suited to the younger
generations. On the other hand, we hear repeatedly of multiple crises linked to monetary issues caused by
uncertain global economics, inflation, budgetary debts etc.To those feeling somewhat less secure, the sheer
pace of developments in information society might seem to be fostering discontent. Such developments as the
gigantism of organizations, dilution of personal responsibility, sliding ethical standards, mounting ecological
problems, standardization of occupations and what Petrella (56) describes as "the diminishing visibility and
efficiency of the nation-state" are growing concerns. These and other trends in the technocratic process impel
us to examine core elements in globalization i.e., change, progress, values etc.

3. ON THE NATURE OF HUMAN VALUES

3.1 THEORETICAL CLASSIFICATION

Human values are associated with many facets of the mental process and are generally understood to include such things as goals, attitudes, choices, decisions, beliefs, judgements, principles and policies. Their criteria include biological, psychological, axiological, epistemological and ontological perspectives. Mukergee (7) develops each of these features into what might be summarised as, a co-ordinated network of dialectical synthesis, assimilated into a sub-conscious process of self-identity and actualization. In any event what we mean is that they are connected with profound human qualities in the fundamental nature of our thinking process. Super and Bohn (73) suggest that types of values vary with the perspective of the philosopher or psychologist, specifically dealing with Edvard Spranger's theory, postulating six types of values : theoretical, social (altruistic), political (prestige and power), economic (material), esthetic, and religious (mystical). Reflecting on a world of cultural determinism, we are interested here in the values of modern social occupational elitism. For as Grant (76) explains, society has fed counterproductive values and expectations into our super-ego. The main thing is to recognise that the process of life is more important than the content. We fail to separate money from the ways of earning it.Gail Inlow (8), takes the approach that different avenues of values are classified as deductivist, pragmatist, existentialist, and Hegelian, crossing the total sphere of philosophical thought. Concentrating on the nature of values in scientific observation, she examines the dual effects of methods and discoveries in a world of mountainous change.

3.2 SPECIFIC ASPECTS

Our choices are based on our values. According to Carl Rogers the psychotherapist "value is the tendency of a person to show preference. They are determines in people that influence our choices in life that decide behaviour. In other words, choices made in response to a given set of determines called values". Gottlieb and Borodin (14); agree, suggesting values are preferred outcomes or goals. Super and Bohn (73) point to ends that people believe to be desirable. Low (40), distinguishes between long and short range goals, pointing out, that our preferences place a valuation on our choices. The aim is directed at a value and every means or tool which enables aiming at a goal is of value, for that particular goal. The possible range of values is limitless. The most important question is whether the goal itself is of value. Short range goals seem to call for skill and techniques, whereas long range goals require character and determination in pursuit of the aims.Ericson (2) refers to values conflict. He clasifies values into clusters or tables of valuations, for business, group and personal goals. Linking mental health to good organisation and the capacity of individuals to produce, be committed, creative and flexible, he concludes we are in a conflict between private prerogative and public right. In reviewing the social responsibilities of business, he endorses the business and industrial machine as one of our greatest inventions. However, he was committed to say "its future - its smooth running - is, in my opinion, no longer dependent on what it is today; it depends rather, on the resolution of some of the larger issues that are eating away at the heart and soul of American society, and I predict that the American business community will in the decades ahead involve itself deeply with these issues."

3.3 GENERIC STRUCTURE

With regard to values ordering or hierarchy, we must distinguish between the supreme values and their lesser or lower qualities. Peace, for example, is of great importance for the individual person and for the wider group and is therefore in the nature of a supreme value. In a values study (81) among the European public, one great cause - peace - clearly holds the prime position in all countries and in all segments of the public. This was followed by other preferences for human rights, freedom of the individual, the struggle against poverty, etc. Low(40), p.191 emphasises this in saying "both the thrills and excitement and the comforts of the lower values are legitimate pursuits if cultivated in moderation. However if they clash with the aims and needs of the supreme value (peace, mental health, etc.), they must be controlled. To know what thrills to tolerate and which comforts to admit within ones scheme of life, requires a delicately balanced sense of values." As an example he suggested that the faithful devotion to a noble profession and the greedy scramble for money cannot possibly have the same values. Although no absolute theory of values may exist, valuations are closely bound up with self-concepts in a world of increasing materialism and complexity. They are influenced to a significant degree by the human external environment and subordinate to individual personal leanings and collective groups of people to which we associate or belong. Also we must distinguish at the group level between the immediate family group, and the wider group dimensions of culture, nation, organisation or universe in accord with Miller (57).

3.4 AETIOLOGY

A primary consideration for self-actualization in mental health is the changing of attitudes, hence values. In the social context, Mannheim (3), suggests the remedy for the wider group is social awareness and structural reconstruction. In the more advanced countries we have reached a point of placing a premium on comfort and convenience, with a high degree of pleasure seeking activities. Mannheim (74) linked the relevance of this to a revolution in the general evaluation of how we assess "survival values". These understandable developments are linked with commercial thinking, which can thrive on the exploitation of innate desires. The endless stimulation of sales and marketing cybernetics, originates in a competitive system, where producers try to compete, to outdo each other. He attributed this to the issue of asceticism, questioning limitless craving as an unnatural response to the business ethic, considering whether we have reached a point where this is detrimental to human consonance. We speak here particularly of workers who stand increasingly in fear of job restructuring, absence of work and technological unemployment and from new sources of stress. That is, people having on the one hand gained employment in producing consumable goods, only to find their positions altered or threatened by the sophistication of the methods they built so creatively. Lasch (83) suggests this culture of consumption organised around mass- production encourages narcissism, based on a seeming limitless array of personal choices formerly restricted to the rich. These symptoms of pathologic "owning" and "consuming" reflect what he calls "a failure of morale, a cultural crisis associated in some way with the collapse of 'traditional values' and the emergence of a new morality of self-gratification." There is a connection between the doctrine of material expansion (helped by automation), and the inevitable impact on the self resulting in many "psycho-spiritual" crises of life.

3.5 MODEL DESIGN CONSIDERATIONS

Given that a value analysis is a difficult undertaking, at risk from prejudice and personal bias, it seems a working mental model would be helpful for easy visualization and understanding of the key features and their relations in the hypothesis. The visual model constructed, see Figure 1, allows for experiment and manipulation of values criteria, hierarchy and interaction, among components or phenomena. The VAL prototype is an attempt in so far as possible in a short paper, at a down-scale representation of economic aspects based on business values in the real world: with their relationship and resulting conflict between social aspects based on human values. The model is a compromise between detail and generality for differing value technics and their comparability, such as developed by Sales (95), Chapter VIII. The impact of automated production is not perceived in isolation outside a total of interrelated elements. Their impact is idealized through the contemporary worldwide trading outlook, with its sovereignty of utility values imposed through social plural consensus over traditional transmitted values connected to the whole history of human enterprise. The resulting model characteristics as treated by Bodily (99), include several key decision making preferences with basic interrelations between multi-objective choices. Quantitative attributes are shown on the left and qualitative on the right.

4. DOMINANCE OF BUSINESS VALUES

4.1 EXIGENCY OF LEADERSHIP

The new methods require a new kind of leadership according to Lawrence (29) which may give realistic and corrective judgement to both social and economic status. Policy making in each area requires planning based on different criteria in respect of new technology take-up. Economic policy is guided by a long history of thought, whereas social policy must be guided by the primacy of labour based on human and artistic scales of value, as new forms of work rapidly develop. Lawrence says "machinery saves labour and makes it possible to do things that were previously impossible. That is good in itself, but it defeats its purpose if it creates millions of unemployed, or it turns men and women into automata. The problem of the next decade is to discover how to keep and develop such economic freedom as we have, while accepting the discipline which is necessary for our survival." Mannheim concurred on this referring to the "method of democratic value guidance" as the only remedy for this possible misuse of social awareness.

4.2 DISCRIMINATIVE LEARNING

With recent advances in informatics, mankind is learning to communicate in a state of hurried excitement. The process of globalization has taken on new dimensions with the collapse of the information float (20). The convergence, integration and interdependence of communications media throws up seeming limitless possibilities for science, technology, business and education. We have moved from an age which revered traditional principles of will practice in the learning process where children were taught the necessity of will power for the mastery for reading, writing and arithmetic. Suddenly in the space of a few short years, we have new value empiricism to deal with. There is it seems, a conflict between traditionalism and liberalism.

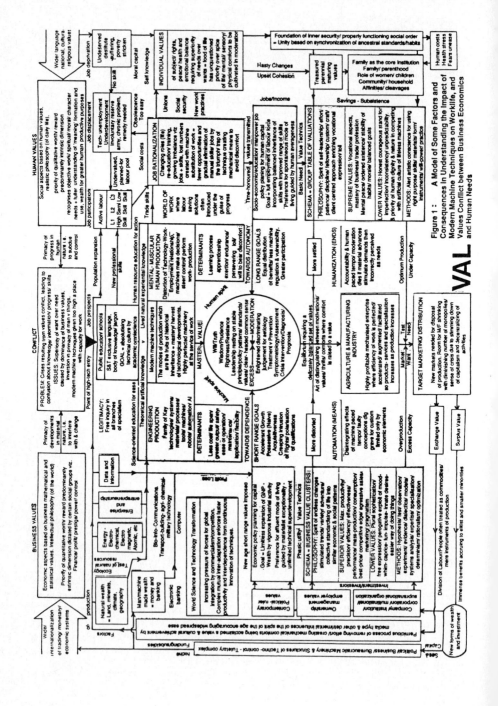

Figure 1 :   A Model of Some Factors and Consequences in Understanding the Impact of Modern Machine Techniques on Worklife, and Values Conflict between Business Economics and Human Needs

The historical view held up the values of the rich disciplines of a learning process dedicated to getting across the "knowhow" of pursuing tasks, of aiming at goals, and accomplishing purposes. This was intended to be brought out in a grinding procedure (learning process) of apprenticeship. It is necessary to stress there are profound differences in approach. The contemplative view according to Low, Mannheim, Lasch etc., sees modern man as a pathetic creature of an extraneous Will, and in abject dependence on forces outside the inner self.

The new liberal attitudes endorse every technological solution as being intrinsically of high value. In this manner of thinking "aids" are encouraged to help us avoid exertion in the workplace, school, home, etc. Children are particularly encouraged to shun mental effort with the advent of calculators, video toys, micro-computers and so forth. In a paper emphasising the need for child advocacy with the newer technologies, Jules Zimmer (98) says "one has to be concerned about the skills and habits that will be acquired by these new interactive devices, since technology seems dedicated to making the educational process as effortless as possible". Zimmer further states that in addition to the potential loss of meaning, "effortless learning often results in a habituation that is typified by mental associations which operate schematically. Children who can control their learning and see themselves as competent learners will be the successful thinkers." The modern trend imbibes the value of techniques and threatens the necessity for learning, patient application and practice of will. Everywhere we are witnessing the growth of new channels of information which encourage the speed-up of the learning curve. The nett effect is the common misconception that to be shown a method means to learn it, and that witnessing a demonstration of a skill means acquiring it. What is in question is not so much the developments, as the speed, impatience and restlessness for change.

4.3 CRISIS OF INFORMATION

Referring to the consequences on mental health, Low (40) stressed that most devastating to the learning process and to the exercise of will power has been the contemporary trend to spoonfeed information since our age is hopelessly addicted to it. He pointed out that in dealing with machines, it may be feasible to avoid the discomfort of mental or physical exertion. In point of dealing with life tasks it is different. He said "my patients will have to realize what former generations always knew: that a life task can be mastered only through a gruelling, enacting learning process in which all the resources of the Will must combine to achieve final fulfillment. It can be secured only if the patient's Will initiates a system of ceaseless trials and trials and trials until in the end the task is accomplished". This is as fundamental to the struggle of a patient in regaining an ordered thinking pattern as the performance of a sales person, in the gruelling daily battle to achieve sales - in effect any form of life apprenticeship.What we may have to realize is, that in spite of the all embracing impact and seeming necessity of communicating and conversing with machines as beautifully illustrated by Gaines & Shaw (58), it is more important to progress in the domain of the human emotions, inter-personal communication and building morale (i.e. the human element). It seems we must be consistently alert to the dangers of putting too much faith and worship in producing sheer information with the consequential health and stress and depersonalization impacts of over-information, disinformation etc. We are torn between the dilemma of the economic (business) values versus the human (character) need values. A crisis of confusion exists, because on the one hand money is information in motion whereas on the other, the implication that correct information is the surest way to correct action is incorrect. For information is merely the preliminary to training and practice, not a substitute for self-leadership. We must beware of the implied values of an information economy where money is needed to acquire it, and question through sustained discussion what kind of future is more realistic, desirable, suitable and attainable.

4.4 SOCIETAL GOALS

Since purpose aims at goals, the unifying purpose of economic planning must be the creation of wealth guided by profit motive. In this primacy of material things over persons, there is the danger of labour being treated as an impersonal productive commodity. It is now well established that global regions and nations are striving to achieve stimulation of economic growth, and in doing so seeking out development opportunities making fullest possible use of skills and resources. In carrying out their objectives, key elements include encouraging modern industry, high-technology investment, and creating a climate that strongly promotes business enterprise (25). The way forward is seen as embracing the emerging technologies in becoming high-income economies.

That wealth generation is an essential task goes without saying. Now more than ever before, manufacturing is the determining factor in success or failure on world markets. With modern methods of universal automation, this process is taken to the point where hardly any human intervention may be required in production, having profound effects on values associated with work, labour and social dislocation.

4.5 PREVAILING VALUE CONSTRUCT

The commercial values embedded in this vision can be described in terms of a commonly viewed approach in capitalist countries at least. Mastery of the means of production is perceived as the determining factor in the future, playing a central role in meeting economic, industrial, and energy challenges. The European Economic Community for example would seem to be prompting concerted action for this strategic dimension (45), of a Euro-culture. European strategy aims towards increasing export of manufactured goods to pay for increasingly large sums in import of raw materials. opening up makes competition vital, which in turn requires industrial specialization and supply markets to dispose of new production. As production expands so does the need for higher productivity and efficiency and technical edge (44). Competition in this sense has a tendency to make labour more productive with consequences for employment and work organisation. Improvement in productivity in turn requires technological innovation, therefore we need ever more research and development and education in the technical culture. Concluding this analogy we see the complex mutual inter-adaptation of the actors accepting a headlong flight into growth, productivity and interdependence as the royal road to satisfy social, political and economic requirements. It is crucial to understand that economic and technology developments are not identical with human progress. We must not be duped on this point, for the means of production are both a threat and a promise. Referring to authentic human development, Sollicitudo Rei Socialis (88), p.47, suggests in the first place that development is not a straight forward process. Such an idea - linked to the notion of progress with philosophical connotations deriving from the enlightenment now used in a specifically economic and social sense - seems to be called into doubt. In spite of better understanding today, the mere accumulation of either goods and services or the real benefits provided by modern science, including the computer sciences, do not free mankind from every form of slavery. Unless these are accompanied by moral understanding and appreciation of true individual needs and the common good, they can have an oppressing effect.

4.6 SYMPTOMATOLOGY

Mass-production is a product of international trade. It evolved over many generations of human history in the activities of warfare, conquest, and colonialism. As Shakespeare said, "others, like merchants, venture trade abroad : others like soldiers, armed in their strings, make boot upon the summer's velvet buds." Massification has produced its own set of cultural values through trans-national business association. With a suitable platform for promoting subjective material wants, albeit satisfying basic needs. The new tools of automated production are important instruments for creating wealth and assisting growth and prosperity, as the conference of Europe and the new technologies pointed out (41). But as Ghandi once said "it was not mass-production that counts, but production by the masses that would do the trick." Given the sophistication of modern marketing methods a crisis of super production was always a possibility. Business values have a tendency to promote extravagant consumption, and speedy or continual acquisition by aggressive practices. In total, a sort of social over-stimulation, which can inveigh against self-equilibrium.

5. MODERN MACHINE TECHNIQUES

5.1 DISCONTINUITY OF RELATIONSHIP

Modern machine techniques serve society well as tools of wealth creation (15). This is their purpose. Development of large-scale commercial production depends upon various forms of mechanization commonly understood to the means of production. These basic factors of instrumentation include four types of instruments: tools, powered tools, machines, and automated machines including robotics. Thousands of variations of these basic aids to the process of production are used across the spectrum of all the trades, professions and farming methods. Increasingly, this highly perfected machinery becomes at the service of work. The scenario varies from the qualitative methods of the craft industries to the more quantative techniques of the mega-industries and mega-technologies. With the advancement of technical and management knowledge, we developed various methods of coping with mass production. Systems analysis, cybernetics, management science and many other soft techniques, extend the efficiency of creating wealth : assisting better organisation of the industrial order. Modern artificial techniques have now brought us to a point where we will soon have fully automated factories to be designed by and for, robot operations. People everywhere it seems will have robot tools, robot machines and robot colleagues. By doing so, man as altered the traditional relationship between the instruments and work itself. These techniques now begin to exert a great influence on the social organisation and self-fulfillment of work. Many new issues are being raised concerning the validity and rightness of giving machines such a powerful capacity to produce. These questions regarding human versus automated production must be treated in a responsible way as they alter the priority and status of man versus machines that should be serving mankind (45). Thus we arrive at Crucial questions of ethics and antagonising disputes arising from technical possibilities and moral dilemmas.

5.2 DELITESCENCE OF KNOWLEDGE

The formidable achievements in theoretical knowledge and communications engineering have enhanced the role of machines to that of subtle, expert assistants. What are the knowledge implications of people in direct competition with machines for jobs. How do we assess the problems of work loss particularly if there is significant evidence to support the fact that the new technologies do not always progress the human performance, but rather just add new effects to the way we do things. Such issues as human copyright and compensation give cause for concern and compassion if work skills are invaded. Are we changing the world too fast by reshaping society without understanding or accepting the humaneness of how we as people are? Is there a crisis about the validity of experiential knowledge in the face of the overwhelming academic success of theoretical knowledge that spurns technology developments? Are we in confusion between expanding human needs and technology needs? Is it disputable whether electronics is an asset in helping inner healing for health and self-growth? There are crucial promises and problems needing total reassessment in the face of increasingly stressful challenges of new technology. In our progressive culture, the only fully acceptable knowledge is based on the scrutiny and required proof of fixed laws of cause and effects (33). Predicted truth is then predominantly endorsed by business activity. We are it seems losing faith in the practical knowledge stemming from humanly acquired experience. Skill, it is said, belongs to workers who cannot be given the scientific knowledge that replaces it, or compete with its autonomous efficiency. But this type of knowledge is vastly informative. Knowledge means experience and the bulk of human experience stems from our actions (40), chapter 4. Practical knowledge of what to do and how to behave in given situations comes from acting and practicing. Knowledge teaches what to do but practice alone teaches how.

5.3 SCIENTIFIC FOCUS

We essentially now live in a monumental world of science. Its breeding ground is research: and its laboratories are education and government. Its method of systematic problem solving and social products consist of the phenomenal spread of advanced techniques. Recent scientific discoveries which in some cases have been impressive in their potential seem to have gone ahead of society's ability to develop ethics or values for them. New reproductive techniques, or brain transplant techniques in medicine for example, or the social accountability of computers. The goal of science is the conquest of nature, manifest in a totally controlled artificial environment. Its purpose is served by the delight of discovery and metaphysical value of penetration into the world of nature and universal existence. Innovation has become a supreme value with rapid developments leading to a mass of instruments. Invention for the sake of invention, can however, gives cause for concern with experimentation going through a period of idealistic and moral uncertainty. This is based on what Ingles (16) refers to as the accumulated body of knowledge and practices, which are founded on a rationale to master and dominate the world. It has been so far proved that the scientific method is the most productive means man has discovered to do this.

5.4 CRISIS OF PSYCHOLOGY

The incomplete framework for an understanding of "mind" or human intelligence is a good pragmatic example. No definitive model has evolved in the interaction of two disciplines, Artificial Intelligence studying intelligence oriented outside of nature, and Cognitive Science studying biologically implemented intelligence specifically the human person (22). Cognitive science is concerned with inquiry into vision, memory, perception, language, inference and action. According to Darrel Ince (100), cognitists use computers for exploring ways in which we think; whereas artefact builders build software systems which inhibit intelligent behaviour, and are not concerned if underlying mechanisms of the software resemble human functions. In each of these domains investigation of human cognitive capacity reveals naturally occurring mechanisms which provide the stimulus for commercial technology. None the less, there is an increasingly thin line between the business research laboratory, and the academic institution throwing up issues about the role of our technical culture (1). New sciences in their relative infancy, with a commonly shared view of man have provided the spring of theoretical knowledge, culminating in a clear image of robotics and unimation as part of the rapid progression of mainstream manufacturing industry.

All life issues are interconnected, as are work issues. The close relationship between psychology and the development of machine techniques is an important factor in present values orientation. The reasons are becoming clearer, as we are at the early stages of identifying social considerations for the empowerment and decision making of machines. The scientific focus apparently neglects experiences occurring within the emotional and intuitive grasp of internal human functioning, in deepest inner environment. These occur within people "affecting" our finest sensibility and are not conveniently measured. It is misleading to believe as is often implied; that science deals with this total inner mental organisation. Emotions do not lend themselves readily to rational analysis, denying the logic necessary for systems theory. Their very essence is their irrationality. It is interesting that psychiatrists, psychologists and theologians with their vast experience in the human, mechanical and spiritual sciences are at such divergence about the uncertain phenomena of human psycho-spiritual Composition and function. The eclectic diversity in ideology lacks a truly unified approach. Broadly we are becoming more mechanistic as evidenced by Minsky (102). In practice the doctrine of human instinct much influenced by Freudian psychology continues in ascendancy. With the ever increasing commercialization of science this is endorsed by developments in information and human communications engineering techniques.

5.5 AUTOMATION - STATUS QUO

Arising in automata and cybernetics theory (19), the goal of automation is the employment of the maximum means of efficiency in industry, implying this process will proceed to the point where hardly any human intervention is required in production. The long range goal being the completely automated factory environment. The implied values include maximum organisation, productivity, efficiency and growth. In spite of what seems enormous change in this field already Lupton (31) believes we are on "the technological and sociological edge of a dramatic increase in the use of computers and microprocessor technology in manufacturing." The constellation of products and design in automation is a vast array of advanced manufacturing techniques (AMT). These include computers in manufacturing (CNC, DNC etc)., Robotics, and so called flexible manufacturing systems (FMS). The indirect applications include production planning and scheduling, factory management, production control, and inventory control. There can be no doubting however the wonderful benefits that modern industrial developments have brought to those countries who have received them. The increased standards of living, sophistication, welfare and prestige of those lucky enough to have skilled jobs provided, have been a high point in material humanistic advancement.

5.6 ROBOT - SYMBOLIC MACHINE

The robot in spite of present limited extensiveness could be interpreted as a symbol of electro-mechanical perfection and the microcomputer and microchip have been the real engines of the robot revolution. The goal of robotics is to mimic human behaviour, producing greater quantity of wealth and work, at faster pace than human industrial workers. In point of value to the commercial enterprise it has superior characteristics such as being economically a better performer, more productive, flexible, has greater lifespan and time utilization, gives better energy conservation and, with increased quality standards. It is commonly considered to be the factory slave/colleague of the future which will serve people in the emancipation of work, to relieve us from hazardous activity and tasks where overall the work is considered too simple, repetitive and stultifying for the human brain. They will serve to eliminate health hazards, increasing safety to its highest level. They will in theory at least, leave people free to develop creativity in other ways with cultured ease, not doing jobs that we don't wish to do. In brief, the basic premise of robotics is to supplant labour by machine, by providing a greater quantity of goods and services with less human effort required in production, at reduced purchase, maintenance and operation cost. How are we to interpret the real social costs in terms of meaningful priorities for our goals?

5.7 HUMAN REPLACEMENT RATIONALE

Whatever the profit motives and financial benefits from using robotics in health-endangering or repetitive activities, there are worrying implications for the reduction of physical demands, and for older workers. In spite of pragmatic statistics, scarce as they may be, a number of issues go unattended. Firstly the replacement of any human function by machine must always be a matter of importance irrespective of the trivial or serious consequences of the work itself. The document, Laborem Exercens (43), says technology is undoubtedly man's ally as long as it is understood not as a capacity or aptitude for work, but rather as a set of instruments which man uses in the performance of work. Given that the goal of robotics is the direct replacement and automation of routine human tasks by machine technique, it is hard to interpret any other meaning of the value analysis techniques (ROI - return on investment), for using robotics, other than that people are treated on the same material level as commodities.

5.8 DICHOTOMY OF REPETITION

In modern China where so much has been done to re-organise and feed the population in their social revolution, manual exertion has a high place in the median values associated with daily routine. Exaggerated futurology, lauding emancipation from lower skilled work by widespread use of robotics such as Gorz (68), embrace widely a working world where new machine families relieve society from much of the drudgery of living. On the factory floor, jobs requiring toil in the sense of muscular industriousness are under severest threat of replacement. According to Leontief (86) p.84, in a study of the impact of machines on man, in this era of automatic control : eliminating the need for muscle power will change the character of our labour force, concluding that naturally, automization, while solving some problems, everywhere creates new and possibly more difficult ones. In former times, physiological work activity was seen as a thing of necessity to man's welfare, and therefore something of moral value. Who sets the new standards. Maybe moral progress has not kept pace with technological advance, or as Low (40) p.106, questions: is it truer to say that the emphasis on technological progress makes us forget the importance of progressing in the domain or morale? A quick glance at the labour statistics of different income economies will reveal the trends away from physical effort to mental effort amongst richer nations. The work ethic (54) has been replaced with the leisure ethic where there is a massive increase in the numbers actually employed in leisure activities now considered socially valuable occupations. No doubt for those countries in former times, heavy labour, sustained exertion, privations and drudgery were regarded as incidental to the sweat and toil of daily existence and borne with patience, resignation and humility. These characteristics are still valued highly in less developed regions of the world.

The tenets of Samuel Smiles (12) are surely equally valid today. He praised practical skills and labour and argued against corrective redistribution replacing individual energy, efficiency, and productiveness at work as a means of widening and deepening prosperity. The transcendental value of the patient and persevering labour of great multitudes of people in all ranks and conditions of life is evidence of the moral character that lies behind it. He concludes that the worth and strength of states depend far less on the form of institutions than the character of its people.

5.9 MUSIC, MUSCLES AND MACHINES

Further illustrating the values impact we can take the case of the planets oldest instrumentalist the drummer, who has been significantly effected by automation. Much of popular music today is drum machine oriented. A whole new generation is being brought up on techno-robotics, were in recent years a gamut of hardware has reached the marketplace with the advent of digital drum electronics. Technology such as Simmons, MIDI electronic drum kits, keyboard pyrotechnics, percussion expanders, detonator triggers-processing units, samplers, electronic pads etc., and techniques such as clicking and triggering have motivated the recording industry to embark on a host of syntho-techno refinements to drum synthesis. The by now universal familiar hard-rocking thumping cult-like sounds of the discotech have helped to foster an immature musical outlook. These developments in synthesized sound production, have at least certainly regarding the art of drumming, created the myth of using electronics to improve musicianship, downgrading its value with enormous consequent loss of work for drummers. It seems the battle between the drum machine and the live instrumentalist has just begun.

Scientific drumming has developed well with advances in new acoustic drum technology but the need to appreciate the finer differences more readily in technical developments. Not all are good in the artistic sense or value-free. The problem we face is one of degree. The smoothest most finessed musicians bring controlled relaxation to their music making, in live performance and in their own unique style and groove, i.e., the human touch. They make it sound easy in creating subtle tensions between brushwork, tone dynamics, combo interplay. The essence of this subtlety of command and touch is developed only through sustained muscular activity.

6. VALUES OF CHANGE

6.1 DUBIETY OF PROGRESS

We mentioned earlier core issues in conflict which arise constantly in analysis of change. It is a breathless subject but we are concerned with the implications of superior value questions underlying the basic thrust with unimation. In a general way we tend to associate the idea of automata with self-acting machines that save labour, and consider such changes to be technically and hence culturally progressive steps for society. Therein lies a challenge of understanding and frequently fuzzy reasoning. Using one example of the notion of progress with its conflicting meaning between human internal and external environments, as previously stated, the perfection of moral character and technical perfection are not synonymous. Recognition of human characteristics are often attributed to robots underservedly according to Weizenbaum (17), in view of their mechanistic nature. The automated machine serves as an autonomous clock with its own inner reality. Physical endurance, and toleration with trivial discomfort would be typical characteristic examples. These have an esteemed value for people, but no place in technical language. It is interesting to note in science literature that the coldness of wordage used chiefly omits references to the warm human qualities we find illuminating other subjects. In this instance there is a high price to pay by ignoring the subjective viewpoint totally.

In common interpretations of "progress" it seems we generally infer or link the concept with motion, advancement, or forward movement indicating a proud record of attainment. In terms of technological development, we specifically put forward this attitude as being of the quality of being modern. Philosophically we arrive at a confrontation between materialistic and idealistic views, having sagacious effect on what we associate as being intrinsically valuable. Opposing views differ in what they perceive as, of nature, and more particularly of human nature. We can say with probability that the scientific method endorses the materialistic view. According to Cornforth (69), "every real social advance, every increase in the productive forces, every advance in science - generates materialism, and is helped along by materialistic ideas." In further examination of present technical culture, we find that this can lead to a crisis of conscience in the idealistic sense. At its most complex formulation we find our quest for humanism is at divergence on the issue of a science of the spirit.

6.2 DIALECTICS AND DUALITY

It is apparently an indication of maturation in social and systemic development, when the necessity is recognised of laying training aside, as proof of presented evidence, confounds deterministic experience. Irrespective of idealistic or scientific perspectives, such for example is the serendipity, when a physician acquires new insights from a patient, learned, in spite of better professional judgement. Contradictions in the natural order are probably best understood in the study of duality. The concept is given different emphasis and expression depending on ones eastern or western philosophy, and technical or non technical background. Essentially it implies there are three basic positions to choose from between two extremes and a middle position. This arrangement of situations into three positions is characteristic of everything that grows and lives, i.e., the "natural" or "normal" mode of distribution. It is natural to think and react in a pulse of two. Most natural physical reactions work in this way, heart beat, walking, eyes, ears etc. The two brain hemispheres right and left are in constant communication, whilst each has its own functions in the unitas multiplex. For example, the fact that there are opposing views in discussion is itself a duality and inevitable to successfully resolving conflicts. We need compromise in any human negotiations and internal conflict. The ancient Greeks and Chinese mostly attributed everything that had life and movement as being made up of a pair of opposites. Heraclitus concurred in his doctrine of the mingling of the opposites maintaining there would be no unity without opposition. Oriental thought endorses primordial and universal Yin and Yang energies in bi-polar opposition, both mutually exclusive and complementary. Harmonization of duality assimilates in triplicity. Most great men of science and philosophy diverge from this juncture, with different genesis of value systems. Marx and Engels (62) dialectical method concur with the polarization in natural forces, reaching climax or balance in synthesis, where as the Leibnizian philosophy is mirrored in pre-established harmony.

6.3 LINGUISTIC MISAPPROPRIATION

In august human action, beyond mechanization, we find how Low (66) discovered the importance of language in patient's progress. The degree of total recovery from nervous or mental symptoms being directly related to the finer appreciation of the meaning of words. He said "language is so constructed so that the meaning of one pair of opposites cannot be understood until it is linked to another." How can right for example, be understood without its counterpart wrong, or comfort, unless contrasted to effort. Synonym-Antonym tests in psychology help science illustrate the catalectic nature of theoretical assumptions in cognitive and artificial intelligence. Low who was ever concerned with the more detrimental influences of contemporary society on mental health and illness, idiographically asserted "it is the curse of our modern life that stability of habits has become impossible. Everything around us is in a state of flux. We have drifted into a mode of life in which change under the guise of Progress has been turned into an ideal. We have adopted the pernicious philosophy that the 'new' is desirable and the 'old' obnoxious. Stable tastes and habits are impossible under a system of this kind which glorifies everything that has no other reason than they are no longer modern. Fellowship is dying under the impact of a system which idolizes novelty and modernity."

Evidence of duality in the psyche is observed in healthy children's behaviour. Their spontaneity in swift mood alterations between healthy stasis, is a phenomenon which happens irrespective of conditioning. In examining the history of psychology, Reisman (77), Chapter 1, concurs that this ebb and flow of ideas is based upon an accumulation of knowledge and a moderation and enrichment in both extremes. Self-synthesis or inner harmony is a central component in different schools of psychological thought each labelled according to the school referred to by Grant (7), i.e., self-actualization, cooperative unity, congruency, peak experience etc. Whichever arguments used in discussing values conflict in modern life, it seems we are firmly entrenched in a struggle for homeostasis. There is a need for better common-sense appreciation of the part language plays in the role of human behaviour. Value assumptions placed on such concepts as unlimited progress, the myth of modernization etc., are clearly misunderstood, in spite of the vast investment in psychological research in the last quarter century. Rychlak concluded (48), "it is in this capacity to know and cultivate the grounding reasons for our behaviour which most definitely established that we are more than simply organic machines."

6.4 CRISIS OF SKILLS

"What a piece of work is man, so noble in reason, how infinite in faculty." So said Shakespeare. Generally speaking, people need to work to Survive. In exploring the inherent psychological significance of work Professor Peter Kelvin (5) says, for the great majority of people work has always been a means to an end for making a living, not an end in itself. They could do without it very well, if only they had an income. This would sum up the attitudes of many people. The goals of factory workers are much like any other occupation. That is, to have a job if one is unemployed, preferably a sense of vocation, good wages, promotional prospects, and a regular holiday. Therefore to develop skills which allow freedom for creative expression. Finally in the performance of work, to be treated much like good average employees. On the other hand many healthy people have an intrinsic need for the satisfaction of work. Doing a job well is a source of spiritual merit. This is not a romanto-intellectual viewpoint, but decidedly realistic. Unfortunately in this age, few people can do the jobs they like, forced by economic necessity to do otherwise. Modern productive enterprises tend to need people with a divergence of work skills, from highly technical expertise on the one hand; to very standardised on the other. The prevailing business model dictates that the work environment much achieve high levels of organisation, competitiveness, efficiency and productivity. Increasingly our latest techniques impact worker security. Reviewing the human side of automated machines (32), the role of people is questioned in an environment ever more determined by computer systems outside their control. Modern means of production require a steady supply of new skills. These tend to become less labour-intensive in the long term, lowering the numbers of skilled people require. In studies on the employment impact of Robotics, recent evidence (31), point to the "skill-twist" in job creation and displacement. Conclusions show that the jobs eliminated are the semi-skilled and the unskilled: whereas the jobs created require significant technical background, with a high degree of skill and high levels of education.

6.5 WORK REORIENTATION

Ever widening social changes bring difficult problems of dislocation and disturbance of those facing job restructure with attended human costs (33). According to Rosenbrock; this often leads to a long period of unemployment for those affected. In a recent conference dealing with the specific problems of a life without work (51), it was highlighted that in the transition phase of re-skilling and re-organising, people can he faced with an unholy baggage of mainly negative characteristics. This often includes protracted periods of "illegitimate" occupation. Governments are lagging far behind in adequately facing up to these problems. Unemployment since the 1970's is rising significantly in western societies, in tandem with the effect of "New Technology." In the EEC now there are 15/16 million unemployed in contrast with a situation of full employment ten years ago. In Ireland the rate of unemployment has grown from 7% in 1980 to 19% in 1987. The Irish White Paper on manpower policy (28), stated this has come about as a result of changing patterns of demand in domestic and international markets and the introduction of new technology. Broadly speaking, manual employment opportunities have decreased mainly in agricultural and low-skilled jobs while there has been a major increase in office and professional employment both in services and industry. In 1987, an Irish government committee report on new technology and small businesses (60), concluded - regarding the effects of new technology on employment, "if the first Industrial Revolution related to the efficient organisation of labour in the context of the assembly line production, the second Industrial Revolution, means the progressive replacement of labour by Advanced Manufacturing Technology on the factory floor." This report also highlighted, that, although new automation technologies have resulted in many new jobs, the net effect on our industrial employment is firmly downwards, with automated production due to the newer techniques being the major reason.

6.6 DEVIATION OF EMPHASIS

It is now apparent that government economic philosophy has moved from employment to wealth expansion. For example, the Irish White Paper on Industrial Policy, in 1984 outlined a change in emphasis from being a provider of jobs to being a provider of wealth. It is clear that the way forward to providing jobs needed for the future whatever the technology labour saving impact, is investment in the transfer of technical solutions, to generate the wealth needed to maintain the highest levels of employment. The technological changes taking place internationally are considered irreversible. Given that underlying trends now are away from industry and agriculture as a major provider of jobs, most of the emphasis is on services. Although there is good evidence to show that in older generations of computers, staff were usually re-deployed, and frequently increased in number, as a result of computers, this is clearly not the case with computer automation. The emergence of sophisticated software technologies has enabled users to exploit the advantages of information technology environments, which deliver measurable increases in productivity and profits. Such corporate and multi- company gains are manifold including extremely low cost entry and reduced life cycle costs. The speed at which automation systems can be designed and installed further the possibilities for adaptability, dependability, and dynamism for effective integration of multiple applications within a business. Such value criteria entwining speed and efficiency, make it imperative for firms to keep abreast of the latest developments. Great emphasis is placed on the values of specialized mental skills which the young have immediate access to as part of their education. Those without these skills such as older workers, particularly the long term unemployed, are becoming obsolete on a widening curve, and the mean age is reducing.

6.7 CONFLICTING VALUES SHIFT

The modern business ethic largely conditioned by the nature of unrelenting and increasing competition is shifting customary values and pressures of work. Jerome K. Jerome said "it is impossible to enjoy idling thoroughly unless one has plenty of work to do." The openings for stable employment and life long occupation are under threat. Traditionally the purpose of work was more to perfect ourselves than to change the world in which we live. In the chain of human civilization, this call to work was connected closely to the individual and group values of the immediate family and the whole human family. The American dream emphasizes that every family deserves the opportunity to earn an income, own a home, educate their children, and afford medical care. The family was considered the core institution, and psychologically, a society without family or social frames of reference encourages escapism in individuals, and primarily in young people.

The emphasis would seem to have shifted. On the one hand we value the removal of effort through the process of modern machine technique. On the other hand we have legions of exploited workers who give far more to their nations efforts than they receive in return, as the obedient servants of a state industrial complex (12). Then in business, great efforts are required by company managers who find it extremely harrowing to negotiate the opportunities and dangers of a fast moving financial world and commercial markets needing continuous insight. The successful piloting of business in a complex industrial driven economy is now a major task, dictated by the export outlook. As we move closer to an internationally regulated global market, great sympathy is apparently required both for beleaguered workers and business people alike.

Reflecting on the modern philosophy of work, society may have reached a point where with increasing affluence, material wants become exaggerated. By what criteria do we seek security in an age where we are exploding from a narrow either/or society with limited choices, into an open free-wheeling, multiple-option society (20). With mass production, the consumer, products and price assume qualities of cardinal value. It is a universal principle that workers have both the right to work and choose their occupation (65). This implies taking the maximum advantage of new opportunities in techniques, which enhance interaction between people on the job, and the mass of tools we use. These give rise to the various forms of limitless wealth and collectivism. Using robots to overcome dangerous and dirty tasks may be desirable, but we must begin a questioning processes along the lines of: at what phase will pursuing ever more stimulating, creative and comfortable work become undesirable for the greater good of all?

Will there be a stage beyond which ambitions based on certain forms of extremism begin to work against society? What we need is a balanced approach. Briefs suggests "we have not thought sufficiently about use to determine the contribution towards new use values" (38). In the face of job losses it seems new technical developments should be weighed against a test of rightness/ usefulness. Ryan (1), believes now that robotics and automation are here, they have a place in the overall scheme of work, and, if properly used, can free and empower us for the better exercise of craftmanship. But we must not lose sight of primary issues: concerning what is desirable and really necessary for human development, the virtue of industriousness etc. Preoccupation with intellectual and physical comforts clouds appreciation for the equal importance of both mental and physical effort. Perhaps if people begin to lower excessive expectations for job satisfaction and rewards, we may very well find as patients do, who imbibe the suggestion, that by lowering unreasonable expectations, we improve overall performance.

6.8 CRISIS OF WORK NEEDS

According to labour statistics published by the ILO in February 1987, about 1,500 million jobs must be created in the world between now and the year 2025. The world is in the midst of massive population increases having just passed the 5 billion mark. It took mankind up to the 19th century to reach the 1 billion level, slightly more than a century for the second billion, and less than half a century for the third. Since then, the billions have followed at intervals of less than 13 years. Six billion will come before the year 2000, but demographers expect the interval to widen after 8 billion is reached in 2022 and halt in about a century at around 10 billion. The ILO study estimates that to deal with this dynamic increase on the one hand, absorb an estimated 90 million unemployed, and provide more equitable conditions of work for about 300 million underemployed on the other, the world is faced with the formidable task of creating more than 1,900 million new jobs in the space of 40 years, an average of 47 million new jobs a year. The distribution of these increases will hardly affect the more developed regions of the highly industrialized countries, with less than 5% of the total increase in job requirements. The African continent has the most alarming problems. Just to keep up the same level of unemployment in the year 2000 as it is at present, 40,000 new jobs must be created every day between now and then.

Against this backdrop of statistics any thoughts or utopian dreams of a world liberated from work seems paltry or trivial. Mankind faces a universal challenge and call to action in meeting a future employment crisis of increasing disproportion. Every effort in future generations will be needed to find meaning in all forms of occupation, however menial, in gaining entry into the world of work. Those presently unemployed, poverty stricken, or ill-disposed serve to remind society of the often forgotten esteem for spiritual values, especially the precious patrimony in the less advanced countries that have not put paid employment at the centre of their existence. The psychiatrist, Professor Ivor Browne (51), reviewing alternative work strategies in a life without work: proposes the concept of "interconnection", believing any alternative strategy of work and living will have to emerge from such a co-operative base. He further stated "Life is work, with or without paid employment and the quality of life must be developed regardless of the nation's unemployment problems."

6.9 SOLEMNITY OF TOTAL VIEWPOINT

The less developed regions have in former times looked openly to the industrial countries to provide jobs, via the multinationals and Mega corporations. What effects unimation will have on these countries is not entirely clear. The sheer number of people raise doubts about further possibilities for exploitation. The uncertainties of the future bring many other latent and intermittent crisis to the fore; for example, deforestation, over-cultivation, exploitation of natural resources, energy shortages, nuclear energy, raw material shortages, the control of change, protectionism, the ecological imbalance, the greenhouse effect, and so on. These must be viewed in perspective. The promise of the alternate technologies is fading and therefore new automation techniques will become ever more on trial. Political and business planning must be far sighted taking rightful account of the meaningfulness of human toil and occupation in whatever legitimate forms are preferenced. The true values of man's need to work are delicate mechanisms, partially bound up with the characteristics of mental-hygiene theory (6) and are interlinked with work in the subjective sense of man the subject of work, and the objective sense of techniques. We must keep correct proportions in different kinds of employment and attitudes towards physical and intellectual efforts.

Science teaches many important things but it does not teach us how to restrain ourselves from upsetting the balance of nature or self-unity. This requires the application of "will" and hindsight it seems, is the most exact science.

7. DETERMINANTS OF RECOVERY

7.1 DIFFERENTIAL DIAGNOSIS

Our societal patient is ill. Its malady in the limited context of this examination reveals pathognomic symphthoms in the form of various crises. There is evidence of significant contradictions in perceptions of technocratic humanization. These have heightened in recent years with the high contemporary disaster of unemployment for many. Increasing tensions are apparent in the work environment which is at least partially fostered by business automation, waves of technology change and the viscious cycle of competition in an ever more brutal market place. The promise of bold new industrial techniques are tempered unfortunately by monopolization of economic values, which threaten to less than recognize in people their full value. These have a tendency to force dependence on transnational economic, financial, and social mechanisms, through the increasingly automated functioning of business bureaucratic apparatus.

The predominant symptoms and values imposed through material idealism, has developed almost obsessive compulsive pathology, in our present society, crossing all boundaries. They can exaggerate the necessity of industrial economic growth and human progress. Work, contrary to its opportune effects can have a tendency when it is more scientific and efficient to develop a risk of dehumanization, for those who perform it, by making them its servants (80). Such can be the situation where automation places the means of production and decision-making process in the hands of the few. While there is undoubted development for some, there is much stagnation and regression for many.

The modern dilemma is clear : how can we alter attitudes if it is not too late and re-address more realistically the balance of human values avoiding the risk of losing an indispensable equipoise.

7.2 INVESTIGATION

The Brindtlana report (1987) by the world commission on environment and development, found in its worldwide study, deep public concern for the environment. It concluded that the challenge is to ensure that these new values are more adequately reflected in the principles and operations of political and economic structures. Our modern productive process has vastly improved living standards and the quality of life. But many of the products and automated technologies are raw material and energy intensive and entail a substantial amount of pollution. The consequent impact on the external environment is greater than ever before and limits the costs of success.The severity of resulting social inequity depends on public interest and awareness and the course of social policy. Given sufficiently enlightened, humane, and far sighted policies, the extent of problems can be mitigated. These include many things but in relation to automation must include transitional counselling, re-education, training, compensatory assistance, proper recognition for the tremendous insecurity associated with the restructuring of lives, legitimising the black economy etc. The alternatives to courageous advanced planning could be severer deterioration of labour relations, more alienation, and a breakdown of public morale. By promoting better long and short range planning for social expenditure, there will be clearer understanding of job displacement and job creation needs. Retraining of workers is pointless without available opportunities for employment, as people often have to migrate/emigrate in large numbers. Rosenbrock (33) investigating the long term survival of human skills in automation suggests we must be more consistent since manufacturing is continually changing. He says some line must be drawn up to which the advance of technology is acceptable and beyond which it is not.

7.3 CRISIS INTERVENTION

Much careful history taking is necessary for wiser understanding of new structured and material value-systems in the public arena, before a clearer helping treatment sequence is possible. Beneficial uses must be measured against relevance to human, social and health questions. The etiology of maladaptive technology change, must become better known. The notions of material. progress weighed realistically against necessity. Many studies will be necessary on how modern technology affects the experienced worker, the unemployed and so on. For example a research report (55), conducted by the psychosomatic unit of the Irish Foundation for Human Development concluded "the new technologies tend to be associated with reduced manpower requirements and thus when introduced by organizations for operational efficiency considerations, and the development of marketable services - need to be viewed in the context of wider social issues especially as these relate to the availability of work within the community as a whole." In the developmental stages of society, each crisis is in a sense a turning point, rather than a threat. If the patient undergoing crisis is amenable to corrective influences through skilled intervention, what must be the case for the contemporary universal disposition.

7.4 ASSESSMENT

It is well documented that forecasting and assessment is a hazardous business. Anticipating potential impacts is fraught with difficulties, especially for decentralized technology such as robotics. However in visualizing trends for the third millennium, we do have many choices in the kind of future we want. It may be an understatement to say that many difficulties lie ahead for civilization, in reversal of the values conflict. World markets are being reshaped by powerful new forces such as global marketing, the rise of the newly-industrialising countries, along with profound technology impacts. The quickening theories of technological interactions cause many shifts in paradigms, often long before their deeper significance becomes evident. The human values associated with our long established traditions and concepts of work are threatened by such events. It is probably reasonable to suggest that no real progress for humanity will be apparent until well into the future to be catalogued by coming generations, say 100 years or so. But how should the confusing transformation effecting our island planet be assessed. Most of the speed up in the techno-evolution seems to have taken place since World War II under the influence of ever present global military tensions. Science and technology forecasting (FAST etc.) is well established with many international forums taking place. It seems however that less attention is given to human issues than to management, organisation, and technology itself, in the philosophy and methodology of futurism. One approach might suggest these discoveries will have to be incorporated into a more prudent understanding of requirements for vocational, economic and industrious needs of ordinary people, in moving towards more humane purpose for the use of new techniques.

7.5 INFORMATION VERSUS LEADERSHIP

It is difficult to relate the serious question of values in a narrow technological sense, outside the much wider vista of conflicts in the social order. The goal of new age industrial policy making, rests on the pursuit of unlimited economic expansion where the free market and price competition is said to create incentive to effort and enterprise. Rising wealth brings rising expectations. Will society eventually become saturated in satisfying ever increasing social demands and material consumption. Endeavouring to equate ways of rationalising automation with the politics of our time, we inevitable seek better strategies for leadership, self-government and human choices. But, the real issues may be associated with economic power and the politics of streamlining social systems too quickly, without a cushion effect for the sake of using automation for better control. The over-emphasis on politics today may indicate how much we choose to be over governed, rather than governing.On the other hand if we are to continue to have such vigorous policy making for competition and trade policies, decision makers must give responsible recognition to the need for thorough assessment, of pathognomic post-marketing conditioning and media social impacts. There comes a time when brilliant macroeconomic solutions are no longer sufficient to meet insatiable demands. Continuous craving for improvements may no longer be in peoples best interest.

It seems clear that the emergence of sophisticated automation technologies is having considerable effect on human self-leadership, as we strive for more benevolent bureaucracies. The spread of technical knowledge and know-how is contributing to social confusion in the shifting currents of a rushing existence. Lasch, Low, Gross, Fromm and many others refer to the crisis of the "self" spanning a whole spectrum of symptoms from self-isolation to self-absorption. For according to Victor Frankl (84) p.24, "technology has deprived us of the need to use our survival skills. The feeling of meaninglessness, the existential vacuum is increasing and spreading to the extent that in truth it may be called a mass neurosis. Today unlike in former times, man is no longer told by traditions and traditional values what he should do, therefore, he is forever more thrown back on his own requirements for personal responsibility". These values based on pragmatic empirical wisdom gained over centuries, guiding conduct and human personality, are disappearing in the face of what Toffler (30) describes as rampant accelerating change overwhelming man's physical defences. By pointing to this most pressing need to halt runaway acceleration he highlights consciousness for the control of change, suggesting we must reach for imaginative use of change to channel change. As change is life itself, and time maintains a constant and slowly unchanging rhythm, excessive reform should not disturb man's core psycho-spiritual composure. Undesirable ratings of change which play on the frailties of human nature while denying its very existence, requires more leadership (not more information) and rests on character and moral fibre.

7.6 CHOOSING GOALS - USE/MISUSE/OVERUSE

Gorz (68) suggests the principle "to each according to his labour" has become obsolete and the socialisation of the productive process has already been completed. Automation therefore, takes us beyond capitalism and socialism. The central issue is what kind of "beyond" in a highly populated world. We sit on the critical threshold of a new journey, and warmly await the potential developments in neural computing and high-performance artificially intelligent machines based on the accumulated learning in biological experimentation. As Fuchs-Kittowski (39) points out "information science and technology is the instrumental force of these processes of change in the immersion of the new societal genesis". Looking to the youth; Mink (23) emphasises the need for certain conditions, to allow advancements, relationships and progressive attainment of long term goals to develop. Chief among these are the commitment to reasonable stable values, and the ability to anticipate and react productively to changing and often ambiguous conditions. In a World where change often for the sake of change has such a high preference, is it any wonder that economic values take precedence. The goals of obtaining sound central finance, letting free markets determine demand can cleverly disguise the resulting poor ecology in manpower and other policies. In this crisis of consumerism according to Lasch (83) p.26, modern technology has the same effect on culture that it has on production, where it serves to assert managerial control over labour. It concentrates economic and political control - and increasingly, cultural control as well - in a small elite of corporate planners, market analysts, and social engineers. Modern machine techniques can serve as effective instruments of social control. The demands of politicians and industrialists for united political and administrative WILL are of little use as long as they continue to promote labour-saving machinery without providing an adequate response to the social problems caused by these technologies.

7.7 THE MASTER VALUE

Mikail Gorbachev (52) in reply to Professor Maurice Maron, head of the Life Institute, agreed the paramount task of our age is proclaiming life, from the biological, philosophical and political standpoint, especially human life to be of the highest value. He further stated "modern science and technology offer the opportunity to improve, in every sense of the word, life on earth, and to create conditions for an overall development of every individual. But it is in the creations of man's minds and hands that jeopardize the very existence of the human race, a blatant contradiction". It is with this apparent dilemma in the investigation of nature and universal dependence that forces us to rethink values in the context of work. In our struggle for liberation we face the greater need for more purposeful activity. Work of any kind can be lifted up with an artistic or divine purpose, and machinery are the result of man's endeavour to create. For according to Hertzberg "man can only be happy by seeking to satisfy both his animal need to avoid pain, and his/her human need to grow psychologically".

To say we have a values conflict indicates we need a clearer recognition of the need for better human interior understanding, before we trust future productivity wholeheartedly to total dependence on technique. Thomas Edison once said "there is a need for regulation today which is a problem of balance and adjustment. Everything has a place under the sun in life - but we need checks and balances. The balance is one of two dynamos, between God's given ingenuity, which is running against the dynamo of God's given humanity. We must put these dynamos in balance as God intended." It seems this is something we need continuous reminding of. There is a danger of excess in society where the great instincts of business enterprise can cloud our reason. As the ancient Chinese discovered interpreting universal change (37). When militarism threatens, purse strings are loosened, so scientific and social changes proceed by leaps and bounds. Thus it may be fairly said that the speed of progress is closely proportionate to the degree of danger. The sober fact is that approximately \$650 billion dollars in 1983 was spent on military weapons and \$14 trillion dollars between 1960-1983 according to the Brandt report.

Living in an age of technique we may boast to have conquered time and space and matter and nature (40), p.106. Well perhaps new technologies involve us in re-defining nature as we may like to perceive it, and in manipulating the process of life and mind by attempting to control their own creation. But if we desire to live in harmony with nature, more particularly human nature, we should be reminded of another thought from Low "control over our internal environment is infinitely more important than all the possible triumphs we can score over external environment", or reflect on ancient regard from another source (53), "for no man can fashion a God like to himself." Mankind faces an immense task in meeting the aspirations and legitimate needs of unborn generations. Given that recent discoveries in agriculture ad so forth: are geared directly towards the mechanization of industrious toil in the speed up of societal production, many uncertainties in this area are unavoidable. Policy makers confidently predicting the uplifting of employment potential, through the pursuit of expanding capital have yet to be totally vindicated. The concerned viewpoint does not argue against machine techniques per se, for this is unreasonable. Rather that they must be used in their due proportion and we must become more alert to the current trend of exaggerated expectations, for their transfer constitutes major problems impacting social international cohesion (88) p.76; and individual human endeavour. It takes many generations of effort to develop cultural habits which can be quickly discarded by simply viewing only economic or technical ends. The "good old days" are still here today but the emphasis is shifting, for according to T.P. O'Neill U.S. Speaker of the House, the new alien philosophy and morality is more self- seeking than group-seeking.

In finding ways to combat fallacies about human progress and the importance and dignity of physiological effort, man must deal both with the realities of the requirements for social production, and strike a balance for more equal distribution of wealth and occupations for the great mass of ordinary people. The master value is embedded in our duty to find solutions to the approaches of dialectical understanding and peaceful cooperation, with an ecology of nature, and the spiritual fountain of universal existence. For example, one of the great insights of modern science was to highlight the role of carbon dioxide in the atmosphere. There is a very delicate earth balance in the ecosystem between the atmosphere and the biosphere.

In a free deterministic society it is becoming more difficult to apportion responsibility for what we do or do not do about new machine techniques. We must not let confusing pseudo-intellectual viewpoints delude us from putting the subject of work and labour to the test of the common man. The importance of the need for useful : purposeful and industrious occupation (5) is a primary necessity and supreme value in the life of every adult human being, however it is defined. In a world increasingly starved of job recognition for every kind of work, job obsolescence is apparently made too easy, and we have evolved a style of introducing machines albeit without extensive social assessment.

7.8 PROGNOSIS

The future is above all hopeful but not without pitfalls. Tremendous cooperation for furthering humanism exists internationally. New communication techniques in spite of excesses and overemphasis, have opened many frontiers and broken down many barriers and prejudice with their penetrating effects. We now have very high quality help in learning and problem-solving. People are more willing than before to pass on knowledge and experience. Professional performance has risen to often extraordinary standards of efficiency, although people previously were of comparable degree in their own area. Still we must be careful of faulty beliefs in the confusion of the times. Material abundance brings its own complications which can distract from primary purpose. The emphasis is shifting from human effort i.e. : in work to machines, in health to pharmacology, and in spirituality to group expression. Perhaps we are more helped presently but also more outward dependent. In a positive sense Sheen (48) reminds us "our exterior world today is in desperate straits, but the inner world of man is far less hopeless. The world of politics and economics lags far behind the psychological development of men themselves. The world is far from God - but human hearts are not."

Whatever the implications for autonomous techniques, we humanly need to adapt to change with greater patience and prudence, beyond the capacity of machines. Low reminds us "the impatient patient refuses to wait patiently." Social re-organisation must be based on the highest order of different group values for the common good, rather than the concentrated interests of the few. We may want the ends but not the means. The Amish community of Pennsylvania serve as one of many inspiring examples to those who lack trust in the values of the old traditions and their survival in harmony with modern trends. The pre-requisites are the necessary WILL, character, determination, courage and resolve, only acquired through settled and consistent leadership. We live in a time where there exists many different conceptions of man, and there arises special tensions between opposing views, traditional and liberal, material and idealistic. etc.

In this planetary journey of human existence we face critical thresholds of communication and find that our trichotomy does not stand outside the historical or moral dimension. Reviewing the pilot conception versus behaviouristic approaches, Stefflre (78) neatly sums up our difficulty - "not surprisingly, none of the theories have been able to unravel one of mankind's oldest, most snarled Gordian knots - free will versus determinism. They explain behaviour in robot terms, while they hope for future adventures in piloting." The patient undoubtedly needs scientific methods of controlled study with its objectivity. However reductionism has a tendency to enforce artificial rigidity and non judgmental attitudes with important consequences for human habits both good and bad. Only we can decide by acts of WILL in what proportion and what limitations we need for our structures and ourselves, and this requires the long drawn out cumbersome machinery of changing attitudes (Will training) on all sides. We need more trustworthy perceptions of balanced work between mental and physical effort. In the course of history we may find that society can still achieve satisfactory good average performances, with lesser degrees of sophistication, such as we have developed in the myriad of new tools and techniques. We may have reached the Moon, but not ourselves. According to Zimmer (98), technology at its best has improved the quality of life in specific situations, medicine, aircraft, etc., but has not done so in a broader context.

Perhaps academic and business people are correct in avoiding value judgements in the objective sense, although Nagel, Weizenbaum and others argue vividly against the intrinsic impossibility of securing value-free and unbiased conclusions. We must be deeply suspicious of any claims that history, morality, and human values are all irrelevant to science and economics with the consequences of such activity. This paper in raising some issues does not aim to discredit any opposing system of ideas, merely to assert an argument the author believes does not get aired sufficiently, and is rightly conscious of Oscar Wilde, who once remarked "moralists are often the biggest hypocrites". We face the growing threat of machine regulated instrumentality and must have at least the courage to make mistakes reaching basic dialogue in mutual concern for the struggles, fulfillment and fellowship of all working people. one must be concerned as Lasch points out in his critique of the modernization process, how these assumptions obviously preclude any public discussion of values at all. Should such a reversal of the conflict materialize, recovery may be at hand, and it not easy to be duped accordingly.

Low puts it firmly: "*Man and human nature have become an anachronism, a relic of that unspeakable imperfect 'horse and buggy age' which to the modern mind is the epitome of clumsiness and ineptitude. In spite of the 'marvellous' advance of technique, man is still in a deplorable state of imperfection. It is he who has failed to measure up to the matchless efficiency of the machine.*"

On a final more idealistic note, perhaps we need a new equilibrium of attitudes, based less on such praise of and reliance on the artificial, but more attuned to and respectful of skilled performance, appreciative of the value of knowledge acquired through the effort and dignity of the human muscle. As could be stated - to live more in harmony with the pace of 'time' itself. Each to their own way.

BIBLIOGRAPHY
1.   Ryan, John Julian, 1972 : The Humanization of Man, Newman Press, NEW York.
2.   Ericson, Richard F., 1969: The Impact of Cybernetic Information Technology on Management Vale Systems, Society for General Systems Research, Lisner Hall 2023 G. St., N.W. Washington.
3.   Mannheim Karl, 1943 : Diagnosis of Our Time, Kegan Paul, Trench, Trubner & Co., London.
4.   Brunwell, J.R.M., 1945 : This Changing World, Readers Union, George Routledge & Sons, 38 William IV Street, London.
5.   Schaff Adam, Fredrichs. Gunter, 1982 : Microelectronics and Society for Better or Worse, Pergamon Press, ISBN - 0-08-028955-Y.
6.   Herzberg Frederick, 1966: Work and the Nature of Man, Thomas Y. Crowell Company, New York, ISBN - 0-690-00371-4.
7.   Mukergee Rodakanal, 1964: The Dimensions of Values - A unified Theory, George Allen & Unwin Ltd.
8.   Inlow Gail M. : 1972 : Values in Transition, A Handbook, John Wiley & Son.
9.   Rokeach Milton, 1973 : The Nature Of Human values, The Free press, New York.
10. Graham A. C.; 1961 : The Problem of Value, Hutchinson University Library, London.
11. Rasmussen, Leif Bloch, 1985: Consequences of Information Technologies, The Design of Inquiring Systems and Culture, Informations Systems Research, Copenhagen School of Economics & Business Administration - Paper.
12. Wolf Marvin, J., 1983 : The Japanese Conspiracy, New English Library, ISBN 0-450-05866.
13. McGuigan Kevin, 1986: ROBOTS - The Pioneering Users, Technology Ireland magazine, January edition.
14. Gotlieb C.C., & Borodin A., 1973: Social Issues in Computing, Chapter 13 Values, Technology and Computers, Academic Press, New York.
15. Share, Bernard, 1987 : Men of Mettle, Aer Lingus "Cara" magazine, feature article.
16. Inglis Tom, 1987: An Ethic of Global Responsibility, The Role of Religion in Post-Industrial Society, Department of Social Science, University College, Dublin. Paper presented to the Sociological Association of Ireland.
17. Weizenbaum Joseph, 1976: Computer Power & Human Reason, W. H. Freeman & Co., San Francisco.
18. Fromm Erich, 1942 : The Fear of Freedom, Chapter V, Mechanisms of Escape Automation Conformity, ARK Paperbacks, London.
19. George F. H., 1971 : Cybernetics, Hodder & Stoughton, 47 Bedford Square, London.
20. Naisbitt John, 1982 : Megatrends, Macdonald & Co., London.
21. Urban G. R. : 1972 : Can we survive our Future, Bodley Head; London.
22. Bertleson P. Imbert M., 1986: Report on the state of Cognitive Science in Europe, presented to programme FAST of the Commission of the European Communities, XII-84-86.
23. Sipe, A.W. R., & Rowe, C.J., 1984 : Psychiatry, Ministry and Pastoral Counselling, The Liturgical Press, Collegeville, Minnesota, 56321.
24. Low, Abraham A. M. D., 1950 : Selections from Dr. Low's Work, Recovery Inc., 802 N. Dearborn Street, Chicago, Illinois, 60610.
25. Fianna Fail, 1987 : The Programme for National Recovery, 13 Upper Mount Street, Dublin, 2.
26. Godet N., Ruyssen 0., 1981 : The Old World and the New Technologies, Commission of the European Communities, The European Perspectives Service.
27. Robertson James, 1983 : The Sane Alternatives - A Choice of Futures, Gibbons Barford Press, Wolverhampton, U. K. ISBN - 0-9505962-1-3.
28. 1986: White Paper on Manpower Policy, Government publications Office, Molesworth Street, Dublin 2.
29. Lawrence John, 1975 : Take Hold of Change, SPCK Publishers, Marylebone Road, London.
30. Toffler A., 1970 : Future Shock, Pan Books, London.
31. Lupton T., 1986: Human Factors, International Trends in Manufacturing Technology, IFS (publications) Ltd., Bedford, ISBN 0-948507-22-5.
32. Wall D., Clegg C. W., Kemp N. J., 1987 : The Human Side of Advanced Manufacturing Technology, John Wiley & Sons Ltd., ISBN 0-471-90867-3.
33. Rhodes E., Weld D., Implementing New Technologies, Choice, Decision, and Change in Manufacturing, Basil Blackwell Ltd. : Oxford : ISBN 0-631-14379-3.
34. Nof Shimon Y., 1985: Handbook of Industrial Robots, John Wiley & Sons, New York.
35. Ayers R. U., Miller S. M., 1983: ROBOTICS Applications and Social Implications, Ballinger Publishing Company, Cambridge, Massachusetts, ISBN 0-88410-891-0.
36. Forrester Tom, 1985: The Information Technology Revolution, Basil Blackwell Ltd., Oxford, U. H., ISBN 0-631-13422-7, Pbk.
37. Blofeld J., 1965 : I CHING, The Book of Change, E. P. Dulton, New York, ISBN 0-525-47212-6.
38. Bjorn-Anderson Niels, 1980 : The Human Side of Information Processing, ISBN 0-444-85415-0.

39. Sackman Harold, 1986: Comparative Worldwide National Computer Policies, North-Holland, Amsterdam.
40. Low Abraham A., M. D., 1950: Mental Health through Will Training, Christopher Publishing House, West Hanover, Massachusetts.
41. Roseingrave, 1986: Europe and the New Technologies, Economic and Social Committee, Brussels, ESC-86-004-EN.
42. Singer Peter, 1980 : Marx, Oxford University Press, ISBN 0-19-287510-8.
43. 1984: Laborem Exercens, Catholic Truth Society, London, ISBN 0-85183-0.
44. Nierhaus, 1986: Europe and the New Technologies, Research, Industry, Social: Economic and Social Consultative Assembly, ESC-86-004-EN.
45. 1984: Europe and New Technologies, conference report, European Communities, Economic and Social Committee, ESC-84-016-EN.
46. Sheen Fulton J., 1949: Way to Happiness, Garden City Books, New York.
47. Letovsky Stanley, 1987 : Artificial Intelligence and the Human Mind : An International, Interdisciplinary Symposium, Conference Report, Roy Arbraham Targhese, Box 59249, Dallas, Texas, 75229.
48. Rychlak Joseph F., 1979 : Discovering Free-Will and personal Responsibility, Oxford University Press Inc., ISBN 0-19-502580-6.
49. Reinecke Ian, 1983 : Electronic Illusions, Penguin Books, ISBN 0-14-00-7103-2.
50. Shallis Michael, 1985 : The Silicon Idol, Oxford University Press, ISBN 0-19-286032-1.
51. Whelan Brian, 1986: Life Without Work - proceedings of conference, Mental Health Association of Ireland : 2 Herbert Avenue, Merrion Road, Dublin, 4.
52. Gorbachev Mikhail, 1987 : For a Nuclear Free world, Novosti press Agency, Publishing House, Moscow, 080201-100.
53. Bible: Book Of wisdom, 15:16.
54. 1972: IS the Work Ethic Going out of Style? Time Magazine, October 30.
55. 1987: Research Report on Impact of New Technology on Experienced Workers Within the Telecommunications Service (Physical & Psychological Stress). Garden Hill, ENB 41A, 1 James Street, Dublin 8.
56. Sizer R., Berleur J., Laufer R., 1985: Can Information Technology result in Benevolent Bureaucracy, North-Holland, ISBN 0-444-87873-4.
57. Miller James, 1976: The Nature of Living Systems, Behavioural Science, Volume 21, President, University of Louisville.
58. Gaines Brown R., Shaw Mildred L. G., 1984: The Art of computer Conversation, a new medium for communication, Prentice/Hall Int., ISBN 0-13-047332-4.
59. Evans Chris, 1979 : The Mighty Micro, Victor Gallancz Ltd., ISBN 0-575-02708-8.
60. 1987 : Seventh Report of the Joint Committee on Small Business. New Technology & Small Business, P. L. 4694 Ireland : Government Publications office, Molesworth Street,
61. Dullforce W., 1987 : Financial Times, Tuesday, 19th May.
62. Engels Frederick, 1934: Dialectics of Nature, Progress Publishers, Moscow.
63. 1987 : Biological Diversity - A Challenge to Science, The Economy and Society. Conference programme and abstracts, FAST programme, National Board for Science and Technology, Dublin.
64. Rau, Neil & Nargaret, 1971 : My Dear Ones - A Biography of Abraham Low, Recovery Inc., Chicago, ISBN 0-13-608470-3.
65. Eppstein John, 1952: Code of International Ethics, Newman Press. Sands & Co., 15 King Street, Covent Garden, London WC2.
66. Low Abraham, A., M. D., 1943 : Peace Versus Power in the Family, Christopher publishing House, Boston, Ref. 67-20567.
67. Cooney Sean, 1985 : Work For All, Glenbar, Kilmacanogue, Co. Dublin, Ireland.
68. Gorz Andre, 1985 : Paths to Paradise, on the Liberation from Work, Pluto Press, London, ISBN 0-86104-762-1.
69. Cornforth Maurice, 1953 : Materialism and the Dialectical Method, International Publishers, 381 Fourth Avenue, N.Y. 16.
70. Miller M. W., 1987 : Securities Industry debates role of Computer in Market Collapse, Wall Street Journal, December 15 edition.
71. Kroll Paul, 1987 : 1988 Economy, Good Times and Bad : feature article, The Plain Truth : P. 0. Box 111, Borehamwood Herts., U. K.
72. Waterman R. H., 1287 : Strategy in a more Volatile World, Fortune Magazine, P. 0. Box 30604, Tampa, Florida, U. S. A. December edition.
73. Super Donald, Bohn Martin, 1971 : Occupational Psychology, Tavistock Publications, 11 New Fetter Lane, London EC4.

74. Adams Brian, 1985 : Sales cybernetics, Melvin Powers, Wilshire Book Company, 12015 Sherman Road, California, 91605.
75. Gross Martin, L., 1978: The Psychological Society, Touchstone, Simon & Schuster, Rockefeller Centre, 1230 Avenue of the Americas, N. Y. 10020.
76. Grant Peter H., 1978 : Holistic Therapy, The Citadel Press, Secancus, New Jersey, ISBN 0-8065-0633-4.
77. Walker Eugene, 1981 : Clinical Practice of Psychology, Pergamon Press, Maxwell House, Fairview Park, N. Y. 10523.
78. Buford Stefflre, 1965 : Theories of Counselling, McGraw-Hill Inc. T 64-25004, 1160970.
79. Bradley Gunilla, 1983 : Computers and their Psychological Impact, RAM Report No. 11, Swedish Work Environment Fund, ISBN 0349-2915.
80. 1967 : The Great Social Problem, Fostering the Development of Peoples Populorum Progressio, Catholic Truth Society, London.
81. 1982 : Young Europeans. An Explanatory Study of 15-24 year olds in European countries, Commission of the European Community - 200 Rue de la Loi, 1049 Brussels.
82. Smiles Samuel, 1859 : SELF-HELP, Sidgwick & Jackson, London.
83. Lasch Christopher, 1984: The Minimal Self Psychic Survival in Troubled Times, Pan Books, Cavage Place, London. ISBN 0330-289977.
84. Frankl Victor E., 19979 : The Unheard Cry for Meaning, Hodder & Stoughton Ltd., 47 Bedford Square, London. ISBN 0340-24153-5.
85. Egan Gerard, 1986: The Skilled Helper, Brooks/Core publishing Company, Monterey, California. ISBN 0-534-05904.
86. Potter David, 1981 : Society and the Social Sciences, Routledge & Keegan Paul Ltd., 11 New Fetter Lane, London EC4 P 4EE. ISBN 0-7100-0943-7.
87. Carkhuff Robert R., 1969 : Helping and Human Relations, Holt Rinehart & Winston, Inc., N. Y. ISBN 0-F-081214-3.
88. John Paul II, 1987 : Sollicitudo Rei Socialis : Encyclical Letter, Liberia Editrice Vaticana, Vatican City.
89. Cavanagh John R., 1963 : Fundamental Pastoral Counselling - Technic and Psychology, The Mercier Press, Cork, Ireland.
90. Hennicot-Schoepges Mrs., 1985 : Privacy of Sound, Council of Europe Report of the committee on Culture & Education, BP 431 R6 : F-67006, Strasbourg Cedex.
91. Kroll Paul, 1988 : Man & Religion, Clothing Naked Greed, Dressing the Economy with Laws and Values, The Plain Truth, P. 0. Box 111, Borehamwood : Herts., England.
92. Ammer C., & Sidley N. T., 1982 : The Common Sense Guide to Mental Health Care, The Lewis Publishing Co., Fassendon Road, Brattleboro, Vermont, 05301. ISBN 0-86616-020-5.
93. Nemeck F. K., Coombs M. T., 1987 : The Spiritual Journey, Michael Glazier, Wilmington, Delaware, U. S. A. ISBN 3-89453-546-3.
94. Mitchell G. Duncan, 1970 : A New Dictionary of Sociology, Routledge & Keegan Paul, 39 Store Street, London. ISBN 0-7100-0327-7.
95. Lindberg D. A. B., Reichertz P. L., 1981 : Computers and Mathematical Models in Medicine, Springer-Verlag, N. Y. ISBN 0-387-10278-7.
96. ITS-ASIS, 1982: Information and the transformation Of society - Conference papers, North Holland.
97. Minirth Frank B., M. D., 1973 : Christian Psychiatry, Fleming H. Revell Co., Old Toppan, New Jersey. ISBN 0-8007-0842-3.
98. Van Rijn Felix, 1987 : Social Implications of Home Interactive Telematics conference papers. Ruysdaelkade I.0. 225.
99. Bodily Samuel E., 1985 : Modern Decision Making, McGraw-Hill Book Co., Singapore. ISBN 0-06-766152-9.
100. Ince Darrel; 1988: AI and Neural Computing - Article, March edition, Computing Magazine, British Computer Society.
101. Grewlich K. W., Pedersen F. H., 1984: Power & Participation in an Information Society, FAST, Published by Commission of the European Communities, EVR 8548 EW. ISBN 92-825-4064-2.
102. Minsky Marvin, 1987 The Society of Mind, Heinemann Ltd., 10 Upper Grosvenor Street, London Wl X 9PA. ISBN 0-434-467588.

Part 5
THE INFLUENCE OF TECHNOLOGY
ON ORGANIZATIONS, SOCIETY
AND THE INDIVIDUAL

The Social Implications of Robotics and Advanced
Industrial Automation / D. Millin and B.H. Raab (Editors)
Elsevier Science Publishers B.V. (North-Holland)
© IFIP, 1989

HUMAN RESOURCES INNOVATIVE ENVIRONMENT - A SYSTEM PERSPECTIVE

Ilan Meshoulam

Faculty of Engineering and Industrial Relations
Haifa Institute of Technology
Haifa, Israel

Intel Electronics Ltd.
Jerusalem, Israel

"Like motherhood and apple pie, innovation is something
everybody favors. What most people don't know is that
you can actually plan and organize for it. No system
ever created an innovation. People make innovations. So,
we have to create an environment in which people will be
stimulated to innovate."
                    (Fred Bucy, President. Texas Instruments)

Introduction - The Changing Environment

During the past two decades an increasing number of
organizations, especially in the USA, have had growing concern for
maintaining and assuring that growing momentum is given to
innovation. They realize that they must be innovative in order to
cope with the rapidly changing forces of their external
environment. Organizations face new constraints as a result of
growing competition in the world market, unfamiliar context of
changing values and demographics of its labor force, new and
rapidly changing technological developments, central government and
local government involvement and changing legislation.
Organizations are under growing pressure to look for new ways to
respond to those rapidly changing elements of their environment.
There is no doubt that since the sixties organizations have been
going through a higher rate of changes, causing a major
transformation of their basic makeup, their structure, people,
processes and more.

Even the most conservative industries, like the financial
industries - banks and insurance companies, have been forced to
react to the changing environment and "wake up" from the many years
of protective and established ways of doing business.
Deregulation, broader financial services, large retail business
entrance into the financial world, like Sears, the penetration of
brokerage firms into the insurance business, all forced major
changes and encourage the industry to innovate - to come up with
new ideas to survive. The industry was not only forced to react to
and align itself with the new demands and the environmental
changes, but also to maintain a constant watch and alertness to the
direction and the continuous trend of those new directions. They
were forced to find new innovative ways to stay flexible, so they
can react quickly to the new changes. "We are currently in the
midst of a great upheaval in our financial systems, and nobody
knows what the upcome will be" (Edwards, 1981). Moving along the
continuum from the traditional, conservative industries to the
newest fast growth industries, like high-technology, the changing

rate staggers.   This new environmental change requires
organizations to come up very quickly with new solutions to the
newly created problems.   Environments that require a totally
different approach to the new demands of the workforce, new ways to
structure the organization, to allow for absorbing the new changing
technologies, new processes to accommodate for the fast needed
reaction, flexibility and leadership to manage the transition.

New strategies are required to motivate people in the
organization to come up with new ideas, to bring forth creative
responses and to take advantage of the new opportunities created by
the changing environment while minimizing risk.   This article will
focus on the organization's need to create such an environment and
the conditions which enable people to be innovative.   Yet we have
to recognize that parallel to the obvious changes in the
environment as the Technology, Government Regulations and Economic
changes, more subtle and very profound human changes take place.
People's work values have changed, influenced heavily by social
movements, demographic changes and new conditions.   Some examples
are the changes in education level.   The workforce has become more
educated.   In 1980 25% are college graduates, compared with 5% in
the 40's (Kanter, 1983).   With increasing education people require
more meaningful jobs.   They want to express themselves, use their
knowledge and be involved in their workplace direction.   They
expect more freedom, more autonomy and flexibility in their work
environment.   This trend has put heavy demands on the organization
to search for new ways and means to provide the appropriate tools
to accommodate those changes.   New issues of career development and
opportunities, dual careers had to be dealt with.   Supervision and
control have to get a different meaning (Edwards, 1979). The change
in the level of education brought with it, therefore, a major shift
in the way organizations manage their people and their new demands
from the organization.   It requires new innovative ways to look at
jobs, culture and structure.   Education is only one of those
changes.

Another example would be the change in the workforce mix.
The number of women entering the workforce has increased
dramatically.   More than 50% of women are now in the workforce.
The population of two-wage earning families has increased to over
50%.   This demographic change has brought revolutionary changes in
the work environment.   More income to spend by the family and less
dependency on the workplace.   This resulted in more freedom of
choice and mobility.   The organization is faced by new issues such
as discrimination, women upper mobility, dual careers (especially
in relocation), daycare, part-time work, appreciation of individual
differentiation and more.   These issues require new solutions, new
tools and new strategies.   They require from the organization to
adjust its processes, tasks and compensation, and in many cases,
the organization has to work on adjusting its culture.

Innovation is influenced by the degree of turbulence in
the environment.   A turbulent environment provides a stimulus
towards innovation (Mohr, 1969).   The more turbulent the
environment, the more pressure there is on the organization to fit
itself to those changing and pressing forces, to be able to react
quickly to its environment. The organization must be flexible, be
open and be predictive of those changes.   The organization will be
able to create an environment of innovation through encouraging
new technologies, new products, new and different skills, accepting
people differentiation.   The organization should create a culture
that encourages the exploration of new opportunities and ideas to
fit itself to the changing environment.

Innovation, the process of implementing new ideas into the organization and its relevant environment (Kanter, 1983; Evan and Black, 1967; Knight, 1967), is an essential ingredient in the recipe of survival.

Holistic Approach to Strategic Innovation

Much research and conceptualization has been done on how the environment affects the organization system, and explaining the relations between the degree of environmental influence, and the process of adaptation to the environmental changes and their effect of the organization system (Terreberry, 1966; Lawrence and Lorsch, 1967; Stinctumbe, 1965). Focussing on the impact of the environment on the organization system, much of this research leaves the impression that the organization only reacts to its environment and that managers react to the broad spectrum of environmental changes. However this relatively deterministic approach is rejected (Child, 1972; Perrow, 1977). "Organizations can exercise a good deal of strategic choice in realizing, perceiving and manipulating the environment" (Gupta, 1980).

Organizations can and should take a proactive role to innovation by applying strategy as the mediating variable that will guide and define the relationship between the organization and its environment. The organization must find ways and means to fully utilize its various internal components to take advantage of the environmental opportunities and minimize the impact of the imposed environmental threats (Cook, 1975; Meshoulam, 1984). The organizations, therefore, have the responsibility to search and apply the appropriate strategies to assure a fit between its changing external environment and its business needs, and an internal fit between the organization's system various components to themselves.

If not done, the organization, as a living system, will react to the imbalance created and look for ways to balance itself. The system, therefore, will take a reactive approach to deal with its changing needs. This reactive process is painful, costly and takes a heavy toll on the participants, and, in many cases, is not directed necessarily to the desired objectives. It prohibits planning, design and application of a proactive strategy of innovation. We believe that the new conditions created by those environmental changes requires a new conceptual frame of mind; a new innovative way to encourage and fertilize new ideas, and new managerial concepts to the organization's life.

Innovation strategies are, therefore, not a set of organization programs, or periodical major adjustments. They require an appropriate change in management philosophy. "The term innovation makes most people think first about technology" (Kanter, 1983), about new products, robots, the use of computer devices, microprocessors etc. Very rarely do people term new ideas about the new work requirements, such as high performance systems, quality circles, involvement programs, work redesign, compensation strategies, as innovations.

Our strategic innovation approach is a holistic concept. Not innovation in technology alone, nor sole rights on innovation in R&D departments, but total system innovation. How do we create a system that fits all of its internal components to allow for innovation? How does the organization set its total system to create such an environment that will cultivate, encourage, enable and open the opportunities for innovation. Answering those questions is the focus of this paper.

The System

    For our analysis purpose we have adopted Galbraith's (1982)
basic model of the organization system, adjusting it to add a major
component - the organization culture.

Organization System Model

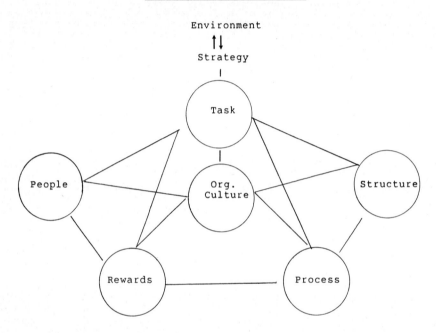

    Under the model the organization consists of five major
subsystems that as a whole must be fit to the organization's
environment to achieve organization effectiveness, and should
internally fit each other to achieve organization efficiency.

    A change in one of the subsystems will carry changes in the
others to achieve a balance between the subsystems.   The
organization will seek to balance itself whether we direct it
(proactive) or not (reactive). It is, therefore, important, when
applying innovation strategies, to look at the total system and
make sure that the organization treats all of its subsystems, i.e.
applying the holistic approach.   Bringing into the organization
"innovative people" without adjusting their tasks to allow for such
innovation, the reward system to encourage them in that direction,
the structure to accommodate for innovation and the process for
smooth flow of innovation, will result in an imbalance and hardship
in achieving the organization's goals.

    All these subsystems must be activated in the context of the
organization culture - that element of the organization which gives
it its uniqueness and holds it together.   It is this total body of
top management values and ideology that is shared by members of an
organization, and sustained over time (Meshoulam, 1984).

Introducing reward programs, processes, new structure changes and innovative people must be done in the context of the organization culture in order that it be accepted and internalized by the organization's participants.

The organization will shift its focus and emphasis on the subsystem as it move along the maturity continuum through growth in complexity and size. As an industry matures, and both its products and technology become more stable, innovation is most likely to shift and center around issues of productivity increases, improving performance, cost saving and maintaining the growth momentum. Our discussion emphasizes social and organizational innovation, highlighting only some of the key strategies that the more innovative organizations apply to maintain that entrepreneurial spirit that produces innovation.

Organization Culture

"Every excellent company we studied is clear on what it stands for and takes the process of value shaping seriously" (Peters and Waterman, 1982).

Creating an innovative environment is not an easy task. Providing the appropriate structure, people, processes and rewards, will not assure a high innovative organization. It is essential that innovation will be a clear top management value (Cummings, 1965). There is a clear relationship between the values of top management, as accepted by the organization members, and innovation (Hage and Dewer, 1973; Mohr, 1969).

The organization value system, its culture, is not easily shaped. For the organization members to accept and internalize any set of values will require a long, obstinate and tedious process. It requires from top management, first, articulation of their values, second, determination and consistency in presenting and managing their values, and third, most important, a behavioral role model. Values must be rooted and recognized by the organization members as a direction for their behavior. Trust in the seriousness of management takes time to develop and has to be slowly supported by positive experience. To install innovation as a value, top management needs to constantly guard their own and the organization's behavior and actions. What takes years to build can be very easily destroyed. For example, to support the innovative value, Digital Equipment Co. introduced into its culture a high tolerance for errors. Making mistakes became acceptable; making mistakes became an integral part of the decision making process; and people were encouraged "to do" things and tolerate errors. It will take only very few cases of intolerance to such errors, to destroy this notion, and a very long time to rebuild it. Yet without a supportive culture for innovation, it will be impossible to encourage it. The deeper the organization believes in the importance of innovation, the more we will find supportive values in the culture to that end. The belief in openness, freedom, free expression, egalitarianism are all supportive values to innovation and all are ways an organization treats its subsystems.

There are many programs that will be needed to support innovation, especially in Human Resources. As Human Resources proactive management in any organization articulates its true culture (Lawler, 1984; Fomburn et al, 1984). Organizations will attempt to fit their Human Resources programs to that culture. Examples are programs such as the Open Door policy to encourage openness (adopted by DEC, IBM, Intel and others), or open and free expression versus structural appraisal methodologies (adopted by Intel and DEC).

The People Subsystem

Gerstein and Reisman (1983) state that employee's characteristics are determined by the strategy or general thrust being pursued by the organization. Therefore, organizations that set their strategy and strive to be innovative, will require different characteristics from their employees, than those pursued by non entrepreneur organizations (Schuler et al, 1985). On one hand the innovative strategy aligns all the organization components to attract and retain people with different characteristics. The various organization policies, its structure and value system, as well as its reward systems, are geared to attract those people that seek challenge of managing and working in high levels of uncertainty. The organization structure is built in such a way that allows cross discipline that can utilize, reward and appreciate their professional knowledge and provide a free hand for expression.
On the other hand, because of the existent set of values of the organization, the people that select the candidates to join the organization, look for people with similar characteristics to their own and the fitness to the culture. Experience tells them what characteristics are needed to survive and succeed in the system. No doubt these characteristics vary from one organization to another, based on the organization culture and its position on the innovation continuum.   Schuler et al (1985) defines the continuum as a highly creative – innovative behavior, on one hand, to a highly repetitive – predictable behavior, on the other. Yet there seems to be a consensus about a set of basic characteristics that apply to the innovative organization (Kanter, 1985; Drucker, 1985; Pinchut, 1984; Miller, 1983). Some of these characteristics are: risk taking, long term focus, cooperation, assuming responsibility, concern for results, creativity, flexibility and being able to live with ambiguity. These people, whenever they are in an organization, must be supported by the internal environment to maintain their innovative spirit. We would expect organizations with a turbulent environment, to cultivate and support the innovative employees, not only in the technical core, but in all of the organization aspects. Innovators should be hired to R&D as well as to Marketing and Human Resources Manufacturing. The organization at large needs to support the innovative spirit. Even those that are not the innovative type need to be indoctrinated to the importance of innovation for the organization's survival. They need to be part of, and carry through the organization, the innovative values, and serve as carriers of the organization culture.

The Reward Subsystem

The reward system's effectiveness is determined by how it fits the rest of the organization systems (Lawler, 1981). The reward system must fit the organizational culture, its processes, its structure and people changing needs. Innovative organizations require the introduction of new approaches to compensation, that will respond to the new demands of the workforce. Keeping the organization open to attract the desired people requires the application of different strategies to employee rewards. Encouraging risk taking behavior, or flexibility, for example, require that the reward tools will support those directions. Lawler (1981) and Kanter (1986) raised a few interesting issues that emerge from the needs to respond to the changing demands of the workforce. Those solutions depend, of course, on the degree of fit of the organization and its various other components.

The innovative organization's direction of autonomy,
freedom, reduction of organization's segmentation, participation,
would imply different strategies and response to compensation as
suggested by the above writers. The following are some examples:
1. Pay for the job versus pay for skills. Traditional
compensations, using typical job evaluation, measure the amount of
responsibility an individual has (number of subordinates, level of
subordinates, available resources etc.) rather than the skills the
individual brings or develops. Pay for the job emphasized the
hierarchial aspect of the organization. Employees are encouraged
to seek managerial jobs, acquire more employees and desire more
resources, even when they are not needed, since they are rewarded
in direct relation to the "size" of the job. One of the
alternatives is to base compensations on skills and abilities that
the individual has. Highly skilled individuals will get higher
rewards. This approach encourages the individual to acquire more
skills without necessary seeking hierarchial promotions or building
empires. Though this approach is relatively new, and does not fit
all levels of the organization, but mainly the professional
employees, it has been successfully tried in companies such as
Proctor and Gamble, TRW and General Foods. This type of
compensation seems to fit better the notion of an innovative
environment. It will, of course, by our systematic holistic
approach, require the adjustment of the other subsystems such as
processes and structure, and would "challenge conventional notions
of hierarchy" (Kanter, 1986).
2. Pay for performance. Pay for performance, again, supports the
notion of hierarchial status. The organization is divided to
different compensation plan scales (management, manufacturing,
engineering etc.), based on organizational levels. It strongly
reflects the power of supervisors over their subordinates, and does
not allow the individual high performer to be paid more than his
boss. The subordinate, who contributes to the organization by his
innovation, is limited by his hierarchial position.
Lawler (1981) suggests to consider a pay scale based on performance
units, which would each have its own performance based pay plan, or
creating multiple pay plans based on vertical and horizontal slices
of the organization. Though not easy to design, the idea is rooted
in the attempt to fit the commonly used tools to the new demands,
and away from hierarchial based compensation, which stifles
innovation, to a more egalitarian system.
3. Combined bonus and salary approach. A third example is the
combined salary/bonus approach. The majority of US merit plans use
salary increases rather than bonuses (Lawler, 1981). The
performers bonus approach creates an opportunity to reward for
excellence and innovation. The bonuses are free from hierarchial
boundaries. Some companies, especially in the High Tech industry,
have been increasingly using financial incentives such as bonuses,
stock options, as a reward independent of job level. It allows
them to reward directly and timely for innovation. AT&T introduced
performance based bonus. The bonus is given to top performers at
all levels, while good performance receive the regular salary
increases. This method opens a new way for creating internal joint
ventures, sharing new startups with internal entrepreneurs,
innovators, based on salary (the organization's contribution) and
contingent bonus (the individual risk and contribution). It
provides the organization with a way to retain its innovators and
reward them.
These three examples and other new methodologies (gain
sharing – group sharing on gains from contributions to the
organization's performance; group bonus – reward on the group
effort) are new ways and tools that organizations seek to respond
to the new needs.

The Process Subsystem

By the process subsystem we refer to the policies and procedures that handle decision and work flow in the organization. "Systematic innovation is strengthened to the extent that the bureaucracy is minimized" (Schuler, 1986). Low formalization in the organization permits openness in the system, which is so necessary to maintaining innovation (Shepard, 1967). It is interesting to note that many organizations which maintain innovative cultures face a dilemma: a strong anti-formalization spirit mingled with the need for control. This dilemma grows parallel to the organization's growth. One can find large organizations debating issues such as whether to introduce written manuals and procedures, which are necessary for control and direction, yet are negatively related to an innovative spirit, or whether to implement formal appraisal systems versus the informal that exist, use organization titles excessively or minimize them, etc. In the large innovative organizations, that strive to stabilize and control as a mean to protect themselves from the turbulent environment, we can observe a constant struggle and tension between those two needs. An anecdote can be found in a statement which appeared in a large corporation as an introduction to their procedures manual: "These procedures serve only as a guidance to management". Guidance, not a rule.

Kanter (1985) identifies few requirements for innovation that "make clear why entrepreneurship challenges the legitimacy of the classic command and control hierarchy".
1. Innovation process is built on uncertainty and doesn't involve planning, forecasting, clear timetables nor exact controllable budgets. Therefore, processes need to be flexible and results built on long term return.
2. The innovation process is "knowledge intensive". Human creativity is its core. Sometimes this knowledge cannot be transferred to others. It requires a high degree of commitment and stability among the participants and the staff teams. Therefore, it requires attention to the group to bring people together and create the atmosphere of partnership.
3. The innovation process is not contained solely in one unit. It requires a cross boundary and interdependent fertilization. Other units will need, in many cases, to adjust their behavior to accommodate innovation. It will require to change the process to encourage innovation and support it, and take in account the needs of the other groups.

The system will require, therefore, policies that rely on mutual relationships, low focus on status, respect for differences. The process should reduce its dependency on the hierarchial command chain. Yet a balance is required to maintain the built-in conflict between the need for uniformity, formalization and control, and the innovative management. It is a conflict between efficiency and innovation which requires the organization to be flexible. It might be necessary, sometimes, to resolve that conflict by putting in place a structure that separates the innovative functions from the daily activities.

The Structure Subsystem

There are a few structural variables that are conducive to maintaining and developing innovation within the organization. We will discuss here three of them: segmentation, differentiation, and decentralization.

Segmentation, a term so clearly described by Kanter (1983), refers to that structure and process that isolates the organization. A segmented structure is "a large number of compartments walled off from one another - department from department, level above from level below, field from headquarters, labor from management or men from women." Segmentation prevents the needed flow of information between units, the exchange of new ideas across the organization boundaries. The Japanese, for example, have built into their organizations many mechanisms to assure such information flow, such as the morning employee meeting and the daily management meetings to exchange ideas. Many western organizations have used the segmentation process in their approach to innovation, by isolating the R&D department. Some organizations have used the concept of segmentation as a mechanism for solving a problems. The problem is identified, isolated in the unit and expected to be resolved by "experts". That way the organization's structure has little incentive for cross fertilization. In order to encourage innovation, the organization must stimulate people to "reach for power despite the box on the organization chart they occupy" (Kanter, 1983).

Differentiation. Galbraith (1982), Kazanjian and Drazin (1986) argue that innovation, in cases of creating new knowledge, will require a different structure, a separate organization unit that will focus on generating new knowledge. Yet generating ideas and formulating of existing information, needs integration with other units, and the structure should be adjusted accordingly. We, therefore, can find in the innovative organizations, a structure that run two or more organizations side by side. It can take various structural shapes from a task force to a complete and separate structure. These approaches, of course, are not free from complications and pull-push relationships. The differentiation approach will decrease the likelihood that new ideas will be transferred back to the operating level. It is important that the innovative organization will learn to appreciate, support and encourage differentiation within the organization - not a cultural one, but among individuals. Accepting new and "crazy" ideas, avoiding stereotyping, will smooth new ideas floating and acceptance in the organization. Coupled with non segmentation, reduction in emphasis on hierarchy and status symbols, will help cultivate innovation.

Decentralization. A high degree of participation in organizations contributes to innovation (Hage and Aiken, 1970; Shepard, 1967). Decentralization will provide for more unit and individual autonomy and freer information flow. Peters and Waterman (1982, p.105) have noted the relationship of decentralization to culture. "In the very same institutions in which culture is so dominated, the highest level of true autonomy will occur". Decentralized organizations increase participation, involvement, which contributes to implementing innovations. A characteristic of the innovation organization structure is an inclination towards local autonomous units that can act on issues immediately and without higher level approval, maintaining high collaboration and interdependency. Examples will be the matrix form of organization which forces the use of multiple source information and interaction of various disciplines in the organization.

The Task Subsystem

Organizations go through stages of development as they grow and develop in reaction to the changing environment (Baird and Meshoulam, 1988). Organizations' tasks will change accordingly, and will provide endless room for innovation in all departments of the organization. An important aspect to watch that the motion on the continuum of maturity does not cause stagnation. Tasks should be designed to help people get involved beyond their narrow jobs. Jobs should be broadly defined, allowing for some ambiguity. The notion of segmentation, or fear of it, should be carefully considered in the allocation of tasks. Traditionally we are locked into thinking on segmentated tasks. We need to look for different ways of structuring the organization's tasks in order to achieve our objectives of innovation. Kanter (1983) states that the appropriate job assignment, broad in scope, stimulates 51% of innovative accomplishments. The Task Subsystem is a dynamic process, like the rest of the subsystems, that needs constant review, alignment and adjustment to fit itself to the changing organization.

Summary

The importance of innovation to the success, and sometimes survival of the organization, in our rapidly changing environment will vary according to the level of turbulence in that environment. More and more traditional organizations face a fast changing environment that they did not experience in the past, such as the finance and automobile industries. Transforming into an innovative mode of operation will take its time, as the organization faces a total change in all of its subsystems and will have to realign accordingly. It becomes very apparent that adjusting, for example, the structure will not do without adjusting to fit it to people needs, their tasks, the organization processes and, in return, the reward system. All of that, of course, in the context of the appropriate culture that will glue it all together. Built-in into the system perspective, presented here, is the need to achieve both internal and external fit, achieving effectiveness and efficiency at the same time.

Much attention is given, both in literature and in the practical world, to technological innovation, yet we believe it is a narrow way to look at the innovative organization. Organizations compete not only on their innovative technology, but also on what they offer as a total: their ability to react, to service, to retain and develop their people, to attract people etc. In each of these areas we must be innovative if we want to survive and lead. In order to keep an innovative, integrated, involved workforce, organizations should balance their efforts in building a system that does it through fitting its culture, structure, processes and to find new ways to reward their people.

BIBLIOGRAPHY

Aiken M. and R. Alford, "Community Standards and Innovation: The
Case of Urban Renewal", American Sociological Review, Vol. 35
(1970), p.650-655.

Baird L. and I. Meshoulam, "Managing Two Fits of Strategic Human
Resources Management", Academy of Management Review, 1988, Vol. 13,
No. 1, p.116-128.

Bucy F., "Fred Bucy of TI Speaks on Managing Innovation",
Electronic Design 19, September 13 1979, p.108-111.

Cook W.E., "Product Life Cycle as Marketing Model", The Journal of
Business, October 1967, Vol. 40, No. 4, p.375-387.

Cummings L., "Organizational Climate for Creativity", Academy of
Management Journal, Vol. 8, 1965, p.220-227.

Drucker P.F., "Innovation and Entrepreneurship", Harper & Row, New
York, 1985.

Edwards F.R., "contested Terrain: The Transforation of the
Workplace in the Twentieth Century", Basic Books, New York, 1979.

Edwards F.R., "The Turmoil in the Financial Market", American
Bankers, October 1 1981, p.3-5.

Evan W.A. and G. Black, "Innovation in Business Organizations: Some
Factors Associated with Success or Failure of Staff Proposals", The
Journal of Business, Vol. 40 (1967), p.519-530.

Fomburn C., Tichy N.M and Devanna M.A., "Strategic Human Resources
Management", John Wiley & Sons, New York, 1984.

Galbraith, J.R., "Designing the Innovating Organization",
Organization Dynamics, Winter 1982, p.5-25.

Gerstein M. and Reisman H., "Strategic Selection: Managing
Executives to Business Conditions", Sloan Management Review, Winter
1983, p.33-49.

Hage J. and Aiken M., "Social Change in Complex Organizations",
Random House, New York, 1970.

Hage J. and R. Dewar, "Elite Values Versus Organizational Structure
in Predicting Innovation"., Administrative Science Quarterly, Vol.
18, 1973, p.279-290.

Kanter R.M., "Supporting Innovation and Venture Development in
Established Companies", Journal of Business Venturing, Winter 1985,
p.47-60

Kanter R.M., "The Change Masters", Simon & Schuster, New York,
1983.

Kanter R.M., "The New Workforce Meets the Changing Workplace:
Strains, Dilemmas, and Contradictions in Attempts to Implement
Participative and Entrepreneurial Management", Human Resources
Management, Winter 1986, Vol. 25, p.515-537.

Kanter R.M., "Work in a New America", Journal of the American
Academy of Arts and Sciences, 107, Winter 1978, p.47-78.

Kazanjian R.K. and Drazin R., "Implementing Manufacturing Innovation: Critical Choices of Structure and Staffing Role", Human Resources Management, 1986, 25, p.385-404.

Knight M.F., "A Descriptive Model of the Intra Firm Innovation Process", The Journal of Business, Vol. 40, 1967, p.478-496.

Lawler E.E., "Pay and Organization Development", Addison-Wesley, Reading, MA, 1981.

Lawrence P.R. and J.W. Lorsh, "Organization and Environment", Division of Research, Graduate School of Business Administration, Harvard University, 1967.

Meshoulam I., "A Development Model for Strategic Human Resources Management", unpublished Doctoral Dissertation, Boston University, Boston, 1984.

Miller D., "The Correlates of Entrepreneurship in Three Types of Firms", Management Science, July 1983, p.770-790.

Mohr L.B., "Determinants of Innovation in Organizations", The American Political Science Review, 1969, p.111-126.

Peters T.J. and R.H. Waterman, "In Search of Excellence", Harper & Row Publishers, New York, 1982.

Pinchut G., "Entrepreneurship: How to Tap Corporate Creative Energies", The Mainstream, 1984.

Schuler R.S., "Fostering and Facilitating Entrepreneurship in organizations: Implications for Organization Structure and Human Resources Management Practices", Human Resources Management, Winter 1986.

Schuler R.S., MacMillan I.C. and Mortocchio J.J., "Key Strategic Questions for Human Resources Management", in W.D. Guth (ed) Handbook of Business Strategy, 1985/1986 yearbook, Warren, Gorham and Lamont, Boston, 1985.

Shepard H.R., "Innovation Resisting and Innovation Producing Organization", The Journal of Business, Vol 40, 1967, p.470-477.

Stinctumbe A., "Social Structure and Organization", In J.G. March (ed) Handbook of Organization, Rand McNally, Chicago 1965, p.142-193.

Terreberry S., "The Evaluation of the Organization Environment", Administrative Science Quarterly, March 1966, Vol. 12, No. 4, p.590-613.

The Social Implications of Robotics and Advanced
Industrial Automation / D. Millin and B.H. Raab (Editors)
Elsevier Science Publishers B.V. (North-Holland)
© IFIP, 1989

ON ROBOTS & SPOUSES: SOCIAL INTERACTION IN AND OUT
THE ROBOTIZED WORKPLACE

Oded Shenkar and Judith Richter

Faculty of Management
Tel Aviv University
Tel Aviv 69978 Israel

One of the major problems in introducing large scale robotization is
the reduction in the level and intensity of social interaction and
its adversary behavioral correlates. The origin and implications of
this problem are discussed in the present study. Coping strategies
for affected employees within and outside the work realm are
proposed.

INTRODUCTION

The number of industrial robots continues to increase at a fast pace. Despite
the revisions of initially over-optimistic forecasts, industrial robots
continue to make strides. With an increasingly sophisticated hardware and
software and the development of visual and tactile capabilities, the range of
robotic applications broadens and robots are introduced to a larger varieties
of industries.

Robots are only one component in a rapidly expanding industrial revolution
leading towards Flexible Manufacturing Systems and the factory of the future.
Thus, robotic applications must be observed within the context of their total
production environment. We suggest, however, that robots are unique and
important enough to merit a separate discussion, at least as far as human
problems are concerned.

A large number of human problems has been identified in studies researching
the impact of robotic technology on employees. Among them are: layoffs and
displacement (Engelberger, 1980; Ayres & Miller, 1981, 1982, 1983), loss of
competence and power (Knod, Wall, Daniels, Shane & Wernimont), loss of
extrinsic and intrinsic rewards (Shenkar, in press), blocked promotion (Zippo,
1980), and the dissatisfaction associated with machine-paced work (Salvendy,
1983). One central problem, however, has been little discussed: The decline
in the level and intensity of human communication and interaction and the
related loss of relationships, isolation, and stress. This problem is the
focus of the present paper.

ROBOTS AND HUMANS: SIMILARITIES AND ANALOGIES

Some observers argue against the uniqueness of robotic technology. They
suggest that robots are just another form of automated machinery and would not
trigger a different response than that encountered in previous rounds of
automation (Foulkes & Hirsch, 1984); or, that robots are initially perceived
as different, and thus tend to stir up reactions, but with familiarity they
are seen as being essentially similar to other machinery (Fey, 1986). Our own

experience suggests, however, that this may not always be the case, and for a good reason: robotics are different from other forms of flexible automation in several important aspects.

One of the unique feature of industrial robots is that they perform tasks in a manner analogous to the human operation. Combined with the flexibility of robot operation and with the mythical ethos of robot replacing man, this human analogy sets robots apart from other new technologies. It is therefore not surprising that unions, like the United Auto Workers in the U.S., have formulated policy guidelines in regard to robotic technology; and that management has sometimes prohibited the use of the word "robot" altogether, referring to it instead as "automated machinery". Indeed, the most popular definition of robot in the US, that of the Robot Institute of America, reflects an effort to preclude any human analogy:

> a reprogrammable multifunctional manipulator designed to move material, parts, tools or specialized devices, through variable programmed motions for the performance of a variety of tasks.

In contrast, many other definitions make direct reference to the similarity between humans and robots. For instance:

> A device that performs functions ordinarily ascribed to human beings, or operates with what appears to be almost human intelligence.
>
> (Computer Aided Manufacturing International (CAM-I), our emphasis)

The human analogy is particularly apparent in the Japanese definitions of a robot:

> An all purpose machine equipped with a memory device and a terminal device (for holding things), capable of rotation and replacing human labor by automatic performance of movements.
>
> (The Electric Machinery Law of Japan, our emphasis)

> A mechanical system which has flexible motion functions analogous to the motion functions of living organisms or combines such motion functions with intelligent functions, and which acts in response to the human will. In this context, intelligent functions mean the ability to perform at least one of the following: judgement, recognition, adaptation or learning.
>
> (Japanese Industrial Standard JIS B0134-1979, our emphasis)

The debate on the similarity and disimilarity between robots and humans involves several fears. The primary fear stemming from the human-robot analogy is that of displacement. And while some observers dismiss as "science fiction" any relationship between robotics and displacement, most systematic forecasts suggest otherwise; Ayres & Miller (1981, 1982) predict that current robots could replace a million employees in the US manufacturing industries, while sensor-based robots could replace 3 of the 8 million current operators by the year 2000. By 2025, almost all operators in manufacturing -- about 8% of the US Workforce -- will be replaced.

Hunt & Hunt (1983) predict that robots will eliminate between 100000 and 200000 US jobs by 1990, 25% of which will be in the car industry. 6% to 11% of all operatives and laborers in that industry will be displaced by 1990. Autowelders (15% to 20% displacement) and auto painters (22% to 37%) will be particularly affected.

The reason why displacement fears have not escalated is twofold: First, in many cases displacement was handled through normal attrition. Second, large scale robotizations which carry the greatest displacement potential are more likely in new or reorganized plants and thus do not encounter employee or union opposition.

Another fear associated with robotization is that it would create a mechanical, isolated work environment. Some of the early predictions foresaw a massive installment of robots with entire assembly lines operating without humans. And while many installations have been modest, with only one or two robots installed at any one time (Fey, 1986), the cumulative impact of such limited installations can be significant. Advances in robot technology and in inter-robot and inter-computer communications are likely to render more and more positions amenable to robotization, thus increasing the likelihood of isolation.

Furthermore, at least in the car industry, some assembly lines have indeed been robotized to a significant extent. To quote one example, a General Motors plant in Pontiac, Michigan, is reported to have 2100 employees vis-a-vis 143 robots. This ratio (15 humans to 1 robot) is still a far cry from the ratio predicted by Susnjara (1982), i.e. one human per six robots; however, the distribution of both humans and robots is uneven across the plant, implying that some employees may already work in a relatively isolated, mechanical environment.

To an extent, this problem is not new: It has been frequently suggested that automation would reduce the amount of social interdependence on the job because human interaction will become neither necessary nor feasible (e.g. Grummon & Petrock, 1984). And while other technological changes severed social relations but created new relationships (Beer, 1980), this has not happened in robotics. Argote, Goodman, & Schkade (1983) found that workers reported less opportunity to interact with others following the introduction of robots, a change they attributed to the increased mental demands of robot operation. Similar observations were made by Howard (1982) and by Anderson & Gartner (1985). The main problems identified were those of operator's isolation and those of lack of communication between the different employee groups involved with robotics, namely operators, programmers, and maintenance personnel.

A mechanical, isolated environment carries further implications: A lack of professional feedback from peers due to the lack of interpersonal contact; a lack of motivating feedback from the group of workers or from the supervisor (Walsh and Ashford, 1985); a lack of exposure and experience in management skills which may limit the scope of jobs available in the future and affect career paths and opportunities; and a weak sense of belonging which implies a declining commitment to the organization.

COPING STRATEGIES

The socio-technical approach assumes that technical and human systems can be "synchronized" in order to incorporate their requirements in the organizational setting. The assumption is that such accommodation of the human and the technical systems is feasible, and that gains in productivity will compensate for the initial investment.

That assumption cannot always be made in the case of robotization. First, the productivity gains from robotics and flexible automation will frequently outweight those of increased human productivity. Second, large installations with isolated work stations may preclude team building and other group processes which are often the socio-technical solution to the problem of employee motivation (Coch & French, 1948; Lewin, 1951).

As a result, conventional socio-technical remedies may be less feasible for robotization in general and in the case of social interaction in particular. It is thus necessary to supplement the traditional coping methods with other, less conventional solutions, which also take into account the multitude of life spheres of employees and which rely on the interface between work and non-work domains of life. Thus, the coping strategies that we shall offer here will be of two types: (1) coping strategies centered on the workplace and (2) coping strategies centered on home.

1 Coping Strategies at Work

One solution is to re-emphasize group activities which are not focused around the work unit: Worker participation and continuous dissemination of information, workplace meetings for supervisors and workers (Argote et al., 1983); and a shift from individual to a system-wide reward system may all contribute to the reaffirmation of group processes in the robotized organization.

From a career point of view, it is important to plan periods of work at less isolated environments where human interaction is frequent. This is imperative for the training of workers in the interpersonal skills required for management jobs later in their career, as well as for the development of organizational identification and esprit de corps.

Another means to increase the level of social interaction is for robot operators to take part in programming and maintenance, instead of assigning the various functions to different individuals. The person who has these various tasks assigned to him is more likely to have opportunities for social interaction with such people as the manufacturer's representatives, quality control engineers, clients, etc.

2 Coping Strategies at Home

Stress is the psychological or emotional response which reflects employees' perception of the characteristics of the job and work setting (Matteson and Ivanovich, 1982). Past research on the general topic of job stress has focused on the effects of stress-related responses on employees and employing organizations, ignoring the employee's total life environment. Recent studies which examine the effects of work-related stress suggest that employee's reactions to their jobs affect their family activities, too (Dubin, 1973 Jackson, Zedeck and Summers, 1985).

Work and non-work activities and concerns are separated by geographical and time boundaries. These two distinctly defined realms induce two different behavior modes, as indicated by Evans & Bartolome (1986) and Richter (1984). The interplay between the two realms evokes either compensation or spillover relationships. In the former, leisure activities compensate for frustration at work, and in the latter, feelings, attitudes and behavior created by and at work spill over into non-work life (Wilensky, 1960).

In the case of robot operators, this means that the home domain may be used to compensate for the deficiency incurred at work; or alternatively, negative effects of the isolation at work may be carried over to home, bringing about stress and alienation.

The problem with the compensation solution is that it could tip the delicate balance between these two central life domains. The employee may come home feeling he has been deprived of a meaningful social interaction and expecting other family members to devote their entire time and energy to his needs. Thus, while he/she will regard home as an instrument in solving his/her work problems (Payton-Miyazaki & Bradfield, 1976), other family members may feel that they are faced with unreasonable demands on their schedules.

The evidence, however, suggests a higher frequency of the spillover effect, leading to a relationship of conflict between professional and private life (Evans and Bartolome, 1986). Spillover may originate in three sources (a) competing time demands (b) strain aroused in one system spilling over to the other, and (c) specific behaviors required by one system being incompatible with the behavior requirements of the other but nonetheless spilling over (Greenhaus and Beutell, 1985).

Spillover leading to conflict may exist as pressures from the work and family domains are mutually incompatible in some respect and the participation in one of the domains is made more difficult by virtue of participation in the other (Richter & Hall, 1987; Greenhaus, 1987). The modalities of strain or behavior spillover may originate from specific contextual characteristics of the job and the work setting. It is our contention that the robotized work environment, which is characterized by isolation, lack of interpersonal communication and limited human interaction, is likely to lead to both strain and behavior spillover from the work to the home setting. The research on strain and behavior in the work setting and their spillover into the home setting provides interesting findings which are applicable to the robotized work context.

Burke, Weir and Du Wors (1980) in their work on strain found that different characteristics of the work environment, such as stress in communication and mental concentration required at work were related to work-family conflict. In addition, Jones and Butler (1980) and Brief, Schuler and Van Sell (1981) found that work and family strain-based conflict was negatively related to task challenges, and variety, and was positively related to task autonomy. Employees suffering from job burnout have been found to display more hostility at home and be more likely to withdraw from their families (Jackson and Maslach, 1982). In this context, the consensus that burnout is accelerated by lack of social support is noteworthy, since this lack is one of the major characteristics of the robotized work environment.

There is some empirical research that directly assesses the link between on-the-job behavior and interaction patterns in the family. Research on managerial behavior (Schein, 1973; Grieff and Munter, 1980) has suggested that managers feel caught between two imcompatible behavior/value systems: the emotional restrictedness presumably reinforced at work and the openness expected by family members. Similarly, Bartolome (1972) showed that when one gets used to masking feelings when at work, he/she may find it difficult to express feelings at home. Indirect evidence has also been provided by Kanter's (1977) observation that employees who experience "interaction fatigue" at work may withdraw from personal contact at home.

The mechanical and isolated work environment associated with robotization encompasses similar hazards. The non-interactional and isolated behavior which is characteristic of large scale robot installations is probably contradictory to the behavior expected in private life. Spillover and penetration of such behavior patterns into the home domain may be a source of tension to the person and his family, and is likely to lead to conflict between the two domains.

The family is recognized as an important source of potential support for workers who experience excessive stress and can help shield workers from the negative effects of their jobs (Haus and Wells, 1978; LaRocco, House and French, 1980). Management, for its part, should take into account the interdependence between the job and the family experience and seek to establish structural conditions at the work place which can be reciprocally supportive and beneficial to both systems of life.

One way the organization can improve the employee's ability to cope with the spillover effects of strain, would be to help strengthen the boundaries between home and work life. For this purpose the establishing of a "buffer zone" to differentiate between the two domains is suggested. In practice such a "buffer zone" is special time scheduled at the end of the working period in a place scheduled for this purpose, where employees may gather together socially. Institutionalizing such work arrangements may help employees in an isolated environment to unfreeze behavior patterns, and unwind from work strain so that work effects would not spillover to home life.

Creating a buffer zone may also provide a solution to another problem of the robotized environment — the lack of group support and cohesiveness, which has been identified as a common source of stress at work (Matteson and Ivanovich, 1982). Meeting in the buffer zone might not only help make up for the isolation experienced during the day but also support a sense of belonging and commitment of the employees to the organization.

CONCLUSION

The robotization of the workplace may require some innovative solutions which go beyond the traditional frontiers of the socio-technical framework. One of these innovative solutions may be to mobilize other life realms to compensate for deficiencies in the workplace. Such strategies, however, must be applied carefully so as to prevent to problems associated with such transfer of boundaries.

BIBLIOGRAPHY

Ayres, R.V.; Miller, S.M. The impact of robotics on the workforce and workplace, Carnegie-Mellon University, Dept. of Engineering and Public Policy, June 1981.

Ayres, R.V.; Miller, S.M. "Industrial robots on the line", Technology Review (May-June 1982), 35-46.

Ayres, R. V.; Miller, S. M. Robotics: applications and social implications, Cambridge, Mass.: Ballinger Pub. Com., 1983.

Bartolome, F. "Executives as human beings", Harvard Business Review, Nov.Dec. 1972.

Brief, A.P.; Schuler, R.S.; Van Sell, M. Managing Job Stress, Boston: Little Brown, 1981.

Burke, R.J.; Weir, T.; DuWors, R.E.; "Work demands on administrators and spouse well-being," Human Relations, 331, 1980, 253-278.

Coch, L.; French, J.R.P. "Overcoming resistance to change", Human Relations, 1, 1948, 512-533.

Dubin, R. "Work and non-work: Institutional perspectives." In N.D. Dunnette (Ed.), Work and Nonwork in the Year 2001. Monterey, CA: Brookes/Cole, 1973.

Engelberger, J.F. Robotics in Practice: management and application of industrial robots, Amacom, 1980.

Evans, P.A.L.; Bartolome, F. Professional lives vs. private lives – shifting patterns of managerial commitment, Organizational Dynamics, 7, Spring 1979, 2-29.

Evans, R.A.; Bartolome, F. "The dynamics of work-family relationships in managerial life", International Review of Applied Psychology, 35, 1986, 371-395.

Fey, C. "Working with robot: the real story", Training (March, 1986), 49-56.

Foulkes, F.K.; Hirsch, J.L. "People make robots work", Harvard Business Review, Jan.-Feb., 1984, 94-102.

Greenhaus, J.H. Career Management, Dryden Press, 1987.

Greenhaus, J.H.; Beutell, N.J. "Sources of conflict between work and family roles," Academy of Management Review, Vol. 10, No.1 76-88, 1985.

Grief, B.S.; Munter, P.K. Tradeoffs: Executive Family and Organizational Life, New York: New American Library, 1980.

House, J. S.; Wells, J.A. "Occupational stress, social supported health." In A. McCleans, G. Black, and M. Colligan (Eds.), Reducing Occupational Stress. Proceedings of a conference. 8-29, Washington, D.C.: U.S. Government Printing Office, 1978.

Hunt, T.L. "Robotics technology and employment." In T. Luton (Ed.), Human Factors in Manufacturing. IFS/North-Holland: Amsterdam, 1984, 9-16.

Hunt, H.A.; Hunt, T.L. Human resources implications of robotics, Michigan: W.E. Upjohn Institute of Employment Research, 1983.

Jackson, S.E.; Maslach, C. "After-affects of job related stress: Families as victims," Journal of Occupational Behavior, 3, 1982, 63-77.

Jackson, S.M.; Zedeck, S.; Summers, E. "Family life disruptions: Effects of job-induced structural and emotional interference", Academy of Management Journal, 28, 3, 1985, 574-586.

Jones, A.P.; Butler, M.C. "A role transition approach to the stresses of organizationally-induced family disruptions." Journal of Marriage and the Family, 42, 1980, 367-376.

Kanter, R.M. Work and Family in the United States. New York: Basic Books, 1977.

Kamali, J.; Moodie, C.L.; Salvendy, G. "A framework for integrated assembly systems: Humans, automation and robots", International Journal of Production Research, 20, 1982, 431-448.

Knod, E.M.; Wall, J.L.; Daniels, J.P.; Shane, H.M.; Wernimont, T.A. "Robotics: Challenges for the human resources manager", Business Horizons, 27(2), 1984, 38-46.

LaRocco, J.; House, J.S.; French, J.R. "Social support, occupational stress and health," Journal of Health and Social Behavior, 21, 1980, 202-218.

Lewin, K. Field theory in social science, New York: Harper, 1951.

Matteson, M.T.; Ivancevich, J.M. Managing Job Stress and Health, New York: The Free Press, 1982.

Nof, S.Y.; Knight, Z.L.; Salvendy, G. "Effective utilization of industrial robots - a job and skills analysis approach", Transactions of the American Institute of Industrial Engineering, 3, 1980, 216-225.

Payton-Miyazaki, M.; Bradfield, A.H. The good job and the good life: relation of characteristics of employment to general well-being. Social reporting, New York: Halstead, 1976.

Richter, J. The daily transitions between professional and private life, unpublished dissertation, Boston University, 1983.

Richter, J.; Hall, D.T. "Managing the work-home interplay in the organizational context," Paper presented at the Academy of Management Convention, New Orleans, Aug., 1987.

Salvendy, G. "Review and reappraisal of human aspects in planning robotic systems", Behavior and Information Technology, 2, 1983, 263-287.

Schein, V.E. "The relationship between sex role stereotypes and requisite managerial characteristics." Journal of Applied Psychology, 57, 1973, 95-100.

Shenkar, O.; Vitner, G. Robot teaching methods and operator job design, working paper, Faculty of Management, Tel-Aviv University, 1987. Press, 1982.

Vitner, G.; Shenkar, O. "Motivational implications of different robot types", International Journal of Operations and Productions Management, 5(2), 1985, 50-57.

Warner, M. "Human resources complications of new technology." Human Systems Management, Vol. 6, No. 4, 1986.

Wilenski, H.L. Work, careers, and social integration, International Social Science Journal, 12, 4 (1960), 543-560.

Zippo, M. "The robot in industry: friend or foe of worker", Personnel, Nov.-Dec., 1980, 51-52.

The Social Implications of Robotics and Advanced
Industrial Automation / D. Millin and B.H. Raab (Editors)
Elsevier Science Publishers B.V. (North-Holland)
© IFIP, 1989

"LAW AND COMPUTER" - SOME SOCIAL ASPECTS
==

Lior Horev, LL.M

Tel Aviv, Israel

Introduction

1. A. Throughout the 20th century, one of the symbols of the tremendous
      technological progress achieved, is the Computer. Nearly every
      field of mankind's activity is influenced by computers, although
      its uses are comparatively in the early stages of their
      possibilities. Computers are not in need of any praise, as their
      usefulness is beyond any discussion. However, the question arises:
      Are we aware of the other side of the phenomenon? The "other side"
      being the negative aspects resulting from the evergrowing use of
      the computer by human society. [1]

   B. This paper does not attempt to point out all the "negative"
      influences, but to shed some light on a few "social" aspects of the
      problem from the point of view of a counsellor-at-law.

   C. What is the reason for using the term "negative" in connection with
      an apparatus or device (computer) which was designed from its early
      beginning to help mankind? -

      The term "computer" is synonymous with "data-processing" - meaning:
      Information. The words "computer" and "information" are linked.

      Information, especially the kind relating to opponents, means and
      capabilities, has always served as a weapon, in military, as well
      as political or economic "battles". If that principle was valid in
      ancient times, it is certainly reinforced nowadays, when industrial
      and political espionage is common and information, as well as
      communication, is the life-blood of human society. In other words
      - having control of a source or means of information equals
      possession of "power". Power can be used either positively or
      negatively. Destructive power can be definitely negative, as is
      every unjustified use of any power. We are witnesses to the fact
      that even something which is good "by nature" might turn out to be
      wrong and evil - computers are no exception.

      If the starting point is that power can be destructive and absolute
      power is definitively destructive, we reach the conclusion that
      power must be controlled and limited to a certain extent.
      As technological progress cannot be stopped, so is the resulting
      power thereof. In such a situation, the practical question is:
      How to dominate, rule and control such a power (without damaging
      technological progress itself) in order to put it to positive use.
      At this point we seek the protection of the "Law", which is the
      correct system to protect accepted principles and ideas, to control
      and shield human society from chaos. All this can be achieved by
      law without damaging technological progress.

D. "Law" is not a just simple word, since it represents rules of
    behaviour and a mode of life. The linkage between social problems
    and law is quite clear, forming the basis for our opinions below.

E. Our purpose is to point out at least 3 aspects of the encounter
    between Law and the computers from the social point of view:
    1) Abuse of the computer:
        a) Aspect of "Private Individual Rights"
        b) Aspect of "Computer Crime" - temptation to commit such
           crimes.

    2) The Need of Survival (active self-defense by software creators
        which causes damage)

    3) Responsibility (typical of computerized services and devices).

Abuse of the Computer

2. Private Individual Rights

A. One of the advantages of using computers is the almost unlimited
    possibility of collecting, storing and using enormous amounts of
    information which can also be easily transmitted. Such informaiton
    may relate to individuals and their personal-confidential private
    condition, such as: health, mental or economical abililities,
    etc.

B. Parallel to the recognition by human society in "freedom of man"
    and the "value" of human beings as such', a concept of private
    secrecy and of the private individual's rights has been
    developed.[2] The meaning of such rights is, in a nutshell, the
    right of the individuum not to be disturbed by intruders and not to
    have exposed to the public his intimate weaknesses and his inner
    world. The term "right" must be understood as some kind of law
    which: -
    1) establishes or declares the existence of such a right;
    2) protects from violation of such a right.

C. "Protection" in the matter under discussion is based on a number of
    elements: -

    1) Prevention of any situation of "secret" data centers, which: -

        a) are uncontrolled by society;
        b) cannot be amended and/or updated by those who are the
           subjects of the data (even erroneous)

    2) Limitation of the use of such information and of transfer or
        exposure thereof.

    3) Protection of the data itself (and the instrument of its
        storage) from harm or destruction.

D. "Rights" and "lawful protection" mean, in the western world, an
    appropriate system of law. It being understood that the elements
    of protection must be implemented on various kinds of data centers.
    Unfortunately (at least in Israel) [3] the main target and "teeth"
    of any such protective law is actually turned against computerised
    data centers only, while other kinds of data centers (such as
    conventional files) are neglected. True, computerised data centers

might be much more dangerous than others, but our opinion, (based on the general public hysteria concerning the issue) is, that the hidden motive behind that phenomenon is people's "fear" of the computer. This fear is so deep and strong, that it over-shadows the positive and justified motives of the people who create this protective system of law. Such fear might lead to extreme measures of proteciton which might miss the main purpose of such law, plus some other "side effects", especially on those who operate computers. What is the clasification of such fear? :-

1) We have all read about workers' fear of the "machine". This fear, which accompanied the Industrial Revolution in its early stages, was, in general, the fear of the worker himself. The modern fear of the computer is no longer such a "private" fear, but of human society represented by its leaders.

2) Since modern democracy is based on representatives, and since these representatives are politicians always engaged in a battle of their own (in order to win the citizen's vote), these social leaders have developed some kind of a "private fear" of their own, relating to computerised data centers. Being so close to the "Seventh Power" (written and transmitted media), it is easier for those political leaders to provoke fear and to cause legislators to reach unexpected extremes, while "fighting" against automatic data centers.

E. As we have already mentioned, politicians and social leaders are not always molded of the same material, and have no one agreed opinion. They are usually looking for some "compromise" among themselves. In order to reach such compromise, they might be looking for someone (or some group) who cannot be identified with any political party, to be the "scape-goat" (mainly because such group is yet without any existing entity and its members are officially anonymous). In our "case", a natural solution to this problem are those who operate computers or are directly connected with them. In Israel it is now a fact that computer workers are those who bear (according to the new law and by-laws) the burden of protecting society from violating the private individual's rights. What is the "social" aspect of this fact? :-

1) Up to now, there was no existing social "group" known as "computer workers" (or similar). Since these workers are identified now (by certain laws) as "dangerous people", or as people who are responsible for a very dangerous device (the computer), they share a spcial kind of problem. These people ought to take defensive measures. In such a situation, I dare say, they are on their way to becoming a unique social group which has not been in existence up to now.

2) Members of this new social group are usually law-abiding and peaceful citizens. Suddenly, they have become the symbol of the negative power existing in computers. These people have become, all of a sudden, the "public enemy", being the target of the law which might turn against them instead of being enforced upon those who really run and manage the system. As a matter of fact, we must admit that instead of taking care of the perils of <u>using</u> computers as an <u>instrument</u> of power and as means of violation of individual rights, all means of protection have been turned against those who technically operate computes. As a final result, we must face the fact

that computer workers in Israel are now under the "pressure" of
the law, in spite of their being "innocent". Such pressure
might have unexpected and undesired results.

3. The Computer and the "Underworld"/Computer Crimes

A. It is a well-known fact that institutions who protect society,
    known as local or international police, use automatic data systems
    in their fight against crime and terror – no doubt that use is a
    blessed one. But we must remember that while talking about crime
    and the computer, two very important and influential social
    problems must be taken into consideration: –

    1) Crimes can be committed <u>against</u> computers;
    2) Crimes can be committed <u>through</u> computers (or while using
        them).

B. The computer is still a very "delicate" device: –

    1) As any other "tool", the computer has a tangible existnece
        which can be physically harmed. But being characterized as a
        very sophisticated and complex apparatus, it is very
        "sensitive" to such damage. Computers are also easily
        influenced by environmental conditions, such as electrical
        induction etc., which cannot be seen or felt. In such a
        situation, one can cause severe damage to any computerized data
        center without even "touching" the machine or being seen, and
        without approaching it. It is far from easy to find such cause
        of damage and to discover who is to blame.

    2) The use of modern computer communication on the one hand, and
        the enormous possibilities of "entering" and controlling
        computer systems even by remote contol on the other hand,
        increase the computer's vulnerability.

    3) A computer is not a device which "stands alone" or exists by
        itself. Computers have always a strong and immediate influence
        on the systems they serve: Industry, finance, administration,
        etc. By causing harm or damage to a computer, one can cause
        much more severe damage to those organizations depending on
        it.

C. Neither violence nor investment of money is essential for the
    purpose of causing such damage. Yet, at the same time, while
    having the "know-how" and possibilities of taking advantage of the
    above facts, one can gain much power and a lot of money without
    being discovered. There is a story of a bank clerk who "entered"
    the bank's software and ordered it to credit, every few days, a
    bank account under his control, with one cent out of every other
    bank account in the area. Needless to say, the man could have made
    a fortune without the crime having been discovered and without
    attacking any person or causing any severe damage to any person in
    particular.

D. It can be imagined that even such crimes, or at least some part of
    it, can be discovered sooner or later. But what happens even if
    the villain is caught and brought to court?[4] Most of the crimial
    codes (or at least those which are based on the Anglo-Saxon system
    of law like the Israeli code) relate to tangible elements and are
    based on "facts" which can be seen or felt, ignoring the intangible

element which is so important when talking about computers. The offence of larceny for example, [5] requires the subject matter of the theft to be a tangible one, and to be taken and carried away from its legal owner for ever — so, how can we talk about software or data "theft" (a term which is so common in the industry). There is no doubt, since the law is so conservative and since computer progress is so fast, that the law has difficulites in catching up with it. There is no legal system or law which has no loopholes [6] (Lacune) through which civil and criminal offences can be committed without any clear possibility of punishment. Moreover, knowing the people who are computer experts and being aware of the fact that these people generally belong to the more sophisticated and intelligent population in any society, we can be sure that they certainly know about the "Lacune" (if not in detail, at least in general), and can use them for their own benefit.

E. From the above descriptions, we can learn that: —

1) Using computers for bad purposes of any kind can be done in a very "elegant" way and also can be the fulfillment of the old and well-known desire of committing the "perfect crime", meaning: easiest, cleanest and most profitable, which is undiscoverable and unpunishable.

2) The above results can lead to a very important conclusion: People might be easily tempted to commit computer crimes, as "temptation" has existed since Adam and Eve as the source of all sins. Computers can be used for crime not only for direct economic benefit or for reasons of causing bodily injuries to some perons (for which most of the "old" traditional crimes are committed), but also for some more sophisticated and "new" reasons, based on motives like "intellectual benefit", or "intellectual challenge": —

    a) "Intellectual benefit" can include a few types:—

        (1) Revenge or demonstration of hard feelings: In order to describe that type we have to mention the famous story of the military clerk who decided to penetrate the salary systems of the I.D.F. with the purpose of causing that system to write a "message" aimed at the Chief of Staff, insulting him disgracefully.

        (2) Unrestricted desire to rule, dominate and run things: there are stories of workers who always try to build up very complex data systems and very complicated communication networks, while keeping the know-how and the "keys" to the system solely in their own hands. By doing this, every single detail in the organization so computerized is totally controlled by them. It is a small step from that stage to abuse of power and crime.

    b) "Intellectual challenge" can include, for example:

        (1) A challenge to commit the "perfect crime";

        (2) A challenge to decipher software codes — a "crime" which is common among youngsters who call it by the nickname "Software Sport".

3) The "temptation" mentioned above is generally identified for the time being with computer workers. But since we are all in the process of becoming computer users and may be computer workers (or slaves), I consider it a social problem we must be aware of. Of course, legislation is one of the means to take care of the problem, but it is not the only one, and not the first step towards a solution.

The Fight of the Computer Industry for Survival

4. A. I have already mentioned above the problem of the existence of "Lacune" in the various legal systems; for example, the problem of software and data theft. I also mentioned the fact that people in the industry are well aware of the said situation. It is a well-known fact that unauthorised copies and use being made of software is the most dangerous threat to every software creator and can even destroy the whole industry.[7]

   B. Experts all over the world are trying their best to solve the problem, usually by developing one kind or another of "chains and locks" on hardware and software alike. Not too long ago we were informed of a new "protective" measure known as "software traps".[8] True, we are already aware of "self-destructive" software: such software can erase or stop its own operation at a given time or occasion, but "software traps" go far beyond that. In the case of unauthorized use of the software, the "software trap" can destroy and cause damage not only to the trapped software itsefl, but to the entire system in which it is installed.

   C. Using such means, software creators and owners are taking advantage of the old principle of law known as "self-defence". Lawyers can elaborate on self-defence in connection with assaults and even with tresspssing, but they all agree: self-defence is legal defense, and as such, it is a "passive right" by nature. Moreover, modern legal systems do not encourage the use of of "self-defence", and try to limit its implications. However, it is agreed that what is alleged to be under the "cover" of self-defence must be performed within reason, and in proportion to the threat or damage it is originally aimed to stop.

   D. Analysis of a "software trap" can indicate that apart from the fact that software traps are a means used by persons possessing lawful rights on the object so protected against a party operating unlawfully in contradiction to these rights, no other characteristic of selfe-defence exists in software traps. This devise is punitive and too offensive (therefore it is more active than passive), there is no obligatory connection between the damage done and the protected right and it is not necessarily reasonable. For example: You can lock your shop if you are a grocer, you can even use force against someone who is trying to rob you, but you cannot poison sugar candies in your shop with arsenic, so that "unauthorized eaters" will die or suffer severe harm (as we have already mentioned above, by using computers one can commit a very "elegant" crime because one does not have to use "arsenic").

   E. The question arises: How much and how far, is human society ready to extend the limits of "self-defence" in order to protect its so valued and important computers. The problem of software theft must be solved soon, but are we prepared to allow to take negative advantage of the sophistication which is in the computer with the purpose of creating a modern by-pass over known legal principles?

5. "Responsibility" or "Liability"

A. Responsibility is one of the key words in every society and legal
    system. Professionalism has created a situation of "mutual
    dependence" in our modern society. The said dependence causes many
    problems of responsibility and liability.[9]   The more complicated
    is any given organization, the more acute is the problem of
    responsibility. Computers in general and computer output in
    particular are almost lost in the depths of that problem.
    Computers are a very complicated device, created and assembled by
    many people, and by a lot of different kinds of "tools",
    constructed of tangible and intangibel elements. Computer output is
    much more complicated, because it is the product of a complicated
    "machine" and of various fragments of data, all operated by many
    different people. The identity of these people, means and date is
    assimilated during the complicated process. The question is, Who
    is to be responsible for what? We shall try to describe the
    problem from three aspects:-

    1) Responsibility/liability of software and hardware manufacturers
       and suppliers for any damage casued by their products or
       services.

    2) Responsibility (or credibility) embodied in computer output.

    3) Responsibility of computer workers for the "fruits" of their
       work, to the systems they operate and the "products" thereof.

B. Responsibility/Liability of Manufacturers and Suppliers [10]

    1) As we have already mentioned, computer hardware and software
       are very complex instruments designed to create products of
       their own and based on various data. The design and planning
       of such software is something which can be called a "calculated
       guess". Every expert in the industry will confirm that the
       existence of some quantity or another of errors ("bugs") is
       almost inevitable. We also mentioned above that computer
       systems never stand alone, but cause or assist the operation of
       other systems. That is the reason why a "small" error in
       software might cause a chain reaction and a lot of dmage to the
       organization which operates the computer and depends on its
       output. Since design and planning are involved in the process,
       it is easy to say that it is the duty of the software and
       computer creator to foresee and expect such damage. It is
       common (in Anglo-Saxon legal systems) to rule that if there
       existed a reasonable expectation, that responsibility must
       follow. In such a situation, software ceators and computer
       manufacturers are doomed to be responsible for almost unlimited
       damages.

    2) Such heavy responsibility might destroy the industry
       (especially when it is multiplied by compensation fees, fines
       and costs set by the courts). This fact has forced the
       industry to use "safety belts" to protect itself from collapse.
       These "safety belts" are devoid of responsibility/liability
       clauses common in contracts and agreements [11] between
       suppliers and buyers. That was the practical solution in
       favour of the computer people, but what about the innocent
       consumer? Can he be exposed to damages without any remedy?
       Why should the consumer be unprotected from negligence and even
       exploitation by such manufacturers and suppliers?

3) This situation constitutes two social problems: –

   a) Which interest is to be preferred in a society which is in
      favour of computers' progress on the one hand, and of giving
      shelter and remedies to consumers on the other hand?

   b) The computer environment appears to be a "dangerous" one,
      and all workers involved are under the pressure of this
      danger. Pressure is not something "pleasant" to live with,
      so some kind of a solution is absolutely necessary.

C. Responsibility for Computer Output

   1) We have already mentioned that computer output (in its general
      and non-specific meaning) is a technical result combinded of
      many machine-processed details, and many human beings (s well
      as their "machines") are involved in its creation. All
      components of such a "creation" lose their identified existence
      and become assimilated in the final product. When talking
      about "final product", we have to be more specific and to
      define in more exact terms what is the relevant "final
      product". "Finality" in data processing can exist only at a
      precise given moment based on the given data – one moment later
      you can have the same "product" identical in shape, but totally
      different in its contents. If your "product" is a written
      report, for example, you can press a small button and get as
      many such written reports as you wish, all identical, every one
      of which appears to be the "original", but in fact they are all
      (from A to Z) copies of the unseen process performed in the
      "electronic brain" of the machine.

   2) Rules of the law of evidence [12] (common in the Anglo-Saxon
      legal system) can demonstrate clearly the problem we are
      talking about: The first rule denies "hearsay" and the second
      rule is the "best evidence rule", demanding the use in court of
      "originals" and not copies. Since we are all slaves to
      computer output, it is almost an every day need to present the
      court with such (receipts, reports, etc.). How can you do
      that? Where and what is the original? Are we not making use
      of pure hearsay? Who is the exact person who can present the
      court with such evidence, testifying under oath and saying: I
      did it personally, and I am responsibile for every single
      detail to be true, because I actually know that it is true". I
      am afraid that any person testifying so (at the present status
      of law), must be a liar: It can be done, but with
      "reservations" – those reservations must be, in my humble
      opinion, an inseparable part of the law.

   3) The conclusion is, that computers have created a problem of
      identification for both man and material. Human society must
      adopt new ways of thinking, accepting assimilation but still
      "keeping alive" the identity of the human individual.

D. Responsibility of the Computer Worker

   1) Our last point on the "responsibility" under discussion is, in
      fact, the result of problems already pointed out above.

   2) The confusion surrounding the "bilateral relationship" between
      man and machine has considerable influence inside and outside
      any organization:

a) Some people, especially those who are living "near" the computer, might find it very comfortable to be covered by and "hidden" at the "back" of the computer, so they will never be responsible for anything and never be found guilty in any way or manner. Such a manner of thinking might create a very undesirable result among computer workers: –

(1) Decline of efficiency and of productivity.

(2) Negligence and even malice. Needless to say, the way to crime is very short from that point on.

b) The phrase, "The computer is to blame", which is so common, is unacceptable by any system of law, since human beings and not machines are the subject matter of rights and obligations recognised by law. No machine, no matter how sophisticated it may be, cannot, from that basic point of view, be a substitute for the human being. Yet the problem of finding the <u>person</u> to be responsible still exists; that fact may cause some kind of "Artificial Responsibility" as a solution. Such a responsibility can be: –

(1) Inside the organization, but towards the whole world: Establishing the solution already found in some laws or codes of ethics known as "ministerial responsibility": According to that concept, one person is to be responsible, not because of his own acts or omissions, but because of his rank and status. In my humble opinion, this solution may be justified, when such a person can lose (because of such artificial responsibility) his rank and status only. But it cannot be applied justly in a case of private responsibility when the person so artificially responsible may lose also his money and property or even his freedom because of being sentenced.

(2) Outside the organization: Establishing the solutions already found in some "Law of Torts", knwon as the responsibility of the "Last Supplier". According to that concept, one person is responsible but not becasue of his own acts or omissions, but because he is the only person known to the person injured. In my humble opinion, such a solution is not the proper one for our purposes. First of all, this concept was originally based on a siutation of personal <u>bodily</u> injury, which is not typical of our problem. Second – the said solution creates an "address" only, but in reality does not solve the problem. The last supplier of food, for example, can always find the remedy by way of suing his supplier. In our case, the problem is how to find responsibility at the last link of that chain of claims and counter-claims, namely the manufacturer himself.

E. Fictitious solutions are not strange to systems of law (see, for example, Company Law), but the question is how and what fiction, if any, is to be used concerning such fundamental problems of responsibility as were described above. The answer is up to the social concept regarding computers and the people behind them.

5. Summing Up

A. The questions which were mentioned hereinabove are not some
   intangible matters for lawyers only and are not a problem of any
   given society or state. Any solution which is to be a general and
   an integral one must cover national and international fields as
   well.

B. Law will follow and enforce any social solution, but such a
   solution must be given soon.

Footnotes

(Prepared especially for readers who are not lawyers, and intended to be
for general ideas only).

[1] Ronen, Moshe, "The Open Eye of Big Brother", in "Meidaon" No. 4, July
          1980 (probably based on "Yediot Ahronot", 11.6.80) (Hebrew)
[2] Lith, Arie, "Privacy Protection Act", in "Ma'ase Hoshev", vol. 9(2),
          app. (Hebrew)
[3] See [2] supra, plus said law itself and its by-laws (Hebrew)
[4] Levenfeld, Barry, "Copyright Protection for Computer Software in
          Israel", in The Computer Lawyer, Vol. 4, no. 8, Aug. 87,
          p. 18.
[5] The Israeli Criminal Punishment Law, Art. 383 (Hebrew)
[6] Rodity-Schachter, Esther, "Software Protection in the Throes of a
          Legal Morass", in Datamation, June 1987, p. 49, (see also
          [4] supra).
[7] Gilber, Harvey and Joseph Jonathan, "Software Piracy", in Computer
          World, 10.5.82.
[8] Avner, Ehud, "The Dark Side of Technology, in "Kesafim" 367, 18.8.87,
          p. 18, (Hebrew)
[9] "The Professional Edge", News 34-38, June 1987.
[10] Kelly, Joseph, "Computer Law", in Datamation 116.
[11] Spanner, Robert A. and Mack, William F., "Sharpening Your Clause", in
          Datamation, Aug. 1980, p. 115.
[12] Compare: R.V. Pettigrew (1980), 17 cr. app. R.39, 206-207,
          Monarch Federal Saving & Loan Association vs. Gazer, 383 A.
          2D. 475 (N.J. 1977).

The Social Implications of Robotics and Advanced
Industrial Automation / D. Millin and B.H. Raab (Editors)
Elsevier Science Publishers B.V. (North-Holland)
© IFIP, 1989

SENSITIVE PROBLEMS OF AN 'INFORMATIONAL SOCIETY': SOCIOTECHNICAL
HANDLING OF COMPLEX ORGANIZATIONS, PEOPLE,
MODERN TECHNOLOGY, STATES, AND SOCIETIES

Alexander J. MATEJKO

Department of Sociology
University of Alberta
Edmonton, Alberta
CANADA T6G 2H4

1. INTRODUCTION

We are gradually moving to an informational society based not so much on
manufacturing or services in general but mainly on the generation, transfer
and practical application of reliable data. The high rate of innovations
will be one of the main characteristics of that socio-economic formation and
therefore the sophisticated handling of innovative projects has the first
rate importance. Sociotechnics is here understood as a scientific approach
to the techno-organizational practice. From this particular perspective the
innovative projects need to be perceived as the transformations of human
relationships done with the minimum harm to the humanistic values and with
the optimal activitization of human potentialities. In order to achieve such
condition it is necessary to take full advantage of the existing sociological
knowledge, the insight available from the large spectrum of positive and
negative practical experiences, essence of the managerial practice, policy
analyses, etc.

This paper contains the review of various problem areas in which
sociotechnics may be applicable: psycho-sociological aspects of innovations,
forms of management and co-operation suitable to the harmonious co-existence
of various people jointly promoting innovative projects, the cause of
industrial democracy, the need to safeguard spontaneity and the grass-root
initiative, the dangers of sociotechnics identified with the manipulation of
people (sociotechnicians as the agents of dominant power), the parameters of
sociotechnical sensitivity (the recognition of external conditioning, the
wholistic approach, the positive orientation of management, disfunctions as
an unavoidable part of calculation, costs/benefits account, handling of
developmental tension, organizational design of information delivery and
transfer, teamwork in both horizontal and vertical dimensions), general
contingencies of sociotechnical success, handling of the cross-cultural
differences, sophisticated planning and computerization of services,
sociotechnical obstacles on a macro-scale (the U.S.A. case), problems of the
modern welfare states, the public and private vehicles of sociotechnical
progress.

This wide spectrum of problems dealt with in this paper is supposed to show
how much the micro-parameters and the macro-parameters of sociotechnical
handling are closely interrelated. Any innovative project is actually
influenced by the large number of internal and external factors. It is
necessary not only to recognize each of them but in addition to analyse all
of them as a network of interdependencies. The first step in this direction
is to sensitize the innovators to the variety of contingencies worth to be
acknowledged.

The designs of innovative projects may gain much in sophistication if the
social interaction model is applied to them: the playground of various social

forces involved in the project and promoting their own concerns, the pecking
order and its transformations, open agenda and a hidden agenda, confrontation
between different perceptions of the same facts, encounter of various values,
the matter of personal dignity, socio-moral bonds and distances, dialectics
of mutual influence, power and dominance, internal system versus the external
system. Technology influences profoundly social interaction but itself is
also much dependent on socio-cultural contingencies. Without an adequate
environmental reinforcement it is very difficult to achieve an effective
technological progress. Local culture and the local power set-ups have much
in common with the success or failure of the innovative projects. It is one
of the vital sociotechnical concerns to mobilize the local socio-cultural
resources in favour of the innovations and the modernization in general
(Matejko 1986c).

2.   THE SOCIAL NATURE OF ORGANIZATIONAL AND TECHNICAL INNOVATIONS

Innovations at work come from a variety of sources: market demands,
technological development, competition, management trying to motivate workers
and better coordinate their efforts, spontaneous organizational initiatives
of the rank-and-file, the union-management-government co-operation,
experimentation by social scientists and management professional consultants,
and even political initiatives (Grootings et al., 1986). The appearances of
innovation may be similar, but the intentions are much different. For
example, the socialist work brigades in the Soviet bloc are somewhat similar
to the autonomous work groups in the West, but their actual nature is much
different.

The humanization in the workplace has been brought into public attention,
both in the West and in the East. However, in the West it is understood as a
valid correction of the status quo dominated by different bodies: the
profit-oriented management or the plan-oriented management, the governmental
bureaucracy or the political body (the one party systems), the technicians
and economists (vulnerable to the "trained incapacity" to see people behind
systems) or the "soulless" administrators, the capitalists or the
apparatchiks, the bosses or the workers.

Innovations in the social organization of work are promoted on the basis of
various manifest and latent intentions. In this respect, it is worthwhile to
look deeper into the power configurations [1] as well as into the
civilizational message. The work life enrichment projects in west Europe
have much to do with the democratic welfare state concepts that include,
among others, public concern about the job environment, promotion of the
co-operative union-state-management relations, etc.

In eastern Europe the organizational consulting of a technical-economic
nature (there is no good reason to identify it with Taylorism!) and the
quality of working life improvement are both productivity oriented. The
party/government bosses hope that people will be ready to work more and
better without necessarily having to obtain higher wages. The employees hope
to earn more without an additional effort and nuisance. Direct promotors of
innovation hope to be rewarded for pet projects which are more or less
successful in softening the negative impact of bureaucratic rigidity. Only
in a few cases are the opposite interests clearly articulated, as in the case
of Poland in 1956, 1970, 1976 and 1980/81. Work remains deeply fragmented
with regard to the actual chance of articulating collective demands and
promoting open bargaining (Matejko 1986a).

There is a growing awareness on the world scale that promise does exist in
recognizing vital human needs and informal social capacities. [2] The
consultative style of management may lead to a harmonious relationship

between the supervisors and the supervised. People organizing themselves
spontaneously into autonomous work groups based on self-management may become
much more committed and trustful contributors the work fulfillment (Matejko
1986c). Management which is conscious of human resources may avoid many
unnecessary troubles. Trade union bodies and local workers' representatives
may act more constructively when they are invited to solve problems jointly
with management. Knowledge originating out of the western and eastern
practical experiences increasingly illustrates how short-sighted it is to
remain doctrinaire and authoritarian. We become alerted to the vital
importance of trust relationships at workplaces.

3. INNOVATIVE SOCIAL ORGANIZATION

So far there are only a few socio-economic forces able and willing to promote
consistently and strongly enough initiatives in the field of the social
organization of work. Norway and Sweden are much positive exceptions, but
even there some difficulties are apparent. For example, in Sweden most of
the innovative projects come from the management side and not trade unions.
This has much to do with the strong local bureaucratic tradition and the high
acceptance of people at the top (Huntford 1972). Trade unions all around the
developed world remain lukewarm in their orientation towards industrial
democracy at the workplace level. Governmental bureaucracies influenced
mostly by lawyers and politicians show a very limited understanding of the
necessity to humanize work. The fear of unemployment contributes to the
passivity of the labour force regarding the internal labour market
innovations.

Actually, only in Yugoslavia is whole work system supposed to be socially
innovative. In reality it does not necessarily function this way due to a
variety of reasons: one party rule, economic difficulties, organizational
weakness, rivalries between various powerful groups. The new ideas promoted
in the Soviet bloc by M. Gorbachev (1987) should, in the long run, open up
much more room for the democratization of workplaces, but, obviously, they
are not that easy to implement as long as in each socialist country there is
enough powerful people defending their privileges at any cost. The case of
Poland illustrates this point.[3]

Democratization of complex organizations may potentially stimulate the
commitment of all organizational members (or at least a considerable part of
them) to mobilize their individual and collective input. It is necessary
here to make a distinction between various models and their implementation.
For example, R.H. Hall claims that in the Yugoslav enterprises "power in the
organization comes from the bottom up, rather than from the top down"
(1986:288). From his perspective, the Yugoslav system represents "a truly
radical organizational form" (Ibid., p. 200). However, the data available
show a lukewarm attitude of the Yugoslav workers towards the system, as well
as mediocre socio-economic results. The centralization of political power in
the Yugoslav one-party state is largely responsible for this condition
(Djilas 1985). [4]

4. THE CAUSE OF INDUSTRIAL DEMOCRACY

The common weakness of present day self-government is the management
participation practiced only on the enterprise level without the interest,
and an adequate effort, to extend it to the lower levels. [5] The elitist
bias of management participation restricted to the top level is quite
obvious. In order to energise self-governmentally the rank-and-file, it is
necessary to implement a social organization of work based on autonomous work
groups as the basic units of co-management. This proposal was formulated by
Jan Wolski (Jain & Matejko 1986) but the actual implementation originated

from Swedish industry, where such groups are intensively promoted by
industrial management of the private companies (Matejko 1986c:150-187). One
of the major weaknesses of workers' self government in Yugoslavia is its much
greatly limited scope; delegates elected by workers make decisions only on
secondary issues, the authoritarian-bureaucratic style of management [6]
remains intact, organization of daily work is not penetrated by the
participatory ideals, and actual power relations are not modified.

It is difficult to imagine any real progress in the quality of working life
without the establishment, in each country, of a public lobby group commited
to promote the cause. Mass media, in general, are positively oriented to
innovative projects, but they usually do not follow up the events. Academics
are more and more in favour of innovative projects and they follow, in this
respect, the progressivistic trends in the university communities. Modern
management training emphasizes strongly the capacity of the manager as a
democratic leader.

It will be interesting to see if and how much the quality of a working life
movement may become an autonomous factor free from any particular political
determination. Could such a movement unite the ideologically diversified
crowd of people who have the desire to enrich the socio-moral value [7] of
collective work? The principle of teamwork has become a vital part of modern
civilization, and economic recovery depends much, among other things, on the
upgrading of this principle. It is quite obvious that the economic success
of Japan originates, to a considerable degree, exactly from a work culture
based on the cultivation of a co-operative approach. The best civilisational
traditions need to be activated in order to make substantial progress, at
least in the cultural international interaction. [8] Now there is more
reason than ever before to hope for success in this respect. The socio-moral
upgrading of collective work in complex organizations is one of the
particularly attractive joint tasks for several countries who are separated
from cooperation in this sensitive field and suffer serious hardships as a
result.

5. A SOCIOTECHNICAL PERSPECTIVE

Sociotechnics as a scientific discipline (Podgorecki 1975; Cherns 1979) must
be value free in order to secure an adequate rational basis for its growth.
However, this should not deny those values which are a vital part of human
existence and wellbeing. For example, in the evaluation of organizational
effectiveness some values and metaphors are unavoidable (Morgan 1986). Any
human activity is based on specific value assumptions and an appropriate
metaphor. The neglect of human dignity and aspirations based on the denial
of values impoverishes any study of human behaviour in workplaces or
elsewhere.

The application of sociotechnics happens always in relation to specific
civilizations (Eisenstadt 1987), and may be successful only if it addresses
civilizational reality: people as carriers of values, and the cultural load
inherited by them from the past. Many policy failures originate from the
unjustified generalization of assumptions and means based on them. What fits
very well into one civilizational framework may be totally ineffective or
even harmful within another framework. Therefore, any sociotechnics has to
be qualified culturally. In this respect the 'humanistic coefficient' of F.
Znaniecki has to be taken into consideration. People acting in their social
roles are culturally motivated.

Sociotechnicians also are not value free; they implement specific values more
or less consciously. Moral confusion among them leads unavoidably to
confusion in sociotechnics. A realistic awareness of circumstances is always

needed in order to act successfully. However, the purpose of actions and the global cost of them (including the human cost) need a clear moral choice. Societies are not only socio-economic and political entities, but also moral communities as E. Durkheim clearly saw. In modern societies, organic solidarity based on the division of labour is not enough to achieve cohesion (Matejko 1986c). There is a great need in the West to enrich the existing work bonds by the socio-moral factors of mutual trust, co-operation, participation, and spontaneity (Matejko 1986b, 1984).

6.   IN DEFENCE OF SPONTANEITY

So far, too much is expected from formal structures and not enough attention paid to the spontaneous social organization initiated by people in accordance with their own potential, imagined by them in their own peculiar way (Morgan 1986). Under state socialism, there is a particularly strong temptation of the ruling elites to form societies according to models that look rational, but lead to a 'truncated' society [9] (Matejko 1986a; Shtromas and Kaplan 1987). Also, in the West, several 'benevolent' policies have actually led to deviant results when the 'humanistic coefficient' was not recognized. [10] For example, industrial democracy remains a window dressing phenomenon as long as participation in decision-making does not penetrate down the hierarchy. The elitist bias of democratization makes most people passive, and, at most, lukewarm towards various participatory schemes.

The assumption that the rulers and experts know better what is actually good for the common people is an obviously wrong moral choice of much social consequence. With the rapid growth of the 'knowledge industry' in modern societies, social scientists gain power without actually recognizing it. The teaching of social sciences on a mass scale, and the impact of 'scientifically' inspired mass media, both shape the public's awareness oof what is possible or not, what is proper, what is worthwhile to achieve in life, etc. [11] Sociologists have a tendency to underestimate their role in shaping societies; actually, they are more and more a substitute for the clergy or even politicians. (It is interesting to watch how much modern theology becomes penetrated by sociological reasoning). Moral relativism becomes reinforced by 'objectivized' sociology which claims to be beyond values. People who are not sensitive enough to the limits of sociological knowledge confuse intellectualism with morality. The developed material civilization multiplies choices available to people in order to avoid ambiguity; it is necessary to depend on moral decisions of an existential nature. The drama of human life is not necessarily easier to deal with uunder the conditions of relative abundance than under the conditions of relative poverty.

7.   DANGERS OF THE MORALLY TRUNCATED SOCIOTECHNICS

Sociotechnicians with a shallow moral orientation may be socially dangerous in a variety of ways. Their claim of rationality is based on the wrong credentials. Knowledge valid for one set of phenomena is not necessarily applicable to another set of phenomena. The universality of rules and observations must be taken with a grain of salt; each situation in time and space needs a different diagnosis. Research data have to be carefully qualified in order to make any practical conclusions. Social reality consists of so many variables that any selection of them is much questionable, the past experience has a limited validity for understanding the present and the future. At best sociotechnicians may act as advisors, tutors, critics, and animators.

Sociotechnical expertise should enrich and inspire practitioners to act more rationally, but this expertise is not a set of ready recipes on how to achieve success. Sociotechnical wisdom depends much more on the intellectual and moral quality of people than on the power of knowledge. It is not in the long range interest of sociotechnicians to claim more than they are actually able to deliver.

Genuine sociotechnics is based on empirical research and insight, praxiological reasoning, and the policy programming/implementation/feedback. Behind all this rationalization and optimalization of social actions, there is a definite place for the moral vision of a better society. Improve, save, simplify, make more effective - but for what ultimate purpose?

In social practice, two concerns appear parallel to each other; how to achieve more expediency, and how to acquire some virtues. Quite often one of these concerns is achieved at the expense of another. Civilizations are based on the mixture of expediencies and virtues, but, ultimately, virtue is much more important. [12]

Sociotechnical programmes and projects have to be designed and implemented with a full awareness of their cultural validity. What is their actual contribution to the enrichment of community values? How much do they reinforce the socio-moral effectiveness of human groups and institutions? Management styles and practices differ in their moral impact, and they need to be evaluated accordingly. Many errors are committed in this respect, not necessarily because of any bad will, but, rather due to the omission of vital factors. The reinforcement of mutual trust and co-operation may be achieved by sociotechnics which are based on moral inspiration and not only on 'cold' scientific calculation. In a whole variety of present day world civilizations, there are many examples of moral growth on the individual and group scale. It would be worthwhile to analyse systematically these examples from a sociotechnical perspective.

8.   SOCIOTECHNICAL SENSITIVITY IN THE TECHNICAL INNOVATIONS

8.1 Technical Equipment as Serving People

Modern machines are products of human thinking and acting. Mechanistic reasoning is a part and parcel of the materialistic reality. When being reduced to a choice between "true" and "false", one is not allowed to deal with the subtleties of a living existence (Bamme et al. 1983). Reasoning applicable only to inanimate matter prevents the effective study of living phenomena. On the other hand, in social reality, there are several practical efforts to use the inanimate matter as a substitute for the animate matter, for example the sex-machines. [13] In modern society there are several serious attempts to reduce living phenomena to objects of manipulation. The marketization of sex is one of them.

On the other hand, there are many evident manifestations of the spontaneous defence of people against the far reaching reification of human relations. Popular music is a new kind of standardized spontaneity, or rather, a commercially channeled illusion of free expression. In reality, man is a part of technology, and technology is a part of man. By studying machines, we are penetrating human thinking and its mechanistic implications. There is nothing else in machines but the input which has originated from human beings. Also, we are not always aware of the artificial nature of machines, and we tend to confuse them with living creatures.

8.2 The Recognition of External Conditioning

Innovations made inside an enterprise are somewhat related to the developments happening outside it. Technological progress is not only a

factor of socio-organizational change. The expectation of the masses for the
good life is growing. [14] The resulting public burden is quite substantial,
[15] which makes it necessary to have reforms not only in the democratic
West, [16] but also in the USSR, [17] and in satellite countries. [18] Even
in Japan there is an evident decline of collectivism, [19] however, it is not
being replaced in any adequate measure by an individualistic orientation.[20]
Secondary Japanese institutions are weakening in their ability to socialize
people; for example, unionization has declined in the period 1949-84 from 56%
to 29% (among teachers only from 70% to 50%). The Japanese are exposed to
several challenges [21] in dealing successfully with modern technology. It
is a fascinating question as to how much the uniquely Japanese mixture of
traditionalism and modernism will fit into the requirements of a
postindustrial era. The social conformism which widely exists among the
Japanese people may be, in the long run, a negative factor in their
technological adaptation. On the other hand, Western social organization
also appears to be obsolete (Matejko 1986c).

The socio-organizational reform dictated by technological necessities cannot
just be neutral in a broader sense. The new shape of society is actually a
continuation of the divisions which are challenged much today:
private-public, collectivistic-individualistic, socialist-liberal-
convervative, etc. We become very confused by these metaphors inherited from
the past which are accepted without a critical reevaluation of them. For
example, the blind following of past practices in dealing with innovation may
be very damaging; on the other hand, nothing is actually brand new.

Innovations on a macro-scale happen within the realities of the present day
world, and these have to be recognized. Our fascination with modern
technology prevents us from recognizing major discrepancies which do exist.
[22] From the world gross product, 65% belongs to 17% of the population and
35% belongs to 83% of the population (1985 data). The per capita
indebtedness of U.S. citizens is per capita $30,000 compared to $400 per
capita in the developing countries (1986 data). Big industrial democracies
actually do not know what to do with their unemployed young people even
though population growth has diminished very considerably. These and similar
facts illustrate the scope of problems which are aggravated by the technical
progress rather than being solved by it. Poor countries do not have
the resources to utilize beneficially modern information gadgets. The
accelerated flow of capital benefits the rich, but exposes to poverty even
more of the majority.

Younger generations have fewer chances of finding a job even in the
relatively low paid services where computerization has lowered the demands on
unskilled personnel. One of the crucial questions we shoudl ask is what is
the actual social utility of products and services? [23] Too many
unnecessary things, or even harmful things, are created in societies.

Another question to be asked is how much may be saved by handling information
in a more efficient manner? For example, in the US economy, around two
thirds of paid labour is devoted to information transfer (Strassmann
198:187); ineffective handling of this business leads to great waste. This
waste occurs mostly in the non-market situations; bureaucratic arrangements
are ineffective buut, nobody cares to eliminate them because cost is
allocated in an arbitrary manner without taking into consideration the
competitive alternatives.

The simplest example of waste is the quasi-monopolistic position of the
producer who ignores cheaper ways of producing and delivering a product
because the consumer has no alternatives. Another example is when public
enterprises are given a privileged position by the government, and actually

function more to please their political sponsors than to follow the
principles of economy and efficiency. [24] Quite often these enterprises
actually fulfill, to a large extent, different functions than profit making.
They offer chances of employment, please clientele who are sponsored by the
politicians, serve localities of some political significance, respond
favourably to pressure groups, etc. Under such circumstances, to fully
utilize modern technology, it is necessary, first of all, to clarify the main
goals of an economic activity and to shape the organization accordingly. A
computerized information flow may be actually beneficial only on a sound
organizational basis, and not as a substitute for it.

8.3 The Wholistic Approach

Innovation appears within a specific framework and this has to be fully
recognized in order to avoid costs and failures resulting from ignorance,
negligence and shortsightedness. The postindustrial age brings variety and
challenge to factory work. "The design and integration of control systems
require extremely detailed knowledge of the specific dynamics of a particular
machine system, not just of machines in general (...) The design of
cybernetic systems is based on the principles of integration and flexibility:
integration, because controls continually regulate the boundaries between
parts of the production process, and flexibility, because these same controls
create machine systems that respond to changing ambient conditions. But
these two principles of design tend to pull in opposite directions"
(Hirschhorn 1984:58,57).

H. Inose and J.R. Pierce in their insightful analysis of information
technology, emphasize "a convergence of service modes in which pictures and
graphs, sound, and data are used together and will be increasingly
intermingled for all purposes: communication, transactions, work, information
retrieval, and so on" (1984:X1). This convergence of modes is a potential
that can be very beneficial depending on how it will be used. "The
convergence of modes and the associated speed, reduction of cost, and
increase in power of information technology can encourage communities of
interest that span many countries" (Ibid.). [25]

Convergence of various factors complicates the innovative process, but also
offers room for new possibilities that can be utilized under the condition of
an adequate organizational set-up which allows the absorbtion of
potentialities.

8.4 The Positive Orientation of Management

Much depends on the goodwill of top management to humanize the workplace in
the face of progressing technicization. The main question is, however, how
to shape employment policies in order to remove the well justified fears of
employees regarding their future. For example, some big Japanese enterprises
temporarily locate their labour surplus in other enterprises, in addition to
widely spread retraining programmes, early retirement plans, and other
measures. Technological unemployment is not only the problem of a much
diminishing income, but also of a declining self-esteem. West German data
show that employees feel insecure when they are denied the assurance that as
permanent staff, they will be taken care of; an assurance that is taken for
granted in big Japanese enterprises (Boethge and Overbeck 1986). As long as
employers are willing and able to invest in their employees - which is much
more typical for the German speaking countries than for the English speaking
countries - there is not much reason for the wide-spread insecurity among
German personnel, especially when co-operation does exist between management
and workers in regard to the implementation of modern technology.

The flow of information dictates, to a growing extent, the activities of people. Quite often, however, they are unaware of a data flood and consequently, are unable to make reasonable use of this information. The reactive style of management is self-defeating in the long run, especially when the people do not actually know what to do with the large number of data arriving to them all the time. Task commitment and work morality are weakened when people are overwhelmed with information and given little time to reasonably digest it. The informational revolution may actually become the revolution of mediocrity and vulgarity unless people are adequately developed, both culturally and morally, to prevent them from making wrong choices. "Everything depends on how we organize, educate, and train managers and employees; how we design our working environment; how we justify and monitor capital investment; how we deal with issues of morale, motivation, privacy, and displaced employees; how we define and measure productivity - in short, how we use the new technology to fulfill the prophecy of information evolution" (Strassmann 1985).

8.5 Disfunctions as an Unavoidable Part of Calculation

As we enter the age of increasingly sophisticated technological equipment and procedures, it is necessary for us to take risks. Nothing is ever free from some sort of cost. The total elimination of failure is impossible even if its achievement remains desirable.

The acceptance of failure as a part of technological reality, makes it necessary to design, accordingly, the social organization of work in order to encourage the conceptual shift (people thinking in a fixed manner are not innovative enough). The reinforcement of diagnostic skills, [26] and the liberation of people from excessive conservatism, helps to expand the breadth of control without necessarily having to increase the depth of theoretical understanding. The reinforcement of fringe awareness (and selective attention based on the dense perception of physical processes, heuristic knowledge of production relationships and theoretical understanding of the production process), promotes the freedom from being overwhelmed with detail, strengthens the capacity of the operators to orchestrate the senses into a heightened awareness of patterns of events, and encourages them to think about themselves as learners. "The control-room operator of a postindustrial society brings his own awareness to consciousness by orchestrating fringe and selective attention into a unified process of pattern-seeking behavior (...) The worker becomes more aware of his work environment, but he also begins to reflect self-consciously on his own actions and becomes aware of how he learns and develops. He learns who he is when he changes" (Hirschhorn 1984:98).

8.6 Cost/Benefits Account

Each technological innovation is based on the calculation of advantages and disadvantages. It is, therefore, a practical problem of how to augument the first and diminish the second.

There are several good reasons why the computer revolution does not lead to the fulfillment of its expected benefits. Employees are not necessarily paid more for their computer literacy. Also, computer systems are widely used to tighten control and increase surveillance rather than to expand personal freedom, and the use of incomprehensible language confuses the public.

Technopragmatists and techno-boosters have a jointly vested interest in isolating and alienating the techno-skeptics (Reinecke 1984). There are several evident dysfunctions of computerization: the concentration of skills at either end of the spectrum, the unequal benefits from microchips (large

organizations are the winners), the chasm that develops between the
information rich and the information poor, the reduction of skills and
employment in several traditional occupations, the use of satellites which
serve mainly corporate interests, the transfer of electronic funds opening up
a greater chance for surveillance, the formalization and standardization of
interpersonal communications, the work-related stress in word-processing
pools, the dehumanizing nature of electronic communication, the transfer of
the main work load from the helping staff to the managerial and professional
staff, the encroachment of electronic inroads into the nonworking life, the
production limits of automation for a large number of products (even in the
US 80% of machined products are made in batches of under fifty), the
reduction of skills due to the use of numerical control, the reduction of
autonomy of working people, the elimination of skills and jobs at the lower
levels, the restrictions of skills and control at the craft level, the
encroachment on professional and managerial tasks, the polarization of those
who possess information, the packaging and marketing of information, the
invasion of privacy, and the lack of good sense and humanity among those who
run big organizations (Reinecke 1984). This is quite a lengthy list!

It is obvious that the introduction of computerization has to be based on a
careful and deliberate calculation of costs and benefits in order to not only
select appropriate and adequate equipment, but also to reduce the risk of
potential negative side effects, and reinforce adequately the positive
effects: lower cost, fast delivery of results, elimination of many potential
errors, etc.

8.7 Handling Developmental Tension

Technologial innovation very often leads to organizational strain which needs
to be anticipated and properly handled. The problem of how to deal
successfully with a crisis needs to be addressed. For most successful
enterprises "developmental tension" is needed in order to mobilize people;
novelty has to be coordinated adequately with controls (Hirschhorn 1984:73).
"The connections between human and machine systems run deep. Indeed, as
automatic systems are developed to control the most obvious kinds of errors,
the patterns of social organization become major determinants of success or
failure" (Ibid., p. 82).

The newer and richer mix of uses makes the machine system vulnerable to
failures and the inappropriate interpretation of signals. The ability to
handle any crisis requires a greater degree of flexibility from the
operators. Therefore, "work designers must find ways to facilitate the
acquisition of trust in symbolically mediated work settings" (Ibid., p. 84).
This may be achieved in a social organization based on co-operation, mutual
responsibility, leadership involving the care of subordinates, long range
commitment, mutual consultation, flexible allocation of manpower, intensive
training, and the promotion of occupational careers on the internal or
external labour market. The quality oriented organizational order is much in
demand in the era of the widespread computerization. It is not enough to
achieve stability. It is actually necessary to proactively take advantage of
shifting circumstances and 'thrive on chaos' (Peters 1987).

8.8 Organizational Design of Information Delivery and Transfer

Productive information handling which leads to high organizational
effectiveness, needs an effective design, a good response to consumer needs,
a transformation of specialists into the generalists (capable of serving all
or most consumer needs), a simplification of case handling procedures, a
readiness and ability to handle nontypical cases, an intensive training of
information users, an actual attainment of promised benefits, a systems

design made to fit well specific users, an elimination of low-value added jobs and an upgrading of people into the high value added jobs, an evaluation of the actual value of information in relation to the consumer (market mechanisms are unavoidable!), on information transfer primarily used as a means for supporting production and distribution rather than an item of consumption, a business executive which serves as a link between information technology and the strategic goals of the enterprise, an analytical utility of upgraded information, a technological priority which does not get ahead of the abilities of the users in applying computers, a global co-operation based on the share of knowledge, and a high appreciation of human capital. "The essence of the new electronic message is its universality - which should not be confused with standardization. The uniform central control and hierarchical structure of the totalitarian state is contradicted by the inherent need for autonomy and decentralization of the effective electronic workplace. The prospect of a workable Orwellian state is, in any case, as yet remote on account of presently excessive costs and incompetence entailed by gargantuan, monolithic control structures" (Strassmann 1985:245-46).

8.9 Teamwork at the Horizontal as well as the Vertical Dimensions

The new team work organization is much different from the traditional hierarchical organization which is based on levels of command, quick and ready responses to a variety of questions, referral to a supervisor, and a minute division of labour. The new model proposes coordination without hierarchy. "It does this by locating initiative in the teams, by providing cross-talk and rotation between the teams, and by supporting a plan governance system that factory members use to monitor the team system and its relationship to the factory's environment. This design can work only if it is embedded in a factory culture that supports learning and development" (Strassman 1985:150-51).

However, there are several obstacles to overcome in this organizational innovation: piece-rate work, difficulty in socializing both employers and employees, management's withdrawal from the shop floor, the dehumanized approach to the design of worker-machine systems, the trade union conservative approach, the short-term determination of profits. On the other hand, there is also a growing evidence that the new work organization is just inevitable (Huse and Cummings 1985).

Modern information systems nencessitate much attention and watchfulness; imperfections and discontinuities have to be immediately recognized and handled accordingly. The operator moves from being a controlled element in the work process to a controlling element; his/her skills have to be upgraded accordingly. The same is valid for structuralization of work. "The sociotechnical system achieves a new and unique integration of individual and group needs. It does not balance the two; rather, it intensifies and highlights both. This is why such settings are particularly stressful, but also why they are flexible" (Hirschhorn 1984:148-49).

The sensitivity of management is particularly needed in this touchy field. The trust relationships will not be established on the basis of manipulation harmful to the autonomy of operators and their sense of integrity. It is necessary to delegate much power to the subordinates, allocate them to specific tasks, secure the adequate input of the support units, recognize the plurality of talents and potential contributions, insist on the loyal fulfillment of duties.

Is the trust on decline in the West? A distinction has to be made between the critical approach to the dominant institutions, an asset under the democratic arrangement, and the actual decline of reliance on leaders,

confidence in the benevolence of various agencies, belief that the fiduciary
obligation and responsibility are fulfilled. The basic norms and values in
order to be valid there must be a substantial acceptance of them. "All
social interaction is an endless process of acting upon expectations, which
are part cognitive, part emotional, and past moral" (Barber 1983:9). The
belief in the persistence and fulfillment of the natural and the moral social
orders, the expectation of the competent role performance, and the
expectation that the parties will carry out their duties - all three are
treated by B. Barber as the foundations of trust. Without enough
predictability of events life becomes very difficult, the costs are growing
(for example, the legal costs), and the sense of insecurity is much growing.

Social changes may reinforce trust or diminish it. The 'revolution of
entitlements' makes people quite critical about the current arrangements.
The 'me' generation puts into the question the traditional duties versus the
others. The growth of the welfare state inspires many people quite
critically toward the authorities as not willing or able to fulfill their
extended duties. The conflict of interests (private gains versus public
duties) makes the public suspicious and defensive.

Trust fulfills the "general function of social ordering, of providing
cognitive and moral expectational maps of actors and systems as they;
continuously interact" (Ibid., p. 19) and in this sense it is essential of
stable social relationships, as well as for the reduction of complexity. The
mechanism for providing the necessary means and goals for the achievement of
social system requirements (social control) is based on trust in the
legitimate power, expression and maintenance of shared values, as well as
rational distrust.

10. GENERAL CONTINGENCIES OF SUCCESS IN INNOVATIONS

Any innovation in organization makes it necessary to consider the following
relevant features of organization design: technology (know-how), structure
(authority and responsibility), culture (values and norms), politics
(negotiation of implementation). Both rationalization (updating) and
routinization (reliability of performance) are needed in order to achieve
positive results (Markus 1984:16). The question to be posed is how to secure
selection of all the basic organizational features so that they take into
account the local conditions of the organization. The combination of these
features must fit smoothly with the contingencies of the given situation.
Obviously, some patterns which fit well into one scene, are out of question
in another situation. For example, the patronalism of big Japanese
industrial enterprises does not fit well into conditions of Western
individualism (Batstone 1984). There are obvious disadvantages to the
employees in patronalism. The long term gains of patronalistic enterpreneurs
appears to be much higher than the advantages acquired by loyal employees.
On the other hand, they have commited their life careers to one company in
the case of an economic recess. The employers are obligated to keep promises
made to the employees and this contributes very considerably to the economic
burden already placed on the company.

Also, one has to take into account the differences between private and public
businesses and their receptiveness to innovation. [27] A fixed budget will
obviously limit an interest in making innovations, especially when
risk-taking operations do not assure adequate rewards, and the penalties for
failures are very painful.

The differences in the perspective on innovation depends on the location of
people in the division of labour. Indirect workers have a vested interest to
preserve designs formulated by them. As a result they are not necessarily

concerned with practical problem solving and the necessity to secure enough
room for the practical inventiveness, freedom to correct errors on the spot,
etc. (Brodner 1985).

Job design as well as matching job/personality has dimensions on both the
individual and job sides that must be considered: personality
characteristics, skills, capacity to handle tasks and people, capacity to
make decisions and take responsibility, capacity to resist the
inconveniences, act securely, etc. The individual who enters the job setting
also brings with him/her several expectations and aspirations that are more
or less realistic, practical, and capable of being fulfilled.
From the perspective of the employer it is very important whether the
operators will be able and willing to handle properly the expensive
equipment. There is quite often just unavoidable to utilize people who do
not have adequate credentials. For example, the women not vocationally
oriented are widely utilized. [28] There is the problem of the loss of
status by people vulnerable to innovations. For example, the supervisors who
are expected more to listen than to make direct orders.

Now can an organization adequately arrange its technological and
administrative systems to maximize and utilize its human potential? Teamwork
may provide many advantages in this respect, but the am
work, an adequate training and instructional support, and a reward which is
more or less adequate to the contribution.

For modern management it is more important to initiate and monitor a highly
motivating organizational set-up than to achieve savings through the division
of labour, mechanization, and control (Brodner 1985:119-21). The rigidity of
traditional organizations does not fit with the modern organizational
requirements of flexibility, speed, punctual deliveries, high quality, and
good interest on invested capital. Differentiation of production requires an
increased mental effort in the design, planning, management and coordination
of organizational activities. However, this can lead to a striving for more
rational mental processes (Ibid., p. 50). Under new technological
circumstances, the greater the degree of technical change, the greater the
need for hybrid skills, with a broader rather than overly specialized
training. However, with the greater need for hybrid skills, there is a
corresponding need for more diverse training, requiring a greater
expenditure of time and expense (Sorge and Warner 1986:177).

The need to upgrade the skills of people facing a computerized society is
growing to an appreciable extent. For example, Marvin J. Centron claims that
"the first step is to begin to encourage the unemployed to upgrade their
skills and take lower-paying jobs as temporary solutions. The next step is
to get the education system back on track to produce educated minds that
accept the challenges of the future and want to learn more (...) We must make
people think and also make them communicate" (Cornish ed. 1985:27).

Market-oriented production depends on the adequate match between
techno-organizational exigencies and changing outlet conditions for its
success. The control of personnel and the work process necessitates measures
which are not always counterproductive; e.g. the formalization of procedures
discouraging the rank-and-file initiative.

The ability to expand the market [29] internally and externally is crucial
for employment and even for technological progress. The automobile industry
is a good example of this (Streeck and Hoff 1983). Only a few producers, for
example Daimler Benz in West Germany, manage to establish a stable market for
themselves. Most others are involved in heavy competition which has major
consequences for their labour power. Technological progress of automobile

production, as well as the saturation of the automobile market, has led to a
slowing down of employment opportunities, a demand in the increase of average
skills, more demanding jobs, a growing concern for productivity and quality,
an insistence on the continuous production, less differentiation between
direct and indirect workers, an incorporation of several other maintenance
duties into the profile of the production worker, and a broader variety of
car models. Rigidities in the external or internal labour market are a
handicap but to successfully overcome them, organizations must depend on a
smooth co-operation in the triangular relationship of management, trade
unions, and government. There appears to be "a strong interrelationship
between an internal pattern of manpower adjustment and manpower planning, the
existence of institutionalized consultation and participation at plant and
enterprise level, a decentralized, flexible work organization, and the
presence of a productivist economic consensus between management and the
workforce. Where one of these elements is present, the others are likely to
be present as well" (Ibid., p. VIII). The cost of consensus may be
considerable, but it is outweighes taken out of its historical context,
important explanatory factors are omitted, as in the case of the comparative
study done by G. Hofstede. [31] The dynamic nature of cultural reality has
to be adequately appreciated. "The organizational culture of a factory or
company is not only a source of stability, orderly functioning, transparence
by familiarity, but also its source of innovation, disturbance, and
elusiveness" (Sorge and Warner 1986:34). [32]

A distinction between the objective and the subjective is quite important in
the practice of management. First of all, the claim of my objectivity over
the subjectivity of others is ill-founded. Secondly, the interpretation by
others of policies originating and promoted from the top plays an important
role in the implementation of those policies. Third, the subjective
calculation of managers influences the willingness and ability of those who
execute orders. Fourth, long-term power considerations have to be reconciled
with the social and economic realities; masters who are not effective in
handling external and internal challenges face defeat. Fifth, in an
environment of changing markets and changing production circumstances, the
flexibility and adaptability of the social organization of work is quite
crucial (Brodner 1985:122). Sixth, the cooperation of management and workers
is necessary to eliminate the many sources of waste, for example, the unused
machine capacity. Seventh, complicated and sophisticated administrative
schemes are quite often more a liability than an asset; dependence on skilled
people is more effective than dependence on impersonal schemes. Eighth, when
the market is limited and very volatile it is not worthwhile to invest into a
permanent and expensive organizational system. Ninth, the capacity of
skilled workers should be reinforced and adequately utilized for the benefit
of a flexible/adaptable production. [33]

11. HANDLING OF THE CROSS-CULTURAL DIFFERENCES

The new informational technologies and among them particularly
computerization, have to be considered also from the socio-cultural
perspective. Different industrial relatiosn and value systems provide the
variety of backgrounds more or less suitable to absorb innovation and allow
it to succeed. Here for illustration the cross-national differences will be
exemplified in order to make clear how much counts in innovation the set of
local circumstances.

The evident difference between various countries is rooted in their local
dominant values and cultures. For example, if one compares West Germany with
France, one finds there ar more workers among the factory labour force, there
are less clerical and commercial staff people, and there are more staff
members in authority positions. [34] "West German factories grow in one

direction, above all: there are more positions of authority than in Britain
and less than in France, relative to works, but these form a much stronger
element of white-collar staff than in France. There seems to be more
restrained growth of both technical and commercial-administrative specialist
components, in favour of the growth of such functions endowed with
hierarchical authority. One might guess that there is a tendency for
functions to be more readily retained within the line of authority in
Germany, and to incorporate specialist functions in the line" (Sorge and
Warner 1986:80). [35] "In West Germany, the application of CNC machines is
more governed by the quantitative and qualitative weight of skilled worker
components of the work-force, by the closer links and cross-fertilization of
line management-supervisory and technical-specialist functions, and by a
blurring of functional distinctions between the workshop and the office,
craft workers and technicians, shop-floor workers and their supervisors. In
Britain, the opposite applies" (Ibid., p. 163). [36]

Occupational identity is particularly strongly pronounced in West Germany and
it is based on the wide spread local tradition of apprenticeship; [37] an
early extraction of elites is less needed to meet manpower demand; the good
quality of skilled workers lessens the need for organizations to apply a
rigid division of labour; there is less dependency on the specialized white
collar staff; there is much more emphasis on co-operation. People from the
lower ranks have a greater chance to advance through employment-related
practice and schooling. Apprenticeship is used less as an instrument to
secure the status of craft-union members.

The quality of vocational learning has an important influence on the flexible
utilization of manpower, professional commitment, amount of control needed,
and job allocation and placement. The economic potential of FRG is
reinforced by the large scope of vocational skills among the population.
This may be expensive but it allows for a better use of personnel.

When comparing per capita industrial productivity between the U.K. and FRG in
the period 1950-78, one finds it has changed from 1.0:0.6 to 1.0:1.3. There
are several reasons for this difference, not only in the external conditions
(export, prices, markets, etc.), but also in the internal conditions as well.
In FRG workers are better trained (Sorge and Warner 1980), supervision is
more oriented toward the participation of blue collar workers in
problem-solving (Maurice, Sorge and Warner 1980), there is less resistance
against job enlargement and a flexible allocation of tasks, and foremen and
higher management personnel have more technical qualifications.

The German labour force has better vocational education. Technician
positions are twice as common in FRG than in the UK. Occupational skills
expected from people with vocational diplomas are better. Sixty percent of
the labour force have completed their vocational occupational training based
on the established standards and certification compared with only 30% in the
UK (Wagner 1986:56). There are more engineers and they have a greater
influence on the organizations they work in. A smooth transfer from school
to the workplace is more assured. Trade unions are more positively oriented
towards the training of employees and payment conditions do not discourage
employers to take them in. General education better prepares youth for an
occupational life (e.g. teaching of mathematics is on a much higher level).

There are also some pockets of waste in FRG. Take the following example:
The sharing of buildings, machines and other production means in the whole
production capital has grown by 63% in the 1970s. But in production period,
only 5-10% of time are the objects actually worked on; the rest of the time
is consumed by transport or storage (Brodner 1985:52-55). There is a
tendency to employ growing numbers of indirect workers, and this is only

partially justified. In German machine building has the ratio of white
collar worker to blue collar workers changed in the period 1960-80s (from
22:68 to 36:55) (Ibid., p. 66).

One of the problems in the U.K. is the major confrontation between the basic
three perspectives on industrial relations: liberal pluralist, unitarist, and
radical (Batstone 1984). The growing concern on "the disorder in factory and
workshop relations and pay structures promoted by the conflict between the
formal and informal systems" (Royal 1968:262) has stimulated practical action
as well as the theoretical discussion. During the 1970s, British management
failed to develop the more coherent personnel and industrial relations
policies. Management strategy was mostly reactive, and responding to trade
union pressures. Personnel management played mainly a procedural role and
its significance was not strong enough to change the traditional neglect of
labour issues by the top management people who are focused mainly on
financial matters. The growth of union stewards in the plants has
intensified collective bargaining at the plant level. "Stewards became
increasingly able to bypass foremen and pursue section interests with higher
levels of management. Formal agreements did not appear to have precluded
'informal' bargaining on agreements" (Batstone 1984:179). Reforms promoted
by management did not increase productivity much, but at the same time they
did not harm workers' interests. Actually "employees had gained considerably
more from reformism than employers" (Ibid., p. 180).

Data for the period 1978-83 shows the increasing role played by personnel
bureaucracy. There was a slight increase in unilateral employer decisions
over manual workers' pay at the expense of plant bargaining, a slight overall
increase in local management discretion, a more developed steward bureaucracy
where personnel bureaucracy is 'complete' as well as where union organization
is more developed, an awareness of plant viability, an increase in attempts
to foster co-operation through union involvement, a growing interest among
employers in developing more direct forms of communication with and
involvement of rank-and-file employees, a reduction in the manual labour
force with associated changes in both management and steward organization,
changes in working practices which has led to major increases in productivity
and efficiency, a growth in the use of job evaluation (but with a fairly
limited impact), a work study which has also not had any major impact, an
increase in union involvement occuring in these plants which faced severe
problems, and an increase in the union stewards' influence. There is a
tendency to involve employees in order to improve general performance by
engaging them in the following strategies: quality circles, autonomous
groups, briefing groups, employee reports, and non-union-based consultation.
However, "direct employee involvement strategies have a marginal impact: this
appears all the more credible when the traditional strength of worker and
steward controls in the 'traditional' industries, in which these techniques
are most common, is taken into account" (Ibid., p. 271-72).

In general, the U.K. scene as well as the French scene seem to be less
suitable for the 'informational' revolution than the German scene. On the
other hand it is necessary to recognize the major differences existing among
various areas of the German socio-cultural zone. In the German speaking
region of Europe there are some very considerable differences in industrial
relations. Not only is GDR's system totally different from the democratic
arrangements of Western Europe, but in addition there are also substantial
differences between the industrial democracies themselves. For example,
there is a neocorporatistic arrangement in Austria based on trade chambers
and labour chambers, a participatory system in FRG secured by law and the
welfare state, and a voluntaristic cooperation between trade unions and
employers in Switzerland.

There is, at least one thing in common for the German speaking territory: so far strikes are rare and most conflicts are effectively solved through established channels. In GDR, industrial peace is imposed by the omnipotent state and the population has nothing to say in this respect. In West Germany, socio-economic growth (three times higher GNP per capita in the period 1950-75 in FRG) so far has kept people satisfied and willing to accept the existing co-operative industrial arrangements.

With growing economic difficulties (tough international competition, unemployment, low rentability of the nationalized enterprises, increasing demands of the population) there is more pressure on existing industrial relations systems of the German cultural zone of Europe. Procedures are perceived as too bureaucratic. Representatives of involved parties tend to alienate themselves from the rank-and-file. The young generation feel they are neglected and handicapped in comparison with the older generation. The high cost of the welfare state costs is criticized by the 10% of the population who are self-employed. [38] With a growing public debt, it becomes more and more difficult to solve the several urgent problems by the appropriate allocation of public funds.

There are some elements of destabilization which need to be acknowledged. One of them is the difficulty, or even the impossibility, of being able to arrest the progress of unemployment in FRG [39] and Austria. Modern information technology has developed so rapidly that the highly formalized industrial relation systems are helpless in dealing with the technological development. The mismatching education and labour market puts additional heavy burdens on public authorities. [40] There is a problem of knowing how to deal with the young people whose life expectations are founded on an expanding economy, when the reality is a constricting economy. Foreign workers have helped to establish the economic well-being of the German speaking countries, but they are treated as inferior creatures. Also, among the native population, there are categories of workers who are discriminated against in the area of wages, promotion, and working conditions. Liberal democratic values and aspirations are wide-spread. but the reality of the workplaces is quite often one of bureaucracy and authoritarianism. Pluralism may look good at the public relations level, but it does not necessarily appear in the daily practice of managing people at work. The cultural gap between the school and the workplaces quite substantial and leads to a reality shock among the young people who enter the workforce. With economic difficulties comes budget cuts on public expenditures. Emigration opportunities are fewer and less attractive than they were in the 1950s and 1960s.

The penetration of the welfare state into the economy has led to many difficulties. The heavy public burden is a sensitive issue in Austria, especially due to the losses in state owned enterprises. There is a feeling among the taxpayers in the better off strata that they receive too little for the amount they pay. [41] According to 1986 data, the upper one third of Austrian households absorb 58.5% of all income and pay 62% of all taxes, but they receive only 36% of all state benefits. The lowest one third of households receive 12.5% of all income, pay 10% of all taxes, but receive 31% of all state benefits. The middle one third of households receive 29% of all income, pay 28% of the whole tax load, and receive from the state 33% of all benefits. Austrian families are taxed according to their income, but the benefits received from the state depend much on household size (Die Presse, 1987, 9th Feb., p. 7).

It is worthwhile to mention here that actually those people who are better off use more of the "invisible" public services (roads, cultural facilities, post services, etc.) but this is not adequately recognized by them. High

additional wage and salary costs in Austria (92% in 1984, of which 39% go to
compulsory social benefits, 23% to vocational and additional payments, 14% to
sickness benefits, 7% to voluntary benefits) discourages employment,
particularly in the private sector (in the period of 1960-85 self-employment
declined from 24% to 14%). Technical and organizational rationalization of
the economy endangers the permanency of many posts. There is some resistance
to the technological and informational modernization. People gaining much
profit from the status quo do not want changes which would undermine their
stability and security.

In the Austrian case, one takes into consideration the continuity of class
differences, social redistribution remains quite improbable for Austria,
especially with the weakening appeal of socialism. The hope, especially for
the growing number of postsecondary graduates, is that economic growth [42]
will be rapid enough to create new chances for everybody, including the poor
and the neglected. In the 1980s, the real Austria GDP growth has declined in
comparison with the 1970s. The same has happened with the real per capita
income. On the other hand, employment has remained on approximately the
same. The social expenditure in % of GDP has grown in Austria since 1960
from 18% to 28% (31% in FRG, 15% in Switzerland, 33% in Sweden). While
Austria's unemployment rate is growing, it still remains much below the
average for West Europe.

The challenge that a postindustrial society faces in Austria - according to
H. Seidel (Bodzenta et al. 1985) - is the fulfillment of a considerable
amount of new expectations, such as: innovative orientation in industry, more
science and development, rationalization of social benefits, achievement of
equilibrium in the public budget, elimination of heavy losses in state-owned
industry, higher efficiency (and rentability) of university education and
public health, and balancing of foreign trade.

The tradition of a centralized Austrian bureaucracy, which took over from the
Austro-Hungarian monarchy, still presents a problem in adaptation to new
technological and trade challenges. Austria's strength rests in its
harmonious industrial relations, however, there is still not enough
flexibility which is required to eliminate the existing pockets of waste and
to insure the appropriate application of modern equipment if Austria wishes
to open new markets for its products. As long as Austria was a part of the
economically growing community of European nations, its internal stability
factors worked much in its favour. Now much more is needed in order for
Austria to activate its internal resources if it wants to successfully
compete with other European nations.

The reality of industrial relations consists of many factors. Only some of
these factors are of a public nature, most, however, are of a private nature.
If trust relationships are to be genuinely effective, the relationship must
be built up from the bottom. The peaceful nature of industrial relations in
the German-speaking nations is only partially founded in the formal framework
of rules, channels, and practices. The spirit of a positive and realistic
mutual relationship between civil servants, employers, trade unionists,
workers, and management is not necessarily based on mutual love. There is,
probably in most of cases, much mutual suspicion. However, in the German
speaking democracies there is enough commonsense and mutual accommodation to
look for peaceful solutions, such as, bargaining instead of striking, and
calculating instead of following emotions. As it is, industrial relations in
Germany, Austria and Switzerland, provide a good a example for other
countries to follow. [43]

Participatory practices in West Germany consist of three elements: management
participation regulated by law, partnership voluntarily established by the

interested parties, and various models of material or nonmaterial
participation (Schanz 1985). Formal channels of co-operation are distinct
from the actual practice of co-operation.

12. WORKERS' PARTICIPATION AND THE GROWTH OF SERVICES

It is not necessarily so that the well functioning formal participation
system means the actual engagement of the rank-and-file. There may be some
obvious good arising from the existence in the enterprises, especially the
larger ones, [44] of the well regulated channels within which various
interest groups may confront each other in a more or less peaceful manner.
However, the activisation of the rank-and-file is possible only as long as
the grass-root people's needs are adequately recognized and articulated.

This means that the social organization of an enterprise has to be reshaped,
managerial practices have to be changed, [45] and the spirit of co-operation
between the management and the workers has to be encouraged. As long as the
practice of participation does not substantially influence the social
organization of work, participation remains at the elitist level and at best
is a continuous bargaining process between representatives of various
interest groups and management. Such bargaining is of some importance for
the rank-and-file, but only to a limited extent. It is quite common for
interest groups to alienate themselves from the common people and to be under
the control of arbitrary leaders. Business between functionaries who
represent management, trade unions, various categories of personnel,
political parties, and ethnic and religious groups, does not necessarily
animate the rank-and-file. [46] The formal democratization of an enterprise
has, sometimes, only a limited impact on the employee community.

In the German-speaking countries, and particularly in FRG and Austria, there
is a major problem with changing industrial profiles and the cost involved.
In the period of 1957-87, employment in West German coal mines declined from
604,000 to 163,000 workers, and in the steel industry, from 294,000 (363,000
in 1962) to 199,000 workers. In order to secure jobs, FRG subsidized
declining industry in the amount of DM 120 billion in 1986 alone (Die Zeit,
1987, 15:1). Industries such as steelworks, shipyards, farms and other
fields are unable to survive without continuous public support. According to
the Institute of World Economy, if FRG cut subventions in half and lowered
taxes accordingly, there could be a million more jobs in the expanding
branches of industry.

Some rigid elements in industrial relation systems originate in a class
structure which is not mobile enough to allow for an intensified vertical or
horizontal mobility of workers. In West Germany, well over half the male
population (56% in the generation of sons and 52% in the generation of
fathers) are blue collar workers. West Germany, specifically, has an evident
differentiation between blue collar workers, office workers, and
administrative elite. This class differentiation is more established and
reinforced by a self-selection processes, than in other countries of western
Europe and North America. German blue collar workers and small enterpreneurs
face considerable difficulties in palcing their children outside their own
social category, and this is much related to the educational system (Kaase
1986:342-353). Class distance is more evident in West Germany than in any
other developed industrial democracy, except Ireland. The gap between the
traditionally lower classes and the top administrative and business elite
remains quite substantial. The progress of computerization may polarize even
more the existing class distances.

One of the problems the German speaking countries face is the burden of taxes
and social insurance. In FRG during the period of 1969-86, the indirect cost

of labour (various benefits, social insurance, etc.) per one employee grew in industry and construction from 46% to 83% of the direct cost (100% in banking and 69% in the retail trade). The whole labour cost per one employee has grown in the same period of time from DM 16,400 to DM 60,100 (Die Zeit, 1987, 10:34). Government's share in the current disbursement/revenue in percent of GDP is in FRG 43%/45%, Austria 45%/48%, and Switzerland 31%/34% (U.S. 35%/31%, UK 45%/43%, Japan 27%/30%).

The substitution of people by machines is attractive for West German employers even when one tenth of the labour force remains unemployed. Around 55% of total civilian employment in German speaking countries is located in the service industry (69% in the US, 56% in Japan) which is becoming incrasingly mechanized. This does not necessarily lead to higher unemployment, [47] but it definitely opens the possibility of it occurring.

Highly organized services are very more depersonalized. Although, they are very sophisticated, they are also costly to operate, and quality suffers. In societies dominated by service industries, customers tend to become objects of manipulation. Consumer needs are artificially created. The social value of services rendered is becoming an acute socio-moral problem. Are services rendered actually contributing to the general well-being of society, or are these services actually doing more harm than good? For example, low quality education is not only very expensive for the society, but in addition, it is obviously performing a disservice to society.

With the growing direct and indirect cost of labour, mechanization also inservices becomes a solution attractive to the employers, especially in the unionized branches. In West Germany, white collar employement has grown during the period of 1950-82 from 22% to 47%, and the service industry has grown in GDP during the period of 1960-85, from 41% to 56% [48] (the growth of private services was much higher than the growth of public services). The socio-economic context of office work is changing. The higher level of education [49] contributes to higher skills, but, also, to expectations of better treatment, more chances of advancement, higher salaries, etc. (another question to consider is how much are these expectations really justified).

13. SOPHISTICATED PLANNING AND COMPUTERIZATION OF SERVICES

The function of planning is gaining importance in organizations, but there is a progressive gap developing between strategic functions and implementation functions. The structural transformations of the labour force influence the power configuration. Complex organizations need more flexibility, translocation, decentralization, and management participation in order to activate fully their great potentials. A better working life has become the vital issue for working people. They expect more now than ever before.

The increasing mechanization of the office has several consequences. There is a reduction of labour power. Chances for internal promotion are reduced due to a demand for externally trained personnel. Men are replaced by women (or vice versa). Competition in the market place forces employers to reduce their personnel on the basis of modern technology. There is a considerable mobility of the personnel due to the change of skill demand. There are a limited number of attractive careers. There is a reduction of lower managerial rank positions. New controls are imposed on people who once enjoyed considerable autonomy. Trade unions face the difficulty of meeting challenges. There is a need for all concerned, to take a long term, cooperative approach in response to technological change.

There are various concepts related to computerization, and organization response must vary with the different demands. Various groups of experts become either reinforced by electronic data handling or they feel the need to defend themselves. Computers may serve as a tool or they may provide a basis for a new management system. The centralization of activities corresponds to the concentration of controls.

The use of modern computerized office equipment in the workplace diminishes the chances for lower personnel to enter upward career patterns. This inhibits people's aspiration to advance to higher levels within the internal market. Although, people in the workplace now have higher levels of education than before, the expectations of autonomy, good salaries, and creative work conditions are more difficult to fulfill. The majority of service employees (4/5) surveyed in West Germany by Baethge and Oberbeck (1986) showed an interest in positions with more responsibilities, interesting work, as well as in the results of their present work activities. However, they were much less optimistic regarding their actual chances for this type of employment (this was particularly valid for women). In financial institutions and communal administration, the awareness of no advancement chances was much stronger than in industry or in trade (Ibid., p. 360). While there was no dominant negative feelings of employees toward modern technology, a major concern for the depersonalization of work was quite evident.

How much can computerization actually stimulate the productivity of service labour? In FRG, the productivity rate per each employee, in thousands of DM, during the period 1960-85, has grown from 7 to 25 in agriculture, and from 26 to 61 in industry, but only from 34 to 63 in services (from 38 to 49 in public services and from 35 to 70 in private services). In the financial field, the productivity rate per employee, in DM, has grown from 49,000 to 101,000. From the 1960s to the first half of the 1980s, the growth of productivity, including services in FRG, has slowed down quite considerably.

The impact of computerization has to be studied systematically in order to make policy judgements according to verified facts and not speculation. Even in FRG, public authority policy making remains at a relatively low level of sophistication. The importance of a close interrelationship between technological facts and socio-organizational facts remains underappreciated.

Computerization may be fully utilized only under certain socio-organizational conditions. Models of socio-organizational structures have to stress flexibility. A close relationship between information and practical activity must be encouraged. The practice of an integrative and cooperative style, the cultivation of personal contacts with clients (electronic communication is not enough), the reinforcement of cost/benefit control, the elimination of the employees' justified fear that they are under too much control, and the prevention of the deterioration of professional self-identity and pride are problems that must be addressed when designing new organizational structures.

Democratic German industrial relations system still function remarkably well because of the following principles which are more or less consistently implemented: a close co-operation between experts who represent divergent interests, but speak the same language of professionalism and rationality, the distinction between entrepreneurship, which is necessary to secure the saleability of the whole enterprise, a practical arrangement of consensus in the fulfillment of specific tasks, the mobilization, at the enterprise level, of various internal bodies (board of directors, director for labour affairs, work council, various managerial levels) to promote jointly common goals of mutual benefit, availability of adequate information for all interested parties (for example, many German enterprises publish regularly the social report on all employees' benefits available), a close contact between the

enterprises and labour unions in order to keep union contracts in accord with
changing conditions, the growing interest of management in motivating people
at the grass roots level (autonomous work groups have been accepted by the
trade unions as a useful innovation), and the cultivation of the bargaining
process, not only as a struggle for power but also as an exchange of
information, consensus building, and motivation device (Endruweit et al.
1985).

It seems that the industrial relation systems discussed here will need, in
the future, much more flexibility and power to absorb novelties. [50] This
can be achieved, not by a multiplication of legal norms, but, primarily, by
focusing on an administrative practice which reinforces trust relationships.
The future is probably in policies that promote the integration of working
people around common tasks, that encourage adequate motivation, that stress
learning from each other, that reconcile occupational commitments with
self-growth, and which pay attention to the well-being of others (clients,
community). The gap between public appearance and private appearance, formal
behaviour and informal behaviour, creates several negative side-effects.
First of all, it prevents people who work together from achieving a full
utilization of their capacities. It also introduces a strong element of
mutual distrust and reinforces disintegrative tendencies. A modern social
technology of collective work has to include such moral aspects as potential
sources of motivation, more positive mutual assessment, and friendly
reciprocity. Industrial relations in German speaking countries are presently
probably shaped too much by lawyers, administrators and politicians.

14. SOCIOTECHNICAL OBSTACLES IN THE U.S.A.

The objective reality of the U.S. appears to be very conservative, but
actually, there is a great need for new organizational approach. According
to L.C. Thurow, "Americans may think that they are great at facing reality,
being flexible, and taking individual initiative (they may even possess these
virtues as individuals), but they have organized a society - and economy,
firms - where they cannot exercise their supposed virtues" (1985:130-131).

The progress of computerization in the U.S.A. is fast and effective but its
actual further chances have to be analyzed from a broad perspective. The
competitiveness of the U.S. products on the world markets is an important
factor. In the mid-1987 productivity and labour cost in manufacturing was in
the U.S. almost the same as in Japan (in 1985 63% higher) but West Germans
still produced per hour 11% more even if they cost 20% more. The unit of
labour cost was somewhat lower in Spain and Britain, but the value added per
working hour was also substantially lower (The Economist 1987, 21-27 Nov., p.
107). With the decline of the US$ value the export capacity is growing. The
technological sophistication of the U.S. products has much common with the
wide utilization of computers.

The optimal utilization and promotion of technical progress needs the
suitable conditions. A wide-spread practice of fairness, the appreciation of
risk-takers in business, an effective management of high quality teams, the
rejection of inefficient personnel in the management ranks, and the
encouragement of direct interest of the labour force in raising productivity,
are all factors which need to be addressed in U.S. industrial relations. [51]
"Motivation, cooperation, and teamwork require the establishment of a
partnership agreement where everyone's interests will be taken into account
and where everyone is secure in the knowledge that they will not be thrown
overboard at the first convenient opportunity or at the first sign of
difficulties (...) Firms should maximize value added rather than profits.
(...) If some variant of lifetime employment were combined with an individual

wage structure that rose rather steeply with seniority and a system of productivity bonuses, the American labour force could become as self-motivated and flexible as any in the rest of the world (...) Conceived as a partnership, structured to promote common long-run goals, and operated to push decision making to the lowest possible echelons - the American firm can succeed. Operated as it is now operated, it can but fail" (Ibid., pp. 160, 177, 180). The greater effort required to train personnel and to involve the employers directly is a necessity.

Other critics of the U.S. economy [52] concur with L.C. Thurow's evaluation. For example, E.F. Denison claims that the "economic performance since 1973 has been grossly unsatisfactory by any standard except comparisons with countries whose performance has deteriorated even more" (1985:8). Output and productivity performance are deteriorating; there is a major underutilization of several basic factors of production. Existing governmental policies do not appear to offer a remedy to the problems. [53]

Increasing individualization does not foster an adequate sensitivity of U.S. institutions to the problems faced by citizens. [54] This is particularly evident in the field of social services, where the role of the household, as a unit, is undermined to the benefit of individual members. The individualized arrangement of social benefits liberates individuals from traditional family authority. There is a greater tolerance to a whole variety of living arrangements. For the administrators and analysts of social policies, modern society becomes definitely less transparent, and more difficult to handle due to the "consumer lobbies". Traditional boundaries between work and leisure become blurred. [55]

One of the problems U.S. society faces, along with other democratic welfare states, is the confrontation between various pressure groups, who, more or less effectively, articulate the collective claims of citizens and consumers as the 'clients' of the welfare state, and the diminishing control exercised by traditional policy makers (Teckenberg 1987). The welfare expectations are growing in the society and the same happens with the criticism of public institutions, but the willingness of citizens to take a higher tax burden remains at the low level. In 1986 the marginal tax on average earnings was around 40% in the U.S. but around 60% in Belgium, Sweden, West Germany and Italy. The Scandinavian level of social welfare has much appeal to many Americans but it is just beyond their imagination to contribute much more (in the period 1960-86 taxes as % of GDP have grown from 28% to 52% in Sweden, from 32% to 48% in Norway, from 27% to 39% in Finland). There is little social discipline preventing the citizens to 'milk' the government on any occasion. Individualization leads to several new phenomena difficult to be recognized by the existing public and private institutions (for example, the whole variety of non-traditional cohabitation patterns). Computerization is much helpful in the registration and analysis of several new configurations of the social and economic life.

The large scale introduction of computers has several consequences typical for the technological revolution in general. Certain categories of the working force gain power and prestige on the expense of others. Some skills become obsolete and the others replace them. Merits change their character. There is a need for reorganization and changing priorities. Management practices have to be modernized and the managerial training is a must. There is a scarcity of jobs which provide subsistence as well as social recognition. Several jobs have disappeared due to technological progress. There has been an export of jobs to cheaper regions, and a do-it-yourself substitution of several services, etc.

One of the basic weaknesses in U.S. management is its focus on short-term profits rather than long-range productivity. This focus is particularly self defeating when entering the electronic era. It is not possible to successfully compete in the international market [56] when there exists such a myopic vision of management duties (Denison 1985:44-47). With the lower classes enjoying a higher level of education and with their exposure to mass media, as well as the changing nature of the trade union movement (only around 20% of the work force are unionized in comparison with 80% in Sweden and Finland), it is necessary for organizations to change their present form. Management needs to be critically evaluated to enable organizations to fit better into present-day realities.

The future of any country which aspires to play a major part in the world market must encourage a social organization based on trust relationships, offer material and non-material incentives to increase productivity, stress team work, decentralize power, support participatory management, encourage an innovative spirit, and foster the co-operation of people who represent a variety of inputs. There are many major obstacles to overcome when one introduces such a model into present U.S. society. Managers have been trained and are motivated to perceive their role as short-term profit makers. Personnel accept their role as one of a passive labour power. Turnover prevents employees from developing genuine commitment to their workplace. Trade unions tend to focus on material gains while neglecting other vital issues. Governmental bureaucracy tends to follow is own vested interests (America 1985).

The domination of the service industry in the U.S. creates new demands and contingencies on the labour market. During 1970-85, most new employment was in the business of health services. Professional services match those of manufacturing (in the period of 1959-85, it has declined from 25% to 18% of the total employment) and they exceed the overall income average, but in personal services average earnings are more than 40% below those in manufacturing (Browne 1987:53). The potential maximization of a service-oriented economy requires a new form of organization. It is necessary to free people from the traps of favored ways of thinking, thereby unleashing their potential power and energy. It is also necessary to emphasize the importance of enactment prowess, and to disentangle the existing webs of interest and power relations. The imaginization of organizational thinking is a necessity (Morgan 1986:382-83).

15. SOCIOTECHNICAL VULNERABILITY OF THE WELFARE STATE

The growth of the modern welfare state creates much demand for the sophisticated informational techniques. The reliable data are badly needed in order to make reasonable decisions. The cost effectiveness of information plays much role. In order to grasp adequately the great informational demand of the modern nation-states it is worth to review the major tasks and problem areas faced by them. Computerization of the governmental services makes the fast progress much due to the obvious necessity to rationalize and modernize the multifaced state business.

The welfare state carries a heavy burden (Rose and Shiratori 1986). For example, in Western Europe during 1950-77, the percent of GDP spent on public health and social welfare grew from 9.3% to 22.4% (16% in Switzerland but 30% in Sweden) (Kaase 1986:33). The state's social welfare expenditure has grown, in the period of 1970-81, in percent of GDP, from 24% to 33% in FRG and from 11% to 21% in Japan. In the U.S., during the period of 1960-85, social welfare expenditure has more than doubled (+123.7%) while armament expenditure has slightly declined (-87%). State expenses in percent of GDP have grown during 1960-85, from 23% to 35% in the US, and from 32%% to 51% in the basic eight countries of the European Community. During 1975-86, public debt in percent of GNP has grown from 25% to 42% in FRG from 45% to 50% in the US, and from 22% to 69% in Japan. It is now 100% in Italy compared to 44% in 1970. In 1986. the current account deficit as a percent of GNP was, -3% in the U.S., -7% in Norway, -6% in Australia, -5% in Denmark, New Zealand and Greece (but around +5% in Japan, Holland, Portugal, and Switzerland) (The Economist, 1987, 17 Jan. p. 105).

With the state taking on the responsibility of maintaining people in need, or to, at least, substantially helping them, citizens experience a change in attitude towards work. There is a growing discrepancy between what citizens feel they are entitled to and what the state is able to afford. The credibility of public institutions declines with the low citizens' sense of public duty. It is generally felt that several branches (in Western Europe, mainly agriculture) are greatly subsidized by the heavy taxes paid by profitable businesses. Politicians, in order to preserve their influence, find it necessary to promote several short range projects over the long range perspectives.

Among the electorate, there are many people who depend financially on the state (on average, 25% in Western Europe) and who exercise their influence in favour of the status quo. Traditionally, that part of the social strata who were against heavy taxation have lost their power to influence events.

The democratic process does not always lead to positive results in the general social well-being. The welfare state, by delegating power to external groups and agencies, feeds its own potential adversaries. On the other hand, the challenges faced by the modern western state are quite often beyond its ability to meet. Some of the challenges it faces are: a permanent unemployment among a very considerable part of the young generation, the growing gap between the "core" workers (unionized, well paid, with the chances to be promoted) and the chronically unemployed (the unskilled, the badly located, women, minorities). There appear new challenges posed by pressure groups which organize for the purpose of squeezing more privileges out of the welfare state (for example, the old people lobby). It becomes evident that there is a great necessity to retrain a considerable part of the labour force to enable them to meet the new needs of the market, to develop a new differentiation of the labour force (several growing professional groups hesitate to join trade unions), to develop an awareness of the dangers related to the escalating contest for power between unions, employers and the state, and an appreciation of the difficulty to integrate diversified interest groups in order to achieve some consensus. A comparison of countries with different levels of consensus definitely shows that a positive relationship exists between a national consensus and economic well-being.[57]

Democracy is not so much a matter of mathematics as a process of integration in which the victorious party prepares itself for the task of assuming responsibility for the whole (Kaase 1986:241). There is nothing wrong with having some elites who are able and willing, to motivate the rest by their own personal example, except that when the elite remains closed to the entrance of others, broader interests are neglected, and the rules of power game become dysfunctional for the democratic system (Ibid., p. 336). The degree to which social system is open or closed to internal mobility is a very important determining factor for the functioning of democracy.

With the growing sophistication of the population (or at least the growing aspirations of the mass in this respect) the social alienation of industrial relations bargaining may become one of the major weaknesses of the democratic establishment. The Marxist critique of industrial relations in the West, which is particularly vivid now in the U.K., makes us doubt where there is an actual chance for honest bargaining that would be beneficial for both involved parties. It also reaffirms the notion that exploitation of the weak by the strong does in fact, exist. On the other hand, the nationalization of the means of production does not necessarily lead to a better system (in the USSR a wide reform is also needed according to Gorbachev 1987). When democracy is missing in a given society, and the working people do not enjoy the freedom of association, the omnipotence of the state as the only employer is enough to put employees into an inferior position. The Yugoslavian example shows that even self-governmental arrangements at the enterprise level do not help much as long as basic freedoms are not acknowledged.

Computerization helps the state to achieve a much higher efficiency in handling the administrative affairs but it does no solve many problems related to the genuine democratization, an authentic satisfaction of human needs, etc. The fear of a major penetration of the state into the private lives of citizens is only partly substantiated. Not only bureaucrats may use data against citizens but also the citizens may defend themselves against bureaucrats on the basis of data more and more available even through the home computers.

The basic question is how much the problem solving of the welfare state will be actually much easier on the basis of the modern informational technology. On the other hand, there is a question how actually successful will be the effort to assure the genuine freedom of information. In Sweden it is already a public fact but in many other contries the citizens face difficulties to enter the governmental files.

16. SOCIAL INEQUALITIES AS A PROBLEM AREA

The 'informational revolution' happens in the period of major discrepancies inside of the societies. On the one hand, more information and the faster delivery of it helps to recognize several sensitive problem areas. On the other hand, the growth of the modern informational industry leads to the transformations which in themselves are painful and put many people on the spot. It is necessary to see the informational progress as a factor of change in relationship to the other factors.

Of course, heavy unemployment in several countries has a major social and moral effect. The concept of work as a duty loses its socio-moral sense when jobs are actually not available and a considerable part of the work force (11% in Western Europe, much more in India or Mexico) ends up becoming just a nuisance for those who are lucky enough to have a permanent job. The 'core' workers are secure and privileged while 'marginal' workers are insecure and underprivileged. Actually, in modern societies, the marginalization of workers is growing. Poorly paid service workers are multiplying. Several workplaces (including universities) take advantage of part-time workers and contract workers (in distinction to the tenured workers). People without credentials (for example foreigners) have to accept poor-paying jobs in other to survive. The unfavourable labour market puts many people at a disadvantage. Under such circumstances, the moral appeal of work as a duty becomes diluted, especially when organizational conditions contribute to a further dehumanizationa nd offend human dignity. The whole problem of freedom and rights at work or outside of it may look very differently depending on the relationship between private good and public good characteristic for a given civilization.

In the present day intensified competition between various societies for profit from export some branches of the economy are in more difficulty than the other. For example, during 1974-85, employment in the U.S. steel industry declined by more than 50% in comparison wtih 45% in the EEC and 20%

in Japan. In several European countries, public subvention kept this
industry alive. This subvention was, in the EEC during 1970-85, US $64
billion (46 billion in the period 1980-85). Per one ton of steel it was from
US $91 to US $144 in Italy, France, Belgium and the U.K., with the average of
US $65 for the whole EEC (the period 1980-85). There is heavy competition in
the steel market, and the U.S. has not had much of a chance to extend its
share on the diminishing market, especially because of a lack of investment
to make U.S. Steel really competitive.

In western Europe, the economic decline has made high unemployment a major
issue. Almost a half of the unemployed have been without work for more than
one year. One of the reasons for this is the tendency for employers to use
machines rather than people when the non-wage labour costs are high. These
costs have grown in the manufacturing industry in the epriod of 1965-83 by 4%
per annum in Sweden an the U.K., 2.5% in the U.S., 2% in Canada, the
Netherlands, Denmark, and Belgium; however, they have almost remained the
same in Japan, France, and Italy (The OECD Observer, 1986, 142:4-11). There
is a growing problem in how wages should relate to the actual performance of
the enterprise. [58] In the hal fof 1987 the living cost of the U.N.
officials taking New York as 100 was 148 in Tokyo, 128 in Geneva and not much
less in Brussels but only 57% in Warsaw and similar in Rio de Janeiro,
Harare, Manila and Cairo. The substantial differences in the living cost
influence much the international cooperation.

The industrialization and modernization of societies leads to an increase in
social anomie. Neighborhood organizations may play a positive role in
diminishing the effects created by the social uprooting of people as well as
in enforcing the need for mobilization of social initiatives at the grass
root level. In the US, neighborhood organizing cuts across the political
spectrum (the process of democracy is very dynamic). There is a tendency for
Americans to transcend their local community borders (external pressures lead
to local response). There is, also, a critical interaction between
neighborhood organizing efforts, national politics, and nationwide social
movements. Problems that beset neighborhoods demand political organization
beyond the local level. Neighborhood organizations are built on more than
material rewards and incentives. Local organization creates and sustains a
galvanizing vision which is rooted in people's lives and traditions. A
gentle balance is strived for between organizing, leading, and education
(Fisher 1984).

17. PUBLIC OR PRIVATE VEHICLES OF SOCIOTECHNICAL PROGRESS

It is a functioning question how much the modern informational technologies
may potentially contribute to more social equality. The dissemination of
information in itself allows to mobilize the public opinion on behalf of
specific issues of a vital importance for the general welfare. For example,
the interest of the well-being of small children and their mothers has led to
a generous maternity leave in several countries [59] (but in the U.S., three
fifths of the female employees do not have ther ight to even an unpaid
leave).

The modern welfare state is in a complicated position with regard to its
policies which are directly or indirectly related to technology, and its
impact on society. Direct interventions quite often have unhappy
consequences. [60] This is quite evident in the case of parastatals, or
state-owned enterprises. The parastatal sector has grown significantly in
the last twenty years. In most countries, public expenditures have risen in
real terms by 2 to 3 percent a year. Parastatals account for 10 to 20% of
GDP in many of the less developed countries, particularly in
manufacturing,[61] and they are responsible for 20 to 60 percent of the
investment in the less developed world (Berg 1987:6-7).

Is privatization the answer to the problems faced by parastatals? Will it
address the problems of lack of skilled manpower, overstaffing, high costs,
bad management, improper handling of several projects, corruption, etc? In
the developing world, markets are thin and there are few potential buyers.
There may not be enough entrepreneurship in the developing world in specific
fields such as the postal services or the railways. Legal sysatems may be
not open to divestiture. Public resistance against divestiture may be very
strong. Contracting out public sector services may be more successful route
to follow than change to ownership. The deregulation of the economy may be
more functional in the long run. "Privatization of management and load
shedding via deregulation or contracting out is probably the next wave of the
future, suitable for economies at all stages" (Berg 1987:?1).

The indirect role of the state seems to be more successful than the direct
role. One such activity is the effort to secure enough funds in order to
finance technical investments. If the tax collection system does not work
properly, or if taxation is commonly felt to be too heavy, the resort to tax
evasion practices will contribute to the growth of a black economy. [62]
However, probably the most important constructive role the state could play
would be in its promotion of an innovative society as a combination of an
intensive market demand, scientific knowledge, business and technical talent,
risk capital, skilled and educated manpower, and a reasonable tax and
regulatory environment (Ayres 1987:38). For example, in Japan where
innovation is well-funded, the capital for internal investment, consisting of
savings and depreciation, contributes 30% of GNP in comparison with 18% in
the US (Ayres 1987:40). In the labour relations the contribution of the
government may be quite substantial, especially when the labour contracts are
dispersed, as this happens for examle in the UK. [63]

The state and public sector can play a very constructive role in technical
innovations in a whole variety of ways. It can assist in the accumulation of
resources needed for investments, the long term collecting of intelligence
and long-range planning, the initiation of co-operation between various
involved institutions, the training of skilled labour power, the retraining
and reallocation of the labour force according to changing needs and
priorities, the stimulation of technical imports and exports, and the
promotion of harmonious labour-management relations.

Direct involvement of the government in economic activities is usually not
successful,[64] except in the case of an emergency situation or the lack of
any other local entrepreneurship. The administrative profile of the state
doeos not fit well into profitable business undertakings. Procedures which
are traditionally followed in running a country are not capable of responding
properly to the typical necessities of enterprises.

A distinction between state and business has to be emphasized in order to
avoid the waste of public funds, the continuation of inefficiency, and the
misuse of enterprises for the sake of protectionism. [65] On the other hand,
it is in the public interest to create conditions for the private,
co-operative and municipal business to grow for the benefit of all. One of
government's main problems is its inability to act in a way that is
convenient for business without being protective or inhibiting
entrepreneurship. The Japanese practice of government-business cooperation
is quite illuminating in this respect, even if the Japanese model does not
fit well into other cultural traditions; another question is how much the
Japanese 'uniqueness' is only an illusion (Dale 1986).

18. CONCLUSIONS

The further development of modern technology is unavoidable due to the long-term and short-term consequences of technical progress need to be analyzed from a sociotechnical perspective, or the application of the social sciences to problem solving. One of the tasks which takes priority in this respect is the extension of sensitivity among management people with regard to the human factor. There must be an adaptation of employees to machines and machines to employees. Job design should be based on the recognition of human potential. Flexible task allocation, career planning, synchronization of business development, system of rewards which motivate people to task fulfillment, imaginative social organization of work that would multiply the collective potential and reinforce the teamwork spirit, co-operation based on trust relationships, and the co-ordination of various activities which is synchronized with the technological potential are all necessary factors to consider.

Modern management badly needs a reinforcement of its professional profile as well as more expanded scope of organizational alternatives. The manager, inspired by the professional values and norms, will commit himself/herself in a much different manner than an administrator. "The ultimate justification for a professional act is that it is, to the best of the professional's knowledge, the right act (...) The ultimate justification of an administrative act (...) is that it is in line with the organization's rules and regulations, or that it has been approved - directly or by implication - from unequal development, and the wide-spread commitment of societies to mechanize work, improve its productivity, and extend its scope. The long-term and short-term consequences of technical progress need to be analyzed from a sociotechnical perspectivae, or the application of the social sciences to problem solving. One of the tasks which takes priority in this respect is the extension of sensitivity among management people with regard to the human factor. There must be an adaptation of employees to machines and machines to employees. Job design should be based on the recognition of human potential. Flexible task allocataion, career planning, synchronization of business development, system of rewards which motivate people to task fulfillment, imaginative social organization of work that would multiply the collective potential and reinforce the teamwork spirit, co-operation based on trust relationships, and the co-ordination of various activities which is synchronized with the technological potential are all necessary factors to consider.

Modern management badly needs a reinforcement of its professional profile as well as more expanded scope of organizational alternatives. The managear, inspired by the professional values norms, will commit himself/herself in a much different manner than an administrator. "The ultimate justificatoin for a professional act is that it is, to the best of the professional's knowledge, the right act (...) The ultimate justification of an administrative act (...) is that it is in line with the organization's rules and regulations, or that it has been approved - directly or by implication - by a superior rank" (Gross and Etzioni 1985:136). The combination of organizational skills, entreneurship, stewardship, and leadership are the necessary components for good management and management training should reflect this need.

The dissemination of modern technology creates an additional demand in this respect. Being open to novelties is obviously needed more when the contingencies of the managerial work are changing under the impact of technological innovations, market transformations, flexibility of organizational settings, international competition, the growing educational level of the personnel, and the mobility of managers themselves.

The rational character of the technology quite often reveals the 'irrational' nature of several factors appearing in the organizational framework of a

given business: dependence on the personnel inadequately selected and
trained, wrong match of people and tasks fulfilled by them, productive
potentials of various organizational units remaining much unequal,
communication gaps, malinformation of the personnel, arbitrary managerial
decisions reflecting personal idiosyncrasies, low motivation of the
subordinates, lack of feedback, etc. Efficient new equipment applied to the
bad organizations may only deepen the existing inadequacies. The mixture of
ratioanlity and irratioanlity puts the business even more in inequilibrium.
Managers need prorfessional awareness which would allow them to make a
reliable diagnosis what will actually work and be beneficial for businesses
run by them. So far due to the bureaucratic managerial tradition there is
too much of the "instrumental/functional" ratioanlity and not enough of the
"substantial" rationality "where people are encouraged to determine whether
what they are doing is appropriate and adjust actions accordingly. Whereas
under the bureaucratic ethos actions are rational because of their place
within the whole, substantial rationality requires actions that are informed
by intelligent awareness of the complete situatoin" (Morgan 1986:37).

FOOTNOTES

(1)   One of the good examples is the controversial insight into the Swedish
      society made by R. Huntford (1972). He emphasizes strongly the
      socialization of Swedes to the omnipotent state bureaucracy and the
      voluntary associations closely co-operating with it. According ot him,
      the basic differences between Sweden and the rest of the Western world
      is exactly in this factor. He emphasizes "an instinct for the
      collective, a suspicion of parliamentary institutions, a worship of the
      State, and a preference for government by bureaucrat rather than by
      politician" (1972:9). Submission to the authority on the side of the
      ruled goes together with the thorough understanding on the side of the
      rulers of the close interaction between power and politics.
(2)   The new line presented by M. Gorbachev and his followers is a testimony
      to the fact that the Soviet bloc is not immune to the awareness
      mentioned above.
(3)   The confrontation between the communist government party and Polish
      society in the early 1980s occurred on several battle fields. One of
      them, industrial democracy was closely related to the issue of economic
      reform. The most enlightened parts of the Polish labour power, mostly
      the technical intelligentsia, supported the idea of self-governmental
      structures within the nationalized enterprises. This was rejected by
      the rulers whose rule depended on their privilege to appoint local
      executives, as well as their making enterprises fully dependent on the
      higher authorities within the tight planning system. The experts
      employed by the enteprises were particularly aware of the existing
      shortcomings: the wide-spread waste of resources, the elimination of
      entrepreneurship, the lack of adequate contact between various
      enterprises which badly needed each other, the inefficiency, the low
      motivation of personnel, the doctoring of the statistical data, the red
      tape, the privileges based on political loyalties and informal liasons,
      and corruption.
      The fast deteriorating economic situation and the evident inability of
      the rulers to offer any remedies, mobilized the rank-and-file
      initiatives towards the autonomy of enterprises, self-government based
      on democratic procedures, the appointment of an executive director by
      the workers' councils, and the involvement of a whole crew in the
      melioratory initiatives. A regular network of communication and
      cooperation was established between many enterprises. They enjoyed
      support from Solidarity even when the free trade union movement was
      hesitant to take direct responsibility for the work democracy projects;
      their intention was to leave it up to individual industrial crews to

promote their own self-governmental initiatives (Lewandowski & Szomberg 1985).

(4) Hall is right that "larger-scale changes would appear to be dependent upon shifts in power, within organizations and in the wider society" (1986:293). However, he misses this point himself when dealing with the Yugoslavian case. Power arrangements within organizations are difficult to change because among the present power holders hesitate sharing their power with the others. Also, change is difficult because "workers appear to be unwilling, even unable, to assume power through participation" (Ibid., p. 300). It would be necessary to flatten hierarchy and to decentralize decision making, open communication channels, and spread the system knowledge around. According to Hall, "the sheer possession of power tends to lead to its perpetuation" (Ibid., p. 312) and any major change is improbable "because owners/managers have more power than workers" (Ibid., p. 312). However, the moral orientation of people located on various levels of organizational hierarchies may be reinforced to open more chances for job reform. This already happens with good results in various countries. The concern for business and management ethics should be systematically reinforced in order to open people up to the new ways of thinking, feeling and evaluating work.

(5) As occurred in 1956, and also in 1980/81, a struggle was promoted in Poland in the name of self-government, to liberate individual nationalized enterprises from the tight control exercised by the higher administrative and political bodies: ministries, industrial "associations" (actually the obedient executors of the orders coming from the top), communist party agencies at the local, regional and central level, and secret police agencies. This struggle mobilized the rank-and-file as long as they felt there was a possibility of improving the general work and salary/wage conditions on the basis of more autonomy. However, much more was actually needed in order to make self-government a viable alternative. Unfortunately, the promotors of self-government seemed not to be aware of the alternative models of social organization at work. In order to establish in the enterprises a new vehicle of social energy mobilization, it would be necessary for sociological imagination to go beyond the traditional bureaucratic pattern. The naive belief that it would be enough to make enterprises fully autonomous in order to improve substantially the work output of the employees, was wide-spread. The direct confrontation with the ruling apparatchiks consumed most of the time and effort of the self-governmental activists, taking time away from the nationalized enterprises.

Unfortunately, under orthodox Marxist rule, there was no chance for Poles to develop a literature on alternative organization which would have supplied interested readers with new ideas and foreign experiences (for example, the fascinating experience of the Israeli kibbutzes). Any long term change, and not just a temporary correction of the status quo, needs to be reinforced by adequate cultural formation. A genuine self-governmental work culture has to be consciously promoted in a variety of ways for it to shape the motivation and the behaviour of people accordingly. Self-governmental reality will never be achieved just by the measure of formal rearrangement. A completely new style of job fulfillment and management practice has to be designed and gradually implemented in order for it to become a dominant factor of work reality. An authoritarian style may be effectively defeated only by a replacement of a democratic style and an appropriate culture of human relations. Unfortunately, economists and technicians who dominate the scene of actual and potential reforms take a very formal and even mechanistic approach to organization. This happens partly because of their lack of a humanistic educational background. Such a mechanistic and formalistic bias is characteristic of many contemporary sociological studies which focus on structural aspects while and missing the psycho-moral and humanistic factors.

Self-government at work can not happen without broad vision. Vague statements about a self-governmental commonwealth are not enough to inspire a democratic culture that would encourage people to relate to each other in a completely new way, be self-critical, and reject the traditional behavioural patterns for entirely new developments. Reform must penetrate human souls for it to be really effective and for it to offer a long-lasting alternative.

(6) The model of bureaucracy created by Max Weber well before the First World War has a universal character. He imagined the world being dominated by this type of organizational system, but, personally. he was far from being happy about it. At least, to some extent, he was definitely right. In the East, a bureaucratic version of socialism has triumphed, and in the West, the growth of the welfare state and of the great corporations, has reinforced the impact of bureaucratization. In the German territory, both these versions of bureaucracy are particularly evident. Both of them mobilize grass-root criticism of the system, and in the eastern part, from time to time, there is a evidence of cladestine criticism. See, among others, Hermann von Berg, Marxismus-Leninismus. Das Elend der halb deutschen, halb russischen Ideologie? Koln: Bund-Verlag, 1986.

The impact of bureaucracy on work relations and attitudes is of particularly great importance. Max Weber was fully aware of the negative side-effect of depersonalization, and, in this respect, his approach already represented an important correction to the visionary analysis of Marx and his followers. There is now a common belief that people who are treated as the obedient servants of the bureaucratic power lose interest in what they are doing, and do not want to involve themselves. As a result, the socializational potential in the workplace has, in general, diminished.

(7) Individual and group responses to work are dependent on the existential situations of people who are members of a given occupation. What is acceptable in one situation may be very dissatisfying in another situation. For example, jobs on the assembly line are quite often hated in developed countries, but they are welcomed in underdeveloped countries. The quality of organizational life influences the a degree of commitment of people to their work. This commitment, as well as the psycho-social correlates of it, have to be placed within specific macro- and micro-constraints. For example, the alleged strong similarities between Poland and the U.S. regarding the reciprocity of individuals and their work (Hall 1986:115) are just confusing when the differences in power relations, the level of work bureaucratization and the standard of living are excluded from the picture.

According to Hall, "By looking at job satisfaction, work centrality, and alienation from work, the importance of work for individuals can be seen. People's socialization experiences and their backgrounds develop their motivation for and reactions to work" (1986:122). What is missing here is the relation between the moral profiles of people, their sense of dignity and accomplishment, and their favourable or unfavourable surroundings. For example, the revolt of Polish workers in 1980-81, was, to a large extent, the violation of their moral conscience by the bureaucratized and dehumanized organizational setup of state socialism. The official status hierarchy was in sharp contradiction to the actual accomplishment and the chance to be socially and organizationally upgraded in the official hierarchy (in a nationalized economy this hierarchy is particularly dominant). There is now, evidently, a tendency in Poland to expand the informal hierarchies. This will create a major challenge to the official system. I am mentioning this case as an example of how much variety actually exists in the modern world in the processes of status attainment through work.

(8) In this respect, the Christian civilization remains very successful despite all its past and present failures. The message around which people group together and commit themselves wholeheartedly to the fulfillment of common goals must have a moral character, and this is historically evident in Christianity. Of course, this appears also in other civilizations but on the grounds of Christinaity, practicality and principiality have been successfully reconciled in a large number of cases (Eisenstadt 1987).

(9) The exaggerated power dimension which suppresses the economic and humanitarian dimensions leads to the lack of balance in the society and a greater waste of resources. The vested interests of power holders prevent them from taking an objective view and inspires the wide-spread manipulation of the collective consciousness. In the societies based on an omnipotent public sector, the manipulation of the masses is particularly penetrative and related to the external control.

(10) Another aspect to consider is the relationship between work/occupation and the life cycle, the latter constituting a vital part of a civilization. For example, the fact that technological changes in housework have not had the effect of reducing the amount of time devoted to housework (Hall 1986:82) has probably much to do with a civilization that keeps people busy (free time is not an idle time) and does not provide room for house servants (they are still common in the developing countries). The division of housework inside the family is again due to a particular civilization.

(11) A very good example of the "sexual branch of social engineering" in Sweden is provided by Huntford (1972:325-337). According to him, Swedes are manipulated to achieve freedom through rationlized sex. "Swedish attitudes to sex may be compared to the classical English public school cultivation of games, but without the character building adjunct" (Ibid. 329-330). Sex as a licenced release provides an outlet for the needs of freedom. "The citizen must feel that the state cares for him, even in what should be the last resort of privacy" (Ibid., p. 337).

(12) Only a limited part of the whole society is able and willing to function on the basis of virtues at the expense of expediencies. One of the potential major sociotechnical tasks may be to reinforce a virtue orientation by providing suitable socio-organizational settings; small circles of people jointly cultivating self-growth, learning from examples, role playing, case study, etc. In the modern management/business circles there is a growing interest to train people in business ethics.

(13) The moral consequences of such substitution need to be acknowledged in order to avoid the traps of innovations that may, in the long run, lead to a major moral impoverishm (International Herald Tribune, 1987, Feb. 14-15, p. 11).

(14) For example, among U.S. college freshmen during 1976-86, those who think that it is essential or very important to be very well off financially has grown from 53% to 73%, and the commitment to develop a philosophy of life has diminished from 61% to 41%. The commitment to legalize abortion (59% in favour) has actually grown. As in the past, half of the freshmen think that a couple should live together for some time before deciding ot get married; the same is valid for the licence for homosexual relationships. Interest has declined somewhat in the promotion of racial understanding, abolishment of death penalty, and in the legalization of marijuana (International Herald Tribune, 1987, Feb. 14-15, p. 11).

Having a good time becomes more and more difficult in developed societies exposed to unemployment and financial difficulties. Tensions develop in several societies in relation to the unequal distribution of

burdens and benefits. On the tensions in modern societies, see Michel
Dobry. Sociologie des crises politiques. La dynamique des
mobilisations multisectorielles. Paris: Presses de la Fondation
Nationale des Sciences Politiques, 1986.

(15) For example, public pension expenditures have grown in big industrial
democracies, during the period of 1960-83, from 5% of GDP to 9% (12% in
France and FRG, 15% in Italy). This rise is attributable to demographic
change, the growth in the number of beneficiaries, and the generosity of
benefits (The OECD Observer, 1986, 138, pp. 3-10). Social insurance, in
percent of GNP, is 33% in France (one third paid by the state), 40% in
Sweden (almost a half paid by the state), 16% in the US (28% paid by the
state), and 13% in Japan (one fourth paid by the state). Social
benefits add substantially to labour cost, for example 92% in Austria:
39% social compulsory benefits, 23% vacations and additional monthly
payments (14 monthly payments!), 14% sickness benefits, 7% voluntary
benefits. Official earnings in Austria are lower than in other
developed industrial democracies, but the benefits are higher (Die
Presse, 1987, Feb. 11th, p. 8).

(16) There is a definite interest in the West to democratize several spheres
of life, including family, workplace, school, and even religious
institutions. One of the problems in the Western world is the
discrepancy between various countries. For example Spain, Ireland,
Greece and Portugal only enjoy 30% to 50% of the US standard of living.
Finland, France, Netherlands, U.K., Belgium and Austria enjoy 60% to
70%, and Italy 57% of US standard of living (The OECD Observer, 1987,
145:16). The tax and social insurance load is 30-40% in Denmark,
Sweden, Holland and Turkey but only 10% in Japan (Ibid., p. 24).

(17) See, among others Seweryn Bialer, Reform und Beharrung im Sowjetsystem.
Ausgangslage, Schwierigkeiten und Aussichten der Politik Gorbatschows,
Europa Archiv, 1987, 42, 2:39-50.

(18) See, among others, Dieter Bingen, ed. Polen 1980-1984. Dauerkrise oder
Stabilisierung? Strukturen und Ereignisse in Politik, Gesellschaft und
Wirtschaft. Koln-Baden Baden: Bundesinstitut fur Ostwissenschaftliche
und Internationale Studien, 1985.

(19) The traditional collectivism of Japan is reinforced by its viable
position in the world markets. Their economy depends much on the import
of energy (two fifths of consumption) even though energy saving devices
has cut energy consumption per unit of GNP by one third since 1973; 27%
of their electricity comes from the nuclear power stations. With 14% of
GNP going on export, Japan only partly depends on foreign export, but
badly needs raw materials. The current Japanese account balance in 1986
in GNP was the same as in FRG (+4%), much better than in the US (-3%).
Export per capita is twice as much in FRG than in Japan.
The continuous exercise of collectivism in Japanese society has met its
limit. See Hiroko Yamane, Les incertitudes d'un people confronte a
l'enrichissement trop rapide Le Monde Diplomatique, 1987, 34, 395, pp.
26-27. On the Japanese university system see Thomas Rohler, Japan's
High School, Berkeley, Cal.: University of California Press, 1983 and
Muriel Jolivet, L'Universite au service de l'economie japonaise, Paris:
Economica. The cost of entering universities has grown very
considerably since the 1950s.

(20) In a survey, Japan was compared with France on the following measures of
personal success: individual effort -74% (62%), diploma -8% (21%),
chance -47% (26%), talent -50% (48%), family origin -3% (37%) (Yamane,
op. cit.). These data show that in Japan there is still a wide-spread
belief that chance, family connection, and diploma actually count less
than individual energy and effort. However, this does not arise from
individualism in the Western sense.

(21) The Japanese are exposed to major challenges related to the high cost of
land and housing, limited social insurance, and the tough competition
for scarce resources (particularly within the school system).

(22) Even in the developed world, there are the major differences in everyday technical equipment. The number of telephones per 1,000 inhabitants in Switzerland is 832 but in Ireland it is 265.

(23) See Es ist eine Explosion des Quatsches (an interview with K. Haefner and J. Weizenbaum) Der Spiegel, 1987, 10:92-113.

(24) For example, the Austrian coalition government has many problems dealing with nationalized industry where, in 1985, there was a deficit of OS 4 billions and the added value per employee is growing much slower in the public industry than in the private industry. Labour cost per capita grew very considerably during 1981-85; from OS 310,000 to OS 396,000, and in the oil industry, from OS 461,000 to OS 602,000. Nationalized Austrian industry remains at one fifth of their whole export (Profil, 1987, 2, pp. 20-22).

(25) The profound impact of information technology on culture needs to be acknowledged. One of the problems societies face is the unequal distribution of electronic information facilities. The developed nations have only 30% of the world's population but around 90% of telephones, TV sets, mail, cinemas, etc. There is a growing information gap between the rich and the poor parts of the world which is intensified by the inability of the governments to overcome the debt crisis. On the other hand, it is just impossible to overcome poverty without redesigning work systems.

(26) An ability to frame problems, infer causes from symptoms, and check resulting hypotheses against one's analytic knowledge (Hirschhorn 1984:90).

(27) Here it is necessary to take into consideration that the perspectives of management from the public and private sector may differ. The management of public enterprises is usually better informed than its governmental superiors and it uses this advantage to enlarge its freedom of action, and among others, to cover its own failures. There is a considerable amount of bureaucratization. Trade unions are in the advantageous position of securing privileged status for their members, especially when politicians have a stake in enlarging employment chances by hiring as many people as possible in local state enterprises.

(28) The mechanization of office work mostly affects women and creates problems related to their specific role in the workplace. Their inferior incomes, the necessity to reconcile work duties with home duties, limited educational background, etc. are just a few of the problems working women have to face. (Aichholzer and Flecker 1986).

(29) There are, in this respect, major differences among various countries. For example, during 1980-86, the developing countries share of world export declined from 28% to 19%, but their steel production has grown by 38% (in North America it has declined by 27%). The developed countries have improved their share of world export from 63% to 70%. The Soviet bloc has improved its share from 9% to 11% (The Economist, 1987, 303, 7429:105-106).

(30) The attractiveness and actual power of trade unionism depends on the public's image of it. "If union density in the United States is declining to its pre-1930s level, it is because the social forces that emerged in the 1930s have experienced a steady decay over the post-World War II era" (Lipset 1987:70). On the other hand, the stronger power of trade unionism in Canada comes mainly from its atmosphere of social solidarity, originating from its massive welfare state support. Different political cultures and social values influence the public's image of trade unionism (Lipset, ed. 1986).

(31) Culture's Consequences: International Differences in Work-Related Values, Beverly Hills, Cal.: Sage, 1980. Hofstede came empirically to four basic dimensions: acceptance of power inequality, elimination of uncertainty, conformism, and masculinity. Managerial approaches are culture-bound, but in order to find their roots, it seems necessary to

appreciate the historical nature of culture as well as its close
relationship with social organization. This is definitely missing in
the approach taken by Hofstede. The phenomenon of 'culture' is related
to the phenomenon of 'civilization' and both of them are having a
dynamic nature. The dominant values of a given culture/civilization
appear in the combination of behavioural patterns and artifacts. As
Sorge and Warner say, "Culture concerns the selection and social
definition of all manner of variables and their dimensions rather than
one set of variables only. It is important at a general, conceptual
level, but not at the level of middle-range theories (...) It is
doubtful whether locating cultural differences in value systems is
compatible with Hofstede's research method; this is to infer values
inductively from preferences manifested in replies to a questionnaire.
The overall gist of method and theoretical approach combined is that
values are thus localised somewhere between loose preferences, ad hoc
rationalization after the act, and basic values which are morally
charged and consciously referred to in actual behaviour. Values are
devalued both morally and in their explanatory function through this
ambivalence" (Sorge and Warner 1986:35, 41).

(32) The phenomena studied by Sorge and Warner (1986) are treated as "an
unending succession of practice and theory where practice sets the pace,
and the speed of evolution depends on the extent to which theory stays
close behind in taking stock, to release creativity, and to which theory
is not used to rigidify practice. Forward-looking theory is not
excluded, but necessarily too general to be of any help in
experimentation in detail. And this, rather than general principles, is
the truly demanding area of social action" (p. 25).
The main value of the above approach is in the investigative search of
facts which affect several current interpretations confronted at the
shop floor reality. There is not much cross-cultural convergence
dictated by modern technology. Social organization of collective work
still remains rooted in the past and the present of a given society.
The growth of unemployment is determined more by changing markets than
by changing technologies. Managerial strategies, in order to succeed,
have to be adapted to the local cultural traditions as well as other
exigencies. A good training of production and maintenance workers still
is of a major importance. It is a great asset for managers to have a
good technical orientation. The dependence on expert staff services, as
this is widely practiced e.g. in Great Britain and France, may be
dysfunctional when the experts take no personal risks in the
accomplishment of production tasks. These and many other research
conclusions are worth serious consideration.

(33) Blue collar jobs differ quite substantially depending on the
fragmentation or integration of tasks/jobs, the isolation or overlapping
of functions, the mobility or fixed allocation of elements, etc. The
practical question of to what extent is it possible to manipulate the
job dimensions in order in order to accommodate their occupants (human
engineering) needs to be addressed.

(34) This is an insightful study by A. Sorge and M. Warner (1986) of the
cross-cultural differences regarding modern technology in British and
West German firms, with some references to French firms. According to
the authors, the progressing change to differentiated markets and the
relatively customised products necessitates a modified division of
labour, flexible technology and a modified flow production - a major
difference in comparison with the relatively inflexible technology,
where a high division of labour and a bureaucratized flow of production
in the factories focuses on homogeneous markets and delivering
standardised products. "The socio-economic context impinges on the
development, selection and application of technology just as much as the
other way around. Technology is not autonomously given but developed to

suit socio-economic purposes. Technical and socio-economic
arrangements, including training and qualification structures, thus
determine each other. Reciprocal determination then means that outcomes
are ambiguous" (Ibid., p. 173).

(35) In the U.K. there is an evident differentiation between management ranks
and professional ranks; it is much less pronounced in FRG.

(36) The impact of CNC technology is modified by the organizational tradition
of a given country. This is evidenced in the comparison of West German
and British businesses.

(37) Over 60% of vocational learners in FRG are in businesses which employ up
to 50 people. The learning programmes and quality of them are
controlled by state authorities.

(38) In Austria during 1960-85, self-employment has declined from 29% to 14%.
Wirtschafts- und social-statistisches Taschenbuch 1986. Vienna:
Österreichischer Arbeiterkammertag, 1986, p. 109.

(39) For example, in West Germany during 1980-84, those who were unemployed
for more than 12 months rose from 17% to 33% of the total unemployed.
Trade unions are having great difficulty handling the conflict of
interest between those members who are employed and pay full union dues,
and those members who are unemployed and push for help from public
funds.

(40) For example, in Austria there is a definite growing interest in
post-secondary education, but it remains an open question as to whether
or not the country will have enough demand for the college educated
personnel. The Austrian population is stratified as follows: 10% -
double average income or more: business people, administrators, experts;
15% - above average: self-employed and professionals; 15% - the upper
limit of the average: civil servants; 30% - average: blue collar
workers; 20% - upper lower: lower levels of the clerical staff; 10% -
below average: the helping hands (Bodzenta 1985). The educational
stratification of society is associated with income distribution.
According to 1984 data, for the population aged 15 and over, 76% (in
Vienna 64%) have only basic education, 10% have secondary education, and
14% have post-secondary education. In 1984, 23% Austrians ageed 25-30
had postsecondary education but only 11% of those aged 50-60 had
post-secondary education (Wirtschafts 1986:100-101).

(41) Socialists, weakened by declining public support have had to enter into
an alliance with the Christian Democrats who are themselves weakened
electorally to the benefit of other political groups. It is significant
that both traditional parties are losing ground because of their
inability to deal effectively with the growing problems of present day
Austria. For example, Austrian society has an increasing number old
people. During 1970-85, the percentage of insured people who are on
pension grew from 49% to 59%. During 1961-85, the number of births per
1,000 population declined from 19 to 11. In 1985, 20% of the population
were aged 60 or over. On the Austrian past see Otto Schulmeister, ed.
Spectrum Austria, Wien: Verlag Harder, 1957.

(42) Due to this past growth in real income in Austria, suit prices have
doubled (5 for the equivalent of one monthly income in comparison with
2.5 in 1965 and 1.4 in 1938), leather shoe prices (17 in 1985 in
comparison with 11 in 1965 and 5.5 in 1938), beef (142 kg in 1985 in
comparison with 80 kg in 1965 and 53 kg in 1938), bread (843 kg in 1985
in comparison with 562 kg in 1965 and 237 kg in 1938), Osterreichs
Wirtschaft in Uberblick 1986/87. Vienna: Wirtschaftsstudio des
Österrechischen Gesellschafts-und Wirtschaftsmuseum, 1986, p. 17.
In West Germany 87% of the elite are from the middle or upper class
compared to 56% in the total population; only 3% are women. There are
some considerable differences between the elites and the general
population but these differences are not of a dramatic nature. I have
here in mind the differences of power, income, education and wealth
(Kaase 1986:320-334).

(43) There is a greater chance that the role of German speaking countries
will increase with the obvious present day need to achieve greater
balance on the European scene. The relative security of the West German
economy and the satisfactory condition of West German democracy may be
an inspiration for the rest of Europe. Located in the centre of Europe,
Germans may be a source of common peace and well-being or a source of
great trouble for everybody, including themselves. There is no reason
to suspect that the best intentions, especially of the young German
generation already educated in democracy, are genuinely dedicated to the
pursuit of peace. The question still remains as to how much, and in
what fashion, present day Germans may help other nations of Europe to
make their economies better and to reinforce the democratic order. The
issue of German unity remains open. There is no good reason to keep the
artificial division of the country. However, only the reapproachment
between the West an the East may open the chance to reunite Germany and
reinforce its positive European role in a whole variety of fields.
(44) In FRG, 0.1% of all trade business firms in total trade volume, has
grown during 1962-80 from 24% to 32%, and 1% of all trade business firms
has grown from 37% to 46%. Computerization is one of the factors in the
change trade, in addition to self-service, centralization of functions,
and core sophisticated personnel allocation.
(45) According to W. Grunwald and H.G. Lilge, the change in West Germany
towards a cooperative-participation style still remains biased by "a
remarkable discrepancy between attitudes and behavior; the statements
about the favoured leadership style are more progressive than is the
actual behavior, from the point of view of both leaders and
subordinates" (Dlugos and Weiermair 1981:721). Even if the
participative style of management is not common in FRG, there are local
traditions that bring business leadership and workers together. For
example, in the German speaking countries the internal labour market
traditionally plays a major role. Enterprises widely practice domestic
training of their personnel. People with post-secondary education are
much more common in the public sector than in the private sector, which
is oriented much more to the practically-oriented vocational background.
The legitimacy of the enterprise is stronger in FRG than e.g. in France,
due to higher achievement levels in the economic field, more recognition
of workers' collective interests, the practice of internal training and
less business centralization. "Even though organizations
cross-rationally face similar contingencies and adapt similar modes of
bureaucratic structures, the people employed in it due to deep-rooted
cultural forces' make different things out of it" (Dlugos and Weiemair
1981).
(46) Voluntarily partnership established by interested parties is much more
authentic than formal arrangements imposed by either law or management.
However, this type of partnership may be also limited in scope and
depth. For example, profit-sharing plans usually have a modest impact
on the motivation of workers because individual performance is not
meaningfully related to collective performance. In order to make
partnership a fact of daily life and work, it is necessary to exercise
more sociotechnical effort. In this deeper sense, partnership is a
matter of reform and education. Both of which need a lot of goodwill to
be actually implemented. It is impossible to expect much from formal
partnerhsip programmes while they remain superficial and primarily serve
the purpose of public relations.
(47) With teh dissemination of electronic hardware, there is a growing demand
for software, and this is a major change to be utilized. Services need
to be upgraded in order to fulfill public expectations. Even "public
expenditure may be encouraged to increase by productivity growth (...).
Intermediate consumer software service production may be the key formal
economic activity in a future 'information society'" (J. Gershuny,

Social Innovation and the Division of Labour, New York: Oxford
University Press, 1983, pp. 172 and 186).
(48) Also, in Austria, services (over 50% of employment) are growing,
agriculture and forestry are declining (in the period 1951-1981 from 33%
to 9% of unemployment). The real GDP has grown over four times larger
since 1950. The real value of the industrial blue collar worker's
income has grown considerably since 1965, and quite dramatically since
1938. Austrian industrial production has grown during 1976-85, by 26%
in comparison with 11% in EC, 50% in Japan, and 15% in FRG; the federal
debt has doubled during 1984-85 (37% of GDP in 1984); agriculture shows
a considerable overproduction and remains subsidized from public funds.
In foreign trade, a considerable deficit remains a matter of fact, even
though tourists bring in considerable income.
The comparison of Austrian society from the interwar period to the
present, shows definite enrichment, stabilization, and equalization. A
substantial decline in food expenditure for the average family budget
(from 50-60% to 23% in 1984), unemployment rate, inadequate housing, and
other poverty indicators is quite evident. An analysis of the Austrian
prewar reality shows that the country was very impoverished due to the
collapse of the Austro-Hungarian monarchy, internally it was very
divided, carrying the remnants of the previous establishment's
military-bureaucracy (thousands of useless pensioend people) (Carsten
1986). Now it is a country structurally similar to the big European
industrial democracies, with a hugh public sector (and a considerable
public debt), intensive foreign trade (mostly with FRG: in 1985 41% of
import and 303% of export), and a distinctive middle class. During
1971-82, the white collar workes in the workforce grew from 36% to 46%.
During 1950-84, the real GDP growth was 419 (if taking 1950 for 100) in
comparison with 224 in the U.K., 282 in Switzerland, and 457 in FRG.
(49) Public educational expenditure, in percent of GDP in 1984, was 4% in
FRG, 6% in Austria and 5% Switzerland (6% in the US, 7% in Canada, 5% in
the U.K.).
(50) In the theory of industrial relations, the German contribution remains
below the practical contribution (Endraweit 1985:305-325). The process
of bargaining, between several institutionalized actors is obviously
very important, but its analysis so far excludes the wide repercussions:
passivity or activisation of people indirectly involved, location of
bargaining within the broader problems of a given society, the
organizational culture and the contribution of bargaining to it; the
establishment of a specific culture of democracy, the elitistic trends
inspired by the alienation of decision makers from the rank-and-file,
the gap between professionalists and their clients.
One problem that has not been adequately addressed is the mass society
model and its application to the German speaking European societies:
passivity of the common people, manipulation of demands and aspirations
by mass media, the making of leadership on the socio-psychological
basis, the ritual of bargaining alienated from the current needs, etc.
The field of industrial relations becomes the domain of professionals
and this serves to discourage ability and willingness of common people
to take care of public duties. The transfer of the general public
interest from work to leisure is of great importance if we are to
understand motivation in the present day. The depersonalization of work
relations lowers the personal involvement of employees who, not only
interact mostly with the pieces of technical equipment, but, in
addition, are surrounded by a machine-like organization.
(51) Major changes in investment, management and training would be necessary
to reinforce U.S. bargaining power in the world market, and this is
exactly what L.C. Thurow advocates. "The changes that will be required
can only be described as fundamental structural change. Every American
and almost every American institution will have to be willing to change

if Americans are to meet the economic challenges facing them as they prepare to enter the third millennium" (19885:381). He wants a much more productive society, but also a more egalitarian one, so that each individual would feel that everyone else is carrying a fair share of the burden. A new social organization is needed therefore, based on team effort, and - according to L.C. Thurow - only democratic leadership is able to offer it. The continuation of the present day Conservative rule would lead to the further deterioration of the economy and a decrease in the standard of living, socio-economic inequalities, and a general dissatisfaction which undermines the credibility of American institutions (which are already low on the credibility scale).

(52) The U.S. society is in major trouble: the federal debt of over $2,000 billion, the credits of around $600 billion, and the trade deficit of $170 billion! In 1985, the trade deficit was $40 billion in motor vehicles, $15 billion in clothing, $114 billion in telecommunication, leisure an electronics, $10 billion in various consumer wares and the same amount in steel. During 1980-85, the trade surplus declined in industrial equipment by -255% (to $2.2 billion), in technical office equipment by -55% (to $3.8 billion), in synthetics by -52% (to $2.1 billion), in scientific equipment by -55% (to 3.4 billion), and in airplanes by -3% (to $11.2 billion) (Der Spiegel, 1987, 3:99).

(53) In 1986, the US cost of living (excluding the rent) was 31% higher than in the U.K. (a little less in Canada), but somewhat lower than in Italy, FRG and France (50% more than the U.K. standard) and much lower than in Japan, Nigeria and Switzerland (two to three times more than the U.K. standard) (The Economist 1987, 27th Jan., p. 99). The progressing deterioration of the U.S. economic balance presents a major danger to the American standard of living and to industrial peace. During 1974-84, strikes on average, took in work days per 1,000 employees, 340 in the U.S., in comparison with 150 in France and Sweden, 74 in Japan, 39 in FRG, 2 in Austria and Switzerland. The number of strikes was higher in the UK (513) and much more in Italy (1239). A substantial growth in industrial conflicts makes it almost impossible to successfully reconstruct U.S. economy.

(54) See James S. Coleman, The Assymetric Society, Syracuse: Syracuse University Press, 1982. Also A.J. Matejko, The Self-Defeating Organization, New York, Praeger, 1986. Chapter 1.

(55) See Harman R. von Gunsteren, The Quest for Control, London: Wiley 91976; Peter Marris and M. Rein, Dilemmas of Social Control, Chicago: Aldine 1973; Martin Rein, From Policy to Practice, Armonk, N.Y.: Sharpe, 1983. Martin Rein, Social Policy, Armonk, N.Y.: Sharpe, 1983.

(56) For example, the U.S. deficit in trade with EEC has grown very considerably during 1981-86. The export of the U.S. wheat to western Europe declined, in tonnes, from 50 million to 20 million.

(57) When comparing the western countries for the first half of the 1960s and the second half of the 1970s, the countries with strong corporatism (Japan, Switzerland, Austria, Sweden, Norway, Holland) appear better off than the rest in stable prices, employment, growth and the cost of state maintenance (Kaase 1986:156-165). The ability of a given society to integrate various interest groups around common welfare goals is of critical importance. Group struggle not only costs more, but, in addition, it makes it impossible to focus the whole society on the practical chances to improve the situation.

(58) In Sweden, Italy, and Austria it is a leave of around 50 weeks, 20 to 40 of them paid 80% to 100%. In FRG and U.K. leave is for around 20 weeks, 18 of them paid 90% to 100%A (The Economist 1986, 301, 7467:40).

(59) For example, in Japan 25% of the cash earned by workers comes from a bonus given twice a year depending on the well-being of the enterprise. See on profit-sharing practices M.L. Weitzman, THe Share Economy. Cambridge, Mass.: Harvard University Press, 1984.

(60) One of the extreme negative examples of governmental intervention is in
the Brasilian economy where around half of the GDP is disposed of by the
government. The net public debt has grown substantially (US $125
billion in 1986). State industry remains in a deficit and the whole
economy is heavily controlled by the civil service. Compared with
Japan, during 1960-85, the Brasilian GNP per capita changed from 1.3:1.0
to 4.0:1.0. This means that the great chances to grow in Brasil
remained unused, even though the real GDP grew two and and a half times
during 1963-86 (160% growth in Mexico and no growth in Argentina) (The
Economist, 1987, 17th Jan., pp. 23-27).
The public sector does not have to be much less effective than the
private sector. The problem lies in teh nature of management. Thurow
himself, distinguishes between the 'administrative guidance' and the
legalistic approach. "What America needs is not more government rules
and regulations but better social organization. Within the firm this
means partnership, value-added maximization, the bonus system, and a
shift away from detailed job classification" (1985:182).
(61) 50% off value added in Turkey, 80% in Egypt.
(62) The 'Black Economy' constitutes axion, in percent of GDP, aroudn 4% in
the U.K., 10% in FRG, 10-15% in the U.S., and around 30% in the U.K. In
addition, it is necessary to also consider the 'self-service' economy,
namely unpaid work within households constituting from 20% to 45% in the
U.S. See Stephen Smith, Britain's Shadow Economy, London: Oxford
University Press, 1986.
(63) In the U.K., the single employer agreements have become dominant
(two-thirds of manual and three-quarters of non-manual employees in
1978). In relation to it, the role of shop stewards has grown,
especially because more of them now have become full-time and the more
sophisticated personnel management has incorporated shop stewards into
the fulfillment of joint tasks. Manufacturing firms have grown in size;
there has been a marked increase in government intervention in
employment relations. Among the hundreds of the largest manufacturing
firms, average employment has grown during 1958-72, from 20,300 to
31,200 employees.
(64) For example, in India the parastatals in mining and steel are very
inefficient. Work productivity in enterprises of equal technology in
South Korea is ten times higher (according to the federal minister of
energy in Times of India, July 1986). Too many people are on the
payroll, too many managerial positions are occupied by incompetent
people, and there is too much intereference from the government.
(65) The political power which deeply penetrates business leads to
corruption. The secret expropriation of business funds for party
dealings, the rewarding of political cronies with profitable posts, and
the decline of a genuine entrepreneurship are some examples of
corruption by political power.

REFERENCES

[1] Abernathy, W.J. und J.M. Utterback. 1982. "Patterns of industrial
innovation," in: M.L. Tushman and W.L. Moore (eds.), Readings in the
Management of Innovation. Boston: Pitman.
[2] Aichholzer, Georg and Jorg Flecker. 1986. Informations Technologien im
Angestelltenbereich. Vienna: Institute for Advanced Studies.
[3] America in Perspective. 1985. Oxford: Oxford Analytica.
[4] Ayres, Robert V. 1987. Technological Protection and Piracy, Economy
Impact, 57, 1:35-41.
[5] Baethge, Martin and Herbert Oberbeck. 1986. Zukunft der Angestellten.
Neue Technologien und beruwfliche Perspektiven in Buro und Verwaltung,
Frankfurt/New York: Campus Verlag.

[6] Bamme, Arno et al. 1983. Maschinen-Menschen, Mensch-Maschinen.
     Grundrisse einer sozialen Beziehung, Reinbek bei Hamburg, FRG: Rowohlt.
[7] Barber, Bernard. 1983. The Logic and Limits of Trust. New Brunswick,
     N.J.: Rutgers University Press.
[8] Batstone, Eric. 1984. Working Order. Workplace Industrial Relations
     over Two Decades. Oxford, U.K.: Basil Blackwell.
[9] Berg, Elliot. 1987. Privatization: Developing a Pragmatic Approach.
     Economic Impact, 57, 1:6-11.
[10] Berger, Peter L. 1986. The Capitalist Revolution, New York: Basic
     Books.
[11] Bodzenta, Erich, Hans Seidel and Karl Stiglbauer. 1985. Osterreich im
     Wandel. Gesellschaft. Wirtschaft. Raum. Wien. New York:
     Springer-Verlag.
[12] Brodner, Peter. 1985. Fabrik 2000. Alternative Entwicklungspfade in
     die Zukunft der Fabrik. Berlin: Sigma Verlag.
[13] Brown, William ed. 1981. The Changing Contours of British Industrial
     Relations, Oxford: Basil Blackwell.
[14] Browne, Lynn E. 1987. Services and Economic Progress: An Analysis,
     Economic Impact, 57, 1:52-57.
[15] Carsten, F.L. 1986. The First Austrian Republic 1918-38. A study
     based on British and Austrian documents. Aldershot: Gower.
[16] Cherns, Albert. 1979. Using Social Sciences, London: Routledge & Kegan
     Paul.
[17] Cornish, Edward. 1985. The Computerized Society. Living and Working
     in an Electronic Age. Bethesda, Md.: World Future Society.
[18] Cox, J.G. and H. Kriegbaum. 1980. Growth, Innovation and Employment:
     An Anglo-German Comparison. London: Anglo-German Foundation for the
     Study of Industrial Society.
[19] Dale, Peter N. 1986. The Myth of Japanese Uniqueness, London: Croom
     Helm & Nissan Institute of Japanese Studies.
[20] Denison, E.F. 1987. Trends in American Economic Growth 1929-1982.
     Washington, D.C.: The Brookings Institution.
[21] Djilas, Milovan. 1985. Rise and Fall, San Diego, Cal.: Harcourt,
     Brace, Jovanovich.
[22] Dlugos, Gunter and Klaus Weiermair, eds. 1981. Management Under
     Differing Value Systems. Political, Social and Economical Perspectives
     in a Changing World, Berlin: Walter de Gruyter.
[23] Eisenstadt, S.N. 1987. European Civilization in a Comparative
     Perspective, Oslo: Norwegian University Press.
[24] Endruweit, Gunter, Eduard Gauler, Wolfgang H. Staehle, and Bernhard
     Wilpert, eds. 1985. Handbuch der Arbeitsbeziehungen.
     Deutschland-Osterreich-Schweiz (Handbook of Work Relations: FRG,
     Austria, and Switzerland). Berlin, New York: Walter de Gruyter.
[25] Firebaugh, Glenn. 1983. Scale Economy or Scale Entropy? Country Size
     and Rate of Economic Growth, 1950-1977. American Sociological Review
     48:257-269.
[26] Fisher, Robert. 1984. Let the People Decide: Neighborhood Organizing
     in America. Boston, Mass.: Twayne Publishers.
[27] Fricke, Werner, Karl Krahn, and Gerd Peter. 1985. Arbeit und Technik
     als Politische Gestaltungsaufgabe. Ein Gutachten aus
     sozialwissenschaftlichen Sicht. Bonn, FRG: Verlag Neue Geselschaft.
[28] Gorbachev, Mikhail. 1987. Perestroika and the New Thinking, New York:
     Harper and Row.
[29] Grootings, Peter, Bjorn Gustavsen and Lajos Hethy, eds. 1986. New
     Forms of Work Organization and Their Social and Economic Development.
     Budapest: Statistical Publishing House.
[30] Gross, Edward and Amitai Etzioni. 1985. Organizations in Society.
     Englewood Cliffs, N.J.: Prentice-Hall.
[31] Hall, Richard H. 1986. Dimensions of Work. Beverly Hills, Cal.: Sage
     Publications.

[32] Hayes, C. 1979. Relationships Between Education, Training and Employment. London: C. Hayes Associates Ltd.
[33] Hirschhorn, Larry. 1984. Beyond Mechanization. Work and Technology in a Postindustrial Age. Cambridge, Mass.: The MIT Press.
[34] Hochgerner, Josef. 1986. Arbeit und Technik. Einfuhrung in die Techniksoziologie. Stuttgart: Verlag W. Kohlhammer.
[35] Huntford, Roland. 1972. The New Totalitarianis. New York: Stein and Day.
[36] Huse, Edgar T. and Thomas G. Cummings. 1985. Organization Development and CHange, St. Paul: West Publishing Comp.
[37] Inose, Hiroshi and John R. Pierce. 1984. Information Technology and Civilization. New York: W.H. Freeman.
[38] Kaase, Max, ed. 1986. Politische Wissenschaft und Politische Ordnung. Analysen zu theorie und Empirie demokratischer Regierungsweise. Festschrift zum 65. Geburtstag von Rudolf Wildenmann. Opladen: Westdeutscher Verlag 1986.
[39] Lewandowski, Janusz and Jan Szomberg. 1985. Samorzad w dobie "Solidarnosci". Wspolpraca samorzadow pracowniczych Pomorza Gdanskiego na tle sytuacji w kraju w latach 1980/81 (Self-government in the time of Solidarity. Co-operation of the self-governmental bodies in the Baltic region and its general background during the period 1980/81). London: Odnowa.
[40] Lipset, Seymour Martin, ed. 1986. Unions in Transition: Entering the Second Century. San Francisco: Institute for Contemporary Studies Press.
[41] Lipset, Seymour Martihn. 1987. Comparing Canadian and American Unions. Society, XXIV, 2:60-70.
[42] Markus, Lynne M. 1984. Systems in Organizations. Bugs and Features. Boston: Pitman.
[43] Matejko, Alexander J. 1986a. Beyond Bureaucracy? Cologne: Verlag fur Gesellschaftarchitektur.
[44] Matejko, Alexander J. 1986a. Comparative Work Structures. New York: Praeger.
[45] Matejko, Alexander J. 1986b. In Search of New Organizational Paradigms. New York: Praeger.
[46] Matejko, Alexander J. 1986c. The Self-Defeating Organization. New York: Praeger.
[47] Maurice, M., F. Sellier and J.J. Silvestre. 1982. Politique d'education et organization industrielle en France et en Allemagne: essai d'analyse societale. Paris: PUF.
[48] Maurice, M., A. Sorge, and M. Warner. 1980. Societal Differences in Organizing Manufacturing Units: A Comparison of France, Germany and Britain. Organizational Studies, 1.
[49] Moore, Barrington Jr. j1987. Authority and Inequality under Capitalism and Socialism, Oxford: Clavendon Press.
[50] Morgan, Gareth. 1986. Images of Organization. Beverly Hills, Cal.: Sage Publications.
[51] Peters, Tom. 1987. Thriving on Chaos. Handbook for a Management Revolution, New York: Knopf.
[52] Podgorecki, Adam. 1975. Practical Social Sciences. London: Routledge and Kegan Paul.
[53] Poster, Mark. 1984. Foucault, Marxism and History. Mode of Production versus Mode of Information. Cambridge: Polity Press.
[54] Reinecke, Ian. 1984. Electronic Illusions. A Skeptic's View of Our High-tech Future. Harmondsworth, Middlesex: Penguin Books.
[55] Rose, Richard and Rei Shiratori, eds. 1986. The Welfare State East and West, New York: Oxford University Press.
[56] Royal Commission on Trade Unions and Employers' Associations. 1968. Report, London: HMSO.
[57] Schanz, Gunter. 1985. Mitarbeiter Beteiligung. Grundlagen-Befunde-Modelle. Munich: Verlag Franz Vahlen.

[58] Shelp, Ronald Kent. 1987. The Service Revolution. Society, XXIV, 2:71-777.
[59] Sorge, Arndt. 1985. Informationstechnik und Arbeit im sozialen Prozess. Frankfurt: Campus Verlag.
[60] Sorge, Arndt, Gert Hartmann, Malkolm Warner, and Ian Nicholas. 1982. Mikroelektronik und Arbeit in der Industrie. Erfahrungen beim Einsatz von CNC - Maschines in Grossbritannien und der Bundesrepublik, Frankfurt/Main: Campus Verlag.
[61] Sorge, A. and M. Warner. 1980. Manpower Training, Manufacturing Organization and Workplace Relations in Great Britain and West Germany. British Journal of Industrial Relations, 3.
[62] Sorge, Arndt and Malcolm Warner. 1986. Comparative Factory Organization. An Anglo-German Comparison of Manufacturing, Management and Manpower. Aldershot, U.K.: Gower.
[63] Strassmann, Paul A. 1985. Information Payoff. The Transformation of Work in the Electronic Age. New York: The Free Press.
[64] Streeck, Wolfgang und Andreas Hoff. 1983. Manpower Management in the Restructuring of the European Automobile Industry. Wissenschaftszentrum Berlin: Dsicussion Paper 83-135.
[65] Teckenberg, Wolfgang, ed. 1987. Comparative Studies in Social Structure. Recent Research on France, the United States, and the Federal Republic of Germany, Armonk, N.Y.: M.E. Sharpe.
[66] Thurow, Lester C., ed. 1985. The Management Challenge. Japanese Views. Cambridge, Mass.: MIT Press.
[67] Thurow, Lester C. 1985. The Zero-Sum Solution. Building a World-Class American Economy. New York: Simon and Schuster.
[68] Trist, Eric. 1981. The Evolution of Socio-Technical Systems. A Conceptual Frameawork and an Action Research Program. Toronto: Ontario Quality of Working Life Centre. Occasional Paper No. 2.
[69] Wagner, Karin. 1986. Die Beziehungen zwischen Bildung, Beschaftigung und Produktivitat und Ihre bildungs- und beschaftigungspjolitischen Auswirkungen. Ein deutsch-britischer Vergleich. Berlin: Europaisches Zentrum fur die Forderung der Berufsbildung (Luxemburg: Amt fur amtliche Veroffentlichungen der EG).

The Social Implications of Robotics and Advanced
Industrial Automation / D. Millin and B.H. Raab (Editors)
Elsevier Science Publishers B.V. (North-Holland)
© IFIP, 1989

NEW TECHNOLOGIES AND NEW PATTERNS OF SOCIAL ORGANIZATION
AND SOCIAL CHANGE

Gert Schmidt

Faculty of Sociology
University of Bielefeld
Bielefeld/W. Germany

Within the thematic area of this title I am going to
present and to discuss findings of research on the
implementation of new information and communication
technologies in industry and administrations in the
Federal Republic of Germany.

1. GENERAL THEORETICAL ORIENTATION

The concept of industrial society - bound up with specific
qualities of socio-economic structure and dynamism - is put into
question by economists, political scientists and sociologists
since about two decades.

There is an inflation of new "labels": Service-Society, Post-
Industrial Society, Information-Society etc. Looking behind the
glittering names for society there is a strong assumption of
change itself: Until recently in general sociological textbooks
as well as in many specific studies on modernization, development, social progress etc. were characterized by three qualities
of change:

1. trend
2. continuity
3. manageability.

These catchwords do stand for relevant "chunks of consciousness"
(Peter Berger) in society and for deep-rooted historical understanding of "Modernity", these catchwords in many ways even are
implemented into the institutional infrastructure of our societies,
moreover these catchwords do represent a particular model of
social consensus on society and organization-level (involved
is a balancing of socio-economic and political interests).
Last not least these catchwords indicate the established
perspective of technology-politics in most industrial societies.

Facing genetics, nuclear-technology and new information and
communication technologies (based on micro-electronics) evidence
of a new change-pattern is strong.

The new three catchwords are:

1. contingency
2. un-certainty
3. self-steering/self-management.

As, of course, contingency, uncertainty and self-management are
not newly discovered elements regarding modern societies and
organizations, it is important, however, that these catchwords
have become the strategically central "notions" for "Modernity".

2.   CHANGES ON ORGANIZATION-LEVEL: RESEARCH FINDINGS

a. I would like to turn now to specific changes on organization-
level. The background-discussion is the fate of the traditional
"Weberian type of bureaucratic organization".

Research on the impact of new information and communication
technologies in industry - under way since 1968 in the context
of a state-financed research program "Sozialverträgliche Tech-
nikgestaltung" - clearly has shown the following:

1. Regarding labor-force politics by management "Taylorism" is
   not anymore the dominant "theory": the need to increase simultaneously process-integration <u>and</u> flexibility of production by using electronic data processing stimulated for
   example new prospects of the qualification-problem.

   Two aspects of utmost importance:

   - The growing relevance of "immaterial labor" compared with
     "material labor" (this holds true down to the shop floor)!
   - The growing relevance of "autonomy" and "self-management"
     in work.

   Both aspects - which are concretely interrelated - have to be
   seen on the background of the "built into" uncertainty of
   high technology production processes.

   And there is another crucial problem of qualification - that
   again is not only one of management, but that hits to shop
   floor level:
   The demand of reorientation from "product"-thinking toward
   "system-efficiency"-thinking.

   Parallel to this goes increased attention to so-called
   "secondary", "cultural" qualification - again: in many branches
   "down to the shop floor level".

   Qualification criteria traditionally relevant more or less exclusively for management and upper level of hierarchy   become
   more and more relevant for positions on the shop floor level:
   flexibility, general intelligence, ability and motivation to
   learn how to learn etc.

   Absolutely crucial - a functional prerequisite - is the ability
   and the willingness of the worker to "self-organization" of
   his work.

2. No doubt: Many traditional patterns of work organization and work-force-politics do not fit with the new technologies: New changes for the valorisation of capital are emerging as well as new limiting conditions and non-predicted side effects.

Effective use of new information and communication technologies based on micro-electronics often requires"dialogue" instead of "monologue" or fixed "down the line" work relations.

Most important not only "functionally", but also regarding status system is an increasing dissolution of the traditional distinction between "production" (mainly the blue collar world) and "administration" (the so-called white collar world).

To put it metaphorically: The processes "informatization" in factories do not care about this traditional scheme.

At least in Western European industry the distinction between production and administration traditionally is of some relevance for career patterns, payment-systems, self-esteem and social status.

3. Our research in machine-tool industry and automobil industry (the latter having been the classical playground for Taylorism) clearly showed a revised "technology-strategy" by management:
Contrasting with former approaches of introducing "socio-technical" systems with the aim to control non-predicted "deviations", "technology systems" and "social systems" in our days are consciously and strategically coupled as "loose" configuration and as open "trial and error" systems.

The installation of loose-coupled systems in non-research and development-departments should be a rather risky measure according to traditional management principles.

Two insights/experiences have been influential in the context of the implementation of new information and communication technologies:

- The introduction of information and communication technologies radically destroys the vision of a "one-best-way" regarding the vision of labor and process organization - the vision itself (as an ideal in the non-Weberian sense of an idealtype!) proves to be a dangerous/deadly "fiction".

  There are cases of organizational breakdown which forced new managements to throw out the new technology altogether as a first step - and start allover again implementing new technology in a more intelligent manner.

- Possibilities to increase productivity on the basis of information and communication technologies often are related to the use of ressources hidden in non-formalized structuring and in self-organization. To be clear: This is not a new round of the informal-group-game we know from the Hawthorne-Studies and Human Relations tradition, but what is important is the "opening" - if you want: the exploitation - of a new dimension of qualification.

One almost obvious aspect of the new situation is the need for
"non-conclusive", incomplete, non-deterministic decision-
making. What sounds obvious from a theoretical point of view,
however, does challenge severely well-proven traditions of
organization-politics and organization-experience.

For example, we found in a big automobile factory in Germany
three different types of the personal computer configurations
implemented into three "technically" almost identical departments of the firm. According to the management, the process
of the installation of the new communication technology had
to be organized on singular department basis. The management
followed the principle : let them decide themselves ...

4. We finally found out that the implementation of the new technology into the organization did enforce a considerable
   "amount" of additional preparatory and side-effect-related
   social politics within the firms. In all cases we studies
   this point was dramatically new to management, workers council
   and union representatives as well. The implementation of a
   personal computer system in administration or production departments proved to be by almost no means comparable to the
   implementation process of a new machine tool aggregate. This
   holds true for the social range of consequences, the timetable
   of the process, and the factual problems arising.

   An almost complementary result of our research is, that the
   implementation of information and communication technologies
   is related to an increasing importance of "specifity of the
   firm".

   There are obviously less egalizing and generalizing consequences of the new information and communication technology
   than differentiating and specifying ones! This is in direct
   opposition to very popular visions about the effects of new
   technologies.

5. Having said this, I would like to avoid a misunderstanding:
   From the point of view of applied social research in industry
   most of the phenomena noticed at first glance look "favorable". But as sociologists we have learned to be sceptical
   towards "self-produced" generalized "positive" or "negative"
   outlooks for the future. We do remember the fate of the old
   "Debate on Automation" in the 50s and 60s, we do remember
   John Diebold, Norbert Wiener and others.

   A closer look at the organization-level does show at least
   the following severe social problems (problems that reach out
   into society!):

   - More qualification no longer means automatically the chance
     for promotion - but has in many branches become for many
     workers the only way to defend "what you have"!

   - More autonomy in work-situation often is de facto connected
     with "improved" centralized control-mechanisms by management
     ("controlled autonomy"):
     From the "foreman"-control to "PIS"-control.

Parallel to this: In many firms we have studied the control-gap between the management on one hand and the workers council on the other hand is substantially widening.

- Related to the argument mentioned last: The power of the traditional workers representative organizations - the unions - has been weakened dramatically during the last 10-15 years - due also to the impact of new technologies in industry. Particularly in Western Germany the strong unions, being traditionally "Blue Collar Skilled Workers"-organizations, are shattered by the consequences of the new technologies.

The growing number of white collar workers is only one factor. The change of the character of work at the shop floor level is another factor.

Put briefly: The union-movement in many industrial societies of the Western World missed the train of "immaterial labor".

6. I can not present any kind of "streamlined" interpretation. But I would like to take the risk of one more general statement - based on a list of individual findings:

The implementation process of new information and communication technologies turns "soft" social facts of factory-life into a kind of social "hardware".

What does this mean?

Traditionally, the introduction of a new technical generation in production-line or administration processes enforced education, sometimes replacement of single workers or groups, consensus with the workers council etc. - all that with the given formal organization in mind.

With new information and communication technologies that strategic focus does shift in many cases: There is also need of (re-)education, replacement and consensus etc. - but to put it briefly, with the non-given ressources and the flexibility of the organization in mind.

And there is still another shift:

Socio-cultural configurations within the firm determine more or less rigidly what the new technology will look like!

We may recall the old question Max Weber put at the beginning of his studies on industrial work:

a. What kind of work-roles and workers are "produced" by factory work?

b. In what way do the social and cultural qualities of the workers influence the organization of the production-process in the factory?

Facing new information and communication technologies <u>the second question</u> becomes the first one, gets priority!

The new situation does fit in with the juxtaposition of "hidden theories" in line with:

trend/continuity/manageability on the one side and contingency/uncertainty/self-management on the other side.

3.   CONCLUSION: THE NEW IMPORTANCE OF "POLITIES".

I would like to introduce a theoretical perspective that could help to understand the nature of what I have called preliminarily "the change of change-pattern".

Taking up Max Weber's general concept of "rationalization" we recall calculability and command of the situation by means of calculation as the most relevant distinctive features. Usually the concept was applied in Industrial Sociology regarding proc- esses of technological change and of organizational change - the social was treated more or less as a "side-factor".

And on these levels "rationalization" has been looked at as a "strategic norm".

Recent organization research shows that firms' political measures, often defined hastily as deviations from the "strategic norm" - as irrational etc. - do relate in fact to social rationalization as a specific dimension of rationalization that is relatively autonomous towards technology and organization.

Social rationalization does not follow the same logical model as technological rationalization and organizational rationalization as the first one is reflected by the inherent tension of "formal rationalization" versus "material rationality" which means exactly nothing else than: "calculability and consensus".

It is my thesis that social rationalization as autonomous dimension of capital valorisation is getting increasingly relevant when new information and communication technologies are implemented in organizations. Firms are forced to change work-organization and management structures substantially utiliz- ing the particular ressources of contingency, uncertainty, and self-management.

During the 50s and 60s we had an intensive and broad discussion on "technocracy" - one thesis has been: Technology will replace politics.
You may remember Ellul, Schelsky, Marcuse.

Put roughly: First empirical evidence about processes of the introduction of new technology points to the contrary: Politics will "place" technology on the background of the in- creasing relevance of social rationalization.

The Social Implications of Robotics and Advanced
Industrial Automation / D. Millin and B.H. Raab (Editors)
Elsevier Science Publishers B.V. (North-Holland)
© IFIP, 1989

THE PROTAGONISTS IN INNOVATION : WHO GAINS WHAT ?

Norbert ALTER

Sociologist at the Direction Générale des Télécommunications
(French Telecom)
Service de la Prospective
20 avenue de Ségur
PARIS 75700

Does the automation of office tasks (more often referred to as office
automation or simply OA) increase productivity?

Does it lead to a reduction in the number of jobs and a derating of
individual tasks?

Can these much discussed but still unanswered questions now be resolved
by examining the experience of leading edge companies?

Certainly, answers Norbert ALTER, but the problem is not so simple
because technological change entails social and organisational change in
which corporate Conservators and corporate Innovators find themselves on
opposite sides of the fence. The author analyses the roles of the social
players, revealing the advantages and the direct and indirect, objective
and subjective costs of introducing new technologies in the tertiary
sector.

The questions most frequently asked concerning office automation in
the business environment are how much does it cost and what productivity gains
does it bring. From observing the changes brought about as a result of this
new technique, it is proving no easy matter to answer the question in simple
terms (1).

The integration of new sociological data into the information fabric
of a business particularly complicates the argument. It seems clear that the
effect of office automation (2) is more to change the process of production
than to increase the amount of work performed at a given workstation.
Furthermore, the economic effect of office automation first passes through the
prism of social relationships and indeed varies according to the results of
these relationships. The price to be paid for the efficient introduction of
office automation cannot therefore be seen as merely a financial investment of
whatever size but also, and more particularly, as a "social" investment, the
institutional capacity of businesses to make the most of the players involved
in the innovation game.

UNFORESEEN BENEFITS

Manufacturers base their sales arguments on the classic, and logical in the case of automating office tasks, theme of substituting capital for labour. However, most businesses, and even those which have extremely thorough management auditing procedures, admit to not knowing the gains in productivity actually achieved. This apparently paradoxical phenomenon can be explained by a number of factors.

The first surprise, if the initial assumption is a rational, classic conception of technological investment, that is substitution of capital for labour, lies in the fact that economic logic applied to office automation does not fit this pattern: often technology does not replace labour but is overlaid upon it (3). The example of pure communication tools is a particularly good illustration of this trend.

- Audio-conference meetings replace conventional business meetings only on a very limited scale; their main function is to increase exchanges between geographically remote partners, thereby increasing the collective dimension of labour.

- the use of facsimile machines or electronic mail rarely responds to a purely economic rationale: rather than replacing conventional mail or telex, the new tool is used for the transmission and reception of written messages between people directly concerned with their content. The advantage here is an acceleration of interaction, through the absence of dedicated transmission services, but also a reduction in formalisation, through the absence of signatories other than the orginator.

In the same light, almost to the point of caricature, the most startling changes can undoubtedly be seen in documentation departments. The mass advent of data banks in these traditionally paper-strewn worlds has not reduced the numbers of personnel. On the contrary, in most cases, these departments are recruiting more staff. Their contribution to corporate life has in fact become far more significant since the change; because the technology cannot itself absorb the workload due to the demand for additional work, numbers are increasing, sometimes in very considerable proportions. In four large businesses analysed (4), the documentation departments have doubled in size over the last ten years. Of course, the number of questions "serviced" has increased in still greater proportion (from 2 to 6 according to the case), which may lead to the supposition that productivity has increased. In fact, the nature of the questions and answers has changed too much for it to be possible to compare the two types of production.

Departments using word processors are experiencing a more complex evolution. In simple typing tasks (basic text entry, in particular) the automation of certain repetitive functions (corrections, justification, page numbering, insertion of words or paragraphs, etc) enables a greater volume of text to be produced by the same number of personnel. In this precise case, there are therefore considerable gains in productivity. These gains are extremely variable, irrespective of the type of machine used. Within the same company, gains can range from 10% to 14%, according to the degree of specialisation of the work: the more repetitive the tasks, the greater and/or more measurable are the gains in productivity. But at the same time, the more repetitive the tasks, the lower the potential efficiency (in terms of optimisation) of the machines. All the functions are not used, particularly the more complex.

But let us not miss the wood for the trees. Most of these gains in productivity are absorbed by a change in the service required of operators: quality of presentation, proliferation of corrections, new services, etc. Gains in working efficiency, unmeasurable qualitative variables, are greater than the increases in productivity (5).

More precisely, in research departments where OA is widespread, a more complex phenomenon can be seen: the technological change has little effect in increasing the productivity of executives, research assistants or secretaries; the main result is in a change in their task, in the organisational environment and in the collective product.

The jobs of these professional categories are becoming more technical through the development of automated information processing applications, more extensive through the substantial increase in versatility, and less well defined through the increase in the lack of precision or uncertainty, concerning the definition of workstations. The introduction of OA also changes the nature of collective production: in a global sense, the major feature of the new environment is that new services are becoming available to businesses leading to diversification of production and a high degree of mobility of the applications used.

Here too, it is proving difficult to obtain quantitative measurements before and after the introduction of OA since the whole process of production is in a state of upheaval. We can see here the effect of an evolutionary trend central to the automation of office work: the effect of the changes may well be accompanied by an increase in the volume of work with the same numbers of staff, but their major result is different products and a different method of production. The measurement tools offered by management specialists seem here to have found their limits: it is proving extremely difficult to evaluate gains in productivity insofar as the nature of the component elements of the task (qualification of the workstation, type of product and organisational environment) change with the installation of OA systems.

OA is more closely related, in fact, to an organisation technique than to a production technique. It is in this context that we should look for value added to the work by the new techniques. If there are gains in productivity, it is not at the level of workstations considered individually but at the level of the whole organisation and the information circuit of a sector or a function of the business. Here we can identify four lines of force:

1) The corporate information fabric is becoming more dense: the accumulation of telephone links, data links and videotex links, the increase in the diversity of "mediatised" interchanges (written, oral and visual) and the relative freedom allowed in the use of these media have led to less formal interchanges: partitions between management levels and between departments are broken down as targets and sources of communication proliferate. Through the increasing versatility, depth and breadth of information interchanges, relations within the work group or establishment increase, and so do relations between groups and establishments.

2) The accumulation in a given business of different information media, OA here representing only an additional (although dynamic) element of a set built up over many years, has three types of effect:

— standardisation of information: enhanced semantic precision;

— expansion of the information field: more data and text are easily accessible;

- faster question and answer cycles: real time interrogation, increased reliability of information and a proliferation of sources leading to increasingly rapid interrogation.

The proportion of uncertainty in all everyday decisions (we are not speaking here of course of "major" business decisions) then becomes sufficiently low to increase the number of decision making choices.   A good example of this development can be seen in technical decision making aid systems, where the "signal"-to-"noise" ratio has been substantially enhanced.

3) The massive development in the use of data banks both within and external to the business deepens and extends the field of knowledge concerning the environment.   It then becomes possible, if not to control it, at least to determine its nature better and therefore to adapt it to corporate production requirements.   The strategic importance of documentary functions is a good example here: in the leading edge sectors, documentation departments are becoming essential staging posts for the research and marketing departments whereas previously they were run basically as libraries.

4) Taken overall, the new information resources must be interpreted as a vast attempt to transform the business environment, in the sense of "de-bureaucratisation" and adaptation to market constraints, which is diametrically opposed to an exclusively productivist rationale.   Thus we see technological investments gradually changing the overwhelming power of the established order, the pyramid structure and secrecy, replacing them with operating standards, mobile structures and less formal communication practices.

COMPLEX SOCIAL COSTS

If the objective of a business is therefore no longer to produce more but to produce differently, the means to achieve this are also original. Capital investment cannot in itself provide technical and organisational success, all the more when there is no pre-established model.

OA is therefore always introduced in an experimental context.   But these social experiments are not in themselves a method of change when we take into account the rationality of the different players involved (6):   they are also an adventure into which everyone is plunged, including the promoters of the change.   The most revealing element of this "wild" form of experimentation lies in the fact that the introduction of technology is not negotiated, but only its use, after some months of practice, and in a durable manner.   This scheme breaks with that of social science practitioners who generally propose negotiation beforehand and only beforehand.

This approach is original at several levels.   Organisation and production represent topics of questionning and evaluation which are conducted in seminars and in "user groups" but above all every day in offices, with regular colleagues, managers and subordinates.   In a manner first confused, then diffuse and finally explicit, the action is evaluated and this evaluation entails modifications which may affect the whole of the department concerned or just one particular point.   This experiment, because it is not recognised as such (7) is a veritable process of permanent change resting successively on obsolescence of techniques, the resulting development of products and the necessary reorganisation which follows.   It is not therefore a question of non-interference for a few months before locking in to a new O&M approach (8): it is a question of durable interrogation and collective evaluation because the mobility of working resources becomes too permanent to accept a definitively acquired organisational scheme.

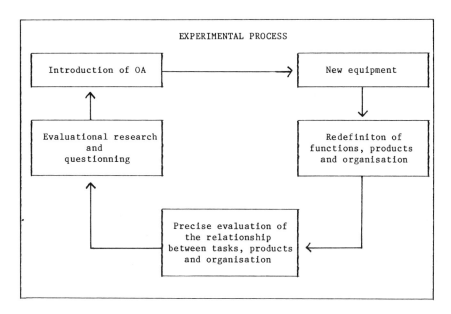

This then is the light in which OA should be considered as a system with a high margin of indetermination: this freedom, in the mechanical sense of the term, simultaneously affects technology, organisation and product. By introducing OA, businesses introduce uncertainties into their operation, and this is diametrically opposed to the scientific rationalisation of work. The fact is original: until now, technological changes have always had the aim or effect of rationalising work; OA, because it is introduced with no explicit organisational reference model, tends on the contrary to "de-regulate" previous practices without immediately replacing them with another form of universal regulation.

The opening of these new areas of uncertainty then introduces into the game players with different talents. Innovators (professionals, secretaries and research assistants) control most of the new "free resources" introduced by OA: directly using most of the techniques, they then become the real experts and essential points of passage for information transmitted via these media. Conservators (middle managers), who use the new techniques either indirectly or only occasionally, have no way of controlling the new areas of uncertainty. Their power, as it was before the technological changes, remains based on exercising and defining the established order and on a thorough understanding of "traditional" information – that which does not pass through the new media.

Between these two groups, conflict, sometimes manifest but more often latent, is always present. The Innovators by optimising technological resources suggest new products and new forms of organisation of work which will reduce the division of work or quite simply the privileges which Conservators enjoy. It is in this light that the pleasure of "playing" with screen terminals should be interpreted: the "games" aspect certainly exists, but only because it enables participants to play a role which emphasises their own rationality. It is also in this light that the "corporate spirit" displayed by Innvovators should be seen: in respect of information, the dominant factors are no longer retention but much rather maximum standardisation and circulation (9). It is through this strategic conduct that they can create products enabling them to gain recognition.

In this way, the Innovators shake off the yoke of the data processing departments by producing local statistics. The decision process, theoretically the domain of the Conservators, is controlled by increasing the number of audio-conference sessions between peer groups. Within the documentation departments, information sources are developped to share the work of professionals ; secretaries tend to acquire maximum technical expertise to avoid the more humdrum tasks. At all levels within the group of Innovators there thus exists cascaded strategies from bottom to top, tending to encroach on reserved territories and based on inventiveness.

Gradually, through these offensive strategies, the Innovators manage to introduce dysfunction with respect to order which is sufficiently great so that the organisation of work is substantially democratised. But territories conquered in this way sometimes do not go well with corporate production constraints: it is sometimes necessary for a secretary to be able to devote herself to typing, for the requirements of the department; it is also quite unbecoming for lower levels of management to bypass their immediate superiors in too public a fashion.

Managers then acts as an arbitrating power between Innovators and Conservators. The "peace treaty" which they establish between partners, the formal organisation, recognises in an institutional fashion part of the advances of the Innovators in the bureaucratic fabric. But only a part, because managers at the same time protects the Conservators so as to preserve a degree of social control over the system of innovation. Institutionalisation of the conflict by managers (10) is therefore always regressive with respect to the attainments of the Innovators; in this way it leaves the door open to a "continuous struggle" the objective of which is to recover the freedom which has been partially lost.

This phenomenon is particularly clear in a department in which the secretaries who, because of the introduction of OA and therefore substantial areas of freedom in the organisation of work, were typing practically no ordinary letters and were reserving their time for more valuable work. The managers, who were not their allies, had been reduced to subcontracting straightforward text entry outside the company. Typing six hours a day before the introduction of OA, secretaries were now down to less than one hour. Managers then acted to recognise the right of access of these personnel to loftier tasks, at the same time imposing a minimum of two hours typing a day.

The most widespread example of these practices concerns the group relationships between Innovators and data processing departments. Schematically, the process is as follows. Firstly, a do-it-yourself approach to word processing (including calculation functions) leads to an avoidance of recourse to central data processing departments for statistical processing. At a second stage, these departments demonstrate the cost of redundancies and their savage application. Managers then intervene to evaluate the respective advantages of the two types of practice ; they accept that certain applications should be totally decentralised at the same time integrating in the central system, and therefore in the data processing department, those which it seems to them could be extensively used by the various establishments of the business. This seriatim incorporation of innovation then tends to place in permanent competition two partners holding different cards and playing for different stakes: on the one hand, the departments where OA has been introduced, who know their own requirements and seek to preserve their autonomy, and on the other hand the central data processing departments who have the advantage of the strength of their resources and who tend to return all innovations straight to the institutional bosom.

Although there is considerable institutional control over the system of innovation, it would be impossible to "finesse" the specific nature of this system through a bureaucratic system: not only does the introduction of a third player, manager, enable the organisation to be transformed and better adapted to the forces in play, but above all, it is the means of taking into account the economic advantages of innovative changes and more particularly, to pay for them (11).

In this light, the evaluation of pilot OA operations is particularly instructive. Much more than a method developed by O&M departments or social experimenters, it is a challenge for the Innovators who are pressing managers to evaluate products and the disadvantages of too formal a respect for regulations. In terms of systems of value or at any event representations, a hint of innovation already exists: henceforth, the production bases become, for management, the harbingers of economic corporate rationality whereas middle management displays a real fear of innovation management.

WHO PAYS THE SOCIAL COSTS?

The social changes related to OA therefore bring about economic rationality. The price to be paid to achieve profitable technological investment can in no case be seen as a simple logical formula, in which capital replaces labour. On the contrary, the more businesses introduce OA into their departments, the more they must invest in training, organisation and reflection on the product. Although there is certainly a social cost in optimising the technique, there is also a parallel "socio-psychological" cost which appears as the result of the interplay of forces.

The Innovators are certainly those who pay the heaviest price for change.

In terms of workload: for them strategic action necessarily involves an increase in their productivity and creativity. Since power does not occupy a strictly defined position in a stable organisation, but rather is the result of an evaluation of the economic results of strategies, intense work becomes the essential medium of these strategies. Let us take two significant examples:

- Secretaries in a department with a high level of OA spend more than an hour every day in learning new technical applications, their only means of avoiding, by "automating" them, some of the more humdrum tasks which they are asked to perform, as well as their only means to acquire the expertise necessary to share tasks with professionals. Since this learning time is not included in the department's budget, they extend the duration and/or intensity of their working day by this amount.

- Particularly innovative professionals in a budget planning department must negotiate acceptance of their requirements with a number of partners who are not always in agreement with them. This results in many meetings, letters and telephone calls which are added to the traditional workload, itself already overburdened with the search for new products.

This situation becomes the essential cause of a mental load which is sometimes difficult to endure. Such circumstances substantially moderate a number of ready made ideas concerning technical change. The strategic action of operators sometimes results in a "self-applied" workload which has the effect of increasing sometimes considerably the fatigue related to the workstation; the existence of this relationship between two forms of professional activity therefore escapes ergonomic analyses through the consideration that the increase in fatigue is directly determined by the installation of a new piece of equipment.

The cost of entry (12) into the system of innovation also results in a number of "cultural separations". For a professional, working for several hours in front of a terminal is never an inspiring proposition, even if it is in this way that he can accede to power: by becoming to some extent a technician, he loses a part of the gloss which also defines his status. But the most evident development concerns secretaries; moving from a business environment in which they were dominated, to another in which they can impose their own rationality, they make a relatively ambiguous discovery concerning the situation: without wishing to return to the previous order, they often miss the "peace" which they enjoyed there.

This is undoubtedly one of the essential regulatory factors of the social system: the psychological cost of strategic action is often too high in terms of mental load or stress for the players to exploit to the full the uncertainties which they control. Often, they prefer to give up, temporarily choosing idleness over action, since action appears as a greater constraint than withdrawal, or even domination.

A secretary, then, can never be propositional and innovative permanently; she will tend to return to forms of bureaucratic behaviour if only to retain control of her resources. Similarly, professional will learn to "stand to attention" to avoid constant confrontation and risk with the powers that be.

But the costs of innovation do not affect only those involved in it. Conservators must henceforth reckon with this offensive base which publically denounces them as the main forces of resistance to change. Some, through the process of institutionalisation of innovation, are however able to achieve a degree of permanence in their function and their role. These are mainly managers in effective charge of a sector or an establishment, heads of particularly dynamic departments who are literally carried by their base and find in this movement as much in the way of rewards as they encounter difficulties in defining their role. Others sometimes become true leaders of innovation in their group and thus opposed to other departments which remain bureaucratic, encroaching on their territories. The example of information distribution departments is a good illustration of this trend: the head of the department and his subordinates form a collective group of Innovators who target themselves on collective groups of Conservators.

Although certain Conservators therefore learn to take an active interest in the system of innovation, others, and this remains the dominant trend, find themselves subjected to a difficult change of identity and culture. Their authority being perceived as legal but not legitimate, with their ideology of progress being taken over by the Innovators and with management only partly supporting them, they can find no way out of a social system which seems to beleaguer them. This fact does not seem to be specific to OA.

The traditional hierarchical function seems gradually to become exhausted under the blows of an economic (13), legal (14) and technological environment, less able than before to preserve the bureaucratic feudalities.

A secretary: "It is more as before, the barriers between them and us are breaking down because everyone must participate in the same work and take part in the free for all (...). For a secretary it is not always easy; we must try to work fast and put aside our little habits, or else we find ourselves once again nothing but housemaids".

A secretary: "We have become highly technical; in a way we are doing the same work even if we do not have the same grade; at this level it is very different compared with what we used to do (...). But for us, the environment is very different. It has become highly technical, highly professional and it is sometimes difficult to put up with working so hard. But we have no choice: if you are not with it, you are rejected".

A research assistant: "To be taken seriously you must be at daggers drawn (...). Documentation is no longer an ivory tower subject, they (the customers) need us".

A research executive: "When you start word processing, you must be able to forget everything you were taught at school. To be versatile, technician and executive at the same time, also involves giving up the privileges of the executive position".

Source: Norbert Alter - "La bureautique dans l'entrprise. Les acteurs de l'innovation" - op cit

---

It is perhaps here that we should examine one of the popular ideas which says that the "old" more than the "young" reject new technologies. At first glance, the idea seems correct, the "old" being more frequently in line management positions than the "young". But on analysis, the comparison does not hold water. If middle managers resist more than they learn, it is because they are more often isolated than the Innovators and therefore have neither the benefit of group support when taking the risk of changing, nor clearly graspable alternative models of authority.

Another reason may explain their difficulty in changing: most of them do not have the minimum technical expertise enabling them to embark on the game of innovation, whereas young middle managers all have at least some experience of computing. At the same time, having little time, let alone the "status", to embark on training, they remain steadfastly outside the process of introducing new technologies into the corporate environment. In more general terms, it seems necessary, even if it cannot be verified by observation, to make the hypothesis of a "cultural contingency" (15). Innovators, because of their age and culture, appear as the corporate "undertow of May 1968", Conservators having certainly played a less prominent part in this crisis of yesterday's street visionary and participating less in its modern corporate equivalent.

Through this conflictual organisational change, a clear phenomenon can be seen: the change for both losers and winners results in an expensive, often too expensive, cultural change so that both, as rational players, use all the resources at their disposal.

This socio-psychological cost of change can then be observed at another level, that of corporate culture, which is itself torn between constraints of permanence and therefore management, and its opportunity for movement and therefore innovation (16).

Two systems of values and management co-exist and suggest a process of production and working relationships which are substantially opposed.

The player's rationale of the Innovators results in a corporate spirit which promotes inventiveness, autonomy and a socio-economic evaluation of strategic action. But this active corporate integration is also proving to be highly critical: the group refuses out of hand everything which may smack of clannishness. This bone of contention first affects the most informal aspects of business life: such as wearing a tie, a certain distance in inter-personal relationships, a private sign language, become incompatible elements, with the "pioneering" spirit. But the more vigorous dispute concerns formal aspects of work. The idea of career is transformed: the positive sanction of success, often resulting in vertical mobility, is frequently called into question, Innovators preferring a "horizontal mobility" in which they retain their distance with respect to the established order and the hierarchical function.

The player's rationale of the Conservators represents the other side of corporate culture. Here the main value is order since it enables, at the worst, the innovation movement to be slowed down, and at best to be institutionalised. But the original features of this group are based on a somewhat contradictory representation of management: thus, a topic dear to line managers, that of the substitution of capital for labour is called into question from the moment when its organisational effects touch upon the privileges of middle managers. Similarly, the transparency of communication, a manifest managerial creed, is latently repulsed as soon as it concerns information previously the exclusive domain of the chain of command.

INNOVATORS AND MANAGERS - THE PLAYERS' RATIONALE

Concerning technical change and its effects on the organisation, the questionnaire shows that desires and expectations are highly dichotomised between the groups

Managers want above all:	Innovators want above all:
- more effective communications - better corporate performance - a more flexible organisation of work	- more effective communications - greater freedom to organise their work - a less hierarchical means of command - "friendlier" working relationships - a career linked to the product made, not to status - better corporate performance

Source: Norbert Alter - "Bureautique dans l'entreprise. Les acteurs de l'innovation" - op cit

The price to be paid for innovation can therefore be seen as socio-psychological rather than economic in nature. It is only by "federalizing" the rationales of opposing players that the business can profit from its technical investment. Arbitration and institutionalisation of power, laid down by managers, can here appear only as the last resort of a business which has not yet really been able to choose between its different component rationalities (17).

Advanced OA sites may therefore lead to situations of incipient anomy. The corporate plan as seen by management itself is very thinly spread.

But beyond this immediate observation of social data, it is possible to distinguish a number of new trends again determining a certain consistency in the corporate identity (18). It is firstly the establishment of an experimental device enabling the costs, and the technical and economic advantages of an operation, to be monitored and evaluated in a less "wild" manner than at present, but also the incidence of strategic or cultural conduct on the product (19). The original feature of this device, when it is established, seems to be that it "fossilizes" within the social system, making the experience/evaluation cycle permanent and institutional. From "wild experiments", businesses move on to "experimental method".

The American example is significant here. To preserve the advantages of deviation whilst eliminating from it its more extreme disturbance--producing dimension, management establishes innovation as an explicit, institutional trend. To do so, it assigns elements specifically based on evaluation, arbitration and distribution of technical and organisational innovation. At the same time, it creates "Communication Systems Departments" incorporating the major part of the activities of the Personnel, Computer and Organisation and Methods Departments.

The other futuristic social fact is the appearance of a technician ideology. Unlike the technocrat ideology the objective of which is to impose, via corporate management, its own system of values on the entire social system, the technician ideology is supported by the innovative base: its objective and effect are to federate its forces around a common culture, that of innovation, but also to be the bearer of the new corporate economic rationale founded on "organisational productivity" and the de-bureaucratisation of structures. Through this cultural diffusion, the Innovators gradually integrate all those who consider that the business of tomorrow will be based on movement and not only stability. In this general context, it seems that in differing degrees the different social groups, including the Conservators, are beginning to take part in this new ideology of progress.

(1) This article has already been published in French under the title "Bureautique, un bilan socio-économique inattendu".

(2) This article is taken from a series concerning research into micro-computing, word processing, data banks, audio-conferencing and facsimile. See Norbert Alter - "La bureautique dans l'entreprise. Les acteurs de l'innovation". - Paris, Editions Ouvrières, 1985.

(3) On this topic, see the works of J L Martineau, and for a more thorough economic analysis of technical change, the works of J L Missika and O Pastré - "Informatique: menace ou mutation?" - Paris, La Documentation Française, 1982.

(4) The figures and examples used in this article are taken from our publication (op cit) or from our thesis "L'effet organisationnel de l'innovation technologique, le cas de la télématique". The survey was conducted from semi-directive interviews (200) and questionnaires (300). The population consisted half of executives and half of non-executives.

(5) On this topic, see the works of L Nauges in "Informatique et Gestion".

(6) Here reference may be made to the theoretical and practical works of the Socio-technical school, the Industrial Democracy and, in France, the Agence Nationale pour l'Amélioration des Conditions de Travail (National Agency for the Improvement of Working Conditions).
In this respect, see O Ortsmann - "Changer le travail" - Paris, Editions Dunod, 1978. For a strategic analysis of the effects of experimentation in business, see the works of R Sainsaulieu, P E Tixier and M O Marty - "La démocratie en organisation" - Paris, Editions Méridiens, 1983.

(7) We return here to the criticism made by M Crozier and E Friedberg concerning the highly formalised forms of participation which tend to create new degrees of unwieldiness and resistance by overlaying other "institutional staging posts" on those which previously existed. See "L'acteur et le système", Paris, Editions du Seuil, 1977.

(8) Organisation and Methods or Taylorism.

(9) We return here to the idea of M Crozier (op cit) according to which information is a source of power. But the author presents dominant strategies for retention of information, which are explained through their belonging to a bureaucratic system. In the social system which we are describing, more open than that examined by M Crozier, information remains a source of power but the dominant strategy is circulation.

(10) On the topic of the "discretionary power" of senior management, see M Bauer and F Cohen - "Qui gouverne les grands groupes industriels?" - Paris, Editions du Seuile, 1981.

(11) See S Mallet - "La nouvelle classe ouvrière" - Paris, Editions du Seuil, 1963.

(12) The costs of entering (and leaving) the world of innovation, cost being understood as the price to be paid by the individual to alter the previously acquired corporate culture, appear as essential factors in the relative stability of inventive working environments. We are using here the term and idea of A O Hirschmann - "Face au déclin des entreprises et des institutions" - Paris, Editions ouvrières, 1972.

(13) See H Savall - "Enrichir le travail humain" - Paris, Editions Dunod, 1975.

(14) See J Gautrat and D Martin - "Cheminement inventif d'une démarche participative" - Paris, Editions du CRESST, 1983.

(15) On this topic and on the process of cultural learning in organisations, see R Sainsaulieu - "L'identité au travail" - Paris, Presses de la FNSP, 1977.

(16) On the theme of corporate culture and its mobility, which seems to be becoming one of the new targets of interrogation by management and research departments, see the various articles published by the Revue Française de Gestion in 1984.

(17) On innovation strategies and their development, see our publication Norbert Alter - "Informatiques et management: la crise". - La Documentation Française - Paris, 1986.

(18) See R Laufer and B Ramanantsoa - "Crise d'identité ou crise de légitimité" - Revue Française de Gestion, September-October, 1982.

(19) We may here refer to the evolution of the "milieu", the best indicators of which are the practices of consultants and the topics of specialised magazines.

Part 6
**TRAINING IN THE AGE OF
CONSTANT TECHNOLOGICAL CHANGE**

The Social Implications of Robotics and Advanced
Industrial Automation / D. Millin and B.H. Raab (Editors)
Elsevier Science Publishers B.V. (North-Holland)
© IFIP, 1989

THE PENETRATION OF TECHNOLOGIES
AND ITS IMPACT ON VOCATIONAL TRAINING
FROM THE POINT OF VIEW OF JOB MOBILITY

Yaacov Hecht
Ministry of Labour and Social Affairs, Israel

The industrialized countries are engaged in a process of constant revolution in the field of production and services to the business sector. This process relates to four fields, which, in fact, are combined with one another.

1. The penetration of new technologies, Shortening of time elapsing from invention stage to production stage, which is expressed, among others, by the increase in R&D budget proportions in industry.

2. Novel administrative and economic concepts.

3. Revolution in the field of computerization.

4. Marketing.

The following may serve to demonstrate the different fields:

1. The penetration of new printing technologies in England left thousands unemployed, because the workers did not adjust themselves for changing to new technologies (the story of Mordoch).

2. The use of "real time", in an international sense, following the full computerization of the London Stock Exchange, is eonnected to new economical concepts.

3. As a result of cometition in the field of marketing, an agreement was signed between the German "Siemens" company and the Dutch "Philips" company for the development of chips for the fifth generation computers, as competitors of Japan and the United States, in the endeavour to be B.J. (Before Japan), or A.J. (After Japan), which obviously is the problem of marketing. Such a joint venture between competing companies is, indeed, a revolution in the field of administration and development. However, the subject of this discussion is not from the point of view of the constant revolution, but rather its consequences on labour training, or more specifically; how would labour be able to adjust to the constant changes. The indicator of this will be the extent of labour mobility and job changes. Paradoxically, this is connected to the conventional conception, the indicator of success having been labour stability. The economical-technological effectiveness of the labour market is measured today by its flexibility. The extent of labour mobility among firms, and occupation is important as an indicator to the degree of flexibility of the economy structure of production.

The concept of labour mobility as opposed to labour stability has today been given a new meaning. For how long is it "good" to stay on a job in light of the fact that the lifespan of production technologies is 3-5 years, and that products must change every 2-3 years?

In any case, it is necessary to re-examine the conventional concepts of:

a.   Life-time jobs and life skills training.
b.   Intra mobility and inter mobility.

The answer is not unequivocal, but the subject is the central problem of the training forms.

Training can lay the foundation for job enrichment through a new method of organisation work and perform an important function in prompting desirable changes in the employment system.

The technological changes, the factors for labour flexibility and job mobility, are, no doubt, connected to the form of training. However, the connection between technological development - vocational training and mobility is not yet sufficiently clear.

The three leading countries in the world in the field of production technologies are the United States of America, West Germany, and Japan. Each one of them has different movability indicators: In the U.S.A. - 77%, in Germany - 48%, and in Japan - 40%. (This refers to young people of the 20-25 age group, over a period of five years.)

In each one of these countries, the form of vocational training differs essentially.

In the U.S.A., the principal emhpasis in on on-the-job training.

In Germany, the principal emphasis in on basic training.

In Japan, the principal emphasis is on plants of a family style, based on values and commitment to the place of work.

Paradoxically, the common denominator of these countries and, infact, of all the educational systems in the industrialized countries (with the exception of the Eastern European countries), is the drastic decline in vocational training. Whereas, still in the 50ies, the vocational training trend in post-primary education had been flourishing, in the last decade voational training went down, sometimes even as far as half of its former extent.

In this development, Israel made an exception. Here, the vocational training trend in post-primary education continues its upward movement, without any plausible explanation in regard to the labour market. In Israel, there is a constant decline in the rate of product per employes person.

It seems there is no special connection between the quantitative rise in vocational training and production quality. It must, therefore, be concluded that the integration of new technologies does not mean only acquiring skills to operate the new type of equipment - but the problem is rather the quality of training than the quantity of training!

The best educational systems lag behind technology by 15 years!

Furthermore, it has been proved that on most labour markets, there is to be observed a considerable extent of alternating between the various specific qualifications (learning of skills being tantamount to specific qualifications) and the ability to be trained on the job.

In other words, - even the most modern equipment available at the schools, will not assure the integration of new technologies. Learning skills will limit the worker, cause stability and not mobility.

The physical mobility between the jobs, or the technological changes altering the character of the job without physical mobility, these are, in fact, the two sides of the same coin! In both cases, the employee must change positions, behaviours, and above all, skills - all these make it necessary for the employee to learn, first of all, on the job, in order to be able to answer the new job requirements, which are, in this case, the result of changes of the new technologies.

As said, the limited learning of skills, be it even for the most modern equipment, will not solve the problem.

I do not have any proven solutions on this subject, but I am giving here some ideas in the right direction:

1.   For many years, there have been talks about a general basic education, but, in fact, nothing has changed in the structure of vocational education. Its teaching programme mostly includes (in varying proportions based only on the student's ability) theortical studies besides the learning of skills, but without any connection whatsoever between them! This connection is, of course, not established automatically by the execution of jobs. It is not sufficient to leave this task to the place of work! It is not for the firm or interplant trainer to translate into the practice of the office or shop-floor what has been taught in theory at school. The present mixture between skills and theoretical studies is worse than theoretical studies only. Students who completed theoretical studies are capable of integrating into jobs, with certain adjustment difficulties, even better than those who acquired skills. The theoretical capability which these students acquired, facilitates their integration with new technologies.

It should be remembered that only a relatively small part of the population is capable of studying theoretical studies, which are based on principles and abstraction. This percentage ranges between 20%-30% of the population. The problem is what to do with the remaining part of the population.

This does not mean, however, that everything is going well in theoretical education. Moreover, most of the graduates of theoretical studies continue their higher education and will not necessarily intergrate into jobs requiring technology in the sense we are meaning!

2.   The vocational education with all its various courses, caters to the needs of those parts of the population who are incapable of studying theoretical studies. How could this population, being incapable, from a cognitive point of view, of learning transferable principles, be prepared for new job situations? Many of today's jobs demand not solely skills anymore, but also more theoretical knowledge. Learning limited skills that are supposed to be suitable for specific jobs, do not answer the requirements of the market, as outlined above. Modern technologies demand the study of principles, learning how to change from one job to another, as well as constant on-the-job training. The conventional didactic methods talk about learning by way of observation and imitation only.

Special thought must be given to didactics, training methods and the organization of training. A good combination of theoretical training in school, systematic practical and theoretical training in the laboratory or workshop and dealing with specific problems at the work place, each of these areas having its own didactics and methods, would seem to be one of the most effective ways of organizing learning, not only as a means of accomplishing short-term adjustments, but also with a view to the implementation of medium and long-term initial and further training concepts.

However, in Israel, there is still made a sharp distinction between the practical and the abstract, between the specific and the general – which sometimes prevents flexibility in moving from one job to the other.

Apparently, in Germany the problem could be solved to a certain extent by training for variable jobs, while making use of socialization systems which encourage job mobility from one task to the other.

Flexibility is created by job rotation, and these jobs are, to a large extent, alternatives to the abstract.

In Israel, it becomes more and more clear that the alternatives to the abstract, the study of principles, may be achieved by social resources. A gradual exposure to the adult world through reference groups, is of decisive importance. Boarding school education, youth movements, voluntary work for public and industrial services, provided, however, that specific training jobs are available, all these are part of a much development field in Germany.

New Technologies can no longer be taught in the framework of conventional vocational courses, but only by didactics, combining the study of principles on the one hand, and job practice under conditions of rotation, on the other hand.

The tendency is to give the student the constant on-the-job study direction, knowing that whatever he learnt, has already become obsolete. It is a fundamental mistake to believe that the introduction of modern equipment into the framework of training and schools will be an alternative to studying in itself.

It would seem that there have not been made yet sufficiently serious attempts to study the principles guiding modern technologies, on the one hand, and the development of didactic methods suitable for a population who finds it difficult to study theroretical and abstract studies, on the other hand.

There are many industrial plants where the available equipment is not put full use, because of a lack of personnel that is capable of operating it. Unemployment is, among others, connected to the failure to intergrate personnel into jobs requiring the performance of new technologies.

The problem of integration and adaption of secondary jobs – which is the main problem facing the penetration of modern technologies, has not yet been solved. This is also a psychological and sociological problem of facing the new and unknown.

Instead of investing funds in the acquisition of equipment, investments should first be directed towards finding a solution for the job mobility problem, the problem of being afraid of a new and changing job, and the problem of didactics connected with the comprehension of the processes and the operation of the new equipment.

The Social Implications of Robotics and Advanced
Industrial Automation / D. Millin and B.H. Raab (Editors)
Elsevier Science Publishers B.V. (North-Holland)
© IFIP, 1989

THE ISSUES OF THE ROBOTIZATION ON QUALIFICATIONS: INELUCTABLE OR NOT ? THE STAKES OF TRAINING.

JACQUES BERLEUR, BERNARD DETREMBLEUR, CLAIRE LOBET-MARIS

U.E.R. META-INFORMATIQUE, INSTITUT D'INFORMATIQUE,
RUE GRANDGAGNAGE, 21, B-5000 NAMUR

Different definitions could be given for the term robotic. We will give three of them. Those definitions are not neutral, since they will influence the statistics of the set-up robots. To present the Belgian situation, we will have to choose one of them.

The first one comes from the "Regie Renault" in France: for them a robot is an universal automatic machine designed for the manipulation of objects. That machine is able to learn a typical behaviour, to perceive its environment, to analyze information and to modify its typical behaviour. This definition is highly restrictive. It seems reasonable to think that the reasons for such a restrictive definition are to be found in the traditional social unrest at the Renault manufactories.From this point of view, the level of robotization is very low and the conflicts induced by the introduction of robots are highly limited.

The second definition comes from the JIRA (Japan Industrial Robotics Association). The association distinghuishes six levels of robots: manipulator robot, sequential robot with a fixed sequence, sequential robot with a variable sequence, learning robot, robot with a digital command, intelligent robot. This definition is very wide. This can be linked with the Japanese will to show their predominance in the introduction of new technologies.

The third definition is the one proposed by OSI in 1982: an industrial robot is a programmable multifunctions manipulator, the position of which is controlled automatically, which has many freedom degrees, and which is able to grasp objects in order to perform a programmed operation on them.

SECTOR	1982 (%)	1983 (%)
Automobile	62.2	58.0
Mechanical manu.	15.5	12.5
Plastics	3.9	3.0
Electronics	2.9	2.0
Smelting-forging	3.3	3.0
Education	2.7	15.5
Others		6.0

(Source: J.V. Philippart,1984)

The definition proposed by OSI is relatively neutral and widely accepted. For these reasons, we propose to keep us to that last definition.

What is the repartition of the robots in the industrial sectors in Belgium? The board shows this repartition and helps to assess the situation. Robots are introduced mainly in two sectors: the automobile and the mechanical manufactories. Indeed, the presence and importance of these two sectors generally explain the level of the robotization in other countries.

As far as we can assess the impact of robotization on employment - since in Belgium there are no official statistics on that question - the robotization seems to lead to a loss of employment mainly in the processes of machining, assembling and quality control. Those losses of employment are not balanced by the creation of employment, up stream (for robot fabrication) or down stream (for robot maintenance). This tends to prove that, in Belgium, robots are introduced to increase the productivity and the competitivity of the firms. We can see therefore that investments in robotics in Belgium are mainly conceived as rationalizing investments.

This quantitative issue is reinforced by a qualitative one. The lost jobs manily concern the unskilled labour force (repetitive manipulations,...). However, it seems to appear that the effects of robotization on the structure of employement are neither automatic nor ineluctable. French surveys [B. Coriat], led in the automobile sector (the Renault manufactories), have shown that inside the same group (Renault) the effects of robotization are different according to the plants they concern. This means that they are linked to various factors i.e. the strategies of the firm, the type of production, organization of the production inside the firm, skill level of the inside workers and skills available on the labour market, division of labour. This means that the dream of a "factory without workers" is only a commercial argument.

However, one can attempt to define, very cautiously, from the few available case studies, the movements that affect the structure of employment.

The integration of work: To the traditional " taylorian " division of labour based on a long hierarchical line made of positions, in charge of work preparation and positions dealing with work execution, would succeed a shorter line composed of polyvalent positions integrating operation units previously separated and various functions intervening in the production process such as fabrication and maintenance.

The recombining of know-how under new forms: The "taylorian" division of labour leads to fragmentation of know-how into small pieces. The robotization introduces to an "objectivation" of those know-how since the required knowledges needed to lead a production process switch from living form on to an object form (software and computer) [CREIS]. This objectivation is, however, never complete : there still are the unforeseeable risks, the programming errors,... The monitoring of those robotized lines of production then requires very qualified control positions, in so far as the operator must possess an integrated knowledge of the whole production line and the whole information flow allowing him to detect an error and to correct whatever the segment where it occurs.

Disqualification and emergence of new qualifications: The monitoring operators or line controllers must than possess a high level of training generally provided by the firm. It remains to know wether the training actions are reconversion actions of workers already present in the company or disqualification operations of them. In the last case, training is detined to new recruits starting with highest diplomas or to members of the technical services moved to the leading of the production lines. Very often, the inside labour-force does hardly allow a reconversion: low-skilled workers, slowly disqualified by a very fragmented process of production. Those are at least the argument stressed by management to introduce "pockets" of new manpower, generally less unionized and closer to the spirit of enterprise. It is a well-known fact that trade-unions traditionnally are better represented in low skilled environment than in technical ones.

As we said earlier, those evolutions are not ineluctable. It appears very clearly however that training, its control, the way it is given, that categories that benefit from it [B. Coriat, op cit.] are today the major stakes of that robotic mutation.

[B.Coriat] B.Coriat, La robotique, Coll. Repère, La Découverte, MASPERO, Paris 1983.
[CREIS]   CREIS, Société et Infomatique, Delagrave Edit., Paris 1984.

The Social Implications of Robotics and Advanced
Industrial Automation / D. Millin and B.H. Raab (Editors)
Elsevier Science Publishers B.V. (North-Holland)
© IFIP, 1989

257

ROBOT ODYSSEY: A MICROWORLD STARRING ROBOTS AS HUMANS' HELPERS

Dr. Teri Perl
Co-Founder, The Learning Company
525 Lincoln Avenue
Palo Alto, California 94301
USA

This conference addresses the implications of robotics and automatons on evolving
social structures. To those of us who are educators, questions arise about the
appropriate education for people in the new society. What kind of education do people
need in order to function effectively in a rapidly changing world?

A clear distinction between education and training should be made since, more and
more, robots and automatons will be performing tasks that require simple training
while people will be performing more complex tasks that require broader education.
Training involves the building of task-specific skills. Education, as distinguished
from training, involves building skills that are less task-specific, skills that help
people learn to learn. Providing an education for people to become livelong learners
requires a curriculum that is focused on building   problem-solving skills.

Robot Odyssey is a computer simulation that provides a powerful environment for
developing problem-solving skills. It is implemented in a graphics environment that
is appropriate for people of different ages and abilities. In addition, its graphics
environment provides a visual learning mode that can be extremely effective for some
learners.

Robot Odyssey simulates a world full of dangerous situations providing challenging
tasks set amid formidable barriers. The successful achievement of many of these tasks
requires cooperation between humans and robots ... some between robots and robots.

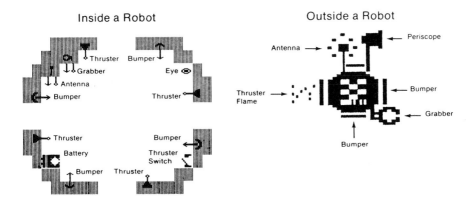

The Robot Odyssey simulation includes three robots that can be programmed to move
through barriers, pick up and carry objects past barriers, and that can communicate
with one another.

Robots, as humans' helpers, can be configured to move through barriers inaccessible to non-robots. In Robot Odyssey, robots are activated by circuits "programmed" by connecting graphic representations of the standard logic elements of computer circuitry, AND-gates, OR-gates, and NOT-gates.

By operating within the Robot Odyssey microworld, users can experience the power of robots as helpers in the accomplishment of tasks that would be difficult or impossible to achieve without them. And yet these robots have been programmed by people. They work **for** people, under people control.

A program such as Robot Odyssey can serve a dual purpose. As an educational tool for developing problem-solving skills, it can help educate members of society to be better learners, more adaptable to retraining, thus better equipped to function in the fast-changing contemporary world. At the same time, this environment provides users with significant insights into how automatons work, opening windows onto several key underlying principles of the mystifying world of technology.

Robot Odyssey is a microcomputer program produced and published by The Learning Company. It is currently available for the Apple // family of computers as well as MS-DOS computers such as IBM, IBM compatibles, and the Tandy 1000.

The Social Implications of Robotics and Advanced
Industrial Automation / D. Millin and B.H. Raab (Editors)
Elsevier Science Publishers B.V. (North-Holland)
© IFIP, 1989

THE ORT ROBOTICS AND AUTOMATION PROJECT

Dan SHARON and Judah HARSTEIN

World ORT Union,
London, England

The Technical Department of the World ORT Union has developed a comprehensive range of Open Learning packages in Robotics and Automation.
In this paper the authors explain the background to this development and
describe the materials, hardware and software which they have produced.

BACKGROUND

ORT has been involved in the teaching of robotics and computerised automation
since 1981. We view it as an important subject for several reasons. Firstly in our
role as an organization specialising in preparing young people for industrial careers
it became obvious that this subject is an essential one to include in our curriculum.
We observed, as did many others, that advanced manufacturing technology can
make a major contribution to improving industry's efficiency and effectiveness.
However, a crucial factor affecting the rate at which we can adopt this technology is
the availability of personnel with the appropriate knowledge.

Secondly, Robotics, being a multidisciplinary subject, is exremely useful for teaching students the inter-relationship between the individual mechanical and electronic
disciplines.

Thirdly, the robot is an excellent educational tool in its own right when teaching the
thinking skills associated with the computer environment. This is because with a
robot it is very easy to physically see the results of one's programmed instructions:
there is a simple correspondence between the position of the robot arm and a sym-
bolic instruction.

ORT and the Open Tech

In 1982, ORT submitted a proposal to the Manpower Services Commission of the
UK for the development, for their Open Tech programme, of an open learning
course in Robotics and Automation based on the principles which we had developed.
The proposed course was seen as an ideal means of overcoming the general lack of
awareness of the subject and was readily accepted. A contract was awarded in 1983.
The course which we developed under this contract has a high practical content and
it was seen from the outset that a "hybrid" arrangement was necessary: When studying theoretical topics students should be able to work at home or at their place of

employment, in true open learning style. They would, however, have to attend a fully equipped centre to undertake the practical work.

The project was developed, therefore, along two principal tracks. Firstly we created a complete open learning course in robotics and automation and, in parallel, we established a network of centres in the UK and overseas where the practical work for the course would be carried out. These centres became known as "nodes" and to date we have established thirty throughout the UK, and one each in Holland, Sweden and the USA. They are situated in Colleges of Further Education, private training establishments and large industrial companies, each of these host organisations having entered into an agreement with ORT. Under the terms of the agreements, nodes provide equipment, premises and tutorial staff, and ORT provides tutor training and continued support.

Many organisations who are using the ORT material find that the hardware and course material can also form the basis of a more conventional course in robotics presented by tutors in a classroom situation. This, too, is encouraged as our aim has always been to provide this essential basic knowledge to as many as possible of the people who require it.

Open Learning

The work carried out by ORT in developing open learning packages has been mirrored by a number of other organisations. As a result, there is now a large body of open learning material on offer covering a wide range of subjects, most of which relate to some aspect of the industrial environment.

These developments have led many companies to set up open learning centres on their premises where these products are presented to trainers and trainees in a type of education "supermarket". Users choose the subject which they wish to study and select the appropriate package accordingly. A number of the companies operating this system have seen the ORT node scheme as being very appropriate to them in this regard and have joined our network.

Although this "supermarket" approach is being adopted initially by industry, ORT sees it as being equally suitable for the teaching of high tech subjects in schools. It must be realised, though, that such an approach requires a great deal of support, both before the product reaches the "shelf" and after it has been selected.

Resource Centres

To provide this level of support, ORT has developed the concept of "resource centres" and the first one for the UK has been set up in North London. The first function of the resource centre is to provide a link with current developments in technology and to feed these into the open learning packages so that they remain up-to-date. This is essential when we are dealing with subjects which develop at such a rapid rate.

The second task for the centre is to provide ongoing support for students studying the material and using the associated equipment. Within the centre are personnel who can provide advice to help any student experiencing difficulties and for which he cannot get help locally.

A third function for the resource centre concerns the equipment itself. Much of the hardware and software required for high tech courses is expensive and, moreover, because of the rapid rate of obsolescence, may need to be replaced after a comparatively short time. This can often place it beyond the budget of many schools. The resource centre, therefore, also houses laboratories containing the appropriate equipment which is then available for use as a centralised facility by students at local schools. For schools in more remote areas ORT operates a mobile classroom, fitted out with all the necessary equipment, which can provide the schools with the required facilities for short lengths of time.

FIGURE 1 THE ORT MOBILE UNIT

Technological Background

The work carried out by ORT in preparing material for a robotics curriculum led us to analyse very clearly how robotics and Automation has developed over the years and how it has reached its current level of importance.

Present day industrial machinery can be analysed in terms of its motive power systems and its control systems. The developments in power systems - from human and animal power to steam and electricity - provided the first industrial revolution.

Current developments centre around the control systems. At first, man was in sole control carrying out all the functions needed to keep the machinery operating in the correct sequences. Then this function began to be taken over first by mechanical and then electrical and electronic subsystems. The role of the human operator then became a supervisory one with the additional responsibility of feeding material and parts to the machines.

The next observable step has been the extension of the control system from the *internal* control of a single machine to the *external* automation of a complete manufacturing system including the material handling functions. This has been made possible by the introduction of the digital computer as the main controlling element.

The advent of the robot on to the industrial scene has heralded some significant changes in approach. Robots do not differ in principle from other computer controlled machines. They make use of similar power devices and controllers and there is very little that is new in basic robot technology. It includes elements of control theory, mechanics, computer science and electronics amongst others. What characterizes the robot is its *versatility*, its *range* and its *programmability*.

Versatility is due to the fact that the physical structure of the robot incorporates a modifiable geometry enabling it to be reconfigured to carry out many different tasks. This versatility is not solely a function of degrees of freedom but also results from other factors such as the structure and capabilities of the end-effectors.

Range is an attribute not possible with traditional machines. By extending itself along its axes the robot can operate anywhere within a volume of space - its work-envelope - which exceeds its own static volume.

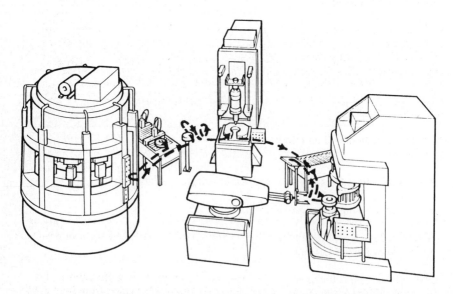

FIGURE 2 A ROBOT SERVING SEVERAL MACHINES

The programmability of robots further extends their versatility. Given the right mechanical parameters a robot can switch between tasks simply by changing the driving software.

But it does not end there. Developments are taking place in both the physical and control subsystems of robots. Developments of the physical subsystem will broaden robot applications. We can expect to see more robots as machine tools. They will actually do the machining, not just feed other tools which do it. To do this they will use advanced machining methods such as water jet cutting and lasers.

Sensor development, particularly vision, will play a vital role in getting the robot from offline programming (eventually by CAD/CAM) to the real world. The really exciting advances will take place in the control subsystem. Developments in control are largely focused on providing robots with intelligence. If successful, and we believe they will be, they will radically deepen robot applications.

Intelligent Robots

Despite there not being an agreed definition of an intelligent robot, a robot that can produce feedback describing its environment and adapt itself accordingly would provide a working definition.

Existing intelligent robots have a limited degree of flexibility. Whilst they can alter their behaviour as the conditions around them change, they can only cope with situations that have been anticipated in every detail by the programmer. The program has a limited number of options depending on certain conditions.

Goal-Seeking Robots

Whilst the step-by-step approach is a fundamental building block of contemporary robot control and will provide the subroutines for all automatic behavior in the forseeable future, researchers are trying to develop robots that can formulate the decision-making rules themselves, and cope with unanticipated events by drawing on their 'experience'. These machines will form the new environment - the task-oriented environment. Preliminary languages such as Prolog already exist to implement this approach.

The basic ingredients of an intelligent system which make up a task-oriented environment are:

* A sensing system to enable it to receive information relating to its environment.

* A problem-solving behaviour algorithm.

* A knowledge base (relating both to the execution of its task and the environment) which is up-dated according to experience.

Concerted research is under way to broaden the theoretical foundations of these three areas, and their application is the aim of all intelligent systems designed today.

As the 'intelligent' machines develop, they are likely to take over tasks not previously considered as candidates for mechanization. Nor need this be restricted to the factory; as these products proliferate, there seems no reason why they should not find themselves in many other areas of our environment. Although currently serious robot application is confined largely to manufacturing industry, the future will see enormous penetration by robots and robot-like devices into other sectors.

In this manner robotics and automation will become part and parcel of our general education. It is in this context that we regard our course as a starting point, providing the building blocks for the future. We at ORT are committed to keeping pace with developments and providing educational material to suit.

Educational Background

It is against this background of technological development that we have identified the need for a new educational approach to cope with the shift in skills needed by industry.

Through the introduction of automatic systems, manual skills, such as the ability to operate a lathe or a milling machine and to ensure that they follow certain desired geometries, become obsolescent whilst other needs become evident. The machine operator no longer requires manual dexterity and good hand/eye coordination, but rather the ability to analyze a procedure logically and express the result in a machine-intelligible form. This changes both the thinking tools with which one approaches the task as well as the way one communicates.

Every environment, including the digital or step-by-step environment, has a language that relates to it and encapsulates the thinking tools required to function in it. Language provides us with the very basic components of thinking. It enables us to construct and calibrate our ideas out of the influx of stimuli to which we are exposed. Language is the library where we store ideas, operators, and images for future formal operations. Therefore, one cannot perceive the necessary change in our system of education as being merely a 'means of translation'. Instead, one is obliged to become adjusted to the idea of creating these new thinking ingredients and building blocks, which are needed in order to be able to act within the new environment, as the basic preparation of manpower for industry.

The very fast developments in our technological environment are regarded by many as revolutionary. The term *revolution* - far reaching and drastic changes taking place within a short period of time - also implies (or, maybe, reflects the hope) that, at a certain stage, not too far in the future, these changes will give way to a more stabilised technological environment. Our view is that fast changes will remain a significant ingredient of our technological environment for many years to come.

This has implications for technological education. In the past, following a technological revolution, a stable period allowed educators to develop their methods of preparing technical staff for various well defined skills in industry. A person could be trained to practise a profession for a life-time. Any changes within trades were sufficiently slow to enable people to pick up the required knowledge whilst on the job. Skills were appropriate educational goals. Today the fast changes do not permit such a luxury. Educationalists are now facing a dynamic problem and not a static one. Contemporary technological changes not only bring about abrupt changes within the trades, but they also break the traditional border lines between them.

This situation leads one to consider a different approach to technological education, in which we recognise that knowledge will need to be continuously updated. This requires preparing the workforce for life-long education and the development of various modes of transmitting the knowledge. It is, therefore, an essential part of the educational system to prepare its graduates not only for their role as professionals within industry, but also as permanent learners.

Educational Model

How do we achieve these goals? Our approach can be illustrated by the thinking pyramid (fig. 3), a multifaced model of human thinking processes. Each facet of the pyramid represents one particular aspect of human knowledge. These aspects may be cognitive ones, such as numerical or linguistic abilities, or more specialised ones. The basic principle of the pyramid model is its hierachy and the way in which it builds up towards higher levels of generalization. The layers are, in ascending order of abstraction:

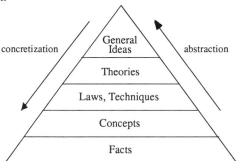

concretization / abstraction

General Ideas
Theories
Laws, Techniques
Concepts
Facts

FIGURE 3 THE THINKING PYRAMID

- Facts and Experiences: where we take in concrete information from the outside world

- Concepts: we develop techniques to organise the data absorbed in the basic layer into a coherent body of knowledge. We learn methods

- Techniques: certain abilities, based on the 'methods' acquired, become ingrained

- Theories: we generalize the lower layers and formulate theories. Many elements are integrated to provide a comprehensive picture

- General Ideas: this is a person's aggregate of theories and outlook that are acquired and developed - one's view of the world

Solving problems usually involves going up levels of of the pyramid seeking theories, procedures and relevant data, while entering different groups of knowledge and information (other facets of the pyramid) and coming down for consolidation, concretization and verification.

Our model, which is shown in figure 3, considers the process of learning as a series of *events*. A learning event occurs when information is absorbed from the outside world and/or generated from within the student. At any stage the student may be on different levels or different faces of the pyramid. At each learning event we move up and down various faces through levels of abstraction. An upward movement indicates a greater degree of abstraction; a downward a search for a more concrete basis for a general idea that has developed. A good educational event will seek to move across as many levels of abstraction and integrate as many faces of knowledge as possible. We have built our course around such events.

Literacy

Generally, one can divide technological education courses into three types:

- skills: the student is taught to respond automatically to a fixed number of familiar situations. The level of abstraction is rarely beyond 'methods'.

- training: the student can respond to new but similar situations. Learned patterns are unified by simple rules, and the learner usually moves up to the third level of abstraction.

- education: the student has a full understanding of the subject and is able to respond to new situations based on his/her understanding of the theory. Students can reach high levels of abstraction in their field.

By *educating* our students we are providing them with the thinking tools and building blocks they require for further development. So equipped they are able to absorb new developments in their field. The belief that education is only for high grade personnel is wrong, vocational education, by being satisfied with merely achieving skills, sent crippled people to work - crippled in that they do not have the tools permitting them to absorb new developments.

To prepare manpower for industry, we need to equip them with the basic tools for thinking and understanding the language of the environment and its concepts.

We see this broad level of knowledge as the "Literacy" level . Literacy is not equivalent to superficial knowledge.

A Robotics Literacy Course, sets the context in which the student's subsequent experience and skill development will take place. It is a course of education rather than specific training. Sufficient for many students, it is a springboard to further study for others.

THE COURSE ITSELF

Based on these principles and also on the requirements of the Open Tech we developed Phase 1 of our Robotics and Automation course to be disseminated via the Nodes.

Structure

The structure of the course can be seen in figure 4 which is a reproduction of the principal items of our course "map". Each entry on the map represents a learning session or group of sessions in the numerous individual disciplines that make up the totality of Robotics. The course is modular and flexible, allowing students to choose their own pathway according to their individual needs and aspirations. Usually the decision as to which modules to study will be taken with the guidance of an ORT-trained tutor.

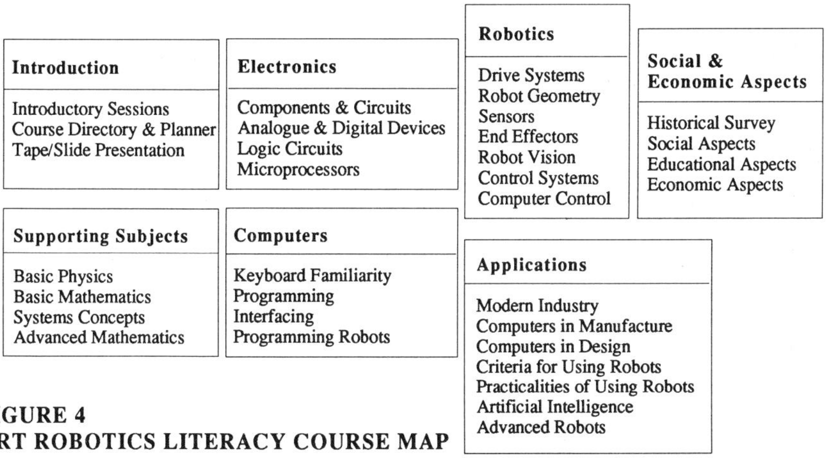

Introduction	Electronics	Robotics	Social & Economic Aspects
Introductory Sessions Course Directory & Planner Tape/Slide Presentation	Components & Circuits Analogue & Digital Devices Logic Circuits Microprocessors	Drive Systems Robot Geometry Sensors End Effectors Robot Vision Control Systems Computer Control	Historical Survey Social Aspects Educational Aspects Economic Aspects

Supporting Subjects	Computers	Applications
Basic Physics Basic Mathematics Systems Concepts Advanced Mathematics	Keyboard Familiarity Programming Interfacing Programming Robots	Modern Industry Computers in Manufacture Computers in Design Criteria for Using Robots Practicalities of Using Robots Artificial Intelligence Advanced Robots

FIGURE 4
ORT ROBOTICS LITERACY COURSE MAP

Style

The course is written to enable students to proceed at their own pace with the minimum of outside help. Particular emphasis has been placed on achieving a friendly style with a clear statement of learning objectives for each session. In addition there are numerous self-evaluation exercises throughout the course.

These exercises are also designed to bring out the creativity of individual students. In accordance with our educational philosophy their purpose is to get the student to find practical applications of ideas, and to try and generalize physical results. Students are encouraged to be as creative as possible in designing their own experiments. They can integrate sensors, actuators, vision systems, computers, robots into a system of their own design.

Content

Within the limits of the student's chosen programme of study, he/she normally pro-
gresses from left to right across the map of figure 4, studying the following sections:

Introduction

The introductory sessions provide an overview of the course and of the general
subject of robotics. This is designed to place in context the material which the
student will study. The Course Directory and Planner, for example, is presented as a
session and contains a description of every session in the course enabling students
to plan their programme of study.

Supporting Subjects

The Supporting Subjects are included to enable students to strengthen their knowledge of basic Physics and Mathematics to help them cope more easily with some of
the later sessions.

We have also included more advanced sessions (e.g. vector transformations) for
those students with the ability or inclination to take their mathematics a little further
and deepen their understanding of robotics.

Electronics

The sessions on Electronics introduce elements of the subject which are relevant to
the operation of robots. A student with no previous exposure to the subject can learn
about basic components and circuits while more experienced students can proceed
directly to a study of transducers and other devices relevant to robotics, and to logic
circuits and microprocessors.

Computers

With the aid of the BBC Model B Microcomputer the student is introduced to the
keyboard and then learns to construct programs using Turtle Graphics (a simplified
LOGO). This is ideal at the literacy level as it quickly enables students to learn the
concepts of structured programming.

The later sessions cover the use of the computer to control external devices and also
show how programming concepts are used when programming the robots.

Robotics

The section entitled "Robotics" deals with the Robots themselves. The robot is
presented as a system having two major subsystems - the physical and the control.

The sessions on the physical subsystem show how robots are constructed and powered. Also included are sessions on sensor devices including vision - which provide
the robot with essential information as to the state of its environment - and end

effectors which are the operational elements of the robot which enable it to carry out its designated tasks.

The sessions on control introduce the principles of closed loop control and feedback and show how these principles are used when the robot's computer is used to control the mechanical subsystem.

Applications

The aim of these sessions is to enable the students to make intelligent decisions about incorporating robots into their own industry. To do this they are introduced to the many parameters that need to be considered when making such decisions.

A second objective of this section of the course is to show how the whole modern factory environment - from product design to manufacture, test and distribution - can make use of information technology. To this end, students are introduced to the techniques of Flexible Manufacturing Systems (FMS), Computer Aided Design (CAD) and to the concept of Information as an industrial resource as vital as energy or manpower.

A number of sessions in this section of the course are devoted to examining the major current areas of research in robotics including Artificial Intelligence and Advanced Manufacturing Systems.

Social and Economic Aspects

The final section of the course deals with the wider implications of robotics and automation. Having learned about the machines and their applications, the students are now shown some of the results of the beast that we have created. No technological development takes place in a vacuum: there are always broader ramifications. It is in these final sessions of the course that the students learn about the economic and social effects of modern industrial practice both from a "micro" and a "macro" point of view.

HARDWARE AND SOFTWARE

Throughout the course there are a number of practical sessions designed to give the students hands-on experience of computers, robots and associated equipment which will reinforce the material taught in the theoretical sessions.

To support these practical sessions a complete package of hardware and software has been developed and is made available at each Node.

The full kit consists of the following items

Computer

We have been using the BBC Model B Microcomputer with 400K disk drive and colour monitor as a basis for the majority of the practical work, and this has been extremely satisfactory. However, to cater for the needs of a large overseas market we are now able to run the course using an IBM PC or compatible machine.

Interface Unit

For the sessions which use the computer as a control device a special interface unit has been developed by ORT. This unit is plugged in to the computer and has a number of sockets which enable input and output devices to be connected all of which are supplied in a specially prepared package.

FIGURE 5 ROBOTICS LITERACY HARDWARE STATION

Simulator

To illustrate the integration of the various computer controlled elements into the factory, the students work with a programmable flexible industrial simulation unit which allows input and output devices to work in conjunction with the miniature robot to carry out a set of tasks defined by the student.

Robots

Two robots are provided for the student to experiment with. Both are six-axis anthropomorphic units (i.e. the articulations resemble those of a human arm on a torso) and interface to the computer. One is an excellent educational robot allowing novices to rapidly familiarize themselves and gain confidence in their ability to manipulate a robot.

The second robot resembles the industrial machines more closely, both in terms of its method of control and its driving software. It is driven by servo motors and is controlled via a special keypad.

Vision System

The vision system consists of a camera, a microprocessor-based control unit, and a vdu screen. It is fully programmable and allows students to carry out object recognition experiments and to learn some of the techniques. This low-cost system can be interfaced to a host computer or to other parts of the system and provides a very worthwhile introduction to this important topic.

Software

The operation of the equipment is controlled by a suite of software programs supplied on disk. This software is used for

- Programming: Keyboard familiarity and basic programming techniques are taught with the aid of the computer.

- Simulations: The computer is used to provide "experiments" in electronics and logic. Circuits are simulated on the screen and the student can examine the effects of changing component values and interconnections.

- Interface control: Software which enables the students student to program and operate the external sensors and actuators and to examine their parameters.

  Our approach enables students to appreciate robots both from a "top-down" systems viewpoint and a "bottom-up" component-oriented viewpoint.

- Robot control: The Robot control software is similar in structure to VAL and allows the robot to be fully programmed. The software features jumps and subroutines and allows the programming of inputs and outputs independently of the interface unit.

Target Group

The initial target group for the course, according to the specifications of the Open Tech were adults in employment. That is members of the workforce and management who needed to be rapidly updated on the latest technology in order to cope with the fast-changing environment of their workplace. Resistance to change comes from fear and fear from ignorance. By providing education at this level we hope to break down the barriers of fear.

As the program developed the target group has been extended to include teachers and regular students and the material has been proving to be extremely acceptable to all groups.

Certification

Students who successfully complete the course are entitled to apply for a certificate issued jointly by ORT and the City and Guilds Institute of London. To obtain this certificate, students have to complete a number of assignments related to the material of the course and to have completed the course practical work to the satisfaction of their tutor. This certificate, having the prestige of being issued by City and Guilds, is of great advantage to students when looking for employment or promotion.

PHASE 2

Our programme has been under continuous development since 1982 and we have now produced our Phase 2 Course under the sponsorship of The Department of Trade and Industry of the British Government together with IBM.

Mechatronics

The purpose of this phase is to build upon the concepts taught in the earlier course and to provide students with a taste of how the principles of Advanced Manufacturing Technology (AMT) are applied in the real world of industry. One of the developments that have taken place since we began our work in the field has been the introduction of a new term "Mechatronics". The term describes the increasing integration of microelectronics and microprocessor technology within the field of mechanical engineering. This affects a wide range of environments from consumer products to automotive and aircraft systems and machine tools. It has resulted in products and systems which are more reliable, flexible and adaptable than their predecessors and has enhanced the development of advanced manufacturing systems.

FIGURE 6 THE ORT MECHATRONICS SYSTEM

As part of our education efforts in this field we have, together with the British Government, initiated a Mechatronics Awareness programme. The central feature of this is the Mechatronics Bus which is equipped with a mechatronics unit. This offers a practical demonstration of the techniques and technologies involved in a mechatronic production process. The example chosen has been the production of a candlestick. An aluminium rod passes down a conveyor to a bandsaw where it is cut to a requisite length. A small robot picks up the sawn off piece and, in a test routine involving a microswitch, measures its length. If correct, it is placed on a carousel where it is picked up by the main robot mounted on a gantry which offers it to a lathe and then a milling machine. A pillar drill then makes the hole for the candle. The robot places the finished product on a vision system which checks the critical parameters. A small robot then places the candlestick in the appropriate base (accept or reject).

A CAD system is linked into the downstream production process. The user can specify the shape of the candlestick to be produced and the requisite cutting paths are downloaded automatically. The entire manufacturing process is under software control and a video system explains all the processes in detail.

The AMT Programme

Our latest and probably most ambitious development is a complete integrated factory package for use in a classroom. Using the system together with its accompanying courseware, students are able to undertake the complete production cycle of Design, Manufacture and Test of a product using state-of-the-art AMT equipment and techniques. As they progress through the programme they acquire first-hand experience of some of the problems encountered in industry and some of the solutions adopted.

Topics which the students have an opportunity to investigate include:

Computer Aided Design (CAD)
Robotic Assembly
Computerised Integrated Manufacture (CIM)
Computerised Automatic Testing (CAT)
Programmable Logic Controllers (PLC)
Sensors
Vision Systems

The striking feature of this package is that the student does not have to sit back and watch a process taking place. He actually becomes a part of that process carrying out the design, programming the manufacture and supervising the testing. At the end of the day he takes home a product for which he has been responsible during all stages of its production.

We have based our programme on a genuine industrial task, namely the automated design and assembly of printed circuit boards (PCBs) for the electronics industry. This choice was influenced by several factors, chiefly that the whole process could be easily contained within a relatively small area and with the minimum of hazards.

To carry out the process we have developed a work cell based on an IBM 7545 SCARA Robot to which we have added component feeders, interchangeable grippers and all the peripheral equipment needed to carry out the planned task.

To operate the cell we have written a high-level, task-oriented programming language. This has been designed to enable students to quickly achieve results in their work with the equipment.

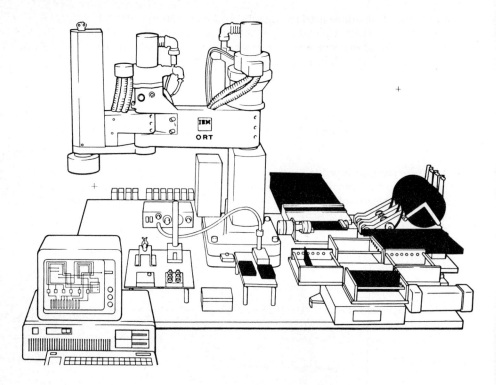

FIGURE 7 LAYOUT OF THE ORT WORK CELL

The driving force behind phase 2 is the need to demonstrate to our students how the modern industrial environment is increasingly becoming an -integrated- environment. What this means is that the previously separate sections of the manufacturing process are now joined together by the common bond of Information. Machines are connected to the computer data network just as they are plugged in to the electricity and compressed air supplies. In today's factory just as we have to consider material and parts flow, we also have to consider data flow.

All this is encapsulated in our Phase 2 programme as the student steers his PCB through the three stages of Design Manufacture and Test.

Design

It is at the design stage that product data is generated. The student works at a CAD terminal and, with the aid of software, first draws the circuit diagram. The next stage is to analyse the designed circuit, simulate its operation and decide whether the design is viable. If it is, then the software goes on to design the final PCB and provide three important pieces of output. These are:

* the artwork that will be used to create the PCB
* a list of components required to build the circuit
* a data file listing the components and their precise locations on the PCB. It is this information which will be used in the manufacturing stage.

Manufacture

The manufacturing process takes place within the workcell. The procedure for the student starts with first learning to operate the robot and other cell components using both low-level and high level software.

Next, a trial program is written, tested and refined using special cell simulation software. When the program appears to be correct it is run on the cell itself. Once the student is capable of operating the cell satisfactorily he then runs the data file created at the design stage to automatically produce a PCB.

FIGURE 8 ASSEMBLING PCBs

Test

At all stages of the production run the student is made well aware that in the real world things seldom go precisely as planned. Testing and inspection have to be carried out constantly. The facilities which we provide include the following:

- Software checks to monitor and report on system behaviour

- Sensors to detect whether for example a tool has been correctly picked up or a component correctly inserted

- A vision system to detect the presence or absence of components on the finished board. This uses information derived from the original data file to create a template against which to test production boards

- A functional testing unit which checks finished boards down to component level. This unit can be operated either on-line by the cell computer or off-line under the control of a PLC.

Other Material

To complement the work that the student carries out on the cell itself, Phase 2 also contains material on more general aspects of AMT. Here the analysis is from an organisational perspective and deals with the problems inherent in adopting AMT. These are considered under the headings of System Design, Specification, Implementation and Operation.

This material is supported by videos, case studies and, importantly, by the use of computerised simulation techniques using the SIMAN simulation system. Simulation, a powerful tool in strategy planning, is of exceptional value in education. The student is given a model of the system under discussion, which can be an individual workcell, a production line or even a national economy and he can see, graphically, the effects of varying individual parameters. At the same time the model itself is capable of constant refinement to take into account the latest information.

SUMMARY

To summarise, ORT is very much involved in seeking to create a general awareness and understanding of the modern manufacturing environment among all those who, knowingly or unknowingly, are affected by it. If people understand the environment they are less likely to be exploited by those who control it.

Part 7
WORKING GROUP REPORTS
AND FINAL PANEL REMARKS

The Social Implications of Robotics and Advanced
Industrial Automation / D. Millin and B.H. Raab (Editors)
Elsevier Science Publishers B.V. (North-Holland)
© IFIP, 1989

INTRODUCTION TO WORKING GROUPS

DISCUSSION GROUP STATEMENTS

Barrie Sherman

The key to the future has to be young people. We all strive to make the
world a better place for them, and in this objective there is clearly a
great role for all the new electronically based technologies. I have a
problem about what is actually being done, however.

It is clear that they can be used for good or for evil purposes. It is
clear that they can be used for socially good and altruistic purposes, or
for selfish reasons.   My problem is that I believe the forces of
darkness, the evil/selfish axis, has the upper hand. Given that human
beings decide what happens, and given the advice which computer
professionals are asked to give, this is an indictment of the profession,
amongst others.

It is possible to develop a wide range of aides for physically
handicapped people (especially children), for mentally handicapped
people, and for elderly people. Surely we should be asking why we have
not done so so?   It is possible to develop ranges of equipment to help
the Lesser Developed Countries (LDC's) find water or help in design and
construction. Again, we should ask, why we have not done so? It is
possible to devise courses on computers to help the educationally
inadequate, but we do not. Why?

The reasons are depressingly simple. Neither disabled nor old people
have clout. They have no strong voice in government, they have no
economic power: they form a lobby which can safely be ignored. The
production runs are too short for a company to recoup its R and D and
variable costs in a period assumed to be reasonable by accountants, so
that without government subsidies the needs go unmet, even though it is
technically possible to meet them.

On the other hand the technologies are used heavily in two areas. The
first is in making better (and often smaller) weapons of war. From
fighter planes to communications and from nuclear submarines to

ciphers, electronics, computers and robots having been playing a full part. The second area is that of 'Candy-floss' investment. This is where a high return can be made, but the net addition to anything other than the profits of the company manufacturing or using the devices is virtually zero. Arcade games, automated check-outs in shops and sexy telephone services are good (or bad) examples.

The real reason for concern is that world-wide there is a shortage of good computer professionals; a shortage of imaginative electronic designers and engineers. Like any human beings they will go mainly to the highest bidder, and this means that the socially useful work will never get done, as they cannot compete in terms of salaries and conditions of service. The military and candyfloss work will always take pride of place.

The only way out of the box is to educate more widely and aquire more of these scarce peoples. But that needs an investment in education which neither governments nor business seem willing to undertake. Wont it be tragic if this technology, so rich in promise, is used only to better the lives of those whose lives are already tolerable. In itself this is not an unlaudable proposition, but to do it at the expense of the underprivileged would be a scandal of historical proportions.

The Social Implications of Robotics and Advanced
Industrial Automation / D. Millin and B.H. Raab (Editors)
Elsevier Science Publishers B.V. (North-Holland)
© IFIP, 1989

Report of Working Group
Impact of Artificial Intelligence

Chairman: Dr. Klaus Brunnstein

Participants: K. Brunnstein, A. Dina, P. Kolm, D. Millin,
T. Perl, Y. Regev, B. Sherman

1. In a 1st approach, the participants defined their
   interest/reason to select this topic. To most, the definitions
   of AI (as known from literature) seemed unprecise and
   controversial, so a need for a broadly acceptable basic
   understanding was predominated. Among the implications, wo/man's
   role when working with such systems the questions of legal
   ownership and responsibility, the need for education, and the
   evident gap between designers and users of the systems were
   mentioned as primary interest. Some of the participants had
   actual background in AI and especially in Expert Systems.

2. In a 2nd round, the definition of AI, areas of work (Games,
   Natural Language Processing, Knowledge Processing including
   Expert Systems, Pattern Recognition) and dominant methods of
   knowledge Representation (Lists, Semantic Networks, Rule based
   Methods; the basic structure of an Expert System including
   Knowledge Base and Consultation Subsystem) were shortly discused
   (essentially following Hal Sackman's definition, as given in his
   conference contribution rather complex, but not available in
   written form). In following discussion, Expert Systems (ES) were
   of predominant interest.

3. The discussion started from the evident analiogy of computers
   being as intelligent as human beings. While "neuronal computers"
   aimed at simulating wo/man's brain are only research tools today
   (also due to problems to simulate effectively and fast enough
   the brains millions of neurous and synapses as well as due to
   limited understanding of the brain functions), AI aims at
   producing a similar behavior as wo/men in specific model
   situations, which - when resulting in "adequate" behavior - is
   attributed to wo/men's "intelligence". Such a computerized model
   must not necessarily work like the human brain; the main effect
   is that observers deduce, from the machine's behavior, the
   impression that the machine "behaves intelligently".

4. On this basis, the question was asked, whether it would be
   helpful to have an expert on one's own desk. As a special (and
   often discussed) example, an "ordinary doctor's" role in a
   process of self-medication was assumed; participants unimously
   stated, on the basis of the heavily critisized "5-minute
   medicine" (where a doctor "processes" diagnosis and therapy of a
   patient within 5 minutes):

   If a doctor reduces a patient to an assembly of symptoms, and if
   a doctor reduces diagnosis to symptom finding, then the use of

an Expert System (assuming best available Knowledge Base as well as diagnostic and therapeutic procedures) is preferable.

Some hope was expressed that an Expert System (in special area) may have the same "good results" for such cases as ordinary doctors. Moreover it was argued, that an ES could send the patient (if "cold" and "concer" were possible diagnosis) to the "natural" doctor.

5. The evident deficits in the described doctor's procedures led to the conclusion that psychosomatic (or very complex somatic) findings might generally not be processed by Expert Systems. The provocative question was asked, whetherems Moliere's "Malade Imaginaire" could have been diagnosed and cured properly by an ES; as this patient's illness evidently has social and psychological (rather than somatic) reasons, an ES (at least in it's contemporary form) could not help him.

6. When discussing wo/man's role in such a decision making process, ES can assist (rather than decide) in those cases, where essential data may be derived in cognitive processes; this implies that emotional aspects (including belief as thrust) cannot be modelled.

7. The question who is responsible for the correctuess and adequacy of an Expert System' diagnostic and therapeutic advice was discussed with initial controversy. While some argued, that due to the complexity of such systems which have been produced by many specialists, any responsibility of the originators vanish, other argued that responsibility is automatically transfered to the user. The evident gap between originators and recipients must be closed by proper education of the users through the originators. Assuming properly educated doctors, they might use Expert Systems as tools to aid in finding a diagnosis and therapy under the doctor's final responsibility.

8. Generalizing the last finding to "traditional" information technologies and other applications, the users should have better education as well as a participation in the design processes of application software, to avoid impacts unforeseen by technique-minded desiners.

The Social Implications of Robotics and Advanced
Industrial Automation / D. Millin and B.H. Raab (Editors)
Elsevier Science Publishers B.V. (North-Holland)
© IFIP, 1989

Workshop on Kibbutz High-Tech

Chairperson: Dr. Michal Palgi, Haifa University

The workshop was opened by three short presentations. The first by Michal
Palgi who described the kibbutz structure, institutions and ideology. Shimon
Shur described the diffusion of computerization in the kibbutzim and Menachem
Rosner showed how the kibbutz can be seen as one successful model for its
diffusion.

The kibbutzim are collective communities that have been built and structures
along some basic values. The most important among these values, from the point
of view of our discussion are, socialism equality and zionism. Socialism is
relevant because it meant that the community would be owned and maintained by
its own members. Self-labor therefore, is one of its basic principles and
this meant that the size of its plants was constricted by it. Equality is
relevant because it means that all spheres of life, like work, consumption and
politics are based on democracy and equality. This in turn determines the
structure of kibbutz institutions. Zionism is relevant because one of its
principles was that Jews should live in Israel and pursue a "normal" variety
of occupations. That meant that the Jewish people in Israel would take part
in all the range of occupations available. The kibbutzim have decided it is
their duty to do the production works and mainly the agricultural ones.

After describing in short the basic relevant values of the kibbutzim I shall
describe the kibbutzim themselves and their organizations. The first kibbutz,
Degania, was built in 1910. Now there are about 280 kibbutzim with a
population of about 120,000 (which is about 3.5% of the Jewish population in
Israel). The size of the average kibbutz is between 300 to 400 adult members
and 100 to 150 children. Each kibbutz is structured so as to comply with its
basic values. In order to free members from household chores and to give them
equal services and education communal consumption was implemented. Thus we
can see that in each kibbutz there is a communal dining hall where all the
meals are served to the members'. There is also a communal laundry and clothes
store where all the members' laundry is washed, mended and ironed. The
communal education of the kibbutzim has started as all inclusive, that is to
say, almost all the needs of the kids were taken care of in the children's
houses, they spent almost all of their days and nights there and came to their
parents' house only for a few hours in the afternoon. This has changed in the
last few years and in about 2/3 of the kibbutzim the children sleep in their
parents houses.

The communities are self-governed. There is a committee responsible for each
sphere of kibbutz life. Thus the work committee is responsible for allocating
members to their workplace. It has to see that also unfavorable places get
their workers, and this by a method of rotation in which all members take turn
in the unwanted jobs. Other committees are, health, education, consumption,
security, economic, special needs, etc. There are also ad hoc committees that
have to deal with specific urgent problems, like, a committee for finding a
new plant, a committee for specific political issues, etc. All these
committees are elected by the kibbutz members in the kibbutz assembly that
convenes once a week. All decisions that are to do with long and medium range
issues are to be made by the assembly. Others, that are concerned with the
every day running of the kibbutz are made by the members or by the elected
office holders (who are, of course, also members). From this description, it
can be seen, that the kibbutz is governed both by direct and indirect
democracy. Direct democracy through members meetings once a week, indirect
democracy through elected committees.

Workplaces are also governed by direct democracy. The head of a workplace is elected by the workers. Almost all decisions are made by the workers together when they convene for meals or especially to deal with a specific issue. The heads of workplace rotate about every second year. This is true for all the workplaces in the kibbutz apart from the kibbutz plants. The kibbutz plants are bigger (on the average between 40 to 50 workers) and the work in there is much more complex. Therefore special norms for keping democracy in them have been established. The manager of a kibbutz plant is to be elected by the kibbutz assembly because he has to have both managerial and human relations skills as he is responsible for a big portion of kibbutz members and kibbutz economy. He is to rotate every 4 to 5 years. All other managerial personnel in the plant are elected by the workers and are rotated every 2 to 3 years. The plant elects committees and in its management workers with no managerial role and kibbutz officials are represented. This in order that the plant would continue both to be democratic and an integral part of the kibbutz. Every week or two the workers of the plant are to assemble for a meeting. In this meeting the problems of the plant are to be discussed. These meetings are not carried out as frequently in all the plants.

The kibbutzim are organized in three federations: The United Kibbutz Movement (with about 165 kibbutzim), the Kibbutz Haartzi (with about 85 kibbutzim) and the Religious Kibbutz Movement (with about 16 kibbutzim). Each of these federations has central offices that advise and guide the kibbutzim. Also all the three federations are organized in one roof organization that represents the kibbutzim to the government and other outside bodies. The workers in all these bodies are elected kibbutz members that rotate every three years. In addition, the kibbutzim are organized regionally mainly for the initial processing of the agricultural products but also for cultural and educational activities.

The diffusion of computerization in the kibbutz was a three-step model:

1. Centralized adoption: 1964 marked the beginning of computerization in the kibbutz movement. This beginning concerned centralized countrywide computer services of Heshev, the national inter-kibbutz unit for economic guidance (with its headquarters and computer centre in Tel Aviv) to about 150 kibbutzim in three spheres:

   a) the application of computerized linear programming, beginning in 1964;

   b) computerized accounting system, beginning in 1970;

   c) computerized kibbutz development analysis system, beginning in 1972.

Regarding the process of accounting service: at the beginning of the week each kibbutz concerned sent its original accounting paperwork to the computer centre in Tel Aviv and these were then returned to the accounting branch of the kibbutz, accompanied by requested outputs (reports). Heshev had at that time 35 standardized computer report forms. In 1974 about 150 kibbutzim (out of 250) used this convenience.

Some of the reasons for the "centralized" beginnings of computerization in the kibbutzim may be:
   a) In the early sixties computerization in Israel was only at its beginnings, hardware was expensive, and experience with computerization rare.
   b) There existed an established central inter-kibbutz unit for economic guidance, with computer equipment and trained experts, on which particular kibbutz accounting systems could lean.

c) Federational departments for economic guidance encouraged affiliated kibbutzim (especially with weak accounting systems) to work with the central unit.

2. Regional Diffusion and Adoption The rise of regional computer centres in the seventies was accompanied by a vehement conflict with the centralized computer unit of Heshev supported by the federational economic departments. While these emphasized the importance of countrywide centralization of information processing experience, the regional enterprises conceived the establishment of regional computer centres as their "natural" growth, leaning on the advantages of geographic proximity and regional integration of particular kibbutz accounting systems.

In the long run, the regional computer centres gained the upper hand, and then diffusion was fast. The first regional computer centre, "Miload", near Acco -- in the Western Galillee -- was founded in 1970. Today there are twelve regional computer centres.

3. Community Diffusion and Adoption By "community diffusion and adoption" we mean the diffusion of computer hardware and software among particular kibbutz communities and the adoption of computer practices by them.

This third step began in the late seventies. Between 1976 and 1979 20 percent of kibbutzim started computerization; between 1980 and 1982 - the number rose to 55 percent; and between 1983 and 1985 another 20 percent. In 1986 approximately 95 percent of the kibbutzim had some sort of computerization.

The transition to the third step of computerization in the Kibbutz Movement, the community computerization, was due to a number of reasons, based on systemic needs of the kibbutzim:
1) the overload on the regional computer centres, that came to be interested in some decentralization;
2) some dissatisfaction in the affiliated kibbutzim with the rate of regional computer outputs, and with regional computer deadlocks;
3) interest of some members in the affiliated kibbutzim in computer practices and their initiative in establishing computer systems in their communities.

Undoubtedly, the kibbutz community inner computer systems are by now heavily dependent on and backed by the regional computer centres, especially in the sphere of software practices. However, owning and controlling their own hardware, and some software, opens an option for at least partial auto-emancipation of their computer systems.

After having discussed the organizational structure of the kibbutz and the diffusion of computerization in it, we looked to see why this was relatively easy, and in what respect its structure and ideology was compatible with the computerization and high-tech diffusion.

In the contradictory forecasts about the impact of technology the kibbutz can be seen as one possible model for coping with it. The reason for this is its community structure and the dissociation between work and need satisfaction. The new technlogies can combine work and community life. It does not necessitate long distance travelling or the performance of work in one central plant. It also raises the need to abolish the fear of unemployment. In the kibbutz there is no such fear and the extra time gained by replacing work with machines can be used for the benefit of the community or its members.

The new technologies require decentralization and self-management - principles that are central to kibbutz life. It also brings with it less standardization and more understanding of everyone's needs. The new technologies can solve problems of size, the advantage to size slowly disappears with the emergence of the advantage to machines.   It enables more access to information and better communication. This in turn can lead to more democratic practices. From this short description it is easy to see that in many aspects the kibbutz structure is compatible with the characteristics of the new technologies.

One of the central discussion issues in the workshop was whether democracy is really possible at the "age" of high-tech.   The general opinion was, that even in the kibbutz the knowledge gaps are getting so big that real participation in decision-making is not possible.   The experts are the ones that would make the most of the technical decisions while the others would receive information and participate in those issues that they have the know how to.   Another issue that is relevant to this one is power distribution.   It was argued that the new technologies require decentralization but the leaders, on the other hand, want to centralize it.   So, maybe they would not enable to open all the possibilities for decentralization, reskilling and democracy that these technologies allow.   In the kibbutz it was not perceived as a major problem now as the principle of rotation is active.   It might be an issue though with the jobs of the professionals (non-managerial) who do not rotate.

The question of secrecy was also raised.   It was argued that if every member had an access to the data bank some might abuse it.   The participants in the workshop from the kibbutz said that this argument is similar to other arguments about kibbutz life, such as how do we know that members who are in office would not use the information they receive through their job for their own personal advantage.   Kibbutz life is based on trust and the identification of its members with the community and its values.   Therefore, there is no place in such a society for secrecy, even though the odd abuser of this right to data might be found.

To sum, the discussants have seen the advantages of a community like the kibbutz for the diffusion of high-tech.   They also realized that it has some very basic problems for this diffusion.   For example, the high investments that the kibbutz has to make for acquiring the machines might determine the work place of many of its members in the future even if they would prefer to work elsewhere.   This because the kibbutz believes in self labor and in order to return the cost of the machines its members would have to work with them.

The Social Implications of Robotics and Advanced
Industrial Automation / D. Millin and B.H. Raab (Editors)
Elsevier Science Publishers B.V. (North-Holland)
© IFIP, 1989

PANEL DISCUSSION: A PUBLIC PHILOSOPHY FOR

SOCIAL EXCELLENCE IN THE INFORMATION AGE

Harold Sackman

Department of Information Systems

School of Business and Economics

California State University, Los Angeles, USA

I have developed the elements of a public philosophy of social excellence for social computerization elsewhere, over the last two decades. The rudiments of this philosophy are as follows.

1. Philosophical Gap: The contention is made that there is a need for a public philosophy of computer system services to help prioritize social values and to help guide long-range policy and social planning in the public interest.

2. Social Control: Information is power, and power is control, and more and more social control is being vested in the form of computer-based social information networks.

3. Democratic and Scientific System Development: The most consistently powerful way to harness information systems to achieve social goals is to use scientific method, which is empirical experimental method, on behalf of users and the public in a participative, democratic setting.

4. Philosophical Pragmatism: The case is made that the American philosophical tradition of "Pragmatism" (e.g. Charles Pierce, William James and John Dewey) particularly satisfies the main requirements for a public philosophy of information systems.

5. Real-World Testing: In particular, the theory of "truth" in pragmatism is based on testing the consequences of a statement, conceptualized as a hypothesis, in actual practice, in the real world. This is essentially what a real-time information system does--it tests expectations against actual outcomes. If there is a mismatch, corrective system action is taken.

6. Computer System Evaluation: The central computer, or distributed computers, in online and/or real-time systems can and should serve as built-in laboratories to record, test and evaluate system behaviors. This facilitates free and open social experimentation with competing systems in the public forum.

7. The Citizen-Scientist: American Pragmatism, structured on democratic values, can serve as an organizing framework for a public philosophy of social excellence with information systems.

For this pragmatic philosophy to work effectively, a higher level of effective, or working intelligence is required in the general public. This is essentially the interdisciplinary citizen-scientist who enjoys, among other traits, computer literacy. Such citizens could provide shared, participative, adaptive feedback with democratic social networks to guarantee continual social improvements in the public and in the individual's interest.

8. <u>Democratic</u> <u>Information</u> <u>Services</u> <u>as</u> <u>a</u> <u>Human</u> <u>Right</u>. To achieve the above philosophy, a new basic human right is required. This is the right of all citizens to have access to computer-communication services in the public domain. This human right is the foundation for democratic information equity and equal information opportunity for the general public.

International legal precedent has anticipated and paved the way for the aim and the spirit of this new human right. Articles 19 and 27 of the Universal Declaration of Human Rights of the United Nations (1967) are prime examples:

Article 19

"Everyone has the right to freedom of opinion and expression; this right includes freedom to hold opinions without interference and to seek, receive and impart information and ideas through any media and regardless of frontiers."

Article 27

"Everyone has the right freely to participate in the cultural life of the community, to enjoy the arts and to share in scientific advancement and its benefits."

Can we develop such democratic vistas by an enlightened, participative public, in ethnically diverse communities throughout the world, to meet the challenge of cooperative global networks of the 21st century?

The Social Implications of Robotics and Advanced
Industrial Automation / D. Millin and B.H. Raab (Editors)
Elsevier Science Publishers B.V. (North-Holland)
© IFIP, 1989

PANEL DISCUSSION - SUMMARY

Barri Sherman

Today, indeed over the conference as a whole, we have talked at length about the world we would like to see. About a technologically literate future, about well educated, happy people; about industrial problems, personnel problems, problems of the kibbutzim (for me utterly fascinating) and the problems in different industrial countries and how they are tackled. But look at life as it is today. Look at the hundreds of thousands of young chldren who will never have the chance of secondary education, perhaps not even to primary standard, let alone be computer literate. Look at the thousands of children who will die from preventable diseases or malnutrition before the next IFIP meeting. Look at the people who will starve, who will lose their livelihoods and homes, perhaps their families, because of drought and crop failures.

Robots and manufacturing technologies are irrelevant to them. They have never heard of them, and as they may well not be anywhere near to an electric supply anyway, couldn't use them even if they had a reason to. The point is that there are more of them, than of us. There are more fundamental human problems to be solved over the coming years in Africa, Central and South America and parts of Asia than have ever presented themselves in the developed world.

This is the challenge isn't it? It is how we as "experts", how the technologists using their sophistications, how the politicians fleshing out their rhetoric, can make the world a better place for these young people. The challenge is to use the technologies in an appropriate way, not to impose them. The challenge has to be far more about trying to help these children and families than about providing more for those who already have.

The concept of a global village is not merely idealistic claptrap. In the last analysis all societies are interdependant. There is an economic as well as a social imperative to direct the newer technologies in this direction. But there is one other imperative, last but definitely not least. It is a concept not often raised at these sorts of conferences, more is the pity. So I am raising it at this one; there is a moral imperative.